CW00735160

Cambridge English

EMPOWER

PRE-INTERMEDIATE

Teacher's Book

B1

Lynda Edwards

with Ruth Gairns, Stuart Redman, Wayne Rimmer,

Helen Ward and Julian Oakley

Welcome to *Cambridge English Empower*

A unique mix of learning and assessment

Cambridge English Empower is a new general English adult course that combines course content from Cambridge University Press with validated assessment from Cambridge English Language Assessment.

This unique mix of engaging classroom material and reliable assessment, with personalised online practice, enables learners to make consistent and measurable progress.

What could your students achieve with **Cambridge English Empower?**

Teacher's Book contents

For Students

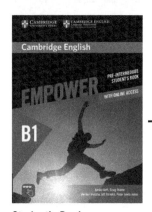

Student's Book
with online access

Online Assessment
Online Practice
Online Workbook

Student's Book also available as Interactive eBook

Also available

- Student's Book (or eBook) without online access
- Print Workbook (with and without answers), with downloadable audio and video

For Teachers

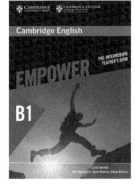

Teacher's Book
with photocopiable activities and online access

Class Audio CDs

Class DVD

Presentation Plus

Student's Book with online access

- Comes complete with access to Online Assessment, Online Practice, and Online Workbook – delivered via the Cambridge Learning Management System (CLMS)
- Syllabus informed by English Profile, the Cambridge English Corpus, and benchmarked to the CEFR

Interactive eBook

- With the Interactive eBook, you can do the Student's Book activities in interactive form (specially designed for tablets), play all Class Audio and Video, check and display answers, control audio speed, create text and voice notes, and more.
- The Interactive eBook can be accessed with the Cambridge Bookshelf iPad app, or using the Cambridge Bookshelf Web Reader on a desktop or laptop computer, and can be used offline (after initial download).

Online Assessment

- Validated and reliable assessment throughout the course – developed by experts at Cambridge English Language Assessment
- A learning-oriented approach – assessment that regularly informs teaching and learning
- A Unit Progress Test for every unit (automatically marked) – covering grammar, vocabulary, and functional language – plus a Unit Speaking Test
- Mid-course and end-of-course competency tests that cover all four skills and generate a CEFR report which reliably benchmarks learners to the target level

For more details about the **Cambridge English Empower** assessment package, and Learning Oriented Assessment, please see pages 7–8.

Online Practice

- Personalised practice – automatically assigned according to each student's score in the Unit Progress Test, so their time is spent on what they need most
- Language presentations, practice activities, and skills-based extension activities for every unit
- Automatically marked

Online Workbook

- Extra practice of all the grammar, vocabulary and functional language, plus extra writing
- Automatically marked

Teacher's Book

- Detailed teacher's notes for every lesson, including extra tips, ideas and support, and answer keys
- Photocopiable activities – a range of communicative extra practice activities for every unit, including grammar, vocabulary, pronunciation, and Wordpower

Online access for teachers

- To access **Cambridge English Empower**'s unique online assessment and practice package, please go to **cambridgelms.org/empower,** select 'Register' and follow the instructions.

Presentation Plus

- With Presentation Plus, you can display all Student's Book material, play all Class Audio and Video, show answer keys, and more.
- Presentation Plus can be used with all types of interactive whiteboards, or with a computer and projector.

Class DVD

- All the video material for the Student's Book, plus Video Extra

Class Audio CDs

- All the listening material for the Student's Book

Print tests

- Downloadable from **cambridge.org/empower**

For more information and extra resources, go to:
cambridge.org/empower

Course methodology

Key methodological principles

A learner-centred approach

Cambridge English Empower, with its unique mix of learning and assessment, places the learner at the centre of the learning process. This learner-centred approach also applies to the course methodology – the Student's Book and additional resources provide a range of classroom materials that motivate learners, address their language needs, and facilitate the development of their skills.

Supporting the teacher

Cambridge English Empower also supports the teacher through classroom methodology that is familiar and easy to use, and at the same time is flexible and creative. A number of key methodological principles underpin the course, enhancing the interface between learners and their learning, and between learners and teachers. **Cambridge English Empower:**

1 encourages learner engagement
2 delivers manageable learning
3 is rich in practice
4 provides a comprehensive approach to productive skills

Measurable progress

This leads to motivated learners, successful lessons, and measurable progress. This progress is then measured by a uniquely reliable assessment package, developed by test experts at Cambridge English Language Assessment.

Key methodological principles

1 Learner engagement

Getting Started

Each unit begins with a 'Getting Started' page, designed to engage learners from the very start of the unit – leading to greater motivation and more successful learning. It does this in three ways:

- **Clear learning goals** – 'can do' statements immediately focus learners on their objectives.
- **Striking images** that take an unusual perspective on the unit theme – this raises curiosity, prompts ideas and questions in the mind of the learner, and stimulates them to want to communicate.
- Short **speaking activities** that prompt a personal response – leading to longer-lasting learning and a sense of ownership from the start. These activities also offer a diagnostic opportunity to the teacher.

Remarkable texts and images

Throughout the course, learners encounter texts and images that inform, amuse, surprise, entertain, raise questions, arouse curiosity and empathy, provoke an emotional response, and prompt new insights and perspectives – this means that learners are consistently motivated to engage, read, listen, and communicate.

The texts have been carefully selected to appeal to a wide range of learners from a variety of cultural backgrounds. They have an international focus and flavour, and each text has a story to tell or a point of view to offer that will be of interest to learners. All texts are accompanied by receptive tasks that support the development of reading and listening skills.

Frequent opportunities for personal response

There are frequent opportunities to practise speaking throughout every lesson. These include **personalisation** tasks which make the target language in every unit meaningful to the individual learner. But not only that – there are also regular activities that encourage learners to respond personally to the content of texts and images. These **personal response** activities foster successful learning because they:

- make learning more memorable – so it lasts longer
- are inclusive – there is no 'correct' answer, so all learners can participate successfully
- promote spontaneous spoken interaction – this further enhances the learner's sense of freedom and ownership, enhances motivation, and makes learning more relevant and enjoyable

2 Manageable learning

A second core principle that informs **Cambridge English Empower** is recognition of the importance of manageable learning. This offers learners (and their teachers) reassurance that they will not be overwhelmed at any point in their learning journey, leading to more successful learning outcomes and sustained motivation. The **Cambridge English Empower** classroom material reflects the concept of manageable learning in three main ways:

- Syllabus planning and the selection of language
- Lesson flow
- Task design

Syllabus planning and the selection of language

A key element in making learning material manageable concerns the selection of target language. In **Cambridge English Empower**, two powerful Cambridge English resources – the *Cambridge Corpus* and *English Profile* – have been used to inform the development of the course syllabus and the writing of the material. These resources provide reliable information as to which language items learners are likely to be able to learn successfully at each level of the CEFR (Common European Framework of Reference). This means learners using **Cambridge English Empower** are presented with target language that they are able to incorporate and use at that point in their learning journey, and they won't encounter too much above-level language in reading and listening texts. It also means that learners are not overwhelmed with unrealistic amounts of language because the *Cambridge Corpus* and *English Profile* are also able to give an indication of what constitutes a manageable quantity of language at each level.

Lesson flow

Learning is also made more manageable through the careful staging and sequencing of activities. Every lesson starts with a clear 'Learn to …' objective and ends with a substantial output task. Each lesson is comprised of several manageable sections, each with a clear focus on language and/or skills. Each section builds towards the next, and activities within sections do likewise. The final activity of each spread involves a productive learning outcome that brings together the language and the topic of the lesson, allowing learners to put what they have learnt into immediate use.

Task and activity design

Tasks and activities have been designed to give learners an appropriate balance between freedom and support. Grammar and vocabulary presentations take a straightforward approach to dealing with the meaning and form of new language, and practice is carefully staged, with additional support in the 'Grammar Focus' and 'Vocabulary Focus' sections at the back of the book. Reading and listening activities allow learners to process information in texts in a gradual, supportive way. Speaking and writing activities are made manageable by means of clear models, appropriate scaffolding, and a focus on relevant sub-skills associated with a specific spoken or written outcome.

As an overall principle, the methodology throughout **Cambridge English Empower** anticipates and mitigates potential problems that learners might encounter with language and tasks. While this clearly supports learners, it also supports teachers because there are likely to be fewer unexpected challenges during the course of a lesson – this also means that necessary preparation time is reduced to a minimum.

3 Rich in practice

It is essential that learners are offered frequent and manageable opportunities to practise the language they have been focusing on – they need to activate the language they have studied in a meaningful way in order to gain confidence in using it, and of course meaningful practice also makes new language more memorable.

Cambridge English Empower is rich in practice activities and provides learners and teachers with a wide variety of tasks that help learners to become confident users of new language.

Student's Book

Throughout each **Cambridge English Empower** Student's Book, learners are offered a wide variety of practice activities, appropriate to the stage of the lesson or unit:

- Ample opportunities are provided for controlled practice of target language.
- Many of the practice activities provide learners with an opportunity to personalise language.
- There are frequent opportunities for communicative spoken practice. Communicative practice activities are clearly contextualised and carefully staged and scaffolded, in line with the principle of manageable learning.
- Further spoken practice is provided in the final speaking activity in each of the A, B, and C lessons, providing the principal communicative learning outcome in each of these lessons.
- In the 'Grammar Focus' and 'Vocabulary Focus' pages at the back the Student's Book, there are more opportunities for practice of grammar and vocabulary, helping to consolidate learning.

- In the 'Review and Extension' page at the end of each unit, there are more opportunities for both written and spoken practice of target language.

Teacher's Book

- Many learners find practice activities that involve an element of fun to be particularly motivating. Many such activities – six per unit – are provided in the photocopiable activities in the Teacher's Book, providing fun, communicative practice of grammar, vocabulary and pronunciation.
- The main teacher's notes also provide ideas for extra activities at various stages of the lesson.

Other components

Through the Cambridge LMS, **Cambridge English Empower** provides an extensive range of practice activities that learners can use to review and consolidate their learning outside the classroom:

- The Online Practice component offers interactive language presentations followed by practice and extension activities. Learners are automatically directed to the appropriate point in this practice cycle, according to their score in the Unit Progress Test (at the end of Student's Book lesson C).
- The Workbook (Online or Print) provides practice of the target language after each A, B, and C lesson.

4 A comprehensive approach to productive skills

Most learners study English because they want to use the language in some way. This means that speaking and writing – the productive skills – are more often than not a priority for learners. **Cambridge English Empower** is systematic and comprehensive in its approach to developing both speaking and writing skills.

Speaking

The **C lesson** in each unit – 'Everyday English' – takes a comprehensive approach to speaking skills, and particularly in helping learners to become effective users of high-frequency functional/situational language. The target language is clearly contextualised by means of engaging video (also available as audio-only via the Class CDs), filmed in the real world in contexts that will be relevant and familiar to adult learners. These 'Everyday English' lessons focus on three key elements of spoken language:

- Useful language – focusing on the functional and situational language that is most relevant to learners' needs, and manageable within the target level
- Pronunciation – focusing on intelligibility and covering many aspects of phonology and the characteristics of natural speech, from individual sounds to extended utterances
- Conversation skills – speaking strategies and sub-skills, the 'polish' that helps learners to become more effective communicators

The final speaking task in each 'Everyday English' lesson provides learners with an opportunity to activate all three of these elements. This comprehensive approach ensures that speaking skills are actively developed, not just practised.

Writing

Across each level of **Cambridge English Empower**, learners receive guidance and practice in writing a wide range of text types. The **D lesson** in each unit – 'Skills for Writing' – builds to a learning outcome in which learners produce a written text that is relevant to their real-life needs, appropriate to the level, and related to the topic of the unit. However, these are not 'heads-down' writing lessons – instead, and in keeping with the overall course methodology, they are highly communicative mixed-skills lessons, with a special focus on writing. This means that writing is fully integrated with listening, reading and speaking – as it is in real life – and is not practised in isolation. Each 'Skills for Writing' lesson follows a tried and tested formula:

1 Learners engage with the topic through activities that focus on speaking and listening skills.

2 They read a text which also provides a model for the later writing output task.

3 They then do a series of activities which develop aspects of a specific writing sub-skill that has been encountered in the model text.

4 They then go on to write their own text, in collaboration with other learners.

5 Process writing skills are embedded in the instructions for writing activities and encourage learners to self-correct and seek peer feedback.

Also, while the **A and B lessons** provide the main input and practice of the core language syllabus, they also provide frequent opportunities for learners to develop their receptive and productive skills.

In line with other elements of **Cambridge English Empower**, the texts used for skills development engage learners and provide them with opportunities to personalise language. Likewise, the tasks are designed in such a way as to make the learning manageable.

The extension activities in the Online Practice component (via the Cambridge LMS) also offer further practice in reading and listening skills.

Learning Oriented Assessment

What is Learning Oriented Assessment (LOA)?

As a teacher, you'll naturally be interested in your learners' progress. Every time they step into your classroom, you'll note if a learner is struggling with a language concept, is unable to read at a natural rate, or can understand a new grammar point but still can't produce it in a practice activity. This is often an intuitive and spontaneous process. By the end of a course or a cycle of learning, you'll know far more about a learner's ability than an end-of-course test alone can show.

An LOA approach to teaching and learning brings together this ongoing informal evaluation with more formal or structured assessment such as end-of-unit or end-of-course tests. Ideally supported by a learner management system (LMS), LOA is an approach that allows you to pull together all this information and knowledge in order to understand learners' achievements and progress and to identify and address their needs in a targeted and informed way. A range of insights into learners and their progress feeds into **total assessment** of the learner. It also allows you to use all of this information not just to produce a report on a learner's level of competence but also to plan and inform future learning.

For more information about LOA, go to
cambridgeenglish.org/loa

How does Cambridge English Empower support LOA?

Cambridge English Empower supports LOA both informally and formally, and both inside and outside the classroom:

1 Assessment that informs teaching and learning
- Reliable tests for both formative and summative assessment (Unit Progress Tests, Unit Speaking Tests, and skills-based Competency Tests)
- Targeted extra practice online via the Cambridge Learning Management System (CLMS) to address areas in which the tests show that learners need more support
- Opportunities to do the test again and improve performance
- Clear record of learner performance through the CLMS

2 LOA classroom support
- Clear learning objectives – and activities that clearly build towards those objectives
- Activities that offer opportunities for learner reflection and peer feedback
- A range of tips for teachers on how to incorporate LOA techniques, including informal assessment, into your lessons as part of normal classroom practice

1 Assessment that informs teaching and learning

Cambridge English Empower offers three types of tests written and developed by teams of Cambridge English exam writers. All tests in the course have been trialled on thousands of candidates to ensure that test items are appropriate to the level.

Cambridge English tests are underpinned by research and evaluation and by continuous monitoring and statistical analysis of performance of test questions.

Cambridge English Empower tests are designed around the following essential principles:

Validity – tests are authentic tests of real-life English and test the language covered in the coursebook

Reliability – tasks selected are consistent and fair

Impact – tests have a positive effect on teaching and learning in and outside the classroom

Practicality – tests are user-friendly and practical for teachers and students

Unit Progress Tests

The course provides an online Unit Progress Test at the end of every unit, testing the target grammar, vocabulary and functional language from the unit. The teacher and learner are provided with a score for each language area that has been tested, identifying the areas where the learner has either encountered difficulties and needs more support, or has mastered well. According to their score in each section of the test, the learner is directed either to extension activities or to a sequence of practice activities appropriate to their level, focusing on the language points where they need most support. This means that learners can focus their time and effort on activities that will really benefit them. They then have the opportunity to retake the Unit Progress Test – questions they got right first time will still be filled in, meaning that they can focus on those with which they had difficulty first-time round.

Unit Speaking Tests

Cambridge English Empower provides a comprehensive approach to speaking skills. For every unit, there is an online Unit Speaking Test which offers learners the opportunity to test and practise a range of aspects of pronunciation and fluency. These tests use innovative voice-recognition software and allow the learner to listen to model utterances, record themselves, and re-record if they wish before submitting.

Competency Tests

Cambridge English Empower offers mid-course and end-of-course Competency Tests. These skills-based tests cover Reading, Writing, Listening and Speaking, and are calibrated to the Common European Framework of Reference (CEFR). They provide teachers and learners with a reliable indication of level, as well as a record of their progress – a CEFR report is generated for each learner, showing their performance within the relevant CEFR level (both overall and for each of the skills).

The **Cambridge Learning Management System** (CLMS) provides teachers and learners with a clear and comprehensive record of each learner's progress during the course, including all test results and also their scores relating to the online practice activities that follow the tests – helping teachers and learners to recognise achievement and identify further learning needs. Within the CLMS, a number of different web tools, including message boards, forums and e-portfolios, provide opportunities for teachers and learners to communicate outside of class, and for learners to do additional practice. These tools can also be used by teachers to give more specific feedback based on the teacher's informal evaluation during lessons. The CLMS helps teachers to systematically collect and record evidence of learning and performance and in doing so demonstrates to teachers and learners how much progress has been made over time.

2 LOA classroom support

Clear objectives

An LOA approach encourages learners to reflect and self-assess. In order to do this, learning objectives must be clear. In **Cambridge English Empower**, each unit begins with a clear set of 'can do' objectives so that learners feel an immediate sense of purpose. Each lesson starts with a clear 'Learn to ...' goal, and the activities all contribute towards this goal, leading to a significant practical outcome at the end of the lesson. At the end of each unit, there is a 'Review your progress' feature that encourages learners to reflect on their success, relative to the 'can do' objectives at the start of the unit. Within the lessons, there are also opportunities for reflection, collaborative learning, and peer feedback.

LOA classroom tips for teachers

In a typical lesson you're likely to use some or perhaps all of the following teaching techniques:

- **monitor** learners during learner-centred stages of the lesson
- **elicit** information and language
- **concept check** new language
- **drill** new vocabulary or grammar
- provide **feedback** after learners have worked on a task

The table below summarises core and LOA-specific aims for each of the above techniques. All these familiar teaching techniques are a natural fit for the kind of methodology that informally supports LOA. An LOA approach will emphasise those parts of your thinking that involve forming evaluations or judgments about learners' performance (and therefore what to do next to better assist the learner). The 'LOA teacher' is constantly thinking things like:

- *Have they understood that word?*
- *How well are they pronouncing that phrase?*
- *Were they able to use that language in a freer activity?*
- *How many answers did they get right?*
- *How well did they understand that listening text?*
- *How many errors did I hear?*
- *And what does that mean for the next step in the learning process?*

The **Cambridge English Empower** Teacher's Book provides tips on how to use a number of these techniques within each lesson. This will help teachers to consider their learners with more of an evaluative eye. Of course it also helps learners if teachers share their assessment with them and ensure they get plenty of feedback. It's important that teachers make sure feedback is well-balanced, so it helps learners to know what they are doing well in addition to what needs a little more work.

	Teaching techniques				
	monitoring	eliciting	concept checking	drilling	providing feedback
Core aims	• checking learners are on task • checking learners' progress • making yourself available to learners who are having problems	• checking what learners know about a topic in order to generate interest	• checking that learners understand the use and meaning of new language	• providing highly controlled practice of new language	• finding out what ideas learners generated when working on a task • praising learners' performance of a task • indicating where improvement can be made
LOA aims	• listening to learners' oral language, and checking learners' written language, in order to: » diagnose potential needs » check if they can use new language correctly in context	• finding out if learners already know a vocabulary or grammar item • adapting the lesson to take into account students' individual starting points and interests	• checking what could be a potential problem with the use and meaning of new language for your learners • anticipating and preparing for challenges in understanding new language, both for the whole class and for individuals	• checking that learners have consolidated the form of new language • checking intelligible pronunciation of new language	• asking learners how well they feel they performed a task • giving feedback to learners on specific language strengths and needs • fostering 'learning how to learn' skills

Unit overview

Getting Started page

- clear learning objectives to give an immediate sense of purpose
- striking and unusual images to arouse curiosity
- activities that promote emotional engagement and a personal response

Lesson A and Lesson B

- input and practice of core grammar and vocabulary, plus a mix of skills

Lesson C

- functional language in common everyday situations
- language is presented through video filmed in the real world

Unit Progress Test

- covering grammar, vocabulary and functional language

Also available:

- Speaking Test for every unit
- mid-course and end-of-course competency tests

Lesson D

- highly communicative integrated skills lesson
- special focus on writing skills
- recycling of core language from the A, B and C lessons

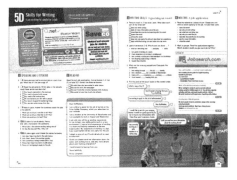

Review and Extension

- extra practice of grammar and vocabulary
- Wordpower vocabulary extension
- 'Review your progress' to reflect on success

For extra input and practice, every unit includes illustrated **Grammar Focus** and **Vocabulary Focus** sections at the back of the book.

Lessons A and B
Grammar and Vocabulary and a mix of skills

Clear goals
Each lesson starts with a clear, practical and achievable learning goal, creating an immediate sense of purpose.

5A I have to work long hours

Learn to talk about what people do at work
G must / have to / can
V Work

Learner engagement
Engaging images and texts motivate learners to respond personally. This makes learning more memorable and gives learners ownership of the language.

THE HAPPIEST JOBS

We spend most of our time at work. When we're not there, we're probably thinking about it. But what makes us happy at work? And which workers are the happiest? Here are twelve of the happiest and least happy jobs in the UK, according to the City & Guilds 'Career Happiness Index'.

% AGREEING THEY ARE HAPPY AT WORK		
1 _____	☺☺☺☺☺☺☺☺☺	87%
2 _____	☺☺☺☺☺☺☺☺	79%
plumbers	☺☺☺☺☺☺☺☺	76%
scientists	☺☺☺☺☺☺☺	69%
doctors and dentists	☺☺☺☺☺☺☺	65%
lawyers	☺☺☺☺☺☺	64%
3 _____	☺☺☺☺☺☺	62%
teachers	☺☺☺☺☺☺	59%
4 _____	☺☺☺☺☺☺	58%
electricians	☺☺☺☺☺☺	55%
IT workers	☺☺☺☺☺	48%
5 _____	☺☺☺☺	44%

1 VOCABULARY Work

a ⚪ Look at the photographs. Which jobs can you see?

b ⚪ Work in pairs. Make a list of as many jobs as you can. You have one minute.

c ▶ Now go to Vocabulary Focus 5A on p.136

2 READING

a ⚪ Work in pairs. Read the first part of the article: *The Happiest Jobs*. Where do you think these jobs go in the list?

bankers   gardeners   hairdressers   nurses   accountants

b ⚪ Check your ideas on p.127. Are you surprised? Why? / Why not?

c ⚪ What do you think makes people happy at work? Make a list of ideas with a partner.

d Read the second half of the article. Was your list correct?

e ⚪ Work in pairs. Answer the questions.
  1 Do you know anyone who does any of the jobs in the article? How do they feel about their job?
  2 Which job in the article is the most similar to your (future) job?
  3 Did anything in the article surprise you? Was there any information that you already knew?
  4 Do you think the results would be the same in your country? Why / Why not?

Regular speaking activities
Frequent speaking stages to get students talking throughout the lesson.

THE HAPPIEST WORKERS: WHY THEY'RE HAPPY

So what makes us happy at work? What you do in your job and where you do it is very important:
✳ 89% of gardeners feel their work is important and useful. Only 35% of bankers feel the same.
✳ 82% of gardeners said they use their skills every day, compared to only 35% of bankers.
✳ 89% of gardeners said they like their working environment, but only 24% of bankers said the same.

The people we work with matter:
✳ The most important thing of all is that other people value your work. 67% of all workers put this first.
✳ Most workers said that good relationships with colleagues are important. Scientists get on best with their colleagues (90%).

More money doesn't make us happier:
✳ 61% of workers said that it is very important for them to earn a good salary, but ...
✳ Workers who earn over £60,000 a year are the unhappiest.
✳ Self-employed people earn less but are much happier at work (85%) than people who work for a company.

PLUMBERS
74% think their work is important and useful.
67% use their skills every day.

HAIRDRESSERS
Only 7% are unhappy in their jobs.
86% get on well with their colleagues.

GARDENERS
89% think their work is important and useful.
35% are self-employed.

48

Manageable learning

The syllabus is informed by *English Profile* and the *Cambridge English Corpus*. Students will learn the most relevant and useful language, at the appropriate point in their learning journey. The target language is benchmarked to the CEFR.

UNIT 5

4 GRAMMAR *must / have to / can*

a Look at the sentences. Match the <u>underlined</u> words with the meanings.
1 To become a nurse you <u>have to</u> do well at school.
2 You <u>don't have to</u> wear a suit or go to many meetings.
3 You <u>can't</u> relax because if something goes wrong, you lose money.

a _____ = this is not necessary
b _____ = this is not allowed or not possible
c _____ = this is necessary

b Compare the written rules from John and Alisha's workplaces with the things they said. Complete the rules below.

> Nurses must not lift patients without another nurse present.

> You can't lift a patient on your own.

> You always have to switch off the mains power.

> Electricians must switch off the mains power before they start work.

In written English, we use:
_____ to say that that something is necessary
_____ to say that something is not allowed or is not possible

c ▶ Now go to Grammar Focus 5A on p.150

d 💬 What do you have to do if you work in these places? What can't you do?
• office   • restaurant   • bank   • school

> In a school, you can't leave children on their own.

> Yes, and you have to wear a suit.

e Write rules for the people who work in each place in 4d. Use *must* and *must not*.

Teachers must not leave children on their own.
Teachers must wear a suit.

5 SPEAKING

a 💬 Choose five of the jobs from the list. Think of three advantages and three disadvantages for each job.
• scientist   • lawyer   • accountant   • electrician
• IT worker   • engineer   • nurse   • pilot
• police officer   • receptionist   • secretary

b 💬 Which job do you think is the hardest? Which job is the most interesting?

> Receptionists don't have to have a university degree. And they can find a job quite easily.

> But they have to work long hours. And they don't earn a good salary.

3 LISTENING

a 💬 What do you think these people like about their jobs?
1 Alisha, nurse
2 John, electrician
3 Miriam, banker

b ▶2.5 Listen to Alisha, John and Miriam and check your ideas in 3a.

c ▶2.5 Listen again and answer the questions about each person's job.
1 What qualifications, experience and other abilities are necessary for the job?
2 What is difficult about the job?

d 💬 Which of the three jobs would you prefer to do? Why? Would you be good at it?

'Teach off the page'
Straightforward approach and clear lesson flow for minimum preparation time.

Rich in practice
Clear signposts to **Grammar Focus** and **Vocabulary Focus** sections for extra support and practice.

Spoken outcome
Each A and B lesson ends with a practical spoken outcome so learners can use language immediately.

49

11

Lesson C
Prepares learners for effective real-world spoken communication

Everyday English
Thorough coverage of functional language for common everyday situations, helping learners to communicate effectively in the real world.

Real-world video
Language is showcased through high-quality video filmed in the real world, which shows language clearly and in context.

Comprehensive approach to speaking skills
A unique combination of language input, pronunciation and speaking strategies offers a comprehensive approach to speaking skills.

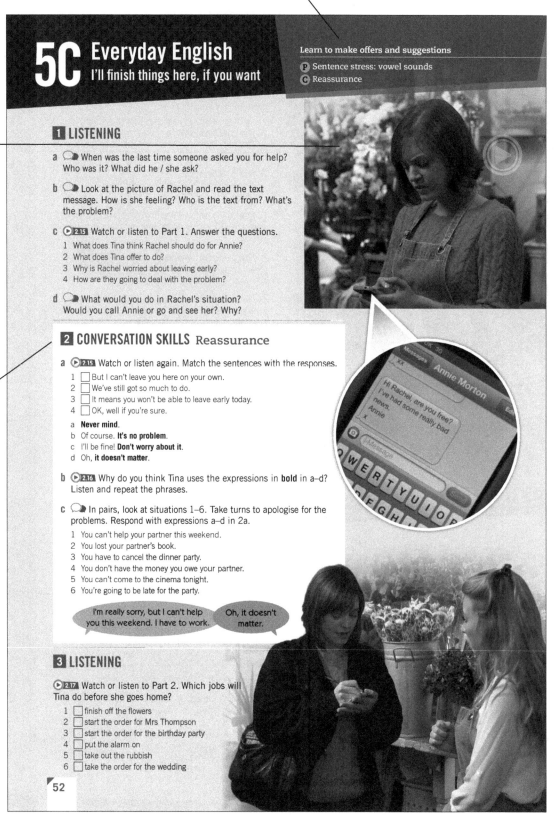

5C Everyday English
I'll finish things here, if you want

Learn to make offers and suggestions
Ⓟ Sentence stress: vowel sounds
Ⓒ Reassurance

1 LISTENING

a 💬 When was the last time someone asked you for help? Who was it? What did he / she ask?

b 💬 Look at the picture of Rachel and read the text message. How is she feeling? Who is the text from? What's the problem?

c ▶ 2.15 Watch or listen to Part 1. Answer the questions.
1 What does Tina think Rachel should do for Annie?
2 What does Tina offer to do?
3 Why is Rachel worried about leaving early?
4 How are they going to deal with the problem?

d 💬 What would you do in Rachel's situation? Would you call Annie or go and see her? Why?

2 CONVERSATION SKILLS Reassurance

a ▶ 2.15 Watch or listen again. Match the sentences with the responses.
1 ☐ But I can't leave you here on your own.
2 ☐ We've still got so much to do.
3 ☐ It means you won't be able to leave early today.
4 ☐ OK, well if you're sure.

a **Never mind.**
b Of course. **It's no problem.**
c I'll be fine! **Don't worry about it.**
d Oh, **it doesn't matter.**

b ▶ 2.16 Why do you think Tina uses the expressions in **bold** in a–d? Listen and repeat the phrases.

c 💬 In pairs, look at situations 1–6. Take turns to apologise for the problems. Respond with expressions a–d in 2a.
1 You can't help your partner this weekend.
2 You lost your partner's book.
3 You have to cancel the dinner party.
4 You don't have the money you owe your partner.
5 You can't come to the cinema tonight.
6 You're going to be late for the party.

> I'm really sorry, but I can't help you this weekend. I have to work.

> Oh, it doesn't matter.

3 LISTENING

▶ 2.17 Watch or listen to Part 2. Which jobs will Tina do before she goes home?
1 ☐ finish off the flowers
2 ☐ start the order for Mrs Thompson
3 ☐ start the order for the birthday party
4 ☐ put the alarm on
5 ☐ take out the rubbish
6 ☐ take the order for the wedding

52

Hi Rachel, are you free? I've had some really bad news. xx
Annie

Comprehensive approach to speaking skills
A unique combination of language input,
pronunciation and speaking strategies offers
a comprehensive approach to speaking skills.

Spoken outcome
Each C lesson ends
with a practical
spoken outcome.

Support for learners
Tasks are scaffolded
to facilitate success.

Unit Progress Test
Learners are now
ready to do the Unit
Progress Test,
developed by experts
at Cambridge English
Language Assessment.

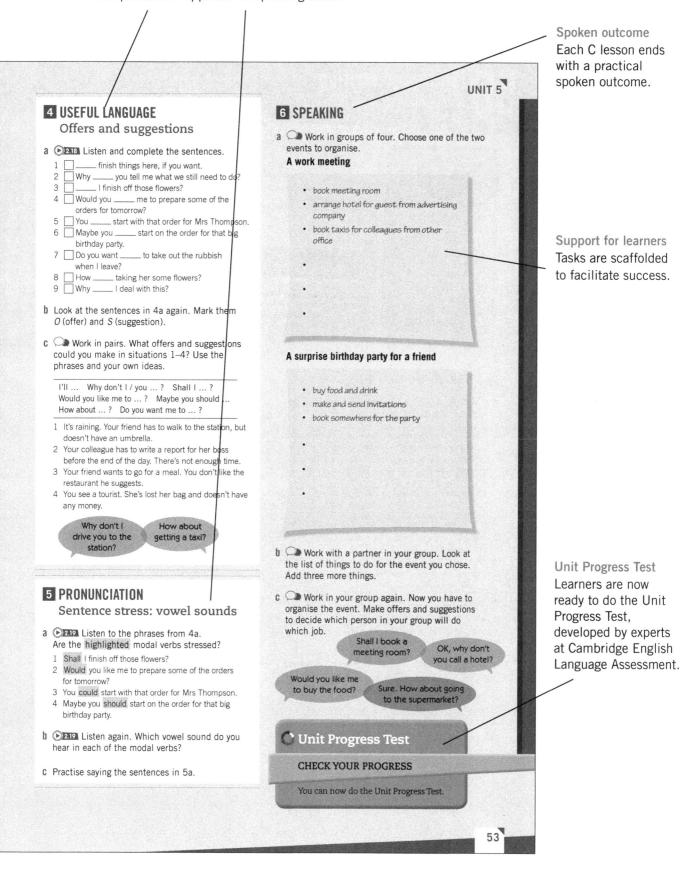

UNIT 5

4 USEFUL LANGUAGE
Offers and suggestions

a ▶2.18 Listen and complete the sentences.
1 ☐ ___ finish things here, if you want.
2 ☐ Why ___ you tell me what we still need to do?
3 ☐ ___ I finish off those flowers?
4 ☐ Would you ___ me to prepare some of the orders for tomorrow?
5 ☐ You ___ start with that order for Mrs Thompson.
6 ☐ Maybe you ___ start on the order for that big birthday party.
7 ☐ Do you want ___ to take out the rubbish when I leave?
8 ☐ How ___ taking her some flowers?
9 ☐ Why ___ I deal with this?

b Look at the sentences in 4a again. Mark them O (offer) and S (suggestion).

c 💬 Work in pairs. What offers and suggestions could you make in situations 1–4? Use the phrases and your own ideas.

I'll ...   Why don't I / you ... ?   Shall I ... ?
Would you like me to ... ?   Maybe you should ...
How about ... ?   Do you want me to ... ?

1 It's raining. Your friend has to walk to the station, but doesn't have an umbrella.
2 Your colleague has to write a report for her boss before the end of the day. There's not enough time.
3 Your friend wants to go for a meal. You don't like the restaurant he suggests.
4 You see a tourist. She's lost her bag and doesn't have any money.

Why don't I drive you to the station?

How about getting a taxi?

5 PRONUNCIATION
Sentence stress: vowel sounds

a ▶2.19 Listen to the phrases from 4a.
Are the highlighted modal verbs stressed?
1 Shall I finish off those flowers?
2 Would you like me to prepare some of the orders for tomorrow?
3 You could start with that order for Mrs Thompson.
4 Maybe you should start on the order for that big birthday party.

b ▶2.19 Listen again. Which vowel sound do you hear in each of the modal verbs?

c Practise saying the sentences in 5a.

6 SPEAKING

a 💬 Work in groups of four. Choose one of the two events to organise.
A work meeting

- book meeting room
- arrange hotel for guest from advertising company
- book taxis for colleagues from other office
-
-
-

A surprise birthday party for a friend

- buy food and drink
- make and send invitations
- book somewhere for the party
-
-
-

b 💬 Work with a partner in your group. Look at the list of things to do for the event you chose. Add three more things.

c 💬 Work in your group again. Now you have to organise the event. Make offers and suggestions to decide which person in your group will do which job.

Shall I book a meeting room?

OK, why don't you call a hotel?

Would you like me to buy the food?

Sure. How about going to the supermarket?

🔘 **Unit Progress Test**

CHECK YOUR PROGRESS

You can now do the Unit Progress Test.

53

13

Lesson D
Integrated skills with a special focus on writing

Skills for writing
The D lessons are highly communicative and cover all four skills, with a special focus on writing. They also recycle and consolidate the core language from the A, B and C lessons.

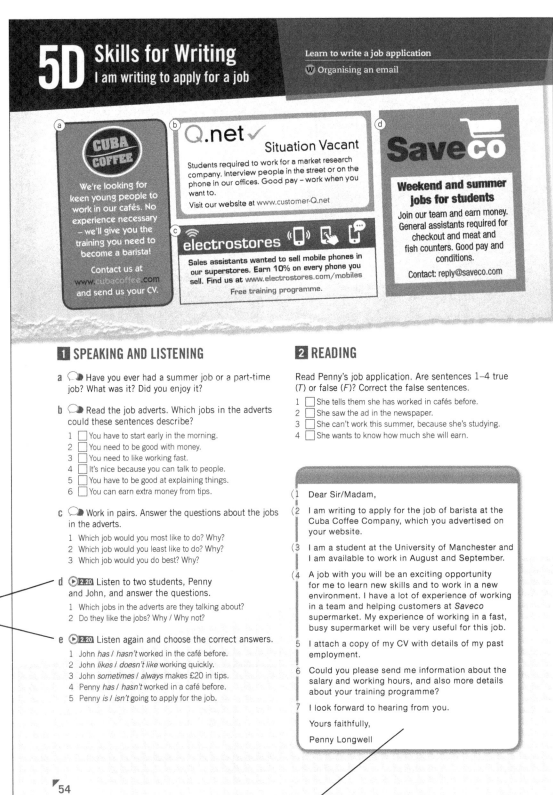

5D Skills for Writing
I am writing to apply for a job

Learn to write a job application
W Organising an email

(a) **CUBA COFFEE**
We're looking for keen young people to work in our cafés. No experience necessary – we'll give you the training you need to become a barista!
Contact us at www.cubacoffee.com and send us your CV.

(b) **Q.net** ✓ Situation Vacant
Students required to work for a market research company. Interview people in the street or on the phone in our offices. Good pay – work when you want to.
Visit our website at www.customer-Q.net

(c) **electrostores**
Sales assistants wanted to sell mobile phones in our superstores. Earn 10% on every phone you sell. Find us at www.electrostores.com/mobiles
Free training programme.

(d) **Saveco**
Weekend and summer jobs for students
Join our team and earn money. General assistants required for checkout and meat and fish counters. Good pay and conditions.
Contact: reply@saveco.com

Receptive skills development
Clearly-staged tasks practise and develop listening and reading skills while supporting learners' understanding of texts.

1 SPEAKING AND LISTENING

a 💬 Have you ever had a summer job or a part-time job? What was it? Did you enjoy it?

b 💬 Read the job adverts. Which jobs in the adverts could these sentences describe?
1 ☐ You have to start early in the morning.
2 ☐ You need to be good with money.
3 ☐ You need to like working fast.
4 ☐ It's nice because you can talk to people.
5 ☐ You have to be good at explaining things.
6 ☐ You can earn extra money from tips.

c 💬 Work in pairs. Answer the questions about the jobs in the adverts.
1 Which job would you most like to do? Why?
2 Which job would you least like to do? Why?
3 Which job would you do best? Why?

d ▶2.20 Listen to two students, Penny and John, and answer the questions.
1 Which jobs in the adverts are they talking about?
2 Do they like the jobs? Why / Why not?

e ▶2.20 Listen again and choose the correct answers.
1 John *has / hasn't* worked in the café before.
2 John *likes / doesn't like* working quickly.
3 John *sometimes / always* makes £20 in tips.
4 Penny *has / hasn't* worked in a café before.
5 Penny *is / isn't* going to apply for the job.

2 READING

Read Penny's job application. Are sentences 1–4 true (*T*) or false (*F*)? Correct the false sentences.
1 ☐ She tells them she has worked in cafés before.
2 ☐ She saw the ad in the newspaper.
3 ☐ She can't work this summer, because she's studying.
4 ☐ She wants to know how much she will earn.

(1) Dear Sir/Madam,

(2) I am writing to apply for the job of barista at the Cuba Coffee Company, which you advertised on your website.

(3) I am a student at the University of Manchester and I am available to work in August and September.

(4) A job with you will be an exciting opportunity for me to learn new skills and to work in a new environment. I have a lot of experience of working in a team and helping customers at *Saveco* supermarket. My experience of working in a fast, busy supermarket will be very useful for this job.

5 I attach a copy of my CV with details of my past employment.

6 Could you please send me information about the salary and working hours, and also more details about your training programme?

7 I look forward to hearing from you.

Yours faithfully,

Penny Longwell

54

Clear models for writing
Clear model texts are provided, on which students can base their own writing.

14

Comprehensive approach to writing skills
Clear focus on key aspects of writing helps develop effective real-world writing skills.

Staged for success
Careful staging and scaffolding generates successful outcomes.

UNIT 5

3 WRITING SKILLS Organising an email

a Penny's email in 2 has seven parts. What does each part of the letter do?

- ☐ says why she's writing
- ☐ asks for more information about the job
- ☐ describes documents she's sending with the email
- ☐ opens the email
- ☐ closes the email
- ☐ says why she wants the job and describes her experience
- ☐ says what she's doing now and when she can work

b Look at sentences 1–5. Which ones are about … ?

- what you are doing now   • past jobs   • skills

1 I am good at working in a team.
2 I have experience of working in a restaurant.
3 I am currently working as a sales assistant in a bookshop.
4 I am studying engineering in Madrid.
5 I speak fluent English.

c What are the missing prepositions? Complete the sentences.

1 I am writing to apply _____ the job _____ barista.
2 I am a student _____ the University of Manchester.
3 I have a lot _____ experience _____ working _____ a team.
4 I look forward _____ hearing from you.

d Put the parts of the email below in the correct order.

I attach a copy of my CV. ☐

I look forward to hearing from you.
Yours faithfully, ☐

I am writing to apply for the job of sales assistant. ☐

Dear Sir/Madam, ☐

I would like to work for your company, because it would be a good opportunity for me to improve my communication skills. I have three years' experience of sales. ☐

Could you send me more information about the working hours? ☐

I am currently working as a sales assistant in a clothes shop. ☐

4 WRITING A job application

a Read the adverts on *Jobsearch.com*. Choose one and write an email applying for the job. Include these parts:

- open the email
- say why you are writing
- say what you are doing now
- say why you want the job
- describe documents you are sending
- ask for more information
- close the email

b Work in groups. Read the applications together. Which student would you give each job to? Why?

◁◇⌂⊕

Jobsearch.com

| Home | New Jobs | Advice |

Use your English … and your local knowledge!
Get a holiday job as a guide for English-speaking tourists to your town.
You will need:
- *a good level of English*
- *knowledge of your local town or area*

VIEW JOB

Work with children and have a holiday
We're looking for people to work on an international holiday camp for children aged 10–15. You will help organise activities and trips, and speak English with the children. We prefer someone with experience of working with children.

VIEW JOB

Evening jobs with Megapizza
We need people to serve and deliver pizzas in the evenings and at weekends.
Good pay and conditions. Must have driving licence.
Contact: *jobs@megapizza.com*

VIEW JOB

55

Written outcome
Each D lesson ends with a practical written outcome, so learners can put new language into practice straight away.

Personal response
Frequent opportunities for personal response make learning more memorable.

Also in every unit:
- Review and Extension page
- Grammar Focus
- Vocabulary Focus
- Communication Plus

15

Syllabus

Lesson and objective	Grammar	Vocabulary	Pronunciationv	Everyday English
Unit 1 Communicating (Teacher's Notes p.20)				
Getting started Talk about sharing things on your phone				
1A Ask and answer personal questions	Question forms	Common adjectives	Syllables and word stress Sentence stress	
1B Talk about how people communicate	Present simple and present continuous	Adverbs	Long and short vowels	
1C Greet people and end conversations			Sentence stress	Greeting people; Ending a conversation
1D Write a personal email				
Review and extension More practice		WORDPOWER *like*		
Unit 2 Travel and Tourism (Teacher's Notes p.33)				
Getting started Talk about holiday activities				
2A Talk about past holidays	Past simple	Tourism	*-ed* endings	
2B Describe difficult journeys	Past continuous	Travel collocations	Sentence stress: vowel sounds	
2C Ask for information in a public place			Joining words	Asking for information in a public place
2D Write a travel blog				
Review and extension More practice		WORDPOWER *off*		
Unit 3 Money (Teacher's Notes p.47)				
Getting started Talk about shopping				
3A Talk about experiences of generosity	Present perfect or past simple	*make / do / give* collocations		
3B Talk about spending and saving money	Present perfect with *just*, *already* and *yet*	Money	Sound and spelling: /dʒ/ and /j/	
3C Talk to people in shops			Sentence stress	Talking to people in shops; Paying at the till
3D Write an update email				
Review and extension More practice		WORDPOWER *just*		
Unit 4 Social Life (Teacher's Notes p.60)				
Getting started Talk about weddings				
4A Talk about your plans for celebrations	Present continuous and *going to*	Clothes and appearance	Sound and spelling: *going to*	
4B Plan a day out in a city	*will / won't / shall*	Adjectives: places	Sound and spelling: *want* and *won't*	
4C Make social arrangements			Sentence stress	Making arrangements
4D Write and reply to invitations				
Review and extension More practice		WORDPOWER *look*		
Unit 5 Work (Teacher's Notes p.73)				
Getting started Talk about people at work				
5A Talk about what people do at work	*must / have to / can*	Work	Word stress	
5B Talk about your future career	*will* and *might* for predictions	Jobs	Sound and spelling: /ʃ/	
5C Make offers and suggestions			Sentence stress: vowel sounds	Offers and suggestions
5D Write a job application				
Review and extension More practice		WORDPOWER *job* and *work*		
Unit 6 Problems and Advice (Teacher's Notes p.86)				
Getting started Talk about being afraid				
6A Give advice on common problems	*should / shouldn't*; imperatives	Verbs with dependent prepositions	Sound and spelling: /uː/ and /ʊ/	
6B Describe extreme experiences	Uses of *to* + infinitive	*-ed / -ing* adjectives	*-ed* endings Word stress	
6C Ask for and give advice			Main stress	Asking for and giving advice
6D Write an email giving advice				
Review and extension More practice		WORDPOWER *verb + to*		

Listening and Video	Reading	Speaking	Writing
Three conversations at a party	Article: *Small Talk*	Getting to know each other	Personal questions
Four monologues about technology and communication	Article: *The Fast and the Furious*	Ways of communicating	Sentences about communicating
Meeting an old friend		Meeting people and ending conversations; Showing interest	**Unit Progress Test**
Conversation: keeping in touch	Three personal emails	Keeping in touch	Personal email Correcting mistakes
Audio diary: *Yes Man changed my life*	Diary article: *Yes Man changed my life*	Types of holiday; A holiday you enjoyed	
Monologue: a bad flight	Two news stories about problems on journeys	Retelling a news story; Problems on journeys	
At the train station		Asking for information in a public place; Asking for more information	**Unit Progress Test**
Conversation: travelling to Indonesia	Travel blog	Writing blogs and diaries	Travel blog Linking words
Radio biography: Philip Wollen	Web forum: *Generosity Day*	Experiences of generosity	
Three monologues: spending habits	Quiz: *What kind of spender are you?*	Spending and saving money	Sentences about spending
Shopping for a present		Talking to people in shops; Changing your mind	**Unit Progress Test**
Four monologues: raising money for charity	Email: update on raising money for charity	Charities	Update email Paragraphing
Interview: May Ball; Audio blog: Indian wedding	Article: *Life in numbers*	Future plans; Preparations for special occasions	
Conversation: Mike and Harry in Tokyo		Tokyo highlights; Planning a day out in a city	Notes on a city you know well
Arranging to meet; birthday dinner		Making arrangements; Making time to think	**Unit Progress Test**
Three monologues: socialising	Two emails: invitations		Invitations and replies
Three monologues: work	Infographic: *The happiest jobs*	What makes people happy at work; Job qualities and requirements	Workplace rules
Three interviews: future careers	Article: *Planning a safe future career*	Your future career; The future world of work	Predictions: finding a job / world of work
Leaving work early		Offers and suggestions; Reassurance	**Unit Progress Test**
Conversation: a summer job	Email: Job application	Summer jobs	Job application Organising an email
	Article: *How to deal with life's little problems*	Common problems and possible solutions; Advice for people who are always late	Advice on a common problem
Two interviews: *Sharks saved my life* (Part 2) / Skydiving accident	Article: *Sharks saved my life* (Part 1)	Emotional experiences; Stories about dramatic events	Notes about a dramatic event
Advising a friend		Asking for and giving advice; Showing sympathy	**Unit Progress Test**
Three monologues: problems	Wiki: Advice for learners of English	Advice	Message giving advice; Linking: ordering ideas and giving examples

Listening and Video	Reading	Speaking	Writing
Two radio monologues: *One minute inspiration, Rivaldo; Sylvester Stallone*	Quotes: life changes	Comparing yourself in the past and now; Life-changing events	Vocabulary definitions
	Article: *1950s and today*	Changes in lifestyle and health	Sentences about changes in health
At the doctor's		Talking to the doctor: describing symptoms; responding to questions	⟳ Unit Progress Test
Three monologues: making a change	Blog: *Living to change*	Making positive changes	Blog: changes / achievements Linking: ordering events
	Article: *Six of the best, biggest and most popular*	Art, music and media	Sentences about art and music
Radio show: *I can't believe it!*		Record breakers; Sports and activities	Sentences about yourself; Notes about sports and activities
Accepting an apology		Apologising; making and accepting excuses	⟳ Unit Progress Test
Three monologues: book reviews	Four book reviews	Books and reading	Book review Positive and negative comments; Linking: *although, however*
Five monologues: study habits	Article: *Unusual degrees*	Degree subjects; Future possibilities	Real possibilities; Future plans
Radio interview: shyness	Article: *The not-so-easy lives of celebrities*	Shyness; Celebrity problems; Actions and feelings	
Telephoning		Telephoning; Dealing with problems on the phone	⟳ Unit Progress Test
Conversation: Online courses	Two student profiles	Advantages and disadvantages of online learning	Personal profile Avoiding repetition
Radio news: illegal downloading		Dishonest behaviour; Honesty quiz	Unreal situations
Radio news: *Complaints around the world*	Article: *The biggest complainers in Europe*	When would you complain?	
Returning goods to a shop		Returning goods and making complaints; Sounding polite	⟳ Unit Progress Test
Three monologues: rudeness	Three emails: apologies	Rude behaviour	Apology emails Formal and informal language
Radio report: inventions	Article: *Science fiction: They thought of it first!*	Definitions; Describing inventions	
	Article: *Lucky discoveries*	Discoveries and inventions	Unexpected events
Lost in a building		Asking for and giving directions in a building; Checking information	⟳ Unit Progress Test
Radio phone in: inventions of the future	Four opinion web posts: important inventions	Useful inventions / important inventions	A web post Giving opinions; Expressing results and reasons
Radio news: *Willie the Parrot*	Article: *Jambo's story*	Experiences with animals; Animal life-savers	Animals causing problems
Three monologues: sibling rivalry	Article: *Brothers and Sisters – The Facts*	Memorable things people say; Family personalities; Sibling relationships	Things people have said to you
Discussion at the gym		Agreeing and disagreeing in discussions	⟳ Unit Progress Test
Monologue: story	Story: unexplained events	Fact or fiction?	Narrative Linkers: past time

Audioscripts p.166   **Phonemic symbols and Irregular verbs p.176**

UNIT 1
Communicating

UNIT OBJECTIVES

At the end of this unit, students will be able to:
- understand texts and conversations about meeting people for the first time and communicating
- discuss attitudes to communication and describe their own communication habits
- exchange personal information
- greet people, show interest in a person and end conversations
- write a personal email

UNIT CONTENTS

G GRAMMAR
- Question forms
- Present simple and present continuous

V VOCABULARY
- Common adjectives: *awful, delicious, gorgeous, perfect, rude, serious, silly, ugly, alright, strange, boring, serious, amazing, lovely, horrible*
- Adverbs: *absolutely, especially, fairly, generally, hardly ever, mainly, normally, particularly, pretty, rarely, really*
- Wordpower: *like* to mean: *for example, if you want, similar to, what is/was your opinion of*

P PRONUNCIATION
- Syllables and word stress
- Sentence stress
- Long and short vowel sounds

C COMMUNICATION SKILLS
- Asking and answering personal questions
- Talk about how you communicate
- Greeting people
- Ending a conversation
- Writing a personal email
- Correcting mistakes

GETTING STARTED

☼ OPTIONAL LEAD-IN

Books closed. Write the following questions on the board: *What time of day do you enjoy most? Who are you with? Why do you like it?* Tell students your own answer, e.g. *I enjoy the early evenings, because I spend time with my children. We have fun together.* Put students in small groups to find out information about each other. Ask some students to share the information they found out with the class.

a Ask students to look at the picture and tell you what they can see. You may want to teach the words *colleague* and *laughing* at this time. Read and talk about the questions. If you wish, give students information from the Culture notes below.

🌎 CULTURE NOTES

The picture shows two workers in London. They are texting and sharing a joke during a work break.

Workers in the UK must have a 20-minute rest break during their working day if they work more than six hours a day. This could be a lunch break or a tea break. Lunch breaks are usually between 30 minutes and an hour long. Most companies in the UK don't allow employees to use personal mobile phones while they are working.

The girl on the right of the picture has a packet of crisps in her hand. Crisps are a popular snack food in the UK. People in the United Kingdom eat 6 billion packets of crisps and 4.4 billion bags of savoury snacks a year – around 150 packets per person, per year.

b Discuss the questions in pairs. Monitor and support students with vocabulary they need to discuss the questions.

☼ EXTRA ACTIVITY

Show students a photo you like on your own phone. Choose a photo with people in it if possible. If your group is large, you could project the photo onto a screen or whiteboard. Encourage questions from the group. Ask the group if they have any pictures on their phone they would like to share with the group. Encourage students to walk around the classroom and show their pictures to other students and ask questions about them in English. Monitor and support students with useful phrases for their conversations.

1A Do you play any sports?

- read and understand a text about having a conversation with someone you don't know
- use some common adjectives correctly
- use question forms correctly
- stress the correct words in questions
- ask for and give personal information

◉ OPTIONAL LEAD-IN

Books closed. Tell students about someone you recently met for the first time. This could be a friend of a friend, someone who you sat next to on a train, etc. Tell them where you met, why you started talking, what you talked about, whether it was an interesting conversation and why or why not. Write on the board: *Where? When? Why? What? interesting?* Then put students into pairs and ask them to tell each other about someone they met for the first time recently. Stop students after a few minutes and ask for examples from their conversations. Find out who had the most interesting conversation.

1 SPEAKING AND LISTENING

a 💬 Tell students to open the book and look at the pictures 1–3 to tell you what they can see. Elicit answers to the three questions and encourage students to justify their answers as far as possible.

b ▶1.2 Tell students that they are going to hear three conversations from the party and they need to identify what the people talk about in the different conversations. Go through the list of topics first to check understanding. Play the recording, pausing after each conversation to take feedback from the class. You may need to play the conversations more than once. With a stronger group, ask students to work individually and then compare their answers in pairs. Check the answers as a class.

Answers
the party: 1, 2, 3; people they know: 1; money: 2; where they live: 1, 2; work: 2; their interests: 3; education: 1

Audioscript

A It's a nice day today.
B Yes, it's a perfect day for a birthday party. It's great that so many people are here.
A So, how do you know Ana?
B We were at university together. We did the same course.
A Oh right. What did you study?
B English Literature. And you? How do you know Ana?
A I'm her neighbour. I live in the house next door.
B Really? It's a lovely street.
A I think so. So did you come …

C How's the food?
D It's great. The pizza is delicious. It's always nice to get good food at a party … Err … So, do you live near here?
C Yeah, I live down by the river. You know those flats …
D Oh yeah! The new ones. They're expensive! How much rent do you pay?
C Err … not much. It's not so … expensive … err …

D So what do you do?
C I work for a bank.
D So, how much do you earn?
C Erm, is that … er … over there … Sorry, I just have to speak to my friend, because …

E What do you think of the party?
F Yeah, it's great. It's really nice to meet all of Ana's friends. You?
E It's all right, but the music is a bit boring.
F Mmm.
E I like your T-shirt. Is it for a football team?
F No! At least I don't think so!
E So, do you play any sports?
F No, not really. I don't really like sport.
E Well, what do you like then?
F I prefer reading, or watching films.
E Oh.
F Yeah, so I might go to the cinema after the party. There's a new film about a man who goes to Peru to visit his brother and …

E Yeah, I saw that last week.
F Oh. What was it like?
E Oh, it's an awful film. Really boring.
F OK, well, I'd like to see it anyway. Perhaps I'll like it.

E No, I don't think so. It's a really strange story. And in the end, the man can't find his brother and he just goes home again.
F Oh, thanks a lot!

c ▶1.2 Play the recording again. Students say if they think the speakers are not enjoying their conversations and give reasons. If necessary, pause after each conversation.

Answer
Conversation 2: The woman doesn't seem happy answering questions about money – she hesitates and then moves on.
Conversation 3: The man isn't enjoying the party. At first, the woman answers but doesn't ask questions. Then they don't agree about a film the woman wants to see and the man tells her how the film ends!

◉ EXTRA ACTIVITY

Give students some lines from the conversations and ask them what the responses were. Don't worry if students don't remember the responses word for word, e.g. Say: *It's a nice day today.* Students: *It's a perfect/great day for a (birthday) party.* Put students in pairs and give them each a conversation to role play. Monitor and help with prompts if necessary. Choose a pair to perform their conversation for the class.

◉ FAST FINISHERS

Ask fast finishers to re-create the other two conversations.

2 VOCABULARY Common adjectives

a ▶1.3 Students complete the sentences. Play the recording again to check.

Answers
1 perfect 2 delicious 3 alright, boring 4 awful 5 strange

b Discuss the questions as a class. Give some practice by asking students to tell you something that they think is perfect/delicious/alright/boring/awful/strange, e.g. *I'm reading a boring book at the moment.*

Answers
positive: perfect, delicious; negative: boring, awful, strange; OK: alright

c ▶ Students complete the exercises in Vocabulary Focus 1A on SB p.133. Play the recording for Exercise a, and encourage students to identify and underline the adjectives. Students complete Exercise b and Exercise c, working individually and compare their answers with a partner. Then check the answers as a class. For Exercise d, check understanding of *syllable* and *stressed* and play the recording twice: once for students to decide how many syllables there are in each word and again for them to underline the stressed syllables. Monitor and correct students' pronunciation as appropriate. Tell students to go back to SB p.8.

> **Answers (Vocabulary Focus 1A SB p.133)**
> a 1 silly; boring   2 rude; serious   3 awful; horrible
>   4 awful; horrible   5 lovely; perfect   6 strange; alright
>   7 amazing; ugly
> b 1 alright   2 strange   3 ugly   4 rude   5 delicious   6 silly
>   7 serious   8 boring
> c very nice/good: gorgeous, lovely, amazing, perfect
>   very bad: horrible, awful
> d de<u>li</u>cious 3   <u>ug</u>ly 2   <u>se</u>rious 3   <u>rude</u> 1   <u>al</u>right 2   <u>sil</u>ly 2
>   <u>bor</u>ing 2   <u>strange</u> 1   <u>gor</u>geous 2   <u>hor</u>rible 3   <u>aw</u>ful 2
>   per<u>fect</u> 2

3 READING

a Read through the questions with the class and then students discuss the questions in pairs.

b Ask students what they think the title of the article means. (*Small talk* is friendly conversation about things that aren't very important, often just to pass the time.) Students read the first paragraph. Discuss the answers to the questions as a class. (The article is for people who don't know what to say when meeting people for the first time. It offers a solution to the problem by giving ideas for some good questions to start a conversation.)

c Read through the questions as a class. Students read the rest of the article individually and use the questions to complete the text. They then check in pairs. Finally, check the answers as a class.

> **Answers**
> 1/2   How do you know Ana? How's the food?
> 3   Where did you buy them?
> 4   Do you play any sports?
> 5   Do you live near here?
> 6   What do you do?
> 7/8   How much do you earn? How much rent do you pay?

d 💬 Students read the article again in pairs and discuss whether they agree with the advice. Ask the class to discuss and explain their opinions.

> 📖 **VOCABULARY SUPPORT**
>
> *relationship* (B1) – the family connection between people
> *topic* (B1) – subject

> 💡 **FAST FINISHERS**
>
> Ask fast finishers to think of some more conversation-starting questions for each section of the article.

4 GRAMMAR Question forms

a Books closed. Put students in small groups. Give them two minutes to remember as many questions from the listening and reading tasks as they can. Ask each group in turn to tell you a question. Write the questions on the board. Which group remembered the most? Ask students to look at the questions in the book. Are any the same as the ones on the board? Individually, students complete the tables. Check answers as a class.

> **Answers**
> Why were you late?
> Are you married?
> Is she your sister?
> Where did you meet?
> Who do you know at this party?
> Do you like the music?

b Ask students for the answers to the questions. You could elicit the present simple third person singular auxiliary *does* at this point.

> **Answers**
> 1 *be*
> 2 auxiliary verb (a verb giving grammatical information, not meaning)

c ▶ Students read the information in Grammar Focus 1A on SB p.142. Play the recording and ask students to listen and repeat. Students then complete the exercises in Grammar Focus 1A on SB p.143. Check the answers as a class, making sure that students are using the auxiliary verbs correctly and that they are not adding 's' to the infinitive. Tell students to go back to SB p.9.

> **Answers (Grammar Focus 1A SB p.143)**
> a 1 live   2 are   3 see   4 know   5 do   6 like   7 's   8 sit
> b 1 3 4 5 6 8
> c 1 What kind of books do you usually read?
>   2 Did you watch the Olympics on TV?
>   3 What was the food like in India?
>   4 Do you go to the gym?
>   5 How much does she earn?
>   6 Is it cold today?
>   7 Where do they go on holiday?
>   8 Am I late?
> d 1 Why do you want to go home?
>   2 Who did you meet at the party?
>   3 How much was your car?
>   4 Which film did you see?
>   5 Whose key is this?
>   6 How many people did you invite?
>   7 What was the film like?
>   8 What kind of music do you like?

d ▶ **1.8** **Pronunciation** Play the recording for students to underline the stressed words. Check as a class. Then play the recording again and students repeat the questions, using the correct stress. If you wish, you can provide more practice by writing some more questions from the lesson so far on the board and asking the class to repeat them, paying attention to reproduce the correct stress pattern.

> **Answers**
> <u>Where</u> did you <u>meet</u>?
> <u>Are</u> you <u>married</u>?
> <u>Who</u> do you <u>know</u> at this <u>party</u>?
> <u>Why</u> were you <u>late</u>?
> Do you <u>like</u> the <u>music</u>?
> Is <u>she</u> your <u>sister</u>?

LOA TIP DRILLING

- Students whose first language is not 'stress-timed' (i.e. all the words in a sentence receive equal emphasis) may have difficulties with word and sentence stress in English. It is helpful to give tasks that help students recognise where word and syllable stress is placed, but it is also important to get students to practise it themselves by repeating.

- Drilling words and sentences in chorus is useful because it encourages students to follow the pattern of the other students. You can vary drilling in chorus with asking individual students to repeat words and sounds.

- It may be appropriate to ask students to overemphasise the stress on the words or syllables to help them at first, then reduce this later.

- Repetition should not continue for too long as you don't want the class to lose interest.

e Students do the task individually and check in pairs.

> **Answers and audioscript**
> Why were you late?
> Are you married?
> Is she your sister?
> Where did you meet?
> Who do you know at this party?
> Do you like the music?

f ▶**1.9** Play the recording for students to listen and check. Then play the recording again for them to underline the stressed words. Check as a class.

> **Answers and audioscript**
> 1 What <u>kind</u> of <u>music</u> do you <u>like</u>?
> 2 What do your <u>parents</u> <u>do</u>?
> 3 Did you <u>grow up</u> in this <u>area</u>?
> 4 How <u>old</u> are <u>you</u>?
> 5 Do you <u>have</u> any <u>hobbies</u>?
> 6 Do you <u>speak</u> any other <u>languages</u>?

g 💬 Students ask and answer the questions in pairs. Monitor for correct word order and stress. Correct any grammatical or stress errors. Help with ideas for kinds of music and hobbies where necessary. Note any interesting answers and discuss them with the class.

5 SPEAKING

a Go through the list of topics and elicit a question for each topic. If necessary, be ready to give some examples yourself, e.g. *Do you live near the school? Do you have a good relationship with your brother?* Students work individually, writing their questions.

b 💬 Students ask and answer the questions in small groups. Before they start, ask them to find out more information after the answer to the first question and read through the examples with them. Monitor the groups but don't stop and correct any mistakes. Note or remember any basic problems to go through afterwards. While monitoring, you can ask and answer some questions yourself to encourage students. After the activity, ask for examples of interesting information students found out.

💡 EXTRA ACTIVITY

Change the groups and give students a different character, name or role, e.g. *Jean, French, 35.* Students think of a background for this person and then ask and answer the same questions as before but this time for their character. Monitor but don't interrupt fluency unless students make mistakes with question forms.

ADDITIONAL MATERIAL

▶ Workbook 1A

▶ Photocopiable activities: Grammar p.204, Vocabulary p.206, Pronunciation p.264

1B I'm really into Facebook

At the end of this lesson, students will be able to:

- read and understand an article about digital forms of communication
- understand speakers giving their opinions about digital technology
- understand and use frequency adverbs correctly
- pronounce long and short vowels accurately
- use present simple and continuous tenses correctly
- discuss digital technology

1 READING AND LISTENING

OPTIONAL LEAD-IN

Books closed. Ask students: *How do people communicate?* Put a list on the board, e.g. *phone conversations (landline and mobile), texts/text messages, emails, instant messages, social networking sites, letters, postcards, face-to-face, skype.* Have a brief discussion with the class about their favourite way to communicate and ask for reasons.

a Students open their books and look at the title of the page *(I'm really into Facebook)*. Elicit the meaning of *be really into* (really like/enjoy). Students discuss the points in 1a with a partner. Ask students to share their ideas with the class. If you wish, give students information from the Culture notes below.

b Tell students that they are going to read an article about different people's views. Ask them to read the introduction and then look at the quote below each picture. In pairs, students guess the missing word. Don't check the answers at this point.

c Read through the questions in 1c with the class. Students then read and answer the questions individually. Check the answers for 1b and 1c as a class.

Answers

b Julie: text message
   Marc: emails
   Gin: forget
   Claudio: instant message
c 1 because she generally does
   2 people's birthdays, and big news
   3 so his friends and family know his news
   4 because it's better than a lot of shouting and crying

VOCABULARY SUPPORT

abroad (B2) – in another country

blog (B1) – information that you put on the Internet regularly for people to read

cancel (B1) – stop something that's arranged

comment (B1) – words or message about something

instant message (IM) – a way of communicating very quickly online

realise (B1) – suddenly start to understand

separate, independent of each other (B1) – different

CULTURE NOTES

In 2014, the social networking site Facebook had around 1.3 billion users, with 654 million using the site every day on their smartphones or tablets. 70 different languages are available for users. Facebook has changed people's lives in various ways because it allows users to stay in touch with friends, relatives and other acquaintances continuously wherever there is Internet access. People with common interests can meet through Facebook groups, and family members and friends can be reunited after losing touch. In 2011, Facebook claimed that 48% of 18–34 year-olds in the US check their Facebook page in the morning when they wake up.

Instant messages (IM) are text messages that are sent over the internet, via social media or special applications (apps). Many different apps for mobile devices allow users to send free messages. The most popular app in 2014 was WhatsApp with over 500 million users. In 2014, WhatsApp delivered more than 10 billion messages, 700 million photos and 100 million videos every day. WhatsApp was bought by Facebook in 2014.

d ▶ 1.10 Tell students that they are going to hear four people talking about communication. Read through the topics with the class and play the recording for students to match the speakers and topics. Listen again, this time pause the recording after each speaker to check the answers.

Answers

Tara: relationships and text messages; Magda: plans and text messages; Chris: important days and Facebook; Mike: blogs and emails

Audioscript

TARA Last year, my ex-boyfriend told me he didn't want to see me any more ... by text message! What kind of person does that? It was horrible. I called him for days, but he didn't answer. I think he just wanted me to go away. What an idiot.

MAGDA When I want to plan something, I generally just send a text. It's the same when I cancel – a text message is easier. You don't need to give a reason or hear the other person's voice. It's better for everyone.

CHRIS Birthdays are different now. I hardly ever get cards or presents from friends, or even my brother, and no one calls. Everyone just writes 'happy birthday' on my wall on Facebook. It's not very friendly, in my opinion.

MIKE My daughter is travelling around Asia at the moment. She's writing a blog so we know what she's doing. But she rarely calls. I'd love to get a postcard or a letter sometimes. Just to know she's thinking about me.

e ▶ **1.10** Play the recording again. You may wish to help students with words in the Vocabulary support box. Students say if each person is happy with the use of technology, and why or why not. Check the answers as a class.

Answers
Tara: unhappy, because her boyfriend ended their relationship by text message
Magda: happy, because it's easy (and you don't have to give a long explanation, with a lot of reasons, or have a difficult conversation)
Chris: unhappy, because it's not very friendly just to write 'happy birthday' on someone's wall and not send a card or give a present
Mike: unhappy, because his daughter rarely calls or sends postcards or letters

---

📖 **VOCABULARY SUPPORT**

ex-boyfriend (B2) – a person who was a boyfriend in the past and isn't now

idiot (B2) – a stupid person

💡 **EXTRA ACTIVITY**

Write these phrases from the listening on the board.

1 I called him for days, but …

2 I think he just wanted me …

3 It's not very friendly, in …

4 She's writing a blog so we know …

Ask students to work in pairs to complete the phrases from memory if they can. Play the recording again to check. (1 *he didn't answer* 2 *to go away* 3 *my opinion* 4 *what she's doing*)

---

f 💬 Elicit some phrases that are useful for agreeing and disagreeing, e.g. *I agree with you. I completely disagree with you!* Check students understand when we use the word *congratulations*, e.g. when someone has done something very good / on birthdays / at weddings and ask them when they last congratulated someone. Students talk about their ideas in pairs before coming together to discuss as a class.

💡 **FAST FINISHERS**

Ask fast finishers to make a list of do's and don'ts for using technology in communication.

---

2 VOCABULARY Adverbs

a Write this sentence on the board: *I often make phone calls at lunch time.* Ask students what we call the word *often* (an adverb). Tell students that an adverb tells us more about the verb, e.g. *often* tells us about frequency. Some adverbs can also be used with adjectives. Such adverbs intensify/make stronger or moderate/make weaker an action (if used with verbs, e.g. *She walks pretty fast*) or a state (if used with adjectives, e.g. *She is pretty clever*). Ask students to look at the highlighted adverbs in the text and answer the questions together. Elicit that the adverbs in 1 are used with a verb and the adverbs in 2 with an adjective.

Answers
1 absolutely, particularly, really, especially
2 pretty, fairly

---

b Read through the sentences with the class and then ask them to complete 1–4 with the frequency adverbs. Practise by eliciting sentences from students about what they often/generally/rarely do in the mornings.

Answers
1/2 generally, mainly   3/4 hardly ever, rarely

📖 **VOCABULARY SUPPORT**

Frequency adverbs generally go *before* the main verb, but they go *after* the verb be: *I usually get up at 7.30.* BUT *I am often late.* Students often make mistakes with this, e.g. *I often am late.* Also note that the adverb *sometimes* can also go at the beginning or end of a sentence, e.g. *Sometimes I go shopping on Saturdays. I go shopping on Saturdays sometimes.*

---

c ▶ **1.11** **Pronunciation** Write on the board: *often* and *normally* and ask students to say them for you. Elicit the difference between the pronunciation of the first vowel in each: *often* is a short vowel and *normally* is a long vowel. Students then decide which column in the table has underlined vowels which are long and which has underlined vowels that are short. Play the recording for students to listen and check. Then play it again for them to listen and repeat.

Answers
Column 1: long vowels Column 2: short vowels

---

d ▶ **1.12** Play the recording and pause after each sentence for students to repeat with the correct pronunciation and stress.

e 💬 Individually, students change the sentences to apply to them and they then compare their new sentences in pairs. Monitor to give encouragement and help where necessary. Note any interesting answers and discuss them with the class.

💡 **EXTRA ACTIVITY**

Students write three sentences of activities they do but without the frequency adverb, e.g. *I go to a restaurant with my friends. I get up early. I play tennis.* Put students into pairs. They read their sentences to their partner who tries to guess the frequency, e.g. *A: I get up early. B: You always get up early! A: No, I hardly ever get up early! I start work at 10.30.* Monitor and check that students are putting the adverb in the correct position in the sentence. Point out errors for students to self-correct.

3 GRAMMAR

Present simple and present continuous

a Books closed. Write three sentences on the board: *I'm talking to my students about communication. I have a Facebook account. I don't go on Facebook every day.* (If the second and third sentences are not true for you, you could change them slightly.) Ask students what the main verb is in each sentence. (*'m talking, have, don't use*). Underline the main verbs as students identify them. Ask students which verb form is different (*'m talking*). Elicit the name of the tense (present continuous). Ask students: *Why did I use the present continuous for this sentence?* (Because it's about right now.) Ask students what the verb form in the other two sentences is (present simple). Open books. Ask students to read the sentences and say which are present simple and which are present continuous.

> **Answers**
> 1/2 simple   3/4 continuous

b Students match sentences and uses in pairs. Check the answers as a class and ask for another example of each use.

> **Answers**
> habits and routines: 2
> feelings and permanent situations: 1
> actions right now: 3
> temporary actions around now: 4

 LOA TIP CONCEPT CHECKING

Ask concept questions to check students understand the different uses of the present simple and continuous as shown in the example sentences 1–4:

Ask: From these sentences, do we know these things?

1 *Is the girl putting her photos on the blog now?* (No / We don't know.)

   Does she often put photos on her blog? (Yes, she does.)

2 *Is she sending a text at this moment?* (No / We don't know.)

   Does she send a text every time she plans something? (Yes, she does.)

3 *How often does she wait for text messages?* (We don't know.)

   Is she waiting for a text message now? (Yes)

4 *Does she write a blog every time she goes away?* (No / We don't know.)

   Is she writing a blog at this moment? (We don't know.)

   Is she writing a blog about this journey? (Yes, she is.)

   When will she stop writing it? (When she comes home.)

c Students read the information in Grammar Focus 1B on SB p.142. Play the recording for students to listen and repeat. Allow time to focus on the spelling notes for verb + *-ing*. Put a short list of verbs on the board for students to spell the *-ing* form, e.g. *put* (putting). Students then complete the exercises in Grammar Focus 1B on SB p.143. Check the answers with the class, making sure that students use the correct forms and, where necessary, put the adverbs in the correct positions. Tell students to go back to SB p.11.

> **Answers (Grammar Focus 1B SB p.143)**
> **a** 1 a1 b2   2 a2 b1   3 a2 b1   4 a1 b2
> **b** 1 I'm eating   2 isn't wearing   3 She normally goes
>   4 I'm studying   5 look   6 hardly ever visit
>   7 we're working   8 Does your brother like
> **c** 1 are you doing?   2 I'm checking   3 do you check
>   4 I usually check   5 my sister is travelling
>   6 She usually sends   7 she's travelling   8 Is she going?
>   9 She doesn't like   10 She prefers   11 She's driving
>   12 It's in   13 There are   14 is she spending

⊙ CAREFUL!

Some learners may overuse the present simple and others may overuse the present continuous if there is no distinction in their first language. If you have a multilingual class, be aware of this. Make sure students don't miss out the verb *be* when using the present continuous, e.g. ~~I watching a good TV programme~~. (Correct form = *I'm watching a good TV programme.*)

📖 LANGUAGE NOTES

There are some verbs we don't usually use in the continuous form, e.g. *think (What do you think about the problem?), know (Do you know Sandy in Class 7?).* However, some of these verbs can be used in the continuous form when they have certain meanings, e.g. *Wait a moment, I'm thinking.*

Other verbs are commonly used in both the simple and continuous, but with different meanings: *I have a big house near Paris.* (state) *I'm having dinner at the moment – I'll call you back later.* (action) This applies to other continuous tenses as well as the present.

4 SPEAKING

a Read through the examples with the class before you start, then put students into pairs to ask and answer the questions. Encourage them to add more information if they can. Monitor and note any common errors. When they have finished, ask students for interesting examples from their conversations. Do a quick survey to find who does each activity most often and who does it least often. Go through common errors together.

💡 FAST FINISHERS

Ask fast finishers to make up some more questions to add to the list. They can ask the rest of the class these questions after the activity.

ADDITIONAL MATERIAL

▶ Workbook 1B

▶ Photocopiable activities: Grammar p.205, Vocabulary p.229, Pronunciation p.266

1C Everyday English
It was really nice to meet you

- understand an informal conversation where people meet each other after a long time
- use phrases to greet people
- use expressions to show interest in a conversation
- use phrases to end a conversation
- use stress to improve pronunciation

OPTIONAL LEAD-IN

Books closed. Tell students about a friend you remember that you haven't seen for a long time (more than two years). Talk about what you remember about them and say what you would talk about if you met again. Give students two minutes to think of a friend they haven't seen for a long time, and prepare to talk about them. Help students with vocabulary if necessary. Put students in pairs to talk about their friends. Ask one or two students to tell the class what they found out from their partner.

1 LISTENING

a Students open their books. Discuss the questions as a class. Look at the examples. You may want to mime the words: *hug, kiss, shake hands*. If you have a multilingual class, the conversation may continue longer as students compare the things they do and say within their different linguistic and cultural contexts.

b Ask students to look at the pictures and tell you what they can see. Then ask them the questions. Don't tell them if they are correct at this point.

c ▶ 1.15 Play Part 1 of the video or play the audio recording for the class to check their answers to 1b.

Video/Audioscript (Part 1)

RACHEL Annie?
ANNIE Rachel!
R Long time no see! How are you?
A I'm great. What a lovely surprise! Great to see you!
R Yeah! You too.
A When did we last see each other?
R Oh, I think it was about … six years ago! So … where are you living these days?
A Oh, not far from here. I live on Hampton Street. Do you know it?
R Yes, I do. That's really close to the centre.
A Mmm. How about you?
R We live on Compton Road.
A Oh – how nice!

MARK My name's Mark, by the way.
A Hi. Nice to meet you.
M Nice to meet you, too.
R Sorry, yes – Mark's my husband!
A Husband – wow! That's fantastic news. When did you get married?
R Six months ago.
M Eight months ago.
R It was six, Mark.
A Well, congratulations! I want to know all the details! Look – I'm going to the café down the street now to meet Leo, my boyfriend. Would you both like to come?
R Yeah, that sounds good.
A Brilliant! Let's go.

Answers
The two women in the first picture (Annie and Rachel) already know each other's names, (*Annie? / Rachel!*), but Annie and Mark in the second picture are meeting for the first time. (*My name's Mark. / Hi. Nice to meet you.*)

d ▶ 1.15 Read through the sentences with the class and play the recording again for students to answer true or false. If necessary, play the recording twice and pause after the information is given. Check the answers as a class and ask students to correct the false sentences.

Answers
1 T
2 F (really close to the centre)
3 F (six months ago – or eight months ago if Mark is right!)
4 T
5 F (to a café)

2 USEFUL LANGUAGE Greeting people

a ▶ 1.16 Students complete the sentences with the words in the box. Play the recording for them to check the answers. Model the sentences for students to copy the pronunciation and intonation.

Answers
1 no see   2 are you   3 to see you   4 these days
5 by the way   6 meet you

b Students answer the questions together.

Answers
1 1, 2, 3, 4
2 5, 6

EXTRA ACTIVITY

Tell students to close their books and see if they can remember all six phrases from 2a.

c ▶ 1.17 Ask students if they can remember the replies to the phrases in 2a that they heard in Part 1 of the recording. Tell them to listen to these phrases and note down the replies, which are the same or similar to the ones in Part 1. Play the recording, pausing after each phrase to give students time to note the replies. Write on the board: *How are you?* Ask one student. Write the reply they give you on the board. Then ask another student. Don't accept the same answer. Elicit another answer, e.g. *I'm fine. / Fine, thanks. / Fantastic. / Not bad.* Go through 2a 1-6 with the whole class (you may want to omit 1 with less confident groups) and write on the board any correct ideas the class give for replies they could use.

Audioscript
1
R Long time no see!
A Yes it is! Great to see you!
2
R How are you?
A I'm great, thanks. How are you?
3
A Great to see you!
R Lovely to see you too.

4
R Where are you living these days?
A I live on Hampton Street. Do you know it?
5
M My name's Mark, by the way.
A Hi! Nice to meet you.
6
A Nice to meet you.
B Nice to meet you, too.

d In pairs, students practise saying the phrases and replying. Demonstrate first with a strong student.

3 CONVERSATION SKILLS
Showing interest

a ▶**1.18** With a stronger group, read through the adjectives in the box before playing the recording and ask students if they can remember the phrases which used these adjectives. Then play the recording for students to complete the conversation and/or check their answers. When feeding back, model the sentences for students to copy the pronunciation and intonation.

> **Answers**
> 1 lovely
> 2 nice
> 3 fantastic
> 4 good

b Elicit from the students that the highlighted phrases don't add extra information but indicate interest and/or surprise on the part of the speaker. Point out the intonation pattern for these phrases (rising then falling).

c Tell students to use the completed phrases in 3a to complete the rules. Then ask for examples of other words to complete the expressions.

> **Answers**
> 1 adjective + noun
> 2 adjective
> 3 adjective
> 4 adjective

d Read through the task and examples and students do the task in pairs. Monitor and help where necessary or quickly correct misuse of the target language. Mention interesting replies during class feedback.

4 PRONUNCIATION Sentence stress

a ▶**1.19** This exercise practises sentence stress. Tell students that English is a stress-timed language which means that certain words in a sentence will be more heavily stressed than others. Say that sentence stress is significant because emphasising some words more heavily than others shows that the information they carry is particularly important. Play the recording, stopping after each sentence for students to repeat and try to reproduce the stress pattern they have just heard.

b Elicit from the students that the stressed words are words that give information.

5 LISTENING

a Students look at the picture and answer the questions. If they are having difficulties, tell them to look back at how the conversation in Part 1 of the recording finished.

> **Answer**
> Leo, Annie's boyfriend. He doesn't know Rachel and Mark.

b ▶**1.20** Tell students that they are going to hear the conversation in the café. In pairs, they predict three things that they think the people will talk about. Play Part 2 of the video or play the audio recording for them to check.

> **Answers**
> sports, plans for next week/weekend, jobs, family

Video/Audioscript (Part 2)

MARK Do you play much sport?
LEO Not really. I occasionally watch the rugby on TV, but I'm not a big sports fan.
MARK Did you see the match at the weekend?
RACHEL Oh, not sport again!
ANNIE So, do you have any exciting plans for next week?
M Well, er …
R No, not really. Just work. I've got a lot to do in the shop this week, because we're going to a wedding next weekend.
A Oh, the shop? What do you do?
R I'm a florist.
A What a great job! Where's the shop?
R Not far from here. I'll show you some time.
A That would be great! And are you the manager, or …
R Well, not really – it's my shop.
A Wow. That's amazing! So you're a businesswoman! Do you work on your own?
R No, I have someone to help. Tina. She comes in for a few hours every day.
A Oh, that's good.
R How about you? What do you do?
A Oh, marketing. Boring!
R Same as Mark. He works in marketing.
A Oh, I'm sorry. I find it boring.
R Do you have any plans for the weekend?
A Actually, yes. I'm going to visit my brother, Dan.
R Oh, I remember Dan. How is he?
A He's fine. He's married now. To Martina.
R Anyway, we really must go. I need to get back to the shop.
A Yeah, of course.
M It was really nice to meet you.
A Yeah, you too.
L Nice to meet you, Mark.
R It was great to see you again, Annie.
A Yeah! We must meet up soon!
R Definitely!
A Actually, it's Leo's birthday in a couple of weeks. Perhaps we can meet then.
R OK, great. I'll give you a call. And say hello to Dan for me!

---

c ▶**1.20** Read through the questions with the class and play the recording again for students to answer them. If students need more support, pause the recording briefly after the information is given to allow students time to note their answers. Play the recording for students to answer or check their ideas.

> **Answers**
> 1 They're going to a wedding next weekend. Rachel has a lot of work to do in the shop.
> 2 She's a florist/businesswoman.
> 3 Tina
> 4 It's boring.
> 5 He works in marketing.
> 6 She's going to visit her brother, Dan.
> 7 Rachel needs to get back to the shop.
> 8 She suggests they should meet up for Leo's birthday in a couple of weeks.

📖 VOCABULARY SUPPORT

florist – a person who sells flowers

marketing (B2) – a job that involves encouraging people to buy a product or service

wedding (B1) – the event when two people get married

---

6 USEFUL LANGUAGE
Ending conversations

a With a strong group, ask: *Can you remember how the people ended their conversations?* Students try to complete the phrases. Then play the recording for students to complete the phrases or check their answers. Model the phrases for students to repeat.

> **Answers**
> 1 go
> 2 meet
> 3 see
> 4 meet up
> 5 Say

b Elicit different ways to say goodbye in English from the class. Then ask students to find a phrase for saying goodbye to someone you have just met.

> **Answer**
> 2 It was really nice to meet you.

c Students do the ordering task in pairs. Monitor and encourage students to look at the start and end of the lines and the use of A/B to give them clues about what went before or what goes after. Point out the example (1) and elicit the next sentence if you think students need more help. Check the answers as a class. Ask students to practise reading the completed conversation in pairs. Remind them to use appropriate intonation to show interest.

> **Answers**
> 6, 5, 1, 3, 7, 4, 2

> ### 💡 FAST FINISHERS
> Ask fast finishers to add some more sentences to the middle of the conversation.

> ### 💡 EXTRA ACTIVITY
> Read the conversation through and stop at different places for students to supply the missing words, e.g. *Do you play much (sport)? Not really, I'm not a big (sports fan).*

7 SPEAKING

a 💬 Tell students that they can now practise all the language from the lesson with a partner. Divide students into pairs and assign A and B roles. Students A read the instructions in 7b. Students B read the instructions on SB p.129. Explain that they will use the information on their cards to have two different conversations with their partner.

b Students look at the information and think about what they're going to say in the first conversation. Suggest that they make some notes about this. Circulate and give help where necessary.

c 💬 Students role play the first conversation. Monitor and listen for correct usage of the target language from this lesson.

> ### LOA TIP MONITORING
>
> Don't interrupt or stop students while they are doing this activity. However, if they have problems trying to think of things to say, give them some help and encouragement by prompting them, e.g. if they don't have an idea of their own, say: *family? recent holiday?* Additionally, if they struggle for phrases to use, prompt by giving one or two words, e.g. say: *Long time …? What a lovely …?* Remember to appear interested and smile while they are doing the activity to encourage further conversation.

> ### 💡 FAST FINISHERS
> Ask fast finishers to role play a similar conversation. Give them some suggestions, e.g. you are on holiday and you meet someone on a trip for the first time.

d 💬 Students have the second conversation. Monitor and help as necessary. If appropriate, nominate a strong pair to perform one of the conversations for the class.

> ### ADDITIONAL MATERIAL
>
> ▶ Workbook 1C
> ▶ Photocopiable activities: Pronunciation p.263
> ▶ Unit Progress Test
> ▶ Personalised online practice

1D Skills for Writing
I'm sending you some photos

At the end of this lesson, students will be able to:

- understand a conversation where people talk about keeping in contact
- discuss ways of and frequency of keeping in touch with people
- understand emails about different language learning experiences
- check and correct mistakes in writing
- write an email to someone they don't often see

☺ OPTIONAL LEAD-IN

Books closed. Ask students *How many texts have you sent today? How many texts have you received?* Ask students to write down an approximate answer for each question. Total up how many texts the class has sent and received on this day. Find out if students are surprised or not.

1 SPEAKING AND LISTENING

a Students open their books and look at the messages. Discuss the questions as a class. If you wish, give students information from the Culture notes below.

> **Answers**
> get in touch – get in contact (*keep in touch* means 'stay in contact')
> get – receive
> haven't heard from you – haven't received a call or a message

🌍 CULTURE NOTES

Salamanca is a city in north-west Spain. Salamanca University was founded in 1218 and for four centuries was one of the greatest universities in the world. Today the university has around 30,000 students and also runs a Spanish language school – one of the largest in Spain. Several thousand foreign students learn Spanish in Salamanca every year.

b Play the recording for students to say who is better at keeping in touch: Nina (the woman) or Chris (the man). Check the answer as a class.

> **Answer**
> Chris

Audioscript

CHRIS So, are you good about keeping in touch with people?

NINA Er, not much. I always plan to write to people, but then I forget. I send emails to my parents sometimes, about once a month, but more often I get emails from them saying 'Are you OK? We haven't heard from you for a long time.' Then I always send them a quick email and tell them what I'm doing. How about you?

c Oh, I like keeping in touch. I think it's important to keep in touch with your family. I write emails to my parents sometimes, but I also phone or Skype. I phone my mother every weekend.

N Every weekend!

c Yes, she gets worried about me and she wants to know what I'm doing.

N I hardly ever phone my parents. I wait until I go and see them, and talk to them then.

c Don't you ever phone them to have a chat?

N No, I only phone if it's something important. You don't have to be in touch with people all the time.

c What about friends? Surely you keep in touch with friends?

N Not very much, maybe I should do. I send texts or messages sometimes, but that's about all. I always think if you have good friends you can talk about everything when you meet. It's more fun to tell people your news when you can have a real conversation.

c Oh well, I often send messages and photos to people so they know I'm thinking about them. And sometimes, when I have a particularly good photo, I send it to everyone by email. I think it's a nice thing to do …

c Read through the questions with the class before they listen. Then play the recording again. Students answer the questions individually. If necessary, pause the recording after the information is given for students to tell you the answers. If you play the recording without pauses, check the answers with the class at the end.

> **Answers**
> 1 She forgets.
> 2 She gets worried and wants to know what he's doing.
> 3 hardly ever – only if it's something important
> 4 when she meets them
> 5 when he has a particularly good photo

☺ EXTRA ACTIVITY

Ask students to write the following adverbs in their books: *always, sometimes*. Ask students to guess which adverb Nina and Chris use most in the interview. Play the recording again. Students put a tick next to each adverb as they hear it. Check the answers as a class: *always* is used three times, but there are four examples of *sometimes*. You could play the recording once more, this time pausing after each instance of the adverb so that students can repeat.

d Write the adverbs on the board. Elicit the phrase which means the same as *rarely (hardly ever)*. Ask students in turn which adverb is correct for them for keeping in touch with family and friends. Put a tick under each adverb for each student and see which adverb is the most common for the group. Remember to add your own tick. Discuss the reasons for students' answers together. Students write down a family member who lives in a different place and a friend who they don't see very often. Then they note down which of the things they do with these people.

e ☺ Read the sentences in the speech bubbles with the class. Student use adverbs to make their own sentences, expanding on the information in 1d. Ask one or two students to give examples of sentences they have made.

f Read through the three opinions with the class. In pairs, students discuss which they agree or disagree with, and why. Check the answers as a class.

☺ EXTRA ACTIVITY

Write some opinions about emailing on the board:

You should always reply to a personal email in 24 hours.

You should never read another person's email.

You shouldn't copy in more than three people on one personal email.

You should invite people to a party in separate emails, not copy them in.

You shouldn't use emails to give bad news.

Students discuss the opinions in pairs. Monitor and discuss any interesting opinions as a class.

2 READING

a Ask students to look at the pictures and tell you what they can see in them. Read the question and ask students for their ideas. Don't check the answers at this point.

b Tell students that the emails are from Simon to three different people. Students read the emails quickly to find out what he is doing in Spain and which email is to which of the different people. Give them a time limit of three minutes and explain that they don't need to read the emails in detail at this point. They need to scan the emails in order to find the answers to the questions. Check the answers as a class. Ask students what language helped them decide.

> **Answers**
> a He's learning/studying Spanish.
> b 2 friend Blake
>   1 uncle and aunt
>   3 younger sister Mika

c Students read the emails, in more detail to answer the question. Check the answers as a class.

> **Answers**
> the weather – uncle and aunt
> what he does in the evenings – Blake
> the family he is staying with – Mika
> learning to speak Spanish – uncle and aunt
> the other students – Blake

d In pairs, students talk about the two questions. Ask for their ideas in class feedback.

> **Answers**
> 1 He's improving. He usually speaks English with his group – which is not very good for his Spanish. He usually speaks Spanish with Blanca (and her friends).

 EXTRA ACTIVITY

Write these prompts on the board. Can students remember the phrases from the reading texts in Exercise 2?

Hope/well (Hope you're (both) well.)

Love/all (Love to all.)

How/going? (How's it going?)

What/Berlin/like? (What's Berlin like?)

I'm/great (I'm having a great time!)

3 WRITING SKILLS Correcting mistakes

a Write on the board: *What Mexico City like.* Ask students to find two mistakes and correct the sentence for you. (What's Mexico City like?) Individually, students check the pairs of sentences for mistakes. They then compare answers in pairs. Check the answers as a class.

> **Answers**
> A punctuation   B capital letters   C grammar   D spelling

↻ LOA TIP ELICITING

Ask students: *Do you usually check your written work for mistakes? What do you check for?* Elicit: grammar/punctuation/spelling/capital letters and put the words on the board. If necessary, put an example of a word or sentence for each kind of mistake on the board. This will make students aware of what they should be looking for in the exercise and also what to watch out for when they are writing.

b Read through the rules with the class and ask students to match them with the mistakes.

> **Answers**
> 1 C1
> 2 A1
> 3 C2
> 4 D2
> 5 B1

c Students correct the mistakes and check with Simon's emails. Check the answers as a class.

> **Answers**
> **A**
> 1 Hope you're both well and you're enjoying the summer.
> 2 Are you having a good time in Berlin?
> **B**
> 1 I'm in Salamanca, in Spain.
> 2 The classes are very good and we also watch Spanish films.
> **C**
> 1 I'm having a great time here and the time's going much too quickly.
> 2 She speaks English quite well, but we usually speak Spanish together.
> **D**
> 1 Here are some photos of my group on the Spanish course.
> 2 We're all from different countries, so we usually speak English.

 FAST FINISHERS

Ask fast finishers to add some more mistakes to the emails. They give them to their partners to correct and explain.

4 WRITING

a Read through the writing task with the class. Ask students to first make notes / write a plan for their emails and then use this to help them write their first draft. Circulate and help where necessary by giving advice, but don't correct any mistakes.

 FAST FINISHERS

Students can write emails to their partners (on any topic), exchange and reply. Then they should check through together for any mistakes to correct.

b Go through the correction code with students. In pairs, students exchange emails, and read and correct them using the code.

c In pairs, students correct the emails together. Circulate to help where necessary. Monitor and point out errors for students to self-correct.

d Choose some of the emails to read to the class yourself, and ask students to vote on the most interesting.

ADDITIONAL MATERIAL

▶ Workbook 1D

UNIT 1
Review and extension

1 GRAMMAR

a Tell students that the first task is to practise the word order in questions. Students do the exercise individually. Check the answers as a class and point out errors for students to self-correct.

> **Answers**
> 1 Did you go out last night?
> 2 Where did you go last weekend?
> 3 What kind of TV programmes do you like?
> 4 Who do you know at this school?
> 5 How often do you play sport?
> 6 What do you usually do at weekends?
> 7 Are you tired today?

b Ask students to ask and answer the questions in pairs. Monitor and encourage students to expand their answers where possible.

c Write the text message on the board: *Sorry. I can't come out tonight because I'm working late. I don't know how long! Every Thursday we get some extra work. See you soon!* Elicit examples of present simple and continuous and check why they are used. Students complete the exercise individually and compare answers in pairs. Check the answers as a class. Nominate a pair to read the correct dialogue for the class and then have students practise the dialogue in pairs.

> **Answers**
> 1 don't call   2 'm working   3 have   4 send   5 like
> 6 calls   7 're speaking   8 is changing   9 phone   10 email

> ### 💡 EXTRA ACTIVITY
> Put some answers to questions about yourself on the board, e.g. *Reading detective books. Sunday lunch with my family. By car. At 5.30.* Ask students to guess the questions, e.g. *What do you like doing in your free time? What do you enjoy most about the weekend? How do you travel to work? When do you finish work?*

2 VOCABULARY

a Students read each sentence carefully before deciding on the missing adjective. Point out that the first and last letter of each adjective is given to help them. Students complete the exercise individually. Check the answers as a class.

> **Answers**
> 1 alright   2 delicious   3 ugly   4 lovely   5 gorgeous
> 6 strange   7 horrible   8 perfect

b Elicit the adverbs students have learned in the unit and put them on the board. Ask students to give you example sentences for each. Students do the exercise individually. Check the answers as a class.

> **Answers**
> 1 absolutely   2 rarely   3 really   4 normally   5 really
> 6 especially

c Discuss the question together, asking students to give reasons for their answers.

3 WORDPOWER *like*

a Tell students to close their books. Write the word *like* on the board and the sentence: *I like learning English!* Then ask: *Can we use the word 'like' in other ways?* Elicit the language in the following ways.

Choose two students with similar phones. Elicit or say: *Helena's phone is really nice. Oh look – Pam's phone is like Helena's.*

Ask students for examples of team sports they know. Elicit or say: *Can you think of some team sports, like basketball?*

Ask students about the last film they saw. Elicit or say: *What was it like?*

Tell them they have a choice about the last activity in the lesson. Elicit or say: *You can play a game – if you like.*

Students open their books and do the matching task. Check the answers as a class.

> **Answers**
> 1 c   2 d   3 b   4 a

b As a class, students match the meanings.

> **Answers**
> a 2   b 1   c 4   d 3

c Ask students to complete the sentences and then check with their partners.

> **Answers**
> 1 like   2 if you like   3 like   4 What was, like

d Tell students we can use *like* in another way too. Read through the first examples of *look like* and *sound like* with the class (first bullet point). Elicit more examples from the class by asking, e.g. *Who do you look like in your family? Does your favourite singer sound like anyone else?* Read through the examples in the second and third bullet points and explain that both can also be used for opinion: *looks like* for an opinion about what might happen; *sounds like* for an opinion about what you've heard or read. Give some more examples to reinforce the concept, e.g. *It looks like you're all going to pass your English tests easily! (I think this because of the results I can see now.) It sounds like Jack's party was really good! (I think this because of what you told me about it.)* Students complete the sentences. Check the answers as a class.

> **Answers**
> 1 sounds like   2 looks like   3 look like   4 looks like

▶ Photocopiable activities: Wordpower p.252

> ### 🔄 LOA   REVIEW YOUR PROGRESS
>
> Students look back through the unit, think about what they've studied and decide how well they did. Students work on weak areas by using the appropriate sections of the Workbook, the Photocopiable activities and the Personalised online practice.

UNIT 2
Travel and tourism

GETTING STARTED

> **⚆ OPTIONAL LEAD-IN**
>
> Books closed. Think of a famous holiday destination or sight in the world, e.g. the Eiffel Tower in Paris. Start to draw the famous sight, drawing a line at a time, and giving students time to guess where it is. If students think they know what you are drawing, they can ask yes/no questions, e.g. *Is it a building?* (Yes, it is.) *Is it in France?* (Yes, it is.) If students can't guess, you can draw clues to help, e.g. the French flag. Put students in pairs to play the game.

> **◗ UNIT OBJECTIVES**
>
> At the end of this unit, students will be able to:
> - understand information, texts and conversations about travel and tourism
> - talk about past holidays and describe difficult journeys
> - express opinions about travel and tourism
> - ask for information in a public place
> - write a travel blog

a 💬 Ask students to look at the picture and say what they can see. Students read and talk about the questions in pairs. Monitor and support students with any vocabulary they may need. Suggested vocabulary: 1 *sand, desert, dune, ride a camel* 2 *excited, be looking forward to, relaxed, be (not) enjoying herself/himself, afraid/frightened/scared* 3 *It's going to be fun. The camel won't hurt you.* Encourage a full group discussion. Do any students have different ideas on how the people are feeling or where they are? If you wish, give students information from the Culture notes below.

> **🌍 CULTURE NOTES**
>
> This picture shows holidaymakers riding camels across the sand dunes on the edge of the Gobi desert. The Gobi desert is in Northern China and Southern Mongolia. It is the largest desert in Asia and the fifth largest in the world. They are at Xiangshawan, which is a theme park for Chinese tourists. The theme here is not Disney, but sand! Visitors can do all sorts of sand-related activities, which include making sand sculptures (models in sand), sand skiing, desert surfing, riding camels and watching spectacular Mongolian dance shows.

b 💬 Students discuss the questions in pairs. Monitor but don't interrupt fluency unless students make mistakes in their choice of vocabulary. Ask one or two students to share their ideas with the class.

> **⚆ EXTRA ACTIVITY**
>
> In pairs, students talk about a holiday experience when they were a child. It could be something they enjoyed or something that frightened them like the child in the picture. Encourage talk about where they went, what they did, how they felt and why. Invite one or two students to share their stories with the class.

2A We had an adventure

- read and understand a text about a holiday
- understand and use vocabulary related to tourism
- use all forms of the past simple
- pronounce past simple regular endings correctly
- talk about past holidays

💡 OPTIONAL LEAD-IN

Books closed. Elicit from the class different kinds of holiday people can go on and write them on the board, e.g. *beach/resort, city break, camping, adventure, cruise, safari, tour.* Ask the class which kind of holiday they would most like to go on today. Take a class vote on the most popular holiday. Put students in pairs and give them three minutes to think of as many different activities as they can for the class holiday. Some suggested activities: *sunbathe, buy souvenirs, go shopping, go sightseeing, go on a trip, meet new people, visit a monument, have a campfire, go surfing, go trekking, go climbing, see wildlife.*

1 READING AND LISTENING

a 💬 Students open their books and discuss the questions. Take class feedback on the kind of new things students like to try on holiday.

b Read the title of the text with students and ask: *What do you think the book is about?* Then ask them to read the text to check their ideas. Discuss the second question as a class. Ask students what problems saying yes to everything might cause. If you wish, give students information from the Culture notes below.

> **Answers**
> 1 It's about a man who decided to say yes to every question for a year.
> 2 He took a holiday from work and became a 'yes man' for a week.

🌍 CULTURE NOTES

Yes Man is a bestselling book by UK writer and comedian, Danny Wallace. Danny's relationship with his girlfriend had finished. He was depressed and avoiding people until a stranger on a bus told him to 'say "yes" more'. Wallace then chose to say 'yes' to any offers that came his way for a year and wrote up the story in his book. As a result, in the year that followed, Danny met some interesting and some strange people and travelled to several countries. *Yes Man* was described by some reviewers as a book that has the power to change your life. A film of the same name was made, starring Jim Carrey and Zooey Deschanel – but the story is quite different.

It is worth noting that there is another meaning for 'yes-man' in English, which is a very different meaning from the one in Wallace's book. A 'yes-man' is someone who agrees with everything their employer says in order to please them.

c Ask students to look at the pictures and describe what they can see. Encourage correct use of the present continuous. (The water sport in the picture is water skiing.) Pre-teach the word *travel agent* in the Vocabulary support box. Ask them to guess what sort of questions Richard said 'yes' to. Students read Day One and answer the questions. Then they read Day Two and answer the questions. Ask them to discuss their answers with a partner. Check answers as a class. You may wish to help students with some of the words in the Vocabulary support box.

> **Answers**
> Day One
> 1 He saw a poster in the window (of the travel agent's).
> 2 a beach holiday in Greece
> 3 No, he usually prefers to go to cities.
> 4 the next day
>
> Day Two
> 1 The receptionist asked, 'Do you want to go?'
> 2 It was very, very hot.
> 3 two pairs of sunglasses, three hats, a watch and a woman's necklace
> 4 He's going to go water skiing. He's very unhappy about it.

📖 VOCABULARY SUPPORT

accommodation (B1) – a place where you stay on holiday, e.g. a hotel, an apartment

check in (B1) – to go to the desk at a hotel or an airport and say that you have arrived

travel agent (B1) – a person whose job it is to sell holidays and make travel arrangements

travel agent's (B1) – a shop which sells holidays and makes travel arrangements

unpack (B1) – to take things out of your suitcase/bag

d 💬 Discuss the questions briefly as a class. Ask what people enjoy or don't enjoy about water skiing. Elicit the words: *stand up on skis, fall off.*

e ▶ 1.23 Ask students to read the sentences 1–5 about Day 3. You may wish to pre-teach the word *instructor* (someone who teaches a particular sport or activity). Play the recording and ask students to decide if the sentences are true or false. When the recording is finished ask students: *What surprised Richard about his day? (He learned to like water skiing.)* Check answers in full group. To extend you can ask more detailed questions, e.g. *How long was the lesson?* (one hour) *How many people were there in the group?* (six including Richard) *How did Richard feel when the instructor asked him to go first?* (sick) *How many times did he fall over?* (two) *How many minutes did he spend in the water?* (ten)

> **Answers**
> 1 T
> 2 F He was really worried.
> 3 T
> 4 F After the third time, he loved water skiing.
> 5 F Later on in the evening he had a drink with the other water skiers.

Audioscript
DAY THREE
So, the next morning, we started with some water skiing practice on the beach. First, they showed us how to stand up on the skis … and then how to fall off safely. The lesson took about an hour, and then we were ready to go out to sea. There were five other people in my group, who were all very excited. But not me – I was really worried. The instructor looked at me and said, "Do you want to go first?" and then everyone looked at me. I felt sick but I said, "Yes" …
Ten seconds after I started, I fell over. I tried again. And I fell over again.

Then the third time, something amazing suddenly happened. I didn't fall over. And I found out that I love water skiing. The ten minutes in the water passed very quickly and I didn't want to stop!
When we got back to the hotel, the receptionist asked me, "So, did you enjoy the water skiing course?" I said, "Yes" which, for the first time, was the truth. And then later on that evening I had a drink in the bar with the other water skiers. I felt really happy. And that was when I realised I was enjoying being a 'Yes Man' after all.

f 💬 Students talk about the question in pairs. Ask students to tell interesting stories to the class.

2 GRAMMAR Past simple: positive

a Books closed. Write on the board: *Richard _____ to change his life. Richard _____ a 'Yes Man' for a week.* Encourage students to call out the missing verbs. Write down any possible correct answers. Ask students to open their books and check with the introduction. (The missing words are *wanted* and *became*.) Ask students *When did Richard become a 'Yes Man'?* (The article does not give an exact time, but this happened before he wrote the article.) Elicit the answer: *in the past.* (If students say: *When he finished the book*, ask: *When was that?*) Elicit that regular past simple verbs end in *-ed*, by asking them which of these verbs is regular and which is irregular. Look at 2a with students. Tell students to find the past simple verb forms, starting at the top of the introduction. The words are in the same order in the article. They underline examples in the texts of the past simple forms. Check answers as a class.

> **Answers**
> became   felt   decided   started   asked   did   changed   had
> wanted   got   saw   slept   went   arrived   gave

b Students say which end in *-ed* (are regular) and what the changes in the other (irregular) past simple forms are. Point out that there is a list of irregular verbs on p.176.

> ### 💡 EXTRA ACTIVITY
> Put students in pairs. Turn to the irregular verb list on SB p.176. Each pair chooses ten verbs from the list that they want to practise. These can be verbs they have not seen before, ones they find difficult or ones they think they will use in today's class. Give them a couple of minutes to choose the verbs and note down the infinitive and the past simple form. Students then test each other: one student reads the infinitive from their list and the other gives the past simple form without looking at the list.

c Students complete the sentences individually. Check as a class. If students made many mistakes with the irregular verbs, look at the list on p.176 with them again briefly. Point out that many of the most common verbs in English are irregular and that it is important to learn these.

> **Answers**
> 1 worked   2 spent   3 stayed   4 won   5 took   6 went

3 LISTENING

a ▶ 1.24 In pairs, students guess which of the activities in 2c Richard enjoyed and give possible reasons. You may wish to pre-teach the words *mosquito* and *bite* in the Vocabulary support box. Explain that *bit* is the past simple of *bite*. Then play the recording of Day 7. Students listen and see if their guesses were right. If necessary, pause the recording after each paragraph to allow students to check their ideas. Take feedback on the information from each section before continuing.

> **Suggested answers**
> He enjoyed working as a waiter for a day, the day he spent fishing and staying at a beach party until six the next morning (he won a dancing competition). He also enjoyed swimming until midnight (but not the mosquitoes).

> ### 📖 VOCABULARY SUPPORT
> *bite* (B1) – to put your teeth into something or someone
> *have control* (B1) – when you can decide things for yourself
> *make friends with* (B1) – to begin to know and like someone
> *mosquito* (B1) – small flying insect that bites
> *souvenir* (B1) – something which you buy to remember a special event or holiday

> ### 💡 EXTRA ACTIVITY
> Ask what the past simple forms of the following verbs are. They are all in the recording:
> *can (could), make (made), come (came), catch (caught), bite (bit).*

> **Audioscript**
> **DAY SEVEN**
> On the last day of the holiday, I couldn't wait for midnight. At 12 o'clock I could stop answering 'yes' to every question. The week had been fun but I wanted some control of my life again! That evening I went for one last dinner with some of my new friends. "So, did you have a good week?" one of them asked me. "Yes," I said. "What was your favourite thing?" she asked.
> And do you know what? I couldn't really answer her. There were so many things I had enjoyed. I worked as a waiter for a day – I didn't get any money for it, but I made friends with some interesting people who came to eat at the restaurant. I also spent a day fishing with five Greek fishermen and caught several fish. I stayed at a beach party until six in the morning. Oh, and I won a dancing competition!
> Of course, some of my experiences weren't very good. I took the same boat trip three times ... I went swimming at midnight – actually, I liked the swimming, but I didn't like the mosquitoes that bit me when I got out of the sea. And I spent over 200 euros on souvenirs that I hate!
> It was great to try new things. But I was glad the week was nearly finished. I wanted to get back home and relax for a day before I started work again on Monday. But Day 7 wasn't finished yet! Without thinking, I asked my new friends what they planned to do next. They were all smiling at me. One of them said, "We're flying to Thailand tomorrow. Do you want to come with us? You'd love it!" I looked at my watch. It was 11.55.

b ▶ 1.21 Ask if students can remember Richard's last question. If nobody in the class heard the question, play the last part of the recording again. (His new friends ask him to go to Thailand.) Ask students to listen and note down any reasons why Richard might say yes, or reasons why Richard might say no. Take feedback, encouraging students to give reasons from what Richard said and their own reasons. You could ask students what they would do in Richard's position.

Answers

Do you want to come with us? (to Thailand)
Possibly he will say yes, because he says Day 7 wasn't finished yet, it is only 11.55, and he is still a 'yes man' for another five minutes. Possibly he will say no because he wants some control of his life again, and he said he wanted to get back home and relax for a day before he starts work on Monday.

c 💬 Students discuss the questions in pairs or small groups. Monitor but do not correct students as this is a fluency activity. Students share their ideas with the class. See how many of the class think being a 'yes man' for a week would be a good idea.

💡 **EXTRA ACTIVITY**

Choose a holiday that you know is not popular with the class and write it on the board. Ask students to work in pairs to imagine a day when someone decided to be a 'yes man' (or woman). First, they think of three questions the person was asked and said 'yes' to. Then they write a paragraph about the day. Circulate and give help where necessary. Encourage students to use the past simple of some of the verbs they have looked at in this lesson. When they have finished, they can read out their paragraphs to the class or exchange with other pairs. The class can vote on the best story.

---

4 GRAMMAR

Past simple: negative and questions

a Tell students to read the sentences from the listening and complete them with the correct words.

Answers

1 weren't   2 didn't   3 Did   4 was

b Discuss the questions in full group and check answers. Write the negatives and questions on the board to reinforce the way that negatives and questions are formed.

Answers

1 1 and 4
2 with the verb *be*: negative – add *not (n't)* to make *wasn't* and *weren't*; question invert subject and *was/were*; i.e. have the subject after *was/were*
   with other verbs: negative – use *didn't* + infinitive; question – use *did* + subject + infinitive

c ▶ Students read the information in Grammar Focus 2A on SB p.144. Play the recording where indicated and ask students to listen and repeat. Students then complete the exercises in Grammar Focus 2A on SB p.145. Check answers as a class, checking the use of regular and irregular past forms and the formation of past simple questions. Make sure that students use inversion for questions with *be* and the auxiliary *did* with other verbs.

Answers (Grammar Focus 2A SB p.145)

a 1 asked 2 bought 3 danced 4 enjoyed 5 found
6 forgot 7 knew 8 learned 9 hurried 10 met
11 offered 12 preferred 13 relaxed 14 said 15 wore
b 1 wasn't; was 2 arrived; didn't arrive 3 were; weren't
4 ate; didn't eat 5 rained; didn't rain 6 spent; didn't spend
7 spoke; didn't speak 8 had; didn't have
c 1 Why was your plane late? 2 When did your bags arrive?
3 What did you wear? 4 Were the people friendly?
5 What was the weather like? 6 What kind of food did you eat?
7 Did you have a good time?

👁 **CAREFUL!**

- One of the most common problems for students when making the past simple is to use *did/didn't* + past form. Make sure that you correct these errors to avoid problems in the future, e.g. ~~I didn't went~~. (Correct form = *I didn't **go**.*) ~~Did you went?~~ (Correct form = *Did you **go**?*)

- Check the spelling of past forms too, especially verbs which end in consonant + 'y', e.g. *carry – carr**ied**, try – tr**ied***, and verbs which double the final consonant in the past simple form, e.g. *plan – plan**ned**, prefer – prefer**red**, stop – stop**ped**, travel – travel**led***.

📖 **LANGUAGE NOTES**

We use points of time with the past simple, e.g. *I arrived at 2.30 / on Monday*. But we use a period with *ago*, e.g. *I arrived an hour ago / two days ago.*

---

5 PRONUNCIATION -ed endings

a ▶ 1.27 Ask students to answer these questions to elicit *stayed* and *visited*: *Where did you stay on your last holiday? What places did you visit on your last holiday?* Put the past forms on the board and ask students to repeat them and tell you the difference in the pronunciation of *-ed* (*visited* has an extra syllable, with the *-ed* pronounced /ɪd/).

Play the recording for students to tick the verbs with the extra syllable. Check answers as a class. Model and drill the pronunciation of the forms.

Answers

change	❯	changed	play	❯	played
need	❯	needed ✓	ask	❯	asked
decide	❯	decided ✓	want	❯	wanted ✓
start	❯	started ✓			

b Give students a short time to complete the rule and then check.

Answers

d, t

c ▶ 1.28 Play the recording for students to listen and choose the correct verbs. Check as a class. Model and drill the pronunciation of these verbs, too.

Answers and audioscript

waited, included, shouted, ended

💡 **EXTRA ACTIVITY**

Divide the class into small groups. They start with five points each. Say the infinitive form of a verb from 5a or 5c to the groups in turn. They must immediately give you the past form with the correct pronunciation of the ending. If they make a mistake, they lose a point. The group with the most points at the end wins. Try to make this a quickfire game.

You can add more regular verbs to your list, e.g. *walk, work, hope, copy*.

---

6 VOCABULARY Tourism

a Students close their books. Ask them what holiday items were in the pictures. Write them on the board. Open the books and check. In pairs, students make a list of other items people often take with them on holiday. Put their ideas on the board.

> **Answers**
> on these pages: sun hat, T-shirt, shorts, sandals, folding chair, sunglasses

> **EXTRA ACTIVITY**
>
> Elicit or input the meaning of *travel light* (take only what you need when you travel). Ask students whether they take too much or just enough with them on holiday. Ask students who travel light to give travel tips to other students.

b ▶ Students complete the exercises in Vocabulary Focus 2A on SB p.133. Play the recordings for students to check their answers to a and c. Ask for students' answers to b in full group and monitor conversations in d.

> **Answers (Vocabulary Focus 2A SB p.133)**
> A 1 guidebook 2 map 3 suitcase 4 sunglasses
>   5 passport 6 foreign currency 7 suntan lotion 8 backpack
> C 1 holiday 2 visa 3 money 4 accommodation
>   5 hotel; luggage 6 sightseeing 7 souvenirs 8 hostel
>   9 campsite 10 adventure

> ⊙ **CAREFUL!**
>
> Students may have problems with spelling with this set, especially *accommodation*, *sightseeing*, *souvenirs* and *adventure*. This is because of the differences between sound and spelling. A common student error is to use *camping* instead of *campsite*, e.g. ~~We stayed at a great camping.~~ (Correct form = *We stayed at a great **campsite**.*)

7 SPEAKING

a Ask students to close their books. Tell students where you went on your last holiday and elicit questions about it. Students open books and check if the questions you elicited are in the task. Ask students where they went for their last holidays and if they enjoyed them or not. Give students a couple of minutes to read through the questions and think about their answers.

> **LOA TIP ELICITING**
>
> Say: *I went on holiday*. Write *When?* on the board and gesture to the class that you want them to ask you a question. Elicit: *When did you go?* Answer the question with information about your last holiday. Write *Where?* on the board to elicit the question: *Where did you go?* and again answer the question. Continue with prompts to elicit the following questions: *How long? (How long did you go for?), Who … with? (Who did you go with?), kind of accommodation (What kind of accommodation did you stay in?)* Finish by eliciting any other questions the class might have without prompting.

b In pairs students take turns to tell each other about their holiday and ask questions about their partner's holiday. Tell them that they can use the questions in the book but if they want more information, they can think of their own questions. Monitor and note any common mistakes to deal with in feedback later. If one student is making the same mistake with the past simple all the time, echo correct to encourage self correction. In feedback, ask students to tell you some interesting or surprising things their partner told them.

> **FAST FINISHERS**
>
> Fast finishers can have another conversation where they tell each other about a holiday they did not enjoy. Ask for examples of these conversations, too, in feedback.

> **ADDITIONAL MATERIAL**
>
> ▶ Workbook 2A
> ▶ Photocopiable activities: Grammar p.203, Vocabulary p.230, Pronunciation p.267

2B Everyone was waiting for me

OPTIONAL LEAD-IN

Ask students: *How did you get here today?* Students tell you what forms of transport they used in their journey. Write a list on the board. Then ask: *What was your journey like?* Encourage students to describe their journey, including any difficulties they may have had. Ask students to tell you what other kinds of problems people can have when using the forms of transport listed on the board.

LANGUAGE NOTES

We usually use *by* + form of transport, e.g. *go/come by car, by bus, by train*. However, when walking, we use on: *go/come on foot*.

1 VOCABULARY Travel collocations

a Read through the forms of transport with the class. Put these phrases on the board: *every day? on holiday? at the weekend?* In pairs, students talk about their preferred ways of travelling and use the phrases on the board to help them. Take feedback as a class. Encourage students to give reasons for liking or disliking the forms of transport.

b Students look at the pictures and describe what they can see as a class. (Top: a traffic jam on an American freeway (=motorway in British English); Middle: commuters on the London Underground; Bottom: passengers waiting for a delayed flight at an airport) Ask some further questions about the pictures: *What is happening? How do you think the people are feeling?*

Where do you think the people are going? What do you think will happen next? Finally, ask the class which situation in the pictures they dislike most, and why.

c ▶ Students complete the exercises in Vocabulary Focus 2B SB p.134. Check answers to Exercise a as a class, then play the recording for students to listen and follow the story on the map. In pairs, students retell the story, using only the picture to help them (Exercise b). If they need further help, give some prompts, either spoken or written, e.g. *Europe / last year*. Students match the problems with the pictures in Exercise c. Play the recording in Exercise d for students to check their answers. Then play it again for them to listen and repeat. Do Exercise e as a class and encourage discussion of questions in Exercise f. When students have finished, ask them to turn back to SB p. 19.

Answers (Vocabulary Focus SB p.134)
A 1h 2i 3d 4g 5e 6c 7a 8b 9f
C 1h 2b 3g 4f 5a 6j 7e 8c 9d 10i

CAREFUL!

Students sometimes overuse *travel* as a noun. *Trip* and *journey* are common nouns associated with travel in English, e.g. ~~It was a business travel~~. (Correct form = *It was a business **trip**.*) ~~The travel was quite long~~. (Correct form = *The **journey** was quite long*.)

2 LISTENING

a Before looking at the picture and text, ask students what problems people can have on a plane. Ask them to look at the picture and title of the text and see if they can guess what happened.

b ▶ 1.33 Tell students they will now hear the woman tell her story. Play the recording for students to compare their ideas.

VOCABULARY SUPPORT

embarrassing (B1) – making you feel silly or stupid when other people are with you

flight attendant – person who works on a plane and helps the passengers

in a rush – when you need to hurry and do things more quickly than usual

seatbelt – a belt that holds you in your seat in a car or a plane

Audioscript
Well, I was in a rush that morning and I suppose I set off a bit late. It was raining when I left the house and there was a lot of traffic on the roads. I got to the airport just before the desk closed.
When I boarded the plane, all the other passengers were waiting for me. It was a bit embarrassing, but we took off OK. I had a seat in the middle of the plane and for the first couple of hours it was fine.
So I was reading my book when one of the flight attendants came over and spoke to me. She said that there was something wrong with **her** seat and that she needed to take mine. I was the last passenger to check in, so they chose me.
I asked the flight attendant where I should sit and she told me that the only place was the toilet. At first, I thought it was a joke, but then I realised that she was serious.
So I was sitting on the toilet when the turbulence started. It was quite frightening because of course there was no seatbelt in the toilet. I almost fell off a few times. After the turbulence stopped, I opened the door. About five passengers were waiting outside to use the toilet. I just closed the door again.
And then to top it all, when we landed at Istanbul there was a delay of an hour before we could get off the plane because of a problem in the airport.
I still can't believe they told me to stay in the toilet for two hours. It was terrible. You just can't treat customers like that.

c ▶ 1.33 Students listen again to give more details about the story. Play the recording and let students talk about the answers in pairs. If necessary, pause the recording to allow time for students to note down their answers before moving on to the next question. Students share their ideas with the class.

Answers
- her journey to the airport: she was in a rush
- boarding the plane: all the other passengers were waiting for her; it was a bit embarrassing
- what the flight attendant said: the only place to sit was the toilet
- what happened when she was in the toilet: there was turbulence; she almost fell off; passengers were waiting; there was no seatbelt
- how she feels about what happened now: still can't believe it; it was terrible

d 🗨 Ask for students' opinions as a class, encouraging them to give their reasons. (You can tell the students that this story is not true, although a man in America claimed something similar happened to him and sued the airline for $2 million in 2008.)

3 GRAMMAR Past continuous

a ▶1.34 Point out that the sentences in 3a are from the story in 2. Read each sentence aloud, missing the gapped word, and see if students can complete them from memory. Play the recording for students to complete the sentences or to check their ideas.

> **Answers**
> 1 was raining   2 were waiting   3 was reading   4 was sitting

b Ask students to underline the past simple verbs in the four sentences. Check together. Elicit what we call the other tense (the past continuous).

> **Answers**
> 1 left   2 boarded   3 spoke   4 started

c Ask students the questions in full group. These concept-check the use of the past continuous.

> **Answers**
> 1 past continuous
> 2 because of the past simple action: 2, 3
>   some time after: 1, 4

d ▶ Students read the information in Grammar Focus 2B on SB p.144. Play the recording where indicated and ask students to listen and repeat. Students then complete the exercises in Grammar Focus 2B on SB p.145. Check answers as a class. When students have finished, ask them to turn back to SB p.20.

> **Answers (Grammar Focus SB p.145)**
> A 1 I was living
>   2 we were sleeping
>   3 were you doing; were watching
>   4 She wasn't studying; she was chatting
>   5 Most people weren't wearing; were they wearing
> B 1 stopped; was watching
>   2 was walking; saw
>   3 left; was studying
>   4 was doing; heard
>   5 were feeling; got home
>   6 didn't visit; was working
>   7 wasn't looking; crashed
> C was walking; found
>   2 was raining; left
>   3 called; was cooking
>   4 weren't working; came

📖 LANGUAGE NOTES

It can sometimes be misleading to talk about long and short actions when discussing the past continuous. It is important that students focus on the fact that the past simple action interrupted the action that was in progress (the past continuous action). Bear in mind that sometimes the past continuous action is fairly short, but it is always longer than the past simple one, e.g. *I was picking up a book from the floor when I heard a strange noise.*

👁 CAREFUL!

- Students make many errors when using the past continuous, often because the tense does not exist in their own languages. Instead, they may try to use past simple all the time and this can result in the wrong sequence of events, e.g. ~~I arrived at school. Jacky played a game with Ella~~. (Correct form = *When I arrived at school, Jacky **was playing** a game with Ella.*)
- Another mistake is for students to use the present tense of *be* in the past, e.g. ~~I am walking home yesterday when I saw a fast car~~. (Correct form = *I **was** walking home yesterday when I saw a fast car.*)

💡 EXTRA ACTIVITY

To review spelling of the past continuous form, write some verbs on the board and ask students to write down the *-ing* form, e.g. *drive, sit, come, make, travel, hit*. They should then spell them back to you to put on the board. Elicit the general rules: 1 a verb ending with 'e' loses the 'e' before adding *–ing*, e.g. *come – coming*. 2 A verb ending with a vowel and a single consonant doubles the consonant before adding *-ing*: e.g. *run – running*.

e ▶1.36 Play the recording for students to notice the stresses (the underlined words) in positive and negative sentences. Point out that in words of more than one syllable, the underlining shows which syllable is stressed.

f ▶1.36 Students listen again to identify the differences in vowel sounds and answer the question. Repeat the sentences, making sure *was* has a weak form /wəz/. Point out the difference between the weak and strong form of *was* and tell students that some words, especially those which don't carry the main meaning, don't have full stress when we're talking.

> **Answer**
> No – The vowel sounds of both *was* and *were* are weak (/ə/) in positive sentences. In negative forms /ɒ/ is the vowel sound in *wasn't* and /ɜː/ in *weren't*.

g ▶1.37 Play the recording for students say whether they hear the words. Elicit that *wasn't* and *weren't* (i.e. the negative forms) have full stress. Drill the pronunciation of the sentences in 3e and g. Model for students to repeat.

> **Answer**
> Yes – but they're clearer/stronger in negative sentences.

> **Answers and audioscript**
> 1 We **were** waiting for the bus.
> 2 He **wasn't** hitchhiking.
> 3 They **were** talking to the driver.
> 4 He **was** travelling by train.
> 5 They **weren't** helping the passengers.

h Students complete the sentences with the correct past forms individually. Check answers in full group. Check pronunciation when students give their answers.

> **Answers**
> 1 was leaving, realised
> 2 was travelling around, lost
> 3 was running, opened, fell
> 4 was driving, stopped
> 5 stole, was standing

i 💬 Tell students about a similar problem you once had (or invent one). Look at the example together and elicit a possible answer to the question, e.g. *I had to send it away and get a new one. It took a long time.* Then ask students to tell their partners about similar problems they had when they were travelling. Monitor and listen for correct use of the past continuous. Ask for examples in feedback and write some of them on the board.

4 READING AND SPEAKING

a Tell students that they are going to read some more stories about difficult journeys. Ask students to look at the map and focus on the two place names. Ask different students to spell the names. Then ask students to describe the picture. Ask: *Where are the people? What are they doing?* They then read the headlines to guess what happened to the travellers. Don't tell students if they are right or wrong.

b ▶ Divide students into pairs and assign A and B roles. Students A turn to SB p.127. Students B turn to SB p.128. Allow some time for students to read their story and answer the five questions. Monitor and help students. Do not check answers as a class. When students have finished ask them to turn back to SB p.21.

> **Answers**
> **Student A**
> 1 travelling around Italy, going to island of Capri
> 2 by car
> 3 they made a spelling mistake on the GPS, typed CARPI instead of CAPRI
> 4 a tourist official, explained their mistake
> 5 the couple got back into their car and started driving south
>
> **Student B**
> 1 from Heathrow airport to Norwich (a city about 150 miles away)
> 2 by coach
> 3 the coach broke down
> 4 ten passengers, strong young men and a couple of women, pushed the coach; a car stopped and pulled the coach
> 5 the passenger waited over an hour for another coach, the driver will get training because he was wrong to ask the passengers to push the coach

c 💬 Ask students to tell the story to their partner in their own words. They should use the questions to help them. Monitor and help where necessary. Encourage students who are listening to ask their partner follow-up questions.

> 💡 **FAST FINISHERS**
>
> Fast finishers can read the complete story to their partner and then ask detailed questions to see how much he/she can remember, e.g. *How many passengers were on the coach? What time did the coach leave Heathrow?*

d 💬 Discuss the question in full group, asking for reasons.

e Tell students that now they are going to tell a story themselves. First, give them some time to think about a difficult journey they once had. Suggest that this could be when they were young or it could be more recent. If they can't think of a story, they can invent one or talk about someone they know. Circulate and help with ideas where necessary.

f 💬 Put students into small groups to tell their stories. The other students can ask questions while they are telling the story. Look at the example together. Monitor but do not stop students if they make mistakes. Clarify these as you check answers as a class.

> 🔄 **LOA TIP MONITORING**
>
> • As this is a fluency activity, do not interrupt the groups while they are talking. However, you want students to use the correct target language from the lesson so listen carefully and note down mistakes students make with the past continuous and any mistakes with vocabulary (that you presented in the lesson). You may need to write notes to remember specific examples to use in feedback – but if you can remember without writing down, this will be less worrying for students.
>
> • During feedback, do not attribute mistakes to individual students, but give the mistake and elicit corrections from the whole group.
>
> • While monitoring, also note any interesting facts about their journeys that students mentioned so that you can bring these up in feedback, too.

g Students discuss each form of transport and describe any other bad experiences they have had. Students decide who has had the worst experience on each form of transport. In feedback, they tell the other groups and give reasons for their decision.

> 💡 **EXTRA ACTIVITY**
>
> In small groups, students each have a piece of paper. Ask them to write down the first part of a sentence in the past continuous: *When I was driving home last week, …* They pass the paper to the student on their right who has to finish the sentence and start the next sentence, also in the past continuous. Students will be building a story so the content of the sentence needs to follow on from the first. Allow about five minutes for the activity. Ask one student from each group to read their story to the class.

> **ADDITIONAL MATERIAL**
>
> ▶ Workbook 2B
>
> ▶ Photocopiable activities: Grammar p.207, Vocabulary p.231, Pronunciation p.268

Everyday English
What time's the next train?

At the end of this lesson, students will be able to:

- use phrases to ask for information in a public place
- link the endings and beginnings of words together
- understand a conversation where someone is asking for and receiving information

---

ⓦ OPTIONAL LEAD-IN

Books closed. Tell students they are going on a train journey but they don't know the train route, timetable or ticket cost. Find out how students prefer to ask for information: by phone, online or in person. Put students in pairs to discuss. Encourage them to explain their reasons. Ask one or two students to summarise the advantages of each.

1 LISTENING

a 💬 Write *train station*, *tourist office* and *airport* on the board. In pairs, students think of two kinds of information they can find out in each place. Compare answers as a class.

> **Suggested answers**
> times of trains, which platforms they leave from
> places of interest to visit, shows and entertainment
> how long a delay is, changing a flight

b 💬 Students look at the pictures and describe them. Then they guess where Annie is and what information she wants. Then ask them to imagine what information she'll ask for. Put a list of their ideas on the board as they might refer to this later in the lesson.

c ▶️1.38 Play Part 1 of the video or play the audio recording for students to check their ideas.

Video/Audioscript (Part 1)

ANNIE Excuse me ... Excuse me!
EMPLOYEE Yes, how can I help you?
A I'm going to Birmingham to visit my brother.
E OK. Erm, which train are you taking?
A Oh, I don't know. What time's the next train?
E The next one leaves in ... four minutes.
A How often do the trains leave?
E Every ... 30 minutes. So the next one after that is at 15.32.
A OK, great. And er, which platform does it leave from?
E That train leaves from ... platform 12. So, it's just over there.
A Sorry, just one more thing.
E Yes, of course.
A Could you tell me where the ticket office is?
E It's over there. But it looks quite busy – there's a long queue. I can sell you a ticket.
A Oh, brilliant! How much is a ticket?
E Well, when do you want to come back?

A Oh, I don't know. Probably tomorrow evening. But on Sunday it's going to be sunny I think and my brother's going to have a party and so maybe I'll stay until Monday.
E The ticket prices change. Sunday is cheaper than Monday.
A Oh, Sunday then. His parties are never very good.
E OK, you want a return to Birmingham. Coming back on ... Sunday?
A Yes, that's right.
E So, that's £26.30.
A Can I pay by card?
E Yes, sure ... OK, so here's your card, and your ticket. Is there anything else I can help you with?
A Actually, there is one more thing. Where can I buy a magazine? Is there a newsagent's here?
E Yes, look – there's one just over there.
A Great. Thanks so much.
E No problem. Have a good journey.

> **Answers**
> Annie is at a train station.
> She wants to know: when the next train leaves; how often the trains leave; which platform the train leaves from; where the ticket office is; how much a ticket is; where she can buy a magazine

d ▶️1.38 Read through the questions with students before they do the activity. You could see if they can answer any of the questions from memory. Then play the recording again for students to answer the questions. If necessary, pause the recording after each answer is given. Check answers as a class.

> **Answers**
> 1 in four minutes
> 2 every 30 minutes
> 3 12
> 4 Sunday
> 5 £26.30
> 6 a magazine

ⓦ FAST FINISHERS

Ask students to cover the exercise. Put the answers on the board to elicit the questions. Students uncover the task and check.

ⓦ EXTRA ACTIVITY

Ask students why the following are mentioned in the dialogue: brother (Annie's going to visit him), a party (her brother might have one on Sunday), cheaper (tickets are cheaper on Sundays).

2 USEFUL LANGUAGE
Asking for information in a public place

a ▶️1.39 Before looking at the exercise, ask students if they can complete the questions from the conversation in 1. Give them the first parts of the questions (1–6). Put their suggestions on the board. Students then look at the task and match the sentence parts. Play the recording for students to check and then compare with their original ideas. You could also ask for examples of other questions beginning with these or similar question starters, e.g. *What time ... does the film start?*

> **Answers and audioscript**
> 1d What time's the next train?
> 2e How often do the trains leave?
> 3c Could you tell me where the ticket office is?
> 4a How much is a ticket?
> 5b Can I pay by card?
> 6f Where can I buy a magazine?

b ▶️1.40 Students listen and complete the questions the assistant asks. Students may be able to do this before hearing the recording again. Play the recording for students to answer the questions or check their answers.

> **Answers**
> 1 can I
> 2 anything else

c Tell students they are now going to look at another dialogue about asking for and giving information. Ask them to read through the gapped dialogue (or read through it with them) and say where they think the conversation happens (information centre / tourist office). Then ask students to complete the dialogue individually.

d ▶ **1.41** Play the recording for students to check. Check answers as a class. In pairs, students practise the dialogue, taking turns to be A and B.

> **Answers**
> 1 could you tell me   2 what time   3 How much
> 4 Where can I   5 Can I

3 PRONUNCIATION Joining words

a ▶ **1.41** Tell students that sometimes it's difficult to understand a person speaking English because they seem to speak very quickly. Explain that often it is about the way they join words together when they speak. Clarify this with an example, exaggerating the way the words are joined, e.g. *my friendAnnie (my friend, Annie)*. Check students know the difference between a consonant sound and a vowel sound and then play the recording of the questions for students to complete the rule and answer the question. Model the questions and ask students to repeat.

> **Answers**
> 1 isn't   2 /naɪ/ /ʧɪ/

b Students underline the letters and spaces where there isn't a pause, i.e. where a consonant sound is joined to the vowel sound at the beginning of the next word.

c ▶ **1.43** Play the recording for them to check their answers. Students repeat to practise.

d ▶ In pairs, students ask each other the questions in 3b. Monitor and point out any errors for students to correct.

> **Answers and audioscript**
> 1 Is anyone sitting here?
> 2 Could I sit next to you?
> 3 What are you reading?
> 4 Do you want a drink?
> 5 Where do you get off?
> 6 Can I have your email address?

↻ LOA TIP DRILLING

- Model the sentences from the recording individually and ask the class to repeat them as a group with the same pronunciation. Start quite slowly and encourage students to repeat at the same speed. Focus on the joining (linking) sounds to make the sentences appear as natural as possible. Then repeat the activity but going slightly more quickly. See how fast students can say the sentences but still remain clear.

- You can then use number 4 in a transformation drill, either together as a class or students can do this in pairs. Say: *Do you want a drink?* Students repeat. Then give different prompts, e.g. a sandwich: *Do you want a sandwich?* This is not to practise the structure but the linking sound: *want + a*.

📖 LANGUAGE NOTES

English speakers also often combine *do + you = /djuː/* Encourage students to use this contraction when they use the form in speaking.

---

4 CONVERSATION SKILLS
Asking for more information

a Read through the exchanges with the class and ask if the underlined phrases mean 1 or 2.

> **Answer**
> 2 ask something else

b ▶ **1.44** Play the recording for students to repeat the phrases. Make sure that they pause after the words *sorry* and *actually*.

📖 LANGUAGE NOTES

In some languages, *actually* (meaning 'in fact' or 'really') is a false friend – a word that looks like a word in their language but which has another meaning. In French, for example, *actuellement* means 'currently' or 'at the moment'.

ⓦ EXTRA ACTIVITY

Ask students to imagine that you work at an airport. One student asks you for some information. Give the information and then ask: *Is there anything else I can help you with?* Another student asks you for information. Reply and ask the same question again. Continue round the class until students finally run out of questions.

---

c ▶ Tell students that they are going to role play a situation where one is a tourist information officer and the other is a tourist. Put students into pairs and give them A and B roles. Give them a short time to look at their roles and the example dialogue, and to think of some extra questions and the kind of answers they might need to use. Give an example if you feel they need extra help, e.g. *How much are the tickets? They're 45 dollars each.* Students practise the conversation. Monitor and prompt or help where necessary. In feedback, ask what additional information they asked for.

d ▶ Students swap roles and do the role play again.

ⓦ FAST FINISHERS

Ask fast finishers to imagine that one is the secretary of your school and the other is a student who wants some information.

---

5 LISTENING

a ▶ Ask students to look at the picture from Part 2 again. Ask: *Why is Annie running back to the assistant?* Take ideas from students and write these on the board.

b ▶ **1.45** Play Part 2 of the video or play the audio recording for students to check their ideas and tell you what Annie's mistake was. Elicit what the assistant says when he doesn't understand: Sorry? Model the correct intonation and ask the class to repeat. Ask if they think she can change her ticket or not.

Video/audioscript (Part 2)

ANNIE He doesn't live in Birmingham any more! He doesn't live in Birmingham any more! He doesn't live in Birmingham any more!

EMPLOYEE Sorry?

A My brother. He moved. He doesn't live in Birmingham any more. He lives in Stratford now! Can I change my ticket …?

> **Answers**
> She needs to change her ticket.
> Her brother doesn't live in Birmingham. He lives in Stratford.
> Her last question was: 'Can I change my ticket?'

c  Students tell their partners about a silly mistake they (or someone they know) made when travelling. Have an example of your own ready to tell the class, e.g. I pushed the wrong button on a ticket machine and got a single instead of a return. I didn't notice until I tried to travel back with the ticket and had to pay again.

> ### ⓦ EXTRA ACTIVITY
> Tell students that many UK stations today have ticket machines and no ticket offices. Is this a good idea or not? Why? Have a short class discussion.

6 SPEAKING

a Put students into pairs and assign them A and B roles. Student A reads card 1 in 6b. Student B reads card 1 on SB p.128. They prepare what they are going to ask/say. Monitor and help with vocabulary as necessary. Each pair role plays the conversation. Student B starts by asking: *How can I help you?* Monitor and check that students are using appropriate language. After the role play, point out any common mistakes with the class. Now Student A reads card 2 in 6b and Student B reads card 2 on SB p.128. Monitor and point out errors for students to self-correct.

> ### 📖 VOCABULARY SUPPORT
> *locker* – a metal cupboard, with a lock where people can leave luggage, e.g. in a station

> ### 📖 LANGUAGE NOTES
> The pronunciation of the town Warwick is /'wɒrɪk/ because the second 'w' is silent.

> ### ⓦ FAST FINISHERS
> Fast finishers should think of extra questions to ask and give more detailed information.

> ### ⓦ EXTRA ACTIVITY
> In pairs, students choose a tourist attraction that they know in the local area and write a section for a guidebook in the style of FAQs (Frequently Asked Questions). Give them an example of this: *Q: Where is the museum? A: It's in the High Street, opposite the church.*

> **ADDITIONAL MATERIAL**
> ▶ Workbook 2C
> ▶ Unit Progress Test
>   Personalised online practice

At the end of this lesson, students will be able to:

- understand a conversation about a travel experience
- read and understand a travel blog
- use linking words *and* / *but* / *so* / *because* / *when*
- write a travel blog

⚲ OPTIONAL LEAD-IN

Put students into pairs. Ask them to write down the name of a country and its capital city that they think other students in the class will not know. Make two or three teams from the pairs. Say: *Jakarta*. Ask students to name the country Jakarta is the capital city of. Only accept one answer from each team. If students know the answer (Indonesia), they win a point for their team. Pairs take it in turns to say their capital cities. If no one knows the answer, the pair wins a point for their own team.

1 SPEAKING AND LISTENING

a 🗩 Students look at the pictures and answer the questions. Take feedback as a class. If you wish, give students information from the Culture notes below.

> **Answers**
> 1 a a traffic jam b a beach in Bali c a storm with lightning in the sky d Barobudur Buddhist Temple e an orang-utan

🌏 CULTURE NOTES

Around 245 million people live in Indonesia (the 4th highest population in the world after the USA, China and India). Indonesia is made up of many islands which include: Java, part of Borneo, Sumatra and Bali. It has a tropical climate with average temperatures ranging between 23°C to 28°C. Jakarta, on the island of Java, is the capital city of Indonesia and the largest city of South East Asia. Around 9 million tourists visited Indonesia in 2013.

- Borobudur Buddhist temple, on the Indonesian island of Java, is the world's largest Buddhist temple. It was built in the 9th century and is a UNESCO World Heritage site. It is Indonesia's most visited tourist attraction. Visitors can see a huge number of Buddhist artworks carved into the stone.
- The Indonesian island of Bali is world famous for its tropical beaches.
- In the wild, orang-utans live only in the forests of Sumatra and Borneo. Both populations are endangered due to deforestation, although charities are working to save them. Specialist guided tours are available to visit orang-utans in the wild.

b ▶ 1.46 Tell students that they are going to hear a conversation between Tim and Karen, his aunt. Read through the questions with the class. Tell them that they don't need to understand every word as they are just listening for the answers to these questions. Play the recording and check answers as a class. Then ask: *Why do you think Tim is going to Jakarta? (on holiday) Why did Karen go to Jakarta? (to work)*

> **Answers**
> 1 to ask for advice about arriving in Indonesia
> 2 about ten years ago
> 3 a (a traffic jam), c (a storm with heavy rain and lightning)

Audioscript

TIM So, when I get to Jakarta, what should I do?

KAREN I'm not really sure. I mean, I left Indonesia about ten years ago and … well … it's probably all changed now.

T So, yeah, I think we'll just get a taxi from the airport to the hostel.

K You could, but if you want to save money, I think there's probably a bus service.

T I suppose so. Is that what you did?

K Well, I was going to Jakarta to work, so someone met us with a car and drove us into the centre of town.

T So what was it like when you arrived?

K It's something I'll never forget. You know, this was the first time I went somewhere that was completely different, the other side of the world. I remember we had a pretty bad flight; there was a long delay at the airport because there was something wrong with the plane. And we had quite a lot of turbulence – and as we were landing I remember thinking 'Is this all a big mistake?'. But no … as soon as we got off the plane and I felt how lovely and warm it was, I began to feel much happier. I loved it there, I'm sure you will too.

T And, so, once you were away from the airport, what did you see?

K Well, the first thing I saw was a traffic jam!

T Oh no.

K Yes, and a traffic jam that was much noisier and longer than in this country. And a storm!

T Oh no! Really?

K Yes, quite often in the spring, the rainy season, there's suddenly a storm with heavy rain and lightning. And you just have to run for the nearest building! For me, it was exciting, though. I expect you'll love it, too.

T You must have so many memories of your time there.

K Yeah … yeah I do.

T Did you write them down? You know, do a blog or something.

K No … I didn't have an internet connection in my apartment.

T Or a diary or something like that?

K No, I never did.

T That's a pity. But you seem to remember it pretty well.

c ▶ 1.46 Tell students that they are going to listen again to answer more detailed questions. Read through the questions first with the class – you may wish to help students with words in the Vocabulary support box at this point. Then play the recording again for students to answer the questions.

> **Answers**
> 1 by taxi 2 long delay at airport, turbulence
> 3 noisier and longer than in this country 4 It was exciting.
> 5 She didn't have an Internet connection in her apartment.

📖 VOCABULARY SUPPORT

have an Internet connection (B1) – if a place has an Internet connection, you can use the Internet there

lightning (B1) – flashes of light in the sky during a storm

rainy season – time of year when there is a lot of rain

⚲ EXTRA ACTIVITY

In pairs, students find a town or area that one of them knows but the other doesn't. Student A is going to visit the place that Student B knows and phones Student B to find out about it. Students role play the conversation.

d 🗩 Students answer the questions, giving reasons where appropriate. If students like reading blogs, ask: *When did you last read a blog? Why did you read it?*

2 READING

a Tell the class that they are going to read two posts from Tim's travel blog about arriving in Jakarta. Elicit what they think he might write about. Students then look at the list of topics and see if it includes their ideas. Students read the blogs quickly to check which topics he does NOT write about. Check answers as a class.

 **VOCABULARY SUPPORT**

flavour (B1) – taste in the mouth when we eat food

humid (B1) – weather that is hot and a little wet

local (B1) – in the area near you

style (B1) – a way of doing something (in this case, building) that is from a particular place, or time

Answers
animals

b Ask students to read the blog again to answer the more detailed questions. Check answers as a class. You may wish to help students with words in the Vocabulary support box.

Answers
1 He slept.
2 There was a huge traffic jam.
3 because they paid him too much
4 delicious; really fresh and full of flavour
5 lots of old buildings in different styles

EXTRA ACTIVITY

Books closed. Read the posts to the class making mistakes in the content, e.g. *It was a short flight …* . Students stop you when you make a mistake and correct it. (It was a long flight.)

3 WRITING SKILLS Linking words

a Ask students if Tim's blog has a lot of short sentences or several long ones. (It has several long ones.) Ask: *Can you find words in the first paragraph in the first blog that Tim uses to join, or link, short sentences?* (He uses *and, but, so, because*.) Individually, students read the examples and answer the questions. Check answers as a class.

Answers
a when   d so
b and   e because
c but

b Students underline more examples of the linking words in the posts. Check answers as a class.

Answers
Tuesday
<u>and</u> it's really exciting; <u>but</u> I slept most of the way; It's really humid, because; <u>When</u> we left the airport; <u>and</u> he brought us here; <u>because</u> he seemed; <u>so</u> I have to finish now
Wednesday
<u>so</u> it seemed to be a place; <u>and</u> fell asleep immediately; <u>and</u> very different from anything

c Explain the activity and do the first one together as a class. Then students complete the sentences individually and then compare answers with a partner. Check as a class.

Answers
1 so   4 but   7 because
2 When   5 because   8 but
3 so   6 when

 EXTRA ACTIVITY

In pairs, each student writes the beginnings of five sentences in the past, finishing with a linking word. They exchange with their partner who has to finish them, e.g. *I went to the cinema last week because … (I wanted to see the new Matt Damon film.)*. Monitor and point out any sentences that don't make sense. Take feedback as a class and ask for examples from the different pairs. Put them on the board. Ask if students can think of other endings, using different linking words.

4 WRITING

a Tell students they are going to write a blog and go through the topics. Ask students to choose a topic. Ask a few students to tell you the specific topic they are going to write about.

b Read through the ideas and give the class three or four minutes to make notes. Monitor and help with vocabulary where necessary.

c When they are ready, students write their blogs. Remind them to use some of the linking words from 3a. Do not monitor closely, but circulate so that students can ask for help if they need it.

FAST FINISHERS

Ask fast finishers to write a second blog for the following day.

d In pairs, students read each other's blogs and compare them. If appropriate, students can suggest changes or improvements to their partner's blog.

EXTRA ACTIVITY

When the blogs are finished and corrected, students can pass them round the class. The readers can add a comment as on a real blog. As the blogs are passed round again, other students can add comments and develop a thread.

LOA TIP REVIEW AND REFLECT

Have a brief class discussion and ask students what new things they learned in this lesson that they did not know before. What was the most interesting thing? Also ask what they can do in English that they couldn't do at the beginning of the lesson, e.g. *I learned some interesting information about Indonesia. I can use linking words better now.*

ADDITIONAL MATERIAL

▶ Workbook 2D

UNIT 2
Review and extension

1 GRAMMAR

a Students complete the sentences individually. Check answers as a class.

> **Answers**
> 1 didn't spend   2 asked   3 needed   4 didn't get
> 5 wore   6 Did, meet   7 learnt/learned

> ### 💡 EXTRA ACTIVITY
> Ask students to think of questions for each of the sentences. Ask them to make the questions for all except 6. Give them the starter words: *1 Why … 2 What … 3 Did … 4 Why … 5 What … 6 Where …* Suggested answers are: *1 Why did you spend a lot of money? 2 What did she ask the bus driver for? 3 Did you need to change your ticket? 4 Why did you get the bus home? 5 What did he wear to the party? 7 Where did you learn to surf?* Students could practise the questions and answers in pairs.

b Write on the board: *I was dreaming about my holiday when my alarm clock woke me up this morning.* Concept check by asking: *Which action started first? (I was dreaming).* Students complete the story with the correct alternatives individually and then compare answers with a partner. Point out that both forms are possible in one case. Check answers as a class.

> **Answers**
> 1 was walking   2 came   3 found   4 were playing
> 5 was reading   6 arrived   7 sat   8 told / was telling   9 got

2 VOCABULARY

a Before students look at the exercise, ask them to make a list of things people can take on holiday. Then they do the matching task. Check answers.

> **Answers**
> 1 suntan lotion, sunglasses   2 foreign currency
> 3 guidebook, map   4 passport   5 backpack, suitcase

b Students complete the sentences. Check answers in full group.

> **Answers**
> 1 travel around   2 get   3 do   4 change   5 go away
> 6 set off   7 check out

3 WORDPOWER *off*

a Write the word *off* on the board. Give students a minute in pairs to think of sentences that use *off* in different ways. Check their ideas as a class. Elicit or put on the board an example for each of the groups of sentences 1–3 in the book, e.g. *1 We had dinner and then Marc went off to play on his computer. 2 I took off the top of the box and looked inside. 3 I checked that the TV was off before I went out.* Ask students to look through the three groups of examples in the book and to match their general meanings with the pictures. Ask them if the sentences on the board are in the same order. (They are in the same order.) Tell them that diagram a shows something divided, or separated, from the whole thing. Diagram b shows power is not on. Diagram c shows the idea of going away from something. Tell students that it is not always possible to guess the general meaning of prepositions and phrasal verbs in these ways, but they can be a useful guide.

> **Answers**
> 1c   2a   3b

b Students match the sentences and replies. Check answers as a class.

> **Answers**
> 1c   2a   3h   4d   5b   6g   7e   8f

c Students cover a–h and try to remember the replies.

▶ Photocopiable activities: Wordpower p.253

> ### 🔄 LOA REVIEW YOUR PROGRESS
> Students look back through the unit, think about what they've studied and decide how well they did. Students work on weak areas by using the appropriate sections of the Workbook, the Photocopiable activities and the Personalised online practice.

UNIT 3
Money

At the end of this unit, students will be able to:

- understand texts and conversations related to money
- talk about experiences of generosity
- talk about spending and saving money
- talk to people in shops
- use phrases to show they are changing their mind about something
- write an update email

UNIT CONTENTS

G GRAMMAR
- Present perfect or past simple
- Present perfect with *just*, *already* and *yet*

V VOCABULARY
- Collocations with *make*, *do* and *give*: *do sth nice (for sb)*, *do well (at sth)*, *give sb a hug*, *give sb a tip*, *give sb directions*, *give sth away*, *make a friend*, *make a joke*, *make sb smile*, *do volunteer work*
- Words and phrases related to money: *bank account, special offers, the sales, pay sb back, lend, cash, borrow sth from sb, get a loan, owe, spend money on sth, cost, save up for sth, afford, discount*
- Wordpower: different meanings of *just*: 1 = only; 2 = soon; 3 = a short time ago; 4 = almost not. Expressions with *just*: *just about, just in time, just like, just over, just under*

P PRONUNCIATION
- Sound and spelling: /dʒ/ and /j/
- Sentence stress

C COMMUNICATION SKILLS
- Talking about experiences of generosity
- Talking about saving and spending money
- Talking to people in shops
- Writing an update email
- Paragraphing

GETTING STARTED

☀ OPTIONAL LEAD-IN

Books closed. In pairs, give students two minutes to write down as many different kinds of shop as they can. Put pairs together. One pair names a shop from their list and the other pair says one item that they can buy there. The students must answer in five seconds. If they answer correctly, that pair gets a point. If they can't answer, the pair asking the question gets the point.

a  Ask students to look at the picture and say what they can see. In pairs, students read the questions and talk about them. Monitor and support students with any new vocabulary they may need. Suggested vocabulary: *jewellers, jewellery, bracelet, gold, coloured glass, stones (diamonds* and *rubies)*. Students share their ideas as a class.

b  Give students one minute to think about their answers to the questions before talking about the picture as a class. Students may also want to include online shopping in their discussions. Give your own opinions to encourage discussion. As this is a fluency activity, don't correct students unless a mistake is making understanding difficult. If you wish, give students information from the Culture notes below.

🌍 CULTURE NOTES

The biggest shopping mall in the world (for its total area) is The Dubai Mall in Dubai, UAE. It is over 13 million square feet – about the size of 50 football pitches! It has over 1,200 shops (including the world's largest sweet shop), a 250-room luxury hotel, 22 cinema screens, 120 restaurants and cafes. It has more than 14,000 parking spaces too. It opened in 2008 as part of the 20 billion dollar Burj Khalifa complex and is now the world's most visited shopping and leisure centre. It has more than 54 million visitors every year. Many people say that men tend to shop quickly and women like to *browse* (look around before buying). Of course, this is a generalisation and there are many men and women who don't shop like this. However, some psychologists believe that male and female shopping habits can be explained by early human history. The woman's job was to gather fresh produce such as plants, nuts, fruit and vegetables and the man's job was to hunt wild animals and take them home!

c  In pairs, students choose their favourite things and talk to their partners about why they like spending money on these things. Take feedback as a class.

☀ EXTRA ACTIVITY

Put students in small groups. Tell them to imagine that they have £1,000 to spend and they have to plan a day's shopping trip. They can choose where they want to go for the trip. Monitor and support students with vocabulary. In feedback, ask for examples of the planned trips and ask the class to vote on the best idea.

3A Have you ever helped a stranger?

At the end of this lesson, students will be able to:

- read and understand a text and posts on a forum about people being generous
- contrast the use of the present perfect and past simple tenses
- use collocations with *make, do* and *give*
- understand a story about a man's favourite charity
- ask and answer questions about generous things they have done

OPTIONAL LEAD-IN

Books closed. Say: *Yesterday a woman dropped her shopping in the street and I helped her pick it up. On the way home, the train was crowded and I let an old man have my seat. A man was playing a guitar in the underground station and I gave him some money.* Ask students to guess the question that the sentences are in answer to, e.g. *How did you help people yesterday? What was the nicest thing you did yesterday?* In pairs or small groups, students talk about and list other things we can do to help other people. Allow a few minutes then ask each pair for one idea. Write these on the board. Take a class vote on which way of helping is the most unusual.

1 READING

a Ask students to look at the picture and describe it. Elicit their ideas about what the situation is and what's happening. (The woman is giving food to hungry and homeless people at a shelter.) Ask students what they think their feelings would be if they were a) the homeless man or b) the girl giving food.

b Elicit the meaning of *generosity*. (It comes from the adjective *generous* meaning giving or being willing to give freely (the opposite of *mean*). In the broader sense of the term, showing generosity doesn't just mean giving money or possessions, it can mean being generous with your time or in your attitude towards people, which is the idea behind Generosity Day.)

VOCABULARY SUPPORT

generosity (B2) – the fact of being generous – willing to give things freely, e.g. money, presents or time

hug (B1) – when you put your arms round someone

LOA TIP ELICITING

- Give an example of someone you know who is generous and say what this person does, e.g. *my friend always buys me a meal when I haven't got any money; he gives people presents on their birthdays; he often gives money to charity.* Elicit the adjective which describes your friend and put *generous* on the board. Then say: *He is well-known for his generosity.* Elicit or point out that there is no letter 'u' in the noun.

- Ask students to look at the title of the article and say what they think *Generosity Day* is. (It's a day when people show generosity to everyone and try to do something nice for people they don't know.) Students read to check their ideas.

- Discuss whether the class think this is a good idea and what they would like to do. Points to consider: Should it just be one day? Do we have too many special days each year? Elicit examples, e.g. Mother's Day / Father's Day / Children's Day / Walk to Work Day.

c Students read the posts on the forum and answer the questions individually. Check answers as a class.

Answers
helping other people: 2 Help@Haiti – volunteer work, paying for someone's education; 3 Neil50 – buying drinks for strangers, leaving a bit tip; 4 ThatGeorgeKid – giving directions, picking up hitchikers, calling an ambulance; 5 Maya_Flower – buying meals for homeless people, giving away clothes to charity, generous in small ways receiving help from other people: 1 Sally_TM – being helped when she hurt her knee; 4 ThatGeorgeKid – details not given

VOCABULARY SUPPORT

charity (B1) – an organisation that helps people

d In pairs, students discuss the meanings of the highlighted words and phrases. Tell them to use the context to work out the meanings. Ask them to explain the new items in their own words. You should encourage them to give an example, too, using the new items, as this makes new vocabulary more memorable. Ask for their answers as a class.

Answers
a stranger: a person you don't know
do volunteer work: do work, usually for a charity, without receiving any money
gave the waitress a big tip: gave someone extra money, e.g. for friendly service
made them smile: made people happy
give directions: tell people how to get to a place
a hero: someone we admire for their courage
save someone's life: stop someone from dying
homeless: not having somewhere to live or sleep
give away: give something to someone without receiving any money in return

EXTRA ACTIVITY

Books closed. Ask: *What is Sally's story?* Choose a student to summarise. Divide students into pairs. Each student chooses one of the stories to retell, but this time they change some of the facts. Give students one or two minutes to prepare before retelling their stories. Their partner listens and corrects the facts, Choose other students to retell the other mini-stories. Be sure to choose students who are quite confident, e.g. Student A: *Sally went to the supermarket to get some ice.* Student B: *No! She went to the corner shop!*

e Students talk about who they think is the most generous, and why. Take a class vote.

EXTRA ACTIVITY

In class or at home, students write another post for the forum in which they tell their own or a made-up story. Circulate the stories in class and vote on the most interesting one. Students can also guess if the stories are true or made-up.

2 GRAMMAR
Present perfect or past simple

a Books closed. Write a question on the board: *Did you help a stranger yesterday?* Ask students: *What is the time word in the question? When am I asking you about?* Elicit the answer: *Yesterday.* Elicit that the question is past simple. Now write: *Have you ever helped a stranger?* Ask students about the time word. Elicit that the word *ever* is a time word. Ask: *What time period is 'ever'?* Elicit that this question asks a person about their whole past life until now. Draw a timeline on the board to show this if you wish. (Example on SB p.146) Open books. Point out that the sentences are from the forum, and ask students to complete them with the verbs in the box individually. If necessary, do the first one together. Check answers as a class. Ask if anyone knows what the difference is between *saw* and *seen*. (*Saw* is the past simple form of *see. Seen* is the past participle.)

> **Answers**
> 1 been   2 saw   3 seen   4 decided   5 done   6 do

b Ask students to identify which sentences are present perfect and which are past simple.

> **Answers**
> present perfect: 1, 3, 5
> past simple: 2, 4, 6

c Students underline the time expressions and complete the rules. Check answers as a class. Elicit other examples of time expressions we can use with the past simple, e.g. *yesterday / last summer / on 15th February / at 12.30.* Then elicit phrases and adverbs to use with the present perfect, e.g. *recently / three times.*

> **Answers**
> Present perfect: *three times, never, ever*
> Past simple: *a few weeks ago, on my fiftieth birthday*

d ▶ Students read the information in Grammar Focus 3A on SB p.146. Play the recording where indicated and ask students to listen and repeat. Students then complete the exercises on SB p.147. For Exercise b, elicit that contractions are natural in spoken English, especially in informal conversations. Note: although the contraction is possible after *How many times* in 9, it would rarely be written as a contraction, even in informal English. Check answers as a class.

> **Answers (Grammar Focus 3A SB p.147)**
> **a** 1 bought   2 done   3 driven   4 given   5 made   6 lent
>   7 ridden   8 saved   9 seen   10 sold   11 smiled   12 spent
>   13 taken   14 wanted   15 written
> **b** 1 I've never given   2 Have you ever sold   3 's lived
>   4 've eaten   5 've never sung   6 Has he ever cooked
>   7 's helped   8 's never broken down   9 have the children
>   10 've never tried
> **c** 2 I've never seen that film.
>   3 Have you ever been to Canada?
>   4 Where did you go on holiday last year?
>   5 She's broken her leg twice.
>   6 I worked in a hospital a long time ago.
>   7 In your life, how many times have you moved house?
>   8 When we went to London we visited Kew Gardens.

> 💡 **EXTRA ACTIVITY**
>
> Give students a past tense forms test with their books closed. Say the infinitive and ask for simple past and past participle forms, e.g. Say: *run* Students reply: *run, ran, run.* Use a mixture of regular and irregular verbs.

e Students complete the questions in 2e individually and then compare answers with a partner.

f Students listen to the recording to check their answers. In pairs, they ask and answer the questions.

> **Answers**
> 1 Have, done; did, do
> 2 Have, driven; did, drive
> 3 Have, bought; did, buy

> 💡 **EXTRA ACTIVITY**
>
> Put some more verbs on the board, e.g. *read, see, write, meet, ride.* In pairs, students choose three of the verbs and write similar pairs of questions to the questions in f with them. They then ask their questions to another pair. Monitor and check accuracy of the verb forms. Encourage students to find out more details about questions their partners answered 'yes' to.

3 VOCABULARY
make / do / give collocations

a Check that students understand the concept of verb + noun collocations by asking what students did last night to elicit, *I did my homework.* Underline *did + homework* and tell students that when the verb and noun go together like this, it is a collocation. Ask students to work in pairs to choose the correct verbs to complete the phrases.

b Ask students to check answers in the text and forum on SB p.28. In pairs, they try to guess the meanings of phrases they don't know by using the context. They can then check their ideas in a dictionary. As a class, ask students to explain the meanings they found.

> **Answers**
> 1 make   2 give   3 do

c 💬 Read through the examples with the class. In pairs, students tell each other which of the things in 3a they've done this week. Conduct group feedback and encourage students to ask each other follow-up questions using the past simple, e.g. *Why did you give them a tip?*

4 LISTENING

a ▶1.49 Tell the class that they are going to read about a man called Philip Wollen, who did something unusual. Students read the information about Philip Wollen to answer questions 1 and 2. Check answers as a class. Check understanding of *life-changing experience* (an experience that changed your life) and ask what this might have been, e.g. a bad accident / winning a lot of money / visiting a very poor country / meeting an inspiring person, etc. Ask students for their predictions for question 3. Then play the recording for students to find out what he has done with his money. Tell the class to listen to get the general idea of who he has helped and where (which parts of the world), but not to worry about understanding every word. You may need to play the recording twice.

📖 VOCABULARY SUPPORT

chemist (B1) – someone who has studied chemistry / works in a pharmacy or the pharmaceutical industry

make a big difference (B2) – improve a situation a lot

organisation (B1) – a group, e.g. a business

orphanage (B2) – a home for children with no parents

Audioscript

After leaving his job, Philip Wollen opened up the Kindness Trust, an organisation that finds small charities in countries where a little bit of money can make a big difference. Wollen then surprises these charities with a gift to continue their good work. So far, he has given money to between 400–500 different charities in 40 countries. His money has built schools, children's homes and homes for animals.

A special charity for Wollen is the Morning Star orphanage in Bangalore. The orphanage started when, 20 years ago, a man called John Samson found a hungry baby boy in the street. He gave him a home and then he looked for more homeless children to help. Today the orphanage looks after 60 children. With money from the Kindness Trust, John has made the Morning Star bigger and opened a new learning centre. Wollen went to India to open the centre, meet the children and hear about their lives. One little girl has won a place at a famous women's college, another child is an excellent chess player and another wants to be a doctor. The little boy that John Samson found in the street has now become a chemist.

And it is not just people that Philip Wollen has helped. He has also given money to a large number of animal charities, such as Edgar's Mission in Australia, a charity that cares for old farm animals and finds new homes for them. The charity also tries to teach people how to look after animals, so they are healthy and happy.

Wollen thinks everyone can help to make the world a better place for other people and animals. He says, 'One man can make a difference and every man should try.'

Answers
1 He was a banker.
2 He had a life-changing experience and no longer needed all his money.
3 He has given his money to different charities.

b ▶1.49 Read through the questions first with the class and then play the recording again for students to answer the questions individually. Pause the recording after the first paragraph to let students answer the first two questions. Check answers together and then play the remaining part of the recording. Pause the recording only if necessary. Check the rest of the answers together.

Answers
1 They are small charities.
2 400–500
3 A man called John Samson gave a home to a hungry baby boy.
4 John used Philip Wollen's money to make a bigger building and open a new learning centre.
5 He's a chemist.
6 old farm animals
7 how to look after animals

c 💬 Discuss the question as a class. Encourage students to give reasons for their answers.

5 SPEAKING

a 💬 To set up the mingle activity, explain to students that they are going to try to find someone in the class who has done each of the things in the grid. Read through the grid and the examples with the class and give them a short time to think about their own experiences. Then start the activity. Students should walk round and ask their questions. Encourage them to talk to different people. When they find someone who has done one thing, they should note down the name and then try to find out an extra piece of information. You can take part in the mingle activity yourself to answer questions. If you decide to observe and monitor instead, don't interrupt students while they are speaking, but note any issues to address during feedback.

When students seem to be running out of things to say, stop the activity, and conduct feedback. Students should tell the class about some of the responses they had. Ask: *Did you find someone for each thing? Was there one thing that no one has done?*

b 💬 Ask *What was the most generous thing you heard?* Ask: *Do you think you will do any of these things in the next few days?* Tell the class that next lesson you will check!

ADDITIONAL MATERIAL

▶ Workbook 3A
▶ Photocopiable activities: Grammar p.208, Vocabulary p.232

3B I've already spent my salary this month

At the end of this lesson, students will be able to:
- talk about saving and spending money
- use a set of vocabulary related to money
- understand interviews about shopping and saving
- use the present perfect tense with *just*, *already* and *yet*

◔ OPTIONAL LEAD-IN

Books closed. The following phrases are often seen in High Street shops in the UK: *3 for 2* and *B.O.G.O.F.* Write them on the board. Can students guess the meaning? (*3 for 2* means: buy 3 items but only pay for 2 – so the cheapest item is free. B.O.G.O.F. stands for Buy One, Get One Free). Are similar offers common in students' own countries?

1 VOCABULARY Money

a ◔ Discuss the question as a class. Encourage students to give reasons for their answers. Ask students to share examples of times they managed to save up and buy something they wanted.

b In pairs, students read the tips and explain the highlighted words and phrases. Remind them to use the context to work out the meanings. Check answers as a class. Ask students if they think the advice is good or not.

> **Answers**
> special offers: products which have lower than usual prices
> the sales: a period of time when shops are offering lower prices on products
> pay it back: give money back to the person who lent it to you / you borrowed it from
> bank account: an arrangement with a bank for you to keep money there

c ▶ **1.50** Students complete the exercises in Vocabulary Focus 3B on SB p.135. Play the recording where indicated and ask students to check their answers to Exercise a. Go through the highlighted words and check students understand what each of them means. Monitor the storytelling in Exercise b and encourage students to tell the stories using the words in the boxes.

> **Answers and audioscript (Vocabulary Focus 3B SB p.135)**
> 1 Carol had a problem. She spent a lot of money on shoes.
> 2 One day Carol and Fay went shopping in the sales.
> 3 Carol saw some shoes she loved, but she didn't have any cash.
> 4 Fay offered to lend her some money, so she borrowed £100.
> 5 Carol now owed Fay £700. So she got a loan for £1000 from the bank.
> 6 She paid back the £700 (and spent the rest on shoes!)
>
> 1 Brian was saving up for a camera.
> 2 He saw a great camera but it cost £499.
> 3 Brian couldn't afford it. He only had £400 in his bank account.
> 4 He asked the shop assistant for a discount but she said no.
> 5 When Brian got home, he found a special offer online.
> 6 So he got the camera for £399! He was very happy!

2 READING AND SPEAKING

a Go through the questions and answers quickly to check understanding. You may wish to help students with the words in the Vocabulary support box. Ask students to choose the answers that are closest to what is true for them. Individually, students complete the questionnaire.

📖 VOCABULARY SUPPORT

balance (B2) – the exact amount of money in your bank account

basic (B1) – only the things that are most necessary

second-hand (B1) – someone else owned or used this thing before you

b ◔ Students compare their answers with a partner. Take feedback from the class to find out which are the most popular answers for all or some of the questions.

c ◔ Ask students to check their results on SB p.130. Take feedback regarding to what extent they agree with the results.

◔ FAST FINISHERS

In pairs, students can ask their partners to find out more about their answers to the survey, e.g. *Why are credit cards useful? Why do you think credit cards are a bad idea? Why are you saving? What kind of special offers do you buy?*

3 LISTENING

a ◔ Students look at the pictures of the people and read the question. Elicit that *a big spender* is someone who spends a lot of money, *a smart spender* is one who looks round to find the best prices and gets good value for money and a *non spender* is one who doesn't spend much at all. Students guess which person in the pictures is which kind of spender and tell the class, saying why they think this.

b ▶ **1.51** Students listen to the recording to check their answers. Stop the recording after each interview to to give students time to make notes about that person's spending habits. At the end, ask students to decide individually which speaker matches with which profile and compare their answers with a partner. Check answers with the class. Encourage students to explain the reasons for their answers.

> **Answers**
> big spender – speaker 3 – some perfume, a necklace
> smart spender – speaker 1 – food (for the week)
> non spender – speaker 2 – (a lot of) suntan lotion

Audioscript

PRESENTER So, in these difficult times, how are people spending their money? Are people still borrowing from the banks? I came to Norwich to talk to shoppers.
Excuse me, sir, do you mind if I ask you a few questions about your spending habits?

SPEAKER 1 Err, OK.

P Can I ask what you've got in your bags?

1 I've just bought my food for the week. They had some special offers on cheese! I think I've got enough for a month.

P Are you saving up for anything at the moment?

1 Yes actually, I'm saving for a car. My girlfriend is moving away to Leeds to study and I want to visit her at weekends. The train is really expensive, so in the end, it's cheaper to drive.

P Why didn't you borrow the money for the car?

1 Well, I don't want to owe money to a bank. I generally don't like borrowing. I've got three credit cards and I've never used any of them. I've only got them, because of the free stuff you get – travel insurance, cinema tickets, that kind of thing.

PRESENTER And what have you just bought?

SPEAKER 2 Not much! It was all too expensive. But I found a good price on some suntan lotion. So I bought a lot.

P Are you saving up for anything at the moment?

2 Well, I'm always saving, but there isn't really anything I actually want to buy. I've already got everything I need. Why should I spend my money on new things when the things I have are perfectly OK? Everyone should save for when they're older. I don't want to be working when I'm an old man.

P So, I suppose you don't need to borrow?

2 No, not yet! And I hope I never do. When I can't afford something, I don't buy it. Simple. And I never lend money to other people. Never. You give them money, and you never get it back. Then you lose a friend.

PRESENTER Have you bought anything nice today?

SPEAKER 3 Some perfume … and a small necklace. The necklace was quite expensive … well, very expensive … but I need a new one to go with a dress I've just bought.

P Lovely! And are you saving up for anything at the moment?

3 No, not really. I don't really save up for things, to be honest. If I need something, I just buy it. I've got credit cards. I've already spent my salary this month, but that's OK. Life's too short to worry about money.

P So you don't mind borrowing money?

3 I don't borrow money. Well, I use my credit cards, but that's not really borrowing, is it? Oh! And I got a small loan last year. I haven't paid it back yet.

VOCABULARY SUPPORT

salary (B1) – the money you receive regularly for work

stuff (B1) – things

---

c ▶**1.51** Ask students if they can complete these questions the interviewer asked:

Can I ask what you have got in your …? (bags) *What have you just …?* (bought) *Have you bought anything … today?* (nice) *Are you … up for anything at the moment?* (saving)

Play the recording again for students to find the answers to the questions for each interviewee. Pause after each speaker to allow students time to note down their answers. Share answers as a class.

> **Answers**
> Speaker 1 – 1 a car 2 generally doesn't like it
> Speaker 2 – 1 nothing specific / He's always saving. 2 He doesn't think it's a good idea.
> Speaker 3 – 1 nothing 2 She uses her credit card but doesn't think that's really borrowing.

📖 **LANGUAGE NOTES**

We *borrow something from someone*, but *someone lends something to us* or *lends us something*, e.g. *I borrowed £10 from my mum to buy a DVD. My mum lent me £10 to buy a DVD. I lent £10 to a friend.*

💡 **EXTRA ACTIVITY**

Ask students to imagine that they are shopping in a large supermarket. They should imagine three things that they have in their shopping bag and write the items down. Then, in pairs, they guess what their partner has in his/her bag. To find out the exact items, students can ask yes/no questions, e.g. *Is it food? Is it expensive? Do people eat it every day?*

---

d 💬 Read through the statements with the class and then ask students to discuss their responses to them in pairs. Monitor and help as necessary. Take feedback from the class, encouraging students to justify their opinions. Find out how many students agree or disagree with the statements, and why.

4 GRAMMAR

Present perfect with *just, already* and *yet*

a Students read the sentences and supply the past participles. Elicit that they are all irregular. Ask students if they can remember which speaker in the listening said each sentence. (They will hear this in b when they listen and check.)

> **Answers**
> 1 I've just bought my food for the week.
> 2 I've already spend my salary this month.
> 3 I haven't paid it back yet.

b ▶**1.52** Students listen to check their answers. Elicit that the tenses are all present perfect.

c Ask students to look back at the sentences in 4a and complete the rules for the use of just, already and yet. Check answers as a class and ask questions to check students' understanding.

> **Answers**
> already; just; yet

Write the sentences on the board:

1 *I've just bought my food for the week.*
2 *I've already spent my salary this month.*
3 *I haven't paid it back yet.*

Ask concept questions to check understanding of the time sequences and whether the actions are completed or not.

Sentence 1:

a *Do I now have the food? (yes)*
b *Did I buy the food a long time ago? (no)*
(The use of *just* tells us that this action was only completed very recently.)
c *Do you know exactly when I bought it? (no)*
(We only know that the action was completed recently.)

Sentence 2

a *Do I have the money now? (no)*
b *Do you know when I spent it? (no)*
(The use of *already* indicates that the action happened before the time of speaking.)

Sentence 3

a *Do I have the money / the time to pay it back? (no)*
b *Am I planning to pay it back? (yes)*
c *Do you know when I'm going to pay it back? (no)*
(The use of yet implies that the action hasn't happened so far, but is going to happen.)

d ▶ Students read the information in Grammar Focus 3B on SB p.146. Play the recording where indicated and ask students to listen and repeat. Students then complete the exercises on SB p.147. If students have problems with the irregular past participles, refer them to the list of irregular verbs on SB p.176. Check answers as a class.

Answers (Grammar Focus 3B SB p.147)

a 1 g 2 f 3 a 4 c 5 e 6 b 7 h 8 d
b 1 Have they paid us yet?
   2 I've already spent all my money.
   3 Our visitors have just arrived.
   4 I haven't been to the shops yet.
   5 It has just started raining.
   6 Has he saved any money yet?
c He hasn't done the shopping yet.
   2 He hasn't paid Mark back yet.
   3 He has already bought paper for the printer.
   4 He has already checked his emails.
   5 He hasn't asked Dad for any money yet.
   6 He has already written to Daniel.
   7 He has already finished writing his project.
   8 He hasn't cleaned the flat yet.
   9 He hasn't taken out the rubbish yet.
   10 He has already had a haircut.

⊙ CAREFUL!

- Students sometimes put *just* and *already* before the auxiliary, e.g. ~~I just have read it.~~ (Correct form = *I **have** just read it.*) They may also add additional time phrases, such as *yesterday* or *a few minutes ago*, e.g. ~~I have already done it yesterday.~~ (Correct form = *I have already done it. I **did** it **yesterday**.*) If they have no equivalent in their first language, students are likely to replace the present perfect with either the simple present or the simple past. Keep reinforcing the idea that the present perfect is used to link things that may have started in the past with now.

- *Yet* is often used in negative sentences, and not *already*, e.g. ~~I haven't already received your letter.~~ (Correct form = *I **haven't** received your letter **yet**.*)

e **Pronunciation** Write this sentence on the board: *Yesterday was the first of July.* Ask students to repeat it. If necessary, correct the pronunciation of the initial *y* = /j/ and *j* = /ʤ/. Then play the recording for students to listen and repeat the words. In pairs, ask students to think of two more words that begin with /j/ and /ʤ/. Ask for the words and write them on the board, e.g. *yellow, yes, year, yoghurt; joke, June, jump.* Students repeat these for practice.

f Students put the adverbs in the correct places in the sentences. They do this individually and then compare answers with their partner. Play the recording for them to check.

Answers

1 I've just spent a lot of money on a new pair of glasses.
2 I bought a new mobile last month, but I've already lost it.
3 I need some winter clothes, but I haven't had time to go shopping yet.
4 I've already bought a card for Mother's Day.
5 I bought some amazing shoes last year, but I haven't worn them yet.
6 I've just seen a special offer on a holiday online, but I haven't decided to buy it yet.

g Ask students to change four of the sentences so that they are true for them. Give them an example of your own, e.g. *I've just spent a lot of money on a new laptop.* Emphasise that *just* is not only used for a few moments ago, but can also mean recently, e.g. *I've just bought a new car.* Elicit that this could be yesterday or last week because for buying something like a new car, a week is quite recent.

h ◯ Students compare their new sentences in pairs. Ask them to add some information as in the example. Students share their ideas with the class.

ⓦ EXTRA ACTIVITY

Ask students to write down five things that members of their family have just done. Three things should be true and two should be false. Their partner has to guess which are true and which are false.

5 SPEAKING

◯ Read through the discussion questions with the class and check understanding. If necessary, remind students of the meanings of *amount, afford, discount, market, owe.* Students discuss the questions in small groups. Circulate and encourage discussion by contributing an opinion or prompting. Note down any repeated errors. Ask students to share any interesting opinions and comments with the class.

ⓦ EXTRA ACTIVITY

Ask students to note down everything that they have bought in the last 24 hours. They compare their list with a partner. The pairs work as a team. Go round the class and ask each pair in turn to say one item on their list. The next pair must give the name of a different item. A pair that cannot give a different item drops out and the winner is the last pair to give an item. This activity could also be done for bought in the last two days or last week.

ADDITIONAL MATERIAL

▶ Workbook 3B

▶ Photocopiable activities: Grammar p.209, Vocabulary p.233, Pronunciation p.269

3C Everyday English
Do you have anything cheaper?

At the end of this lesson, students will be able to:

- understand a conversation in a shop
- use sentence stress correctly
- use phrases to pay at a till
- use phrases to change their minds

💡 OPTIONAL LEAD-IN

Books closed. Put students in small groups. Give them two minutes to note down different places where we can buy things, e.g. *supermarket, shopping centre, department store, online, market, gift shop, sports shop, chemist, vending machine*. Monitor and support students with vocabulary. The winning group is the one with the most ideas. Ask them to read their ideas to the class. Put any new words on the board.

1 LISTENING

a 💬 Look at the photo. Say: *Mark and Rachel are shopping. Where do you think they are?* Elicit: *a shopping centre.* Read the questions and the examples. Students discuss the questions and give reasons for their comments.

b 💬 Ask students to summarise what has happened in the video story so far. Students look at the picture and guess what Rachel and Mark are shopping for.

c ▶ 1.56 Play Part 1 of the video or play the audio recording for students to check their ideas.

> **Answers**
> a birthday present for Leo

Video/Audioscript (Part 1)

RACHEL OK, what's next? Oh, we need to buy a present for Leo.
MARK Really? Why?
R It's his birthday, remember. Annie told us last week.
M Well, we don't know him very well.

R Oh, come on. We need to buy him something. Oh, look – how about this shop? I'm sure we can find something in here.
M Hmm.

d 💬 Ask students what the last present was that they bought someone and the last present that they received. Then they work in pairs and answer the questions about the pictures of products. Students share their ideas with the class.

> **Answers**
> One is a game, you play football with it by putting your fingers into the boots and kicking a ball. Two is a clock that you can use to see what the weather is like as well as to tell the time. Three is a clock which you use for telling the time; it is shaped like a football. Four is a piggy bank shaped like a book and you use it to keep money in.

e ▶ 1.57 Tell students that they are going to listen to or watch Part 2 from the video story. They should listen for general understanding, and to find out which product they bought and not worry if they don't understand the details. Check the answer as a class.

> **Answer**
> the football clock

Video/Audioscript (Part 2)

MARK This place is great! I could stay here all day!
RACHEL Well, we're only here for Leo, remember.
SHOP ASSISTANT Hi, can I help you?
R Er, yes. We're looking for a present for a friend. It's his birthday.
SA OK. Are you looking for anything in particular?
R Umm, I don't know …
M Something fun!
SA OK. What sort of thing does he like? Is he a sports fan?
M Yeah.
R Is he? Does he like sport?
M Yeah, I'm sure.
SA OK … How about this? 'Football in a tin'. Perfect for a birthday present.
R What is it exactly?
SA It's a football game. Look, you put the boots on your fingers, there's a ball …
M This looks perfect! He loves football.
R Does he? I'm not sure. What else do you have?
SA What about this? A weather station.

M Oh – what does it do?
SA Well, it tells you the weather now, and the next day. It's also an alarm clock.
M Do you have anything cheaper?
SA Well … well, this is a great product. A book money bank.
R A book money bank?
SA Well, you open it here and there's a place to put your money. To keep it safe.
R Oh, that's quite nice.
M Yeah, I suppose he might like that.
R OK, we've decided.
SA Great …
M On second thoughts, I really think we should get something sporty. Could you show us something else?
SA Oh, I know. What about this? A football clock.
M Brilliant! Let's get that!
R Well, if you really think he likes football.
M Yeah, of course. He was talking about football last time we saw him. We'll take it.
R Was he? I don't remember that.

f ▶ 1.57 Read through the questions with the class. Ask if they can remember the answers. Play the recording again for them to find or check their answers. Elicit further details of the products, e.g. you put the football boots on your fingers. You may need to play the recording again for students to hear these details.

> **Answers**
> 1 Because Leo loves football.
> 2 She isn't sure Leo loves football.
> 3 It's expensive.
> 4 Mark thinks they should get Leo something sporty.

g 💬 In pairs, students discuss the question. Conduct feedback and ask for their ideas. Ask: *Which present would you have got Leo? Why?*

2 USEFUL LANGUAGE
Talking to people in shops

a ▶ 1.58 Ask students in groups of three to imagine that they are in the shop. One student is the shop assistant and the other students are Mark and Rachel. They role play the conversation from memory. Monitor and help but don't interrupt fluency to correct students. The focus here should be on re-creating the situation and not on complete accuracy and the aim is to activate existing knowledge and memory. Then ask students to complete 2a and 2b individually and compare their answers with a partner. Play the recording to check their answers.

> **Answers**
> 1 help   2 looking   3 anything   4 sort   5 do   6 cheaper
> 7 show   8 take

b Ask the questions as a class

> **Answers**
> 1 1, 3, 4
> 2 2
> 3 6, 7
> 4 5
> 5 8

3 PRONUNCIATION Sentence stress

a ▶ 1.59 Books closed. Write sentences 1 and 2 on the board with no stress indicators. Remind students how important sentence stress is by saying that English is a stress-timed language and the words that carry the most important information or emphasis in a sentence are stressed more heavily than the other words, which gives the English language its distinctive rhythm. Ask students to copy the sentences and say them aloud, marking the words they think are stressed in each one. Then play the recording. Students open their books and listen. They study the marked stressed pattern in the book and compare it with what they hear. Point out that the underlining represents the stressed words/syllables.

b ▶ 1.59 Play the recording again for students to answer the questions. Alternatively, ask the questions first and then play the recording to check answers. Tell students that we say the syllables between stressed words quickly and that the vowel sounds are often 'weak' (the full vowel is not pronounced, but is replaced by another sound), e.g. *for* /fə/. Ask students to repeat the sentences to practise.

> **Answers**
> 1 sentence 1 four; sentence 2 seven
> 2 three
> 3 quickly

> **LOA TIP DRILLING**
> • Drill the phrases by asking students to repeat them after your model. Use a transformation drill to give variety and make the repetition more interesting, e.g. *This looks perfect/wonderful/fantastic/horrible. We're only here for Leo/Katy/Marcia.*
> • Encourage students to emphasise the word stress in order to 'feel' the rhythm of the sentences.

c ▶ 1.60 Tell students that they need to complete the sentences with the unstressed words. Remind them that the vowel sounds will often have been replaced by the weak /ə/ sound. Students listen to complete the sentences. Check answers as a class. Model the sentences again for students to repeat.

> **Answers and audioscript**
> 1 I'd like **to** look **at a** different one.
> 2 Can you show **me the** first one again?
> 3 I'm looking **for a** present **for my** brother.
> 4 Do you have this **in a** different size?
> 5 It'll cost **a lot of** money **to** fix.

4 USEFUL LANGUAGE Paying at the till

a ▶ 1.61 Ask students what *till* means (a place or machine in a shop where you pay). Elicit ideas about what Mark and the shop assistant say when he buys the clock at the till. If students don't mention a credit card, ask: *Mark wants to use a credit card. What do they say then?* Play the recording for the students to answer the question regarding what Mark changes his mind about. Check the answers and ask students to compare the conversation at the till with their version. Do Mark and the shop assistant use the same phrases?

> **Answer**
> how to pay

> **Audioscript (Part 3)**
> **SA2** Who's next, please?
> **MARK** Oh, yes. Just this, please.
> **SA2** How would you like to pay?
> **M** Cash.
> **SA2** OK.
> **M** Actually, I think I'll put it on my credit card.
> **SA2** OK. Can you put your card in, please? … And can you enter your PIN, please? … Thank you. OK, here's your receipt, and here's the clock.
> **M** Thanks a lot.

> 📖 **VOCABULARY SUPPORT**
> *PIN* (B1) – number you need when you pay by card (Personal Identification Number)

b ▶ 1.61 Play the recording for students to complete the questions. Play the recording again for students to check their answers.

> **Answers**
> 1 next, please   2 you like   3 put your   4 enter your
> 5 receipt

c 💬 In pairs, students take turns to practise the conversation at the till. Monitor and check pronunciation, especially sentence stress.

5 CONVERSATION SKILLS

Changing your mind

a Read through the sentences with the class and ask if the underlined phrases mean the same or different things. Ask students to tell you about the last time they changed their minds about something. Give an example of your own, e.g. *This morning my daughter said at breakfast, 'I'd like some orange juice.' Then she changed her mind and said, 'On second thoughts, I'd prefer some milk.'* Now ask them to tell you their experiences, but this time using one of the phrases above.

> **Answer**
> The same – both are used when we want to change our mind.

b 💬 Elicit that the response to someone changing their mind is usually *OK* or *Fine*. In pairs, students take turns to change their minds in the different situations. Encourage them to add a reason, too, where appropriate, e.g. *I'd prefer a cup of tea because I've already had five coffees this morning!*

> 💡 **FAST FINISHERS**
>
> Fast finishers can think of more situations when we sometimes change our mind. During feedback, they can ask other students what they would say in those situations.

6 SPEAKING

Tell students that they are going to role play buying a present for a friend in a shop. Divide the class into groups of three and assign A, B and C roles. Students A and B are buying the present and read the instructions on SB p.130. Student C is the shop assistant and reads the instructions on SB p.127. Students then role play the conversation. Monitor and help where necessary but don't interrupt fluency to make corrections. Students then swap roles and role play the conversation again.

> 📖 **VOCABULARY SUPPORT**
>
> *atmosphere* (B1) – feeling in a room
>
> *candle* (B1) – something we burn to give light
>
> *pine* (B2) – tall tree that gives a special smell
>
> *rack* (B1) – small shelf
>
> *ringtone* – sound of a phone
>
> *scented* – with a special smell
>
> *slippers* – shoes we wear in the house
>
> *spice* (B1) – something we add to give flavour to food
>
> *stylish* (B1) – fashionable and attractive
>
> *vanilla* – a flavour used in ice cream and cakes

> 💡 **FAST FINISHERS**
>
> Fast finishers should think of some additional fun products to buy for a present and write short descriptions of them. During feedback, ask which items students chose, and why. Also ask for examples of the language they used and deal with any common mistakes.

> 💡 **EXTRA ACTIVITY**
>
> Have a short class discussion about the pros and cons of shopping online. Ask: *How many of you regularly shop online? What kinds of things do you buy? Is it better to shop online or in a store? Why? What are your favourite shopping websites? Why do you like them?*

> **ADDITIONAL MATERIAL**
>
> ▶ Workbook 3C
>
> ▶ Photocopiable activities: p.270
>
> ▶ Unit Progress Test
>
> ▶ Personalised online practice

3D Skills for Writing
We've successfully raised £500

At the end of this lesson, students will be able to:

- understand people talking about charities
- discuss opinions about charities
- use paragraphing correctly when writing an email
- write an email update

1 LISTENING AND SPEAKING

a 🗪 Students look at the pictures and describe what
they can see. Then they look at the names of the
charities and say what they know about them and guess
what they do. Ask them to match the charities with the
sentences. Elicit the names of other charities students
might know, e.g. World Wildlife Fund or The Heart
Foundation. Ask what these charities do.

Answers
1 Greenpeace   2 the National Trust   3 Oxfam

🌍 CULTURE NOTES

Oxfam is a global organisation which works to find solutions
to poverty. Volunteers from the organisation work in local
communities to help provide food, water, healthcare and
education for poor people worldwide. Oxfam also sends aid
and volunteers to the scenes of emergencies and disasters
around the world. In the UK Oxfam has almost 700 High
Street shops which raise money by selling second-hand and
fairtrade goods.
The National Trust is a UK conservation charity. They protect
historic buildings, gardens and green spaces such as forests,
coastline and moorland in England, Wales and Northern
Ireland. The aim of the charity is to open the places to the
public and protect them for future generations.
Greenpeace is an environmental organisation which
has offices in 40 countries worldwide. The group
organises campaigns and carries out research into global
environmental issues including climate change, protection
of habitats such as the rainforests and oceans, as well
as worldwide peace. Greenpeace has a history of direct
action and is credited with raising public awareness of
environmental issues.

b 🗪 Before looking at the exercise, ask students to tell
you what people can do to raise money for charity. Put
their ideas on the board. Read through the examples
and see if students had thought of them. In pairs,
students spend a minute thinking about additional ways
to raise money. Ask for ideas during class feedback and
put them on the board. Tell students that this list may
be useful later in the lesson. If you wish, give students
information from the Culture notes below.

📖 VOCABULARY SUPPORT

raise money (B2) – to earn or collect money for a charity

sponsor (B2) – to give money to someone who is doing
something for charity

📖 LANGUAGE NOTES

Students sometimes confuse raise and rise. Raise is a regular
verb. The past tense forms are: raise, raised, raised and it
takes an object, e.g. The student **raised** his hand to answer
the question. Rise is irregular. The past tense forms are: rise,
rose, risen and it doesn't take an object, e.g. The sun **rises**
very early these days.

🌍 CULTURE NOTES

In the UK, there are several big television events that help
raise money for charities. Celebrities take part and viewers
can give money online or by phone during the show. The
public is also encouraged to organise money-raising events.
One of the most famous shows is Red Nose Day run by the
charity Comic Relief which takes place every two years. In
2013, with the slogan 'Do something funny for money' Comic
Relief raised over £100 million for projects to help people in
need in the UK and other countries, especially Africa.

c ▶️ 1.62 Tell students that they will hear four people
talking about giving money to charity. They need to
listen to say which of the charities on this page each one
gives money to. Tell them that there is one speaker who
doesn't give money to any of them. Play the recording
and pause after each speaker to let students note down
the charity. Check answers together.

Answers
1 Shona – Oxfam; 2 Jack – Greenpeace; 3 Jessica – no; 4 William –
the National Trust

Audioscript

SHONA I support Oxfam. You
see, I had a really happy
childhood myself and I think
it's important to help other
people in poorer countries have
happy childhoods. I haven't
got a lot of spare money, but
I try and help them in other
ways. For example, last year
I ran a marathon and people
sponsored me, you know, gave
me money for doing the run.
I made just over a hundred
pounds. And then, once a
month, I make cakes and take
them to my office. I sell pieces
of cake to my colleagues for
morning tea and give the
money to Oxfam.

JACK Well, giving to charity is quite
easy really. You can go online
and pay with your credit card.
I've given money to Greenpeace
that way a few times recently.
And once a year, I sell their
calendars – mostly to friends
and the people I work with.
I think that helping to save

our natural world is the most
important thing you can do. I
think I should do something
now – so that my children and
my children's children can enjoy
the kind of world that I live in.

JESSICA Of course, I think it's
important to … well, that
people give money to charities.
But actually, I haven't got a lot
of money myself. I owe money
to my parents and I have to pay
back the government for my
university study and … In fact,
I've never given any money to a
charity. I can't really afford it.

WILLIAM Our history is really
important and we need to
protect it. When I think of all
the old buildings that we've
already lost, it's terrible. So,
once every six months I go
around my neighbourhood and
collect money door-to-door for
the National Trust. I tell people
about local places the National
Trust want to protect and they
are usually very generous.

d ▶️ **1.62** Play the recording again for students to make notes about why the people do or don't support a charity. If students find this activity challenging, do the task in sections. Play the first part of the recording and then allow students to discuss what they've heard with a partner. before noting down the reasons. Tell them that they can do this in their own words, not necessarily using the exact words from the recording. Check their ideas as a class.

Answers
1 Shona: wants people in poorer countries to have happy childhood, like hers; ran a marathon last year; sells cakes at work
2 Jack: wants to save our natural world so children and children's children can enjoy the world; gives money online; sells calendars
3 Jessica: owes money to parents and government and can't afford it
4 William: thinks history is important and we need to protect it; collects money door-to-door

e Students make notes on the questions individually. Prepare to give your own answers to the questions later.

f 💬 Students compare their ideas in small groups. Students share their ideas with the class and discuss points of interest. See if one charity is more popular than others in the class. Also allow for the fact that some students may not give money to charities for financial or other reasons: some people prefer not to give or raise money, believing that it is the responsibility of governments rather than individuals.

2 READING

a Read through the question and the possible reasons for writing the email message with the class. Then ask students to read the email and tick the correct reasons. Check answers as a class and elicit phrases that give the purpose of the message and helped students understand the reason for writing. Put them up on the board: *We'd like to thank everyone / thanks again; We've successfully raised; we'd just like to let you know about; The NT will use the money to*

Answers
1, 3, 4, 5

b Students read the text again to answer the questions. Conduct feedback and check answers. Ask them if they think the National Trust is a good charity to support, and why or why not.

Answers
1 making and selling cakes; selling old books, DVDs and clothes online; paying to wear casual clothes to work
2 repair historic buildings and keep them open for the public to visit
3 visiting a historic building

3 WRITING SKILLS Paragraphing

a Ask students to look at the email again. Ask: *Is the email organised well? Why / Why not?* (By looking at the email, you can see how the paragraphs divide the points so that it is clear for the reader.) Remind students that good organisation is important when writing any text. Then ask them to match the descriptions with the paragraphs. Check answers as a class.

Answers
1 d 2 a 3 b 4 c

b Ask students what information is included in the introduction and the closing paragraph. Point out that the introduction must tell the reader the main reason the person is writing. Another common way of starting an email is: *I am writing to* ... . Also point out that a closing paragraph is often quite short and usually summarises what has been said in the email or makes a request, e.g. *Thanks for* ... *Apologies for* ... are good ways to start this final paragraph.

Answers
introduction: the amount of money they raised (£500)
closing paragraph: the next event

c Give students time to read through the paragraphs and put them in the correct order. Ask students to underline phrases that helped them. Check answers as a class.

Answers
1 This email is to say a big 'Thank you!' to everyone who ...
2 Many of you have bought tickets ... Your money and time will help Oxfam to continue their important work.
3 Oxfam will use the money on projects ...
4 Would you like to help ... Thanks again for all your help.

4 WRITING

a Read through the choice of emails 1 and 2. Ask students to choose which email to write and underline the important information that they need to include, and the best order for it (1 thank the people; 2 say how much money was raised; 3 tell them something about the charity).

b Remind students how important it is to plan their writing well before they start. Give them some time to think about the email and make notes for each paragraph. Monitor and give help and advice where necessary.

c Students write their emails. Continue to monitor.

 LOA TIP MONITORING

- While students are writing their emails, monitor and give help where necessary. Students should know that you are available to answer questions when they have a query about language, including paragraphing, spelling, punctuation or tense use.

- If you notice an error, encourage students to self-correct. Point out the mistake and ask them to look at it again. You may need to prompt by asking, e.g. *You've said 'last week', so which tense do you need?*

d When they have finished, ask students to swap emails with a partner and to look at the organisation in particular. Ask them to think about the number of paragraphs, the content of each paragraph and if the paragraphs follow on clearly from each other.

💡 **FAST FINISHERS**

Fast finishers can swap emails with another fast finisher and write another email to that charity. They could ask for some particular information about a future event or suggest another event that might help them raise more money.

ADDITIONAL MATERIAL

▶ Workbook 3D

UNIT 3
Review and extension

1 GRAMMAR

a Students do the task individually. Check answers as a class.

> **Answers**
> 1 Have you ever bought something you didn't need?
> 2 Have you ever given money to a stranger?
> 3 Have you ever been to a very expensive restaurant?
> 4 Have you ever driven an expensive car?
> 5 Have you ever lost money on the street?

b 💬 In pairs, students ask and answer the questions. Ask for examples in class feedback.

c Give students a quickfire test of past forms of irregular verbs by giving the infinitive and asking the class to supply the past simple and past participle forms. Do it again, but speed up so that the responses become quicker and quicker. Students then do the exercise. Check answers as a class.

> **Answers**
> 1 's done   3 's raised   5 's been   7 've had
> 2 's run   4 's spent   6 's helped

d Students do the exercise individually, check in pairs and then give answers in class feedback.

> **Answers**
> 1 A Have you spoken to John yet?
>   B Yes, he's just called me.
>   A Did you ask him about the party?
>   B Yes, he's already bought the food.
>   A Great. I haven't been to the shops yet.
>   B Have you already decided what music to play?
>   A Yes, I've just made a list.

e 💬 Students practise the exchanges. You could divide the class in half and nominate one student from half A to ask the question to a student in half B, e.g. *A: Katya – have you spoken to John yet? B: Yes, Julia, he's just called me.*

> 💡 **EXTRA ACTIVITY**
>
> Write these questions on the board: *1 What have you just done? 2 What did you plan to do earlier but haven't done yet? 3 What have you already done this week that you didn't expect to do?* Give students a short time to write two answers for each question. Put students into three or four teams. Go round the class and ask for an answer from each student to question 1. If their answer is different from a previous student's answer, they earn a point. Do the same with questions 2 and 3. The winner is the team whose combined score is the highest.

2 VOCABULARY

a Students complete the sentences individually. Check answers in class feedback. Point out that verbs that always go with a certain noun like the ones in this exercise are very common in English. It's important for students to record the noun and the verb together in order to remember the collocation.

> **Answers**
> 1 hug   2 directions   3 volunteer   4 joke   5 something

b Ask students to complete these sentences to see if they can remember the new vocabulary related to money. *I've left my money at home and I need to buy a coffee. Can you … ? (lend me some money) I'd like to buy a new car but unfortunately I can't … (afford it). We're going on an expensive holiday this summer, so at the moment we're … (saving up). If you want to buy a new TV and you take in your old one, you can sometimes get a … (discount). I lent my sister a hundred pounds last month and fifty pounds last week so now she … 150 pounds. (owes me)* Students then do the matching task. Check answers as a class. Ask students to cover questions 1–5 and try to recall them by looking at the answers.

> **Answers**
> 1 d   2 c   3 a   4 e   5 b

3 WORDPOWER *just*

a Students close their books. Write some sentences on the board:
I've recently finished reading a good book.
Ben doesn't really understand you. He's only a dog!
At the last moment, I remembered to take the chicken out of the oven before it burned.
Can you wait a moment? I'm finishing my homework now. I won't be long.
Ask which word can be used instead of the underlined words: *just.* Elicit that *just* goes between *I* and *remembered* in the third example. Students open their books and do the exercise. Check answers as a class.

> **Answers**
> 1 c   2 a   3 d   4 b

b Students do the matching task. Check answers in feedback.

> **Answers**
> 1 e   2 a   3 d   4 c   5 b

c Write the expressions in bold from 3b on the board and tell students to use them to complete the sentences. Check answers as a class.

> **Answers**
> 1 just under   2 just like   3 just in time   4 just over
> 5 just about

d 💬 In pairs, students make sentences about their lives using the expressions on the board. Give an example of your own first, e.g. *My journey to work today took just over an hour because there was a traffic jam in the town centre.* Circulate and help where necessary. Ask for examples in feedback.

▶ Photocopiable activities: Wordpower p.254

> 🔄 **LOA REVIEW YOUR PROGRESS**
>
> Students look back through the unit, think about what they've studied and decide how well they did. Students work on weak areas by using the appropriate sections of the Workbook, the Photocopiable activities and the Personalised online practice.

UNIT 4
Social life

UNIT OBJECTIVES

At the end of this unit, students will be able to:
- understand texts and conversations about celebrations
- talk about plans for celebrations
- plan a day out in a city
- make social arrangements
- write and reply to an invitation

UNIT CONTENTS

G GRAMMAR
- Present continuous and going to
- *will / won't / shall*

V VOCABULARY
- clothes and appearance: *bracelet, high heels, sandals, sweatshirt, tracksuit, underwear, flat shoes, top, tights, earrings, gloves, tie, socks, shorts, necklace, belt, scarf, handbag, boots, trainers, raincoat, suitcase, jumper*
- collocations: *get a new outfit, go to the hairdresser's, have a shave, look one's best, go to the beautician, wear sth*
- adjectives to describe places: *ancient, high, huge, low, magnificent, modern, narrow, ordinary, outdoor, peaceful, pretty, tiny, ugly, crowded, quiet, indoor, wide, noisy*
- Wordpower: look with different meanings, including + adjective and + preposition(s): *look excited/happy/tired/well, look after, look around, look forward to, look up*

P PRONUNCIATION
- *going to*
- *want* and *won't*
- Sentence stress

C COMMUNICATION SKILLS
- Talking about plans for celebrations
- Planning a day out in a city
- Making social arrangements
- Writing notes on a city you know well
- Inviting and replying

GETTING STARTED

⚑ OPTIONAL LEAD-IN

Books closed. Write: *wedding* in the centre of the board. (If you wish, you could project an image from a wedding, and elicit the word). Around *wedding* write: *people, things, places, activities.* Ask students: *Who are the most important people at a wedding?* Write words on the board as students call them out. Input any vocabulary they do not know – *bride, (bride)groom, the best man, bridesmaid, guests* etc. List as many different types of people involved with a wedding as possible. Then move on to places that are important at a wedding – e.g. *church/temple/mosque, town hall, registry office*, etc. Stop the activity when the students run out of ideas. Open books.

a Ask students to look at the picture and tell you what they can see. In pairs, they read and talk about the questions. Monitor and support students with any vocabulary they may need. Students share their ideas with the class. If you wish, give students information from the Culture notes below.

🌍 CULTURE NOTES

A wedding in Southeast Asia takes months of planning and can last several days. Southeast Asian weddings are big, colourful events with many different rituals and ceremonies and a large number of guests.

The picture shows a wedding in Karachi, Pakistan. It was taken on the first day of a four-day-long wedding party. The people in the picture are the bride, the groom, female members of both families and female friends. The custom is for male friends and relatives to sit in a separate tent. The bride and groom drink a cup of sweet milk, which is a symbol of their love.

b In pairs, students describe a typical wedding photograph from their country. Ask students if they have any wedding photographs on their phones or tablets to show the other students in small groups. Monitor but don't interrupt fluency unless students make mistakes in their choice of vocabulary. Ask students to share any interesting photos or stories with the class.

⚑ EXTRA ACTIVITY

In pairs, students tell each other about a wedding they have been to. They ask and answer questions about it using *Where, When, Who, What,* etc. Ask for examples from the class. Finish by asking the class: *Do you think it's better to have a big or a small wedding? Why?*

4A I'm going to the hairdresser's tomorrow

At the end of this lesson, students will be able to:

- use a vocabulary set related to clothes and accessories
- understand a conversation about preparing for a celebration
- talk about future plans using the present continuous and *going to*
- read and understand a text about celebrations in different countries
- talk about their plans for celebrations

OPTIONAL LEAD-IN

Books closed. Talk about an item of clothing that you are wearing. Say why you like it, where you bought it and when you wear it, e.g. *I really like this jacket. I bought it in 'Blacks'. It's a nice colour and it's really warm. I wear it all the time. Maybe I'll buy another one!* Put students into pairs to talk about their own clothes. Are any students in the class wearing similar clothes?

1 VOCABULARY Clothes and appearance

a Books closed. Ask students what kinds of clothes they like wearing to parties. Ask if there is a difference between what they wear to formal and informal parties. Put the clothes items they give you on the board. Then students open the book, look at the pictures and tell you what the pictures show. They then discuss the questions with a partner. (You might want to explain the meaning of *accessory* – a thing you wear or carry that matches your clothes, for example a belt, bag or piece of jewellery.) Circulate and make comments yourself to encourage discussion. Ask students to share any interesting ideas with the class.

b Students complete the exercises in Vocabulary Focus 4A on SB p.135. Play the recordings where indicated for students to check their answers and ask them to listen and repeat. Monitor and correct students' pronunciation as appropriate for the pairwork in g and listen for correct use of the target language. Tell students to go back to SB p.38.

> **Answers (Vocabulary Focus 4A SB p.135)**
> b 1 tie 2 bracelet 3 high heels 4 tracksuit 5 underwear
>   6 sweatshirt 7 top 8 gloves 9 tights 10 earrings
>   11 sandals 12 flat shoes
> e 1 c 2 a 3 e 4 d 5 b 6 f

2 LISTENING

a Students look at the pictures of Marta and Craig and the captions. Students say what Marta and Craig are doing. Elicit or explain that a ball is a formal dance. Explain that a May Ball happens at many universities and colleges, and that students will find out more about this and the wedding in the listening.

b ▶ 1.65 Tell students that in the recording they will hear an interview with Marta about going to a May Ball and Craig talking about his Indian wedding. They need to decide which person, Marta or Craig, says the different things. Read through the sentences with the class first and check the vocabulary. Ask students to work in pairs to guess who said which things. Then play the recording for them to check. You may need to play the recording twice.

> **Answers**
> 1 M 2 M 3 C 4 C 5 M 6 C

VOCABULARY SUPPORT

ceremony (B1) – formal event performed on important social or religious occasions

DJ (B1) – person who plays music at a party or club

entertainment (B1) – shows (music / TV / film etc.) that people enjoy watching

marriage (B1) – the event when people get married and become husband and wife

rub (B2) – to move your hands backwards and forwards over the skin

spice (B1) – a substance made from a plant which is used to give flavour in cooking

turmeric – yellow spice, common in Indian food

Audioscript

INTERVIEWER So Marta, what exactly is a May Ball?

MARTA Well, it's a huge party at our college. They have it every summer after we finish our exams because we need to celebrate after all that stress. Everyone gets dressed up, and there's food and drink and entertainment. There are eight different stages and over 70 bands. This year one of my favourite DJs is playing. I really can't wait.

I What are you going to wear?

M I've just bought the dress I'm going to wear – it's dark blue and I feel really good in it. I'm going to wear it with high heels and some nice jewellery!

I Is there anything else you need to do?

M Get ready and sleep! I need to look my best ... I'm going to the hairdresser's tomorrow. And a beautician is doing our make-up. Apart from that, I'm not going to leave the house on Saturday. I'm going to get as much sleep as possible!

I What time are you leaving?

M The ball doesn't start until 9 pm but I'm meeting the others at 7 pm so we can start queuing. Everyone says it takes a really long time to get in ... but then we're going to stay the whole night – until 6 am, when they serve breakfast!

CRAIG So, hi, everyone – welcome to today's audio blog. Well, today is the fourth day of my wedding. Everyone's going to be back here again in a few hours. There's going to be more dancing and food, of course. And today they're going to make a special cream from a spice called turmeric and rub it on my face and arms. The idea is that it cleans your skin and makes you ready for marriage. I hope it doesn't hurt ... Then tomorrow is the wedding day. It starts at 9 am, so quite early. But it finishes in the afternoon, after lunch. My friends are arriving early tomorrow to help me get ready and take me there. I'm going to wear a traditional Indian suit called a 'kurta pajama'. It's actually really comfortable. I'm really excited now. I'm looking forward to seeing all my friends and relatives, and, of course, my new wife! But I need to be patient ... the first part of an Indian wedding is breakfast with all the guests. The bride eats in a separate room with some of her friends. So I'm not going to see Monisha until the ceremony actually begins, later in the morning.

c **1.65** Tell students that they are going to listen again, this time for detailed information. First, read through the questions with the class. Then play the recording for students to answer the questions. If necessary, pause regularly to give time for students to write down the answers. Don't check as you go through but check answers as a class at the end of the recording.

Answers
1 to celebrate finishing exams
2 She feels really good in it.
3 to get as much sleep as possible
4 They serve breakfast.
5 They're going to rub it on his arms and face.
6 They start at 9 am and finish in the afternoon, after lunch.
7 It's called a 'kurta pajama' and it's really comfortable.
8 Everyone has breakfast together, apart from the bride and her friends.

💡 EXTRA ACTIVITY

Put the numbers *8, 70, 9, 6, 4th* on the board and ask students what they refer to in the recording (*8 stages, 70 different bands, 9 pm (start of the ball) / 9 am (start of the wedding), 6 am (end of the ball), 4th day of the wedding*).

d 🗨 Students discuss the questions in pairs. Monitor and help with vocabulary as necessary. Ask students to share their ideas with the class.

3 GRAMMAR
Present continuous and *going to*

a Books closed. Write *My friends ... early tomorrow. I'm ... the house on Saturday. I'm ... the whole night. A beautician ... our make-up.* on the board. Ask students if they can complete the sentences. Ask the class to try to remember what Craig and Marta actually said in the previous listening task. If students find the task difficult, give them the verbs as a clue (*arrive, do, leave, stay*). Students compare their answers with the sentences in 3a. Elicit which sentence Craig said (1). Students answer the question.

Answers
the future

b Students read the task and answer the questions as a class.

Answers
1 present continuous   2 *going to*

↪ LOA TIP CONCEPT CHECKING

Ask yes/no questions to concept-check students' understanding of the verb forms used in the sentences in 3a.

My friends are arriving early tomorrow. Ask: *Are we sure this activity will happen?* (yes)

A beautician is doing our make-up. Ask: *Has the speaker already asked the beautician?* (yes) *Does the speaker have another option?* (no) *Have they probably agreed a time?* (yes)

I'm going to stay the whole night. Ask: *Do you know exactly when the speaker will leave?* (no) *Is it possible for the speaker to change her mind when she's there?* (yes)

c ▶ Students read the information in Grammar Focus 4A on SB p.148. Play the recording where indicated and ask students to listen and repeat. Students then complete the exercises in Grammar Focus 4A on SB p.149. Check answers as a class, then tell students to go back to SB p.38.

Answers (Grammar Focus 4A SB p.149)
a 1 are buying   2 's studying   3 I'm not walking
   4 Are you wearing; I'm not   5 is your sister moving
   6 We're going   7 I'm not coming; I'm going
b Suggested answers:
   1 The parents have already ordered the computer.
   2 He has paid for a course.
   3 He has booked a taxi.
   4 He has chosen a different outfit.
   5 She has bought her flight tickets.
   6 They have arranged where to meet and the time.
   7 He's already told the boss and made an appointment.
c 1 'm going to invite   2 are you going to do
   3 'm not going to play   4 're going to ask
   5 we're going to write   6 Is there going to be
   7 she's going to make   8 she isn't going to pay
   9 're going to pay   10 am I going to do
   11 You're going to clean
d 1 a2 b1   2 a1 b2   3 a2 b1   4 a1 b2   5 a1 b2

◉ CAREFUL!

Some students use only *will* to talk about the future. Encourage them to use the present continuous and *going to* as appropriate.

📖 LANGUAGE NOTES

• Sometimes the two verb forms can be used interchangeably, but the use of the present continuous is more likely than *going to* when a specific time or date is given, e.g. *We're leaving tomorrow; They're meeting outside the leisure centre at six thirty; I'm getting married on the 14th October.* The more specific the arrangements are and the more preparations have already been complete, for example tickets bought or flights booked, the more likely it is that speakers will use the present continuous rather than *going to* when discussing their plans.

• If a *going to* intention is followed by the verb *go*, it is often replaced by the present continuous to avoid repetition, e.g. *I'm going shopping on Saturday* rather than *I'm going to go shopping.*

d **1.67** Pronunciation Write a sentence with *going to* on the board: *I'm going to play you a recording.* Read it in two ways – one with *going to* pronounced /ˈɡəʊɪŋtə/ and the other pronounced /ˈɡənə/. Ask students to tell you the difference. Play the recording. Students listen and decide which pronunciation is used. Explain that the second form is often used in less formal speech.

Answers
1 I'm going to get a new outfit.
2 We're gonna stay out late.
3 He's gonna have a shave.
4 I'm not going to worry.
5 The taxi's not gonna wait.

e Read through the task and time expressions in the box with the class. Give an example of your own, e.g. *This weekend I'm playing tennis with Sam on Saturday morning. I've just called the club to book.* Ask students to note down some ideas of their own. They can invent plans and arrangements if they like.

f Students talk about their plans with their partners. Monitor but don't interrupt fluency unless students make mistakes with future forms. Point out mistakes for students to self-correct.

4 READING

a Ask students to look at the pictures in the article and describe what they can see. They should guess what kind of celebration is taking place in each one. Discuss the questions about birthdays as a class.

b Students read the article quickly to find out what the numbers refer to. Check ideas as a class.

> **Answers**
> 1: Vietnamese New Year, or 'Tet', when everybody gets one year older
> 15: the age a girl becomes a woman in Latin America; the birthday girl often gives out 15 candles
> 20: the age when Japanese people become adults
> 100: the age when people in the UK receive a birthday card from the Queen; on New Year's day in Vietnam, children greet older people with 'Long life of 100 years!'

📖 VOCABULARY SUPPORT

fireworks (B1) – small objects that make loud noises and colours in the sky

kimono – traditional Japanese dress or robe

take to the streets – to go out into the streets

c Read through the questions with students. Students answer the questions individually and compare their answers with a partner. Check answers as a class.

> **Answers**
> 1 20, Japan   2 100, the UK   3 15, Latin America   4 1, Vietnam
> 5 15, Latin America   6 20, Japan

💡 EXTRA ACTIVITY

Students cover the text. Ask a student to tell you something he/she can remember about one of the events. Then choose a student to add another piece of information. Do this until students have remembered everything about the event. In pairs, students do the same activity for some or all of the events.

d Read through the task and questions. Students discuss the questions in pairs. Monitor and contribute yourself to encourage discussion. Take feedback and ask for examples from the discussions. If your class is multilingual, students can ask each other more questions about different festivals or celebrations in their countries. Monitor and help with vocabulary as necessary. To finish, ask which celebration the class found most interesting and/or unusual.

5 SPEAKING

a Read through the task with the class and give students a short time to note down their three events.

b Think of an event of your own and write *When, What, Where, Who* on the board and verbs such as *happen, go with, wear, eat,* etc. and elicit questions that students can ask you in order to guess the event. Remind them at this point that they should think carefully about the future forms they choose to use. Since students will be discussing definite arrangements on a fixed date, it's probably more natural to use the present continuous. However if the question concerns something they might still have to make a decision about, students can use *going to,* e.g. *Are you going to take a present?* Put students into small groups to ask questions to guess each other's events. At the end of the activity, take feedback and find out the most popular kind of event and any more examples of questions they asked.

👁 CAREFUL!

Make sure students don't miss out the verb *be* when using *going to,* e.g. ~~They going to visit us~~. (Correct form = *They're going to visit us.*)

ADDITIONAL MATERIAL

▶ Workbook 4A
▶ Photocopiable activities: Grammar p.210, Vocabulary p.234

4B Shall we go to the market?

At the end of this lesson, students will be able to:
- use *will / won't / shall* when talking about the future
- understand and use correct pronunciation of *want* /wɒnt/ and *won't* /wəʊnt/
- use a set of adjectives to describe places
- understand a conversation about what to do in a city
- talk about and plan a day out in a city

OPTIONAL LEAD-IN

Books closed. In pairs, students draw a table with two columns on a piece of paper. They write down the name of a city in one of the columns and a famous sight from that city in the other. They cannot write the same city twice. Give students three minutes and see which students have the most city/sight pairs after that time. Don't ask for examples at this point. Then students fold the paper in half so that only the famous sights are showing and swap lists with another pair. They then have to see how many of the cities they can name. At the end of the activity, students unfold the paper and check their answers.

1 LISTENING

a In pairs, students talk about the questions. Take feedback and ask for comments. See which Tokyo sights were most popular in the class. Ask: *Do you use a guidebook when you visit different places? Why / Why not?*

CULTURE NOTES

The capital city of Japan, Tokyo is located in the centre of the country, around 100 kilometres from Japan's highest mountain, Mount Fuji. Tokyo is considered to be the world's largest city. Around 13 million people live in the city but the number rises to around 37 million in the surrounding area. Many people commute to work from here to the centre of the city every day. Tokyo grew from a small village called Edo and in the 1720s became the first city in Asia to have a population of more than one million. The city is still proud of its traditions despite being one of the world's technology capitals and the richest city in the world.

b ▶1.68 Read through the task and the questions with the class. The recording is quite long. Pause the audio as needed for students during playback. Students share their answers with the class.

Answers
1 Yoyogi Park, Akihabara
2 A noodle restaurant, karaoke (private room), Tsukiji fish market

Audioscript (Part 1)

HARRY Hello?
MIKE Hi, Harry! It's me! I'm here! I've just arrived at my hotel.
H Welcome to Tokyo! Did you have a good journey?
M Yeah, it was fine. I was so lucky to get a stopover in Japan!
H And lucky that I'm here to show you around! I've already got a few ideas about what we can do.
M OK, but I really don't want to go where all the tourists go. I want to see the real Tokyo.
H OK, so we won't go to Disneyland then! And I won't take you to the Imperial Palace, either.
M OK.

H I mean, the palace is nice but it's so crowded. It's really just a place for tourists.
M Fine.
H So … shall we start with something to eat?
M OK.
H There's a great noodle restaurant I know. The noodles are delicious, some of the best in Tokyo. And it's also really simple. You just eat quickly and then you leave. So we won't waste any time!
M Brilliant.

H After that, I'll take you to Yoyogi Park. It's a huge park and it'll be really busy at the moment because everyone's going to see the cherry blossom.
M The cherry blossom?
H Yeah, it's beautiful. You see young people, businessmen in suits, families – everyone goes to look at the pretty flowers. There are also lots of musicians there, and the teenagers doing 'cosplay' …
M Who?
H Well, basically they're people who dress up as characters from computer games and cartoons. That kind of thing. They just do it for fun but they spend a lot of time and money on it so they look incredible.
M Wow – I think I've seen pictures of them before. I'd love to see them in real life. And after that?
H Well, do you want to do any shopping?
M Actually, yeah – I want to look for a new camera.
H Excellent. I'll take you to Akihabara, then. There are lots of electronics shops there. And they often have special offers.
M Perfect. And what are we doing in the evening?

H I've already booked a room for karaoke.
M Really? I don't really like karaoke that much. I'm a terrible singer.
H Yeah, but you haven't tried karaoke Japanese-style! I've booked a private room for six people. So, you, me and four of my friends. You'll love them – they're really good fun. Anyway, I've booked it till 2 am.
M 2 am?! Remember my flight leaves at 7 am tomorrow!
H Don't worry – you won't miss your flight! I promise. Anyway, we won't be finished at 2. After that we're going to the Tsukiji fish market!
M A fish market? In the middle of the night?
H Yeah, it's the best time to go. They bring in all the fish they've just caught. Trust me, it's an amazing sight.
M OK. This is going to be an interesting day …
H So, shall I come to your hotel in about an hour?
M OK, see you in a bit.
H Bye!

VOCABULARY SUPPORT

cherry blossom – flowers on cherry trees
noodles – typical Asian food, often in soup
private (B1) – only for one person or group and not for everyone
stopover (B2) – a short overnight stop between parts of a journey, especially a plane journey

c ▶1.68 Tell students that this time they are going to listen for more detailed information. Read through the questions with students and then play the recording for them to answer. Pause after *It's really just a place for tourists / Fine* and elicit the answer to question 1. Then play the rest of the recording without stopping and let students answer the questions individually before comparing their answers with a partner. At the end, they can compare their answers with a partner. Check answers as a class. Ask students: *Would you like a friend to arrange everything for you like this? Why / Why not?*

Answers

1 It's crowded and just a place for tourists.
2 The noodles are delicious – some of the best in Tokyo. You eat quickly and then you leave.
3 They do it for fun. (They dress up as characters from computer games and cartoons.)
4 There are lots of electronics shops there.
5 in a private room
6 They bring all the fish they've just caught. It's an amazing sight.

d 💬 Discuss the questions as a class and encourage students to give reasons for their answers.

2 GRAMMAR *will / won't / shall*

a ▶️ **1.69** Books closed. Write these two questions on the board: *… we start with something to eat? … I come to your hotel in about an hour?* Can students think of one word which was used to complete both questions in the previous listening task? (*Shall*) Play the recording for students to complete the sentences. Check answers as a class.

Answers
1 won't   2 Shall   3 'll   4 won't   5 Shall

b Elicit the answers to the questions and the full and short forms of each of the examples.

Answers
the future
'll = will; won't = will not

c Students match the sentences and uses of *will* and *shall* as a class. Elicit another example of each function.

Answers
make promises 4
make decisions while we are speaking 1, 3
make offers 5
make suggestions 2

d ▶ Students read the information in Grammar Focus 4B on SB p.148. Play the recording where indicated and ask students to listen and repeat. Students then complete the exercises in Grammar Focus 4B on SB p.149. Check answers as a class. Tell students to go back to SB, p.40

Answers (Grammar Focus 4B SB p.149)
a 1O 2S 3O 4D 5P 6S 7P 8S
b 1 I'll   2 won't   3 Shall   4 I'll   5 Shall   6 Will
c 1 Shall we go   2 I'll cook   3 I'll pay   4 shall we eat
   5 Shall I book   6 I'll do   7 I'll call   8 Will you call
   9 I'll call   10 I won't forget

📖 LANGUAGE NOTES

- It can help students to understand when to use *will* and *shall* if they match them with certain functions. Tell students that we use *will* to make promises (e.g. *I won't be late tomorrow.*) and spontaneous decisions (e.g. *Is that the telephone ringing? I'll answer it*). We use *shall* in the first person only for offers (e.g. *Shall I do that?*) and suggestions (e.g. *Shall we stop for lunch now?*).

- Students often want to know the detailed differences between the different future forms. However, the differences are often complex and difficult to explain. In many cases, more than one form can be used.

e ▶️ **1.72** **Pronunciation** Students listen to the recording to identify the different vowel sounds. Model the sentences again for the class to repeat.

Answers
1 /ɒ/   2 /əʊ/

f ▶️ **1.73** Students listen and circle the correct words. Check answers as a class.

Answers
1 won't   2 won't   3 want to   4 want to   5 won't   6 won't

g ▶️ **1.73** Students listen and repeat the sentences as a class. Nominate individual students to repeat sentences for additional practice.

h ▶ Divide the class into pairs and assign A and B roles. Student As read the instructions on SB p.131 and Student Bs read the instructions on SB p.132. They read out the sentences and choose the best reply. Check the answers as a class.

Answers Communication Plus 4B SB p.131 and 132
Student A (correct responses from Student B)
1 I'll meet you at the airport.
2 Shall we go to a shopping centre?
3 Shall I read it for you in English?
4 OK – so we won't go to the market.
5 Shall we go to a gallery?

Student B (correct responses from Student A)
1 I'll find a good place to eat nearby.
2 I'll take you to a nice park.
3 I'll take you to the airport soon.
4 Shall we visit the castle?
5 Shall I come and pick you up?

3 VOCABULARY Adjectives: places

a Elicit adjectives from the conversation by asking: *Can you remember the adjectives Harry and Mike used in the dialogue to describe these things?* the noodle restaurant (*great*), the noodles (*delicious*), the cherry blossom (*beautiful*), Mike's singing (*terrible*), the day (*interesting*). Put the adjectives on the board and elicit the opposites: *great – terrible, awful; delicious – disgusting, horrible; beautiful – ugly; terrible – great; interesting – boring.*

Students complete the sentences with the correct opposites.

> **Answers**
> 1 quiet 2 tiny 3 ugly

b In pairs, students match the adjectives and their opposites.

c ⏵**1.74** Play the recording for students to check answers and to underline the stressed syllables in words of more than one syllable.

> **Answers**
> 1 c m<u>o</u>dern, <u>an</u>cient 3 d <u>in</u>door, <u>out</u>door   5 b <u>na</u>rrow, wide
> 2 e high, low   4 f mag<u>ni</u>ficent, <u>or</u>dinary 6 a <u>noi</u>sy, <u>peace</u>ful

d ⏵**1.74** Students listen and repeat. Then nominate individual students at random to say a word. If a student makes a mistake in the stress pattern, repeat the error with an upward questioning tone in order for him/her to correct it. If they can't manage to do so, elicit the correction from the class.

e Put the students into groups. Ask the groups to think of some places everyone in the group knows, e.g. the school buildings, places in the local town. Students match each of the places they think of with a suitable adjective from 3b to describe it (they need to use all the adjectives). Check the answers as a class.

> 💡 **EXTRA ACTIVITY**
>
> Draw a grid on the board with numbers 1–12. Make a list of the 12 adjectives from 3b mixed up and numbered, e.g. 1 *magnificent*, 2 *wide* etc. Read out the list to the students and tell them to try to remember which adjectives and numbers go together. (They aren't allowed to write anything down). Students then take turns to choose a pair of numbers, trying to match pairs of opposites. When they find a pair, cross them off the grid.

4 LISTENING

a ⏵**1.75** Tell students that they are going to listen to the first part of Mike and Harry's conversation on their way to the airport the next morning. Ask them to listen to find out Mike's favourite part of the day. Play the recording and check answers.

> **Answer**
> the karaoke

> **Audioscript (Part 2)**
>
> **HARRY** Airport, please.
> **TAXI DRIVER** OK.
> **MIKE** Ooof!
> **H** Tired?
> **M** Yes, and I'm a bit worried about my flight. It leaves in two hours …
>
> **H** Don't worry – you'll be fine. It only takes half an hour to get there. We've got plenty of time.
> **M** Hmm.
> **H** So, what was your favourite part of the day?

> **Audioscript continued**
>
> **M** Difficult question. I liked all of it. The food was great. The fish
> **H** Yep!
> **M** But I think I liked the karaoke best. It's such good fun in a private
>
> market … well, I've never seen anything like that.
> room. I hate it in England, when you do it in front of 50 strangers.
> **H** Yeah, absolutely.

b ⏵**1.76** Tell students that they are going to hear the next part of the conversation and ask them to tell you what the problem is, and what Harry suggests. Play the recording twice if necessary, once for students to answer the first question and a second time for the next question. Check the answers as a class.

> **Audioscript (Part 3)**
>
> **M** Can you ask the taxi driver to go a bit faster? I really am worried about this flight.
> **H** Yeah, he is a bit slow. Can you go a bit faster?
> **M** This is a nightmare now! The flight leaves in an hour.
> **H** Yeah, I'm really sorry about this. We stayed too long at the fish market. And I didn't know there'd be so much traffic.
> **M** Mmm.
> **H** Look – I've got an idea. You enjoyed your day, right?
> **M** Definitely. Well, until now anyway.
>
> **H** Well, change your flight and stay another day. I'll take the day off work. There are lots more places in Tokyo I want to show you.
> **M** I don't know … what about the flight?
> **H** You can change the flight! Come on, it'll be great!
> **M** Yeah, but …
> **H** Come on … shall I tell the taxi driver to turn round?
> **M** Well …

> **Answers**
> The traffic is bad and Mike will probably miss his flight.
> Harry suggests that Mike stays another day.

c 💬 Ask students to discuss the question in pairs and take feedback from the class about the reasons why students would or wouldn't choose to stay another night.

d 💬 Discuss the question in pairs or small groups. Then take feedback from the class about which cities students would like to live in or spend time in. Encourage students to justify their answers, giving reasons why these places are attractive to them.

5 SPEAKING

a Prepare students for the role play by reading through the task. Give students some time to note down their ideas. Circulate and help where necessary.

b 💬 Read through the examples before students start the activity and put some useful phrases on the board: *That's a good idea. I'm not very keen on … I'd love that. That sounds interesting. That might be a bit boring.* In pairs, students tell each other about the places they can go to and the things they can do. They should discuss which they prefer, and why, and decide on plans for the days. Monitor and help as necessary. Note any common mistakes and deal with these during class feedback.

c 💬 Students describe their days out to the rest of the class. They vote on the best day out.

> **ADDITIONAL MATERIAL**
>
> ▶ Workbook 4B
>
> ▶ Photocopiable activities: Vocabulary p.235, Pronunciation p.269

4C Everyday English
Are you doing anything on Wednesday?

At the end of this lesson, students will be able to:
- use phrases to make arrangements
- understand a conversation where people make arrangements
- use phrases to give time to think
- give correct stress to auxiliaries
- make and respond to an invitation

☼ OPTIONAL LEAD-IN

Books closed. Put students into small groups. Ask them to choose a celebrity who they are all familiar with. Give students five minutes and ask them to imagine all the arrangements the celebrity has for the next week. Ask one or two groups to share their ideas with the class. Which celebrity has the busiest week?

1 LISTENING

a 💬 Ask students if they make arrangements by phone, and what kind of arrangements they make. How else do they arrange things – by text, email, letter? Which is the most common way in the class?

b ▶1.76 Tell the class that they are going to hear a phone conversation between Annie and Rachel. Ask students what has happened previously in the story and ask them to guess what the phone call is about. Play Part 1 of the video or play the audio recording. Students listen to the recording to check their ideas. If necessary, play the recording again.

> **Answer**
> to invite her for a meal (for Leo's birthday)

Video/audioscript (Part 1)

RACHEL Hello, Fantastic Flowers.
ANNIE Oh, hi. Rachel?
R Yes?
A It's Annie.
R Oh, hi Annie! How are you?
A I'm OK, thanks. You?
R I'm great.
A Listen – you know it's Leo's birthday this week?
R Of course!
A Well, are you doing anything on Wednesday? Would you like to come round for a meal?
R Oh, that sounds nice. I'll just check. No, we can't do Wednesday. Sorry. We're meeting some friends.
A Oh, OK. How about Thursday? Is that OK for you?

R Thursday ... hang on a minute ... oh, no, sorry. I'm working on Thursday evening.
A Oh.
R This week's really busy for us. Next week?
A OK. What are you doing on ... Monday?
R Er, just a moment ... Nothing! We can do Monday – perfect.
A Great!
R What time shall we come round?
A Let's say ... seven o'clock.
R OK – and would you like us to bring anything?
A No, nothing! See you on Monday then!
R Great! See you then.

📖 VOCABULARY SUPPORT

hang on (a minute) (B1) – wait (a moment)

c ▶1.77 Read through the questions with the class. Play the recording again for students to listen and answer the questions. Check answers as a class.

> **Answers**
> 1 They're meeting some friends.
> 2 She's working.
> 3 Monday
> 4 7 o'clock
> 5 nothing

2 USEFUL LANGUAGE
Making arrangements

a Before looking at the phrases in 2a, ask the class: *How did Annie invite Rachel for dinner? How did Rachel say that they couldn't go on certain days?* Put their ideas on the board. Then read through the phrases with them and see if they remembered any correctly. Students decide which phrases are invitations and which are responses. Check answers as a class.

> **Answers**
> 1 I 2 I 3 R 4 I 5 R 6 I 7 R 8 R

b ▶1.78 Play the recording for students to note down the replies. They may need a pause after each exchange to note down their answers. Check answers as a class.

Answers and audioscript

ANNIE Would you like to come round for a meal?
RACHEL That sounds great.
ANNIE Are you doing anything on Wednesday?
RACHEL Sorry. We can't do Wednesday.
ANNIE How about Thursday? Is that OK for you?
RACHEL No, sorry, I'm working. This week's really busy for us.

ANNIE What are you doing on Monday?
RACHEL Nothing. We can do Monday.
RACHEL What time shall we come round?
ANNIE Let's say seven o'clock.
RACHEL Would you like us to bring anything?
ANNIE No, nothing.

c ▶1.79 Students can do the gap fill task individually or in pairs. Play the recording for them to check their answers.

> **Answers**
> 1 Are you doing   2 Would you like   3 can't do   4 How about
> 5 Is that OK   6 busy   7 are you doing   8 shall I

d 💬 Go through the examples with the class. In pairs, students practise the conversation but change some details. Monitor and help as necessary, note interesting conversations. Ask students to share interesting conversations with the class.

☼ FAST FINISHERS

Put pairs together to make groups of four. Students make an arrangement for their group. If students are finding it easy to make an arrangement, tell one of the students to pretend he/she is only free on one evening in the week. Students make invitations until everyone in the group accepts.

3 CONVERSATION SKILLS
Making time to think

a Elicit what students do to give themselves thinking time during a conversation in their own language. This may be fillers like *well, erm,* etc. or there may be phrases like *let me think ...* . Ask if students remember what Rachel used when she was talking to Annie. Then read through the examples and ask students to underline and tell you the phrases.

> **Answers**
> 1 I'll just check.   2 hang on a minute   3 Just a moment

b ▶**1.80** Students listen and repeat the phrases. Encourage them to try to imitate the speaker's intonation as well as the words.

c 💬 Ask students to get out their phones or diaries and check when they have free time next week. Give them a short time to think of things they could invite their partner to do. Then put them into pairs to take turns to make invitations and respond. Remind them to use the phrases in 3a to give themselves time to think whilst they are checking their diaries. Monitor and point out errors for students to self correct.

> ### 💡 EXTRA ACTIVITY
> Give students a couple of examples of difficult social events, e.g. your ex-girlfriend's wedding, a leaving party for a colleague you don't get on with. In pairs, students choose one of these events and think of some good excuses for not accepting the invitation. Suggestions don't have to be serious! Students share their ideas with the class and vote on the best excuse.

4 LISTENING

a ▶**1.81** Students look at the pictures to tell you what they can see and answer the questions. Then play Part 2 of the video or play the audio recording for them to check their ideas.

> **Answers**
> They are at Annie's house. Leo probably doesn't like his present (even though he says he does!). He isn't a sports fan and he can't stand football.

> **Video/audioscript (Part 2)**
>
> **MARK** That was great!
> **RACHEL** Yeah, thanks, Annie. You're a great cook.
> **ANNIE** Thanks! I'm glad you enjoyed it.
> **M** Enjoyed it? I don't think I can move!
> **A** Excuse me for a moment.
> **M** I think I need to go for a run tomorrow.
> **R** I always tell you not to eat so much.
> **A** Rachel, can you come here for a second? I need you to help me carry something.
> **R** I'll send Mark. He needs the exercise! Go on.
> **LEO** I think I need to get some exercise as well!
> **R** Mark said you're a big sports fan.
> **L** No, not really. I mean – I like to keep fit, so I go to the gym. But I don't really like sport. It's a bit boring. And I can't stand football.
> **R** Oh.
> **A** Happy birthday, Leo!
>
> **M&R** Happy birthday!
> **L** Thanks, everyone. What an amazing cake!
> **M** Oh ... we've got this for you, Leo.
> **R** Yes, happy birthday!
> **L** Oh, you really didn't need to! (VIDEO ONLY ... Ha, thanks ...) Wow, that's great. I love it! That's very kind of you.
> **M** I knew you'd like it! Actually, Leo, I was thinking ... since you're a sports fan, maybe we could do something together some time. Maybe go to a football match?
> **L** Well ... sure, or how about a workout? I like going to the gym. How about that? Do you want to come with me some time?
> **M** Oh, OK. Why not? The gym sounds great.
> **L** When are you free? I normally go in the evening.
> **M** Well, are you going next Tuesday? I'm free then.
> **L** I can't Tuesday. How about Thursday?
> **M** OK. Sounds great!

> ### 📖 VOCABULARY SUPPORT
> *for a second* (B1) – for a very short time
> *work out* (B1) – to exercise

b ▶**1.81** Read through the questions. Play Part 2 of the video or play the audio recording again for students to answer. You may need to play it twice and/or pause after each question is answered. If you play it all the way through, allow students to talk about their answers in pairs before checking answers as a class.

> **Answers**
> 1 because he's eaten too much   2 He doesn't like sport, especially football. He likes to go to the gym to keep fit.
> 3 go to the gym next Thursday

> ### 💡 EXTRA ACTIVITY
> Ask students: *Did Mark and Rachel enjoy the meal? What did they say? (*That was great! You're a great cook.*) What did Annie say when she wanted to leave the room to get the cake? (*Excuse me for a moment.*) How did Leo thank them for the present? (*Wow, that's great. I love it! That's very kind of you.*)
>
> Model the pronunciation of the sentences for students to repeat. Point out that Leo's thanks could have been more enthusiastic if he had really liked the present. Show this by modelling his sentences with more exaggerated stress and intonation.

c 💬 Students discuss the questions together. Take feedback from the class about the most interesting things they have learned about their partner's attitude to presents and present giving and receiving.

5 PRONUNCIATION Sentence stress

a ▶1.82 Write the two sentences on the board and play the recording for students to listen for the difference in stress. Students repeat to practise. Ask for a volunteer to come up to the board and underline the stressed syllables.

> **Answers**
> 1 can't   2 long

b ▶1.83 Nominate individual students to read the sentences aloud with the correct stress pattern before playing the recording for the class to listen and repeat. Ask students to find and circle the negative auxiliaries in the sentences before eliciting the rule.

> **Answer**
> always

c ▶1.84 Students listen and repeat the sentences.

> **Answers and audioscript**
> 1 I can't do next week.
> 2 We don't have time.
> 3 I won't be late.
> 4 I could see you tomorrow.
> 5 We didn't go to the party.
> 6 We can come at six o'clock.

LOA TIP DRILLING

Students repeat the sentences as a class but to provide variety and keep focus, occasionally nominate a student after modelling the sentence, e.g. You say: *We don't have time. Nicole!* / Nicole says: *We don't have time.* You say: *Everyone! We don't have time.*

6 SPEAKING

a ▶ Divide the class into pairs and assign A and B roles. Student A reads the instructions in 6b and Student B reads the instructions on SB p.132.

b Students role play the conversations. Student As arrange plans for three evenings and write them in the diary. Monitor and help as necessary.

c Students role play the second situation. Monitor but don't interrupt fluency. Note any particular problems to discuss later. At the end of the activity, ask students what the final arrangements are and what B is going to bring. Discuss your feedback with the class.

💡 FAST FINISHERS

Ask students to change roles and repeat the activity.

ADDITIONAL MATERIAL

▶ Workbook 4C

▶ Photocopiable activities: Grammar p.211, Pronunciation p.272

▶ Unit Progress Test

▶ Personalised online practice

At the end of this lesson, students will be able to:

- understand speakers talking about arrangements
- read and understand written invitations and replies
- write and reply to invitations

💡 OPTIONAL LEAD-IN

Books closed. In small groups, students plan an end-of-term party for the class. Tell them to choose a theme for the party. Students note down what is going to happen at the party, if there will be games or not, where it will be, who is going to bring or prepare different things, and who to invite. Conduct feedback and ask for ideas from the groups. The class vote on the best ideas for the party.

1 SPEAKING AND LISTENING

a 💬 Ask students to match the pictures to some of the things in the list before they discuss the questions in small groups. Take feedback to find the most popular activities in the class.

b 💬 Discuss the question as a class and also ask when students last did each of the activities in the list.

💡 EXTRA ACTIVITY

In pairs, students talk about the best way to celebrate some or all of these events: 1 a five-year-old's birthday; 2 an 18th birthday; 3 a 21st birthday; 4 a wedding; 5 a new baby; 6 a 50th birthday; 7 retirement; 8 a 100th birthday. Ask students to share their best ideas with the class.

c ▶ **1.85** Tell students that they will hear three people speaking. Each person is talking about a different weekend activity. They listen to find out what the three activities are. Play the recording and pause after each speaker to ask the class for answers. Elicit brief answers.

> **Answers**
> Susanna: She's having her 21st birthday party.
> Barbara: She's having a barbecue.
> Sven: He's going to the countryside / a lake with some old friends.

🌍 CULTURE NOTES

A barbecue (or BBQ, barbie) is a social gathering outdoors where most of the food is cooked over wood or charcoal. Barbecues are popular in many countries around the world. In the UK, many people have a small barbecue grill in their gardens for use on hot summer afternoons or evenings! Pubs and restaurants will also organise larger barbecues in the summer months.

📖 VOCABULARY SUPPORT

function room (C1) – a large room which you can pay to use for different activities such as parties

go bowling – to do the sport where you throw a heavy ball along the floor to knock things down

stressed (B1) – feeling worried and anxious

Audioscript

SUSANNA I don't really like having a party at home to celebrate. It's too much work. I think it's better to go out together and find a nice place where you can celebrate. Then you can all have a good time together.
This weekend, it's my 21st birthday and we're going to book a function room at a hotel and have a big party there. All my friends are coming and we're going to have a band and a DJ. Everyone's going to look their best – all the men are going to wear suits and I'm going to buy a new dress. I'm really excited about it!

BARBARA I like inviting friends to my home, but I'm not a very good cook. I always get very stressed if I have to cook meals for people. Everyone else is having a nice time, but I'm just worrying if the food's OK. So, I don't really enjoy it. What I do like is if we all cook something together, or if everyone makes something and brings it. I think that makes it more relaxed. We're doing that on Saturday. We're having a barbecue, but I'm just going to make some salads and I'm going to ask everyone to bring something for the barbecue. I'm looking forward to it.

SVEN I sometimes enjoy parties, but they're all the same really: you just sit around and talk to people about all the usual stuff until it's time to go home. With friends, I think it's better to do something together, then you don't get bored – like going to the cinema or bowling maybe, or going out somewhere nice together. This weekend, I'm going to the countryside with some old friends I haven't seen for a long time. We're going to a lake to swim and have a picnic together, and maybe we'll play volleyball. That'll be fun.

d ▶ **1.85** Play the recording for students to listen and answer the more detailed questions. Ask them to compare answers with a partner before checking as a class.

> **Answers**
> 1 It's too much work.
> 2 in a function room at a hotel
> 3 a new dress
> 4 She isn't a very good cook and gets very stressed.
> 5 It's more relaxed.
> 6 some salads
> 7 They sit around and talk to people about all the usual stuff until it's time to go home.
> 8 He prefers to do something together because you don't get bored.
> 9 swim, have a picnic, play volleyball

e 💬 In pairs or small groups, students talk about who they are most similar to, and why. Take feedback from the class and find out which of the three speakers the highest number of students are similar to.

2 READING

a Ask students to imagine that they are Barbara and they are sending invitations to her barbecue. Ask: *What would you include in the invitation?* Write some ideas on the board. Read through the questions with the class. Students read the two emails to check their ideas and answer the questions.

> **Answers**
> 1 no   2 Saturday, around 8 o'clock
> 3 Martina: something (for the barbecue) Bill: meat

📖 VOCABULARY SUPPORT

chance (B1) – opportunity

for ages (B1) – for a long time

b Students answer the question as a class and give their reasons.

> **Answers**
> Bill because she knows what activities he did recently. She says she hasn't seen Martina for ages.

3 WRITING SKILLS Inviting and replying

a Ask students: *Do you think Martina and Bill are good friends of Barbara's?* Elicit that the language in the email to Martina suggests that she isn't as close a friend as Bill. They have seen Bill recently and know he has been cycling, but they haven't seen Martina. The language in the message to Martina is more formal. Ask for examples of the difference in language, e.g. *How are you? How are things?* Ask students if they use different phrases when they write to people they know well compared with people they don't know well. Students complete the table with the correct phrases from the emails. Check answers as a class.

> **Answers**
> 2 free 3 Would you like 4 would be lovely
> 5 are things 6 doing anything 7 Can you 8 be great

b Students read the two replies and answer the questions. Check answers together as a class.

> **Answers**
> The first email is from Martina. She talks about her job.
> The second email is from Bill. He talks about his legs hurting from the bike ride; he includes kisses (xx). Martina is coming to the BBQ.

c Students underline the appropriate phrases individually and then compare their answers with a partner. Check answers as a class. Point out the slight differences in formality of the phrases.

> **Answers**
> 1 Thanks for inviting me on Saturday. / Thanks for asking.
> 2 I'm free that evening and I'd love to come.
> 3 I'm really sorry, the BBQ sounds great, but I'm afraid I can't come.
> 4 I'm staying with my sister at the weekend.
> 5 I'm looking forward to seeing you and having a good chat. / See you soon anyway.

LANGUAGE NOTES

It is important for students to see how formal and informal language is used, depending on who is going to read the email. Usually it is quite clear that we use more formal language when we write/speak to someone we don't know. However, as shown here, our language also changes a little depending on how friendly we are with the person and sometimes on how old they are.

EXTRA ACTIVITY

Ask if students know any more phrases that they could use to do the things in 3c. Suggest/ or elicit:
1 Thank you for your invitation. Thanks a lot.
2 That'd be great.
3 I'm really sorry, but I have to say no. I can't make it.
4 I'm away for the week.
5 It'll be good to catch up. Must get together soon.
Match students from one half of the class to students in the other half of the class. Students all imagine they are Barbara and write a short email to their partner in the other group. They exchange the emails. Students reply to the emails using some of the above phrases.

d Students read and correct the sentences. Check answers as a class.

> **Answers**
> 1 Would you like to come to my birthday party?
> 2 Thanks for inviting me to your wedding.
> 3 I'm afraid I can't go to the cinema with you.
> 4 I'd love to come, but I'm busy that weekend.
> 5 I'm looking forward to seeing you tomorrow.

4 WRITING

a Tell students that they are going to work in pairs to first think of an activity and then write an invitation to it together. They need to consider the points in the task. Give students a short time to do this. Monitor and help with ideas or language where necessary.

b Students swap invitations and write replies, including the points given.

c Students exchange replies and check whether the points have been included. Take feedback and ask some pairs to read their invitation and reply to the class.

LOA TIP REVIEW AND REFLECT

Ask students to say which phrases that they have learned in this lesson will be most useful to them, and why. Ask them if they think formal and informal English phrases for inviting and replying are more or less different than the equivalent phrases in their own languages.

FAST FINISHERS

Fast finishers can write a further email to the guest to thank them for their quick reply, say it'll be good to see them or, to those who can't make it, arrange another meeting.

EXTRA ACTIVITY

Ask students to tell you their experiences of teenage parties, both good and bad! If students are not happy to talk about their own experiences, perhaps they have seen a film about this topic. Ask them if they have any tips or advice for arranging a party for teenagers including how many people to invite and how to avoid gatecrashers (people you haven't invited but hear about the party and come anyway).

ADDITIONAL MATERIAL

▶ Workbook 4D

UNIT 4
Review and extension

1 GRAMMAR

a Students complete the sentences individually. Check answers as a class. Ask students to repeat the sentences and focus on the pronunciation of *going to* /ˈɡənə/.

Answers
1 'm going to watch   2 're going to travel   3 are going to go
4 'm not going to take   5 's going to buy   6 're going to meet

b Remind or elicit from students that we use the present continuous for definite arrangements, and ask for a few examples of what they have planned or someone in their family has planned over the next few days. Students complete the sentences individually. Check answers as a class.

Answers
1 Are you doing   2 'm going   3 's having   4 'm not doing
5 'm having   6 are coming   7 'm making

c 💬 In pairs, students practise the conversation in 1b.

d Students complete the text message and check with their partners. Check answers as a class. Students can then write a follow-up text answering the question from the second text and asking one more question of their own. Students share their questions with the class.

Answers
1 I'll get   2 Shall I get   3 I'll have   4 I'll eat
5 Shall we go   6 I won't be

2 VOCABULARY

a Students do the task individually and then compare answers with a partner. Check answers as a class.

Answers
5, 6 tights 4 bracelet 1 earrings 2 tie 2 scarf 6 high heels 6 sandals
3 sweatshirt 3 top 3, 5 tracksuit

> 💡 **EXTRA ACTIVITY**
>
> Ask students to work in pairs and make a word search puzzle using ten items of clothing. They swap them with another pair and solve the puzzles. This will focus on correct spelling as well as practising the vocabulary.

b 💬 In pairs, students talk about the clothes and accessories they are wearing. To extend, ask students to close their eyes and see if they can remember what the other students are wearing today.

3 WORDPOWER look

a Write *look* on the board and ask students to work in pairs and see if they can write sentences that use the word *look* in different ways. Check their ideas and write correct examples on the board. Students match the sentences and definitions. Check answers. Point out that *look* can be used a) to show how someone seems from their appearance, e.g. He looks tired. b) as an activity, e.g. He is looking at the book. c) with a preposition to make a multi-word verb. This can sometimes change its meaning a little, e.g. He looked up the word in the dictionary.

Answers
1 c   2 e   3 d   4 b   5 a

b Students choose the correct alternatives to complete the sentences. Check answers as a class.

Answers
1 after   2 forward to   3 up   4 at   5 for   6 look   7 around

> 📖 **LANGUAGE NOTES**
>
> - There is not a lot of logic to the use of the prepositions in multi-word verbs. It's important that students don't try to learn a lot at once. Point out the importance of recording them by writing them in sentences so that they see how the verbs work.
> - Some multi-word verbs take objects and some don't. Some can be separated, e.g. *look up a word/look a word up*, and some can't, e.g. ~~look the children after~~ (correct form = *look after the children*).

c 💬 In pairs, students talk about which sentences from 3b are true for them. Ask for example comments in feedback.

▶ Photocopiable activities: Wordpower p.255

> **LOA REVIEW YOUR PROGRESS**
>
> Students look back through the unit, think about what they've studied and decide how well they did. Students work on weak areas by using the appropriate sections of the Workbook, the Photocopiable activities and the Personalised online practice.

UNIT 5
Work

GETTING STARTED

> ### ⓦ OPTIONAL LEAD-IN
> Books closed. Students work in pairs to name three jobs. Then they swap partners and mime the jobs for their new partner to guess. Choose some students to show their mimes to the class.

a ▶ 2.2 Ask students to look at the picture and say what they can see. You can pre-teach *twin building, crane* and *tower* using the picture. Ask students what they think the people are doing, then play the recording for students to check their ideas. If you wish, give students information from the Culture notes below.

UNIT OBJECTIVES
At the end of this unit, students will be able to:
- understand texts and conversations about work
- talk about what people do at work
- talk about future careers
- make offers and suggestions
- write a job application

> **Answers and audioscript**
> The men are window cleaners at the Petronas Towers in Kuala Lumpur, Malaysia – the world's tallest twin buildings. There are two towers and they have 32,000 windows. Several teams of brave window cleaners are employed to clean the tower windows. It takes a month to wash the windows of one building! Once they finish they begin again at the top.

> ### 🌍 CULTURE NOTES
> The Petronas Towers are twin skyscrapers in Kuala Lumpur, Malaysia, with 88 floors each. The towers have appeared in many films and have also attracted climbers and jumpers. In 2009, a French urban climber, Alain 'Spiderman' Robert, climbed the outside of the tower without any safety ropes. It took him two hours. At 452 metres high, the Petronas Towers were the tallest buildings in the world until 2004, when the skyscraper Taipei 101 was completed in Taiwan. Since then a number of taller buildings have been built, including Burj Khalifa in Dubai (828 metres), which was completed in 2010. In 2014, work started in Saudi Arabia on building the Kingdom Tower in Jeddah which aims to be 1 kilometre high.

b 💬 Discuss the questions as a class. Encourage students to give reasons for their answers. Ask students to imagine what a typical working day is like for these people.

c 💬 Give students a short time to talk about the questions in pairs. Elicit or input *stretch your arms up*. Ask students to share their ideas with the class.

> **Suggested answers**
> He's getting ready to start work in the early morning.
> He's giving instructions to a co-worker.
> 'OK! Let's start!'

d 💬 Tell students that they are going to role play the conversation between the man and his co-worker. Monitor and help where necessary. Nominate a pair to role play their conversation for the group.

> ### ⓦ EXTRA ACTIVITY
> Put students into pairs. Ask: *Should people who have dangerous jobs earn a lot of money? Why / Why not?* Ask students to share their reasons with the class.

5A I have to work long hours

At the end of this lesson, students will be able to:

- use a set of vocabulary related to work
- understand people talking about their work
- use *must*, *have to* and *can*
- discuss different kinds of work and what people do at work

OPTIONAL LEAD-IN

Students think about their job or a job that a friend or someone in their family has. They write down two things they like about their job and two things they don't. Put students in small groups to compare their lists. Now ask the groups to discuss whether there are similar things that they like or don't like about their jobs. Ask one or two students to share their ideas with the class.

1 VOCABULARY Work

a Students look at the pictures and describe what they can see. Ask what jobs the people are doing and write them on the board. The woman on the telephone is an inve stment banker. Accept the answer *businesswoman* from students, then input her job title.

> **Answers**
> gardener   scientist   banker/businesswoman   nurse/doctor
> electrician

b Put students into pairs and ask them to note down as many different jobs as they can in a minute. When they have finished, ask for a job from each pair in turn. Put the jobs on the board. Turn this into a game: each pair drops out when they have no more jobs left to add and the winner is the last pair who can name a different job.

c ▶ Students complete the exercises in Vocabulary Focus 5A on SB p.136. Play the recording where indicated and ask students to listen and repeat and check their answers. Ask them to underline the stressed syllable in each job title. Give students two minutes to discuss Exercise c in pairs then take feedback from the class about which are the most popular jobs. Tell students to go back to SB p.48.

> **Answers (Vocabulary Focus 5A SB p.136)**
> a 1 i 2 f 3 a 4 e 5 c 6 d 7 b 8 g 9 h
> b Xx: gardener, plumber, lawyer, banker   Xxx: hairdresser,
>   scientist   xXx: accountant   xxXx: electrician
> c 1 have 2 work 3 need 4 deal with 5 earn
>   6 am 7 make

2 READING

a Ask students to read *The Happiest Jobs* and the list. Check understanding of the list. Ask: *What does IT workers 48 per cent mean?* (It means only 48 per cent of IT workers in the survey say they are happy at work). In pairs, students talk about where they think the jobs go in the list. Take feedback to see how far students agreed.

CULTURE NOTES

The City & Guilds (C&G) Group offers 500 vocational qualifications in many different industries. Around two million people start C&G qualifications every year and these are well-recognised by employers. They are also the UK's leading provider of apprenticeships. C&G qualifications are also available in 80 countries around the world. The 'Career Happiness Index' was published in 2012 and involved asking 2200 workers about what they considered to be the most important factors in their happiness at work.

b Students turn to SB p.127 to check answers and to see who in the class was right. Ask the class if they are surprised by the the information and why / why not.

c In pairs, students make list of what they think makes people happy at work. Give them a few minutes to do this before eliciting suggestions from the class, e.g. *people, workplace.*

d Ask students to read the second half of the article to see if any of the ideas on the board are mentioned.

VOCABULARY SUPPORT

get on with (B2) – have a good relationship with

least (B1) – opposite of *most*

skill (B1) – ability to do a job well

e In pairs or small groups, students talk about the questions. Monitor but don't interrupt fluency unless students make mistakes with the word stress on job titles.

FAST FINISHERS

Fast finishers can role play an interview with a person who has one of the jobs in the list. The interviewer should ask questions about their job and how happy they are.

EXTRA ACTIVITY

Ask students to think about their own town(s). Do they think the top twelve jobs would be similar where they live or might there be differences? Ask students to think about jobs where they live which might be towards the bottom of the list. Students share their ideas with a partner and then with the class. Encourage them to justify their ideas as far as possible.

3 LISTENING

a Elicit from the class what kinds of things the people listed do in their work and then ask what they think the people like about their jobs.

LOA TIP ELICITING

To elicit the activities that the people do in their jobs, you can do a mime and ask students to say what you're doing, e.g. *nurse* (making a bed / taking a temperature / checking blood pressure). If students don't know a word, put it on the board after the mimed activity.

b Tell students they will hear the three people talking about their jobs. Play the recording for students to listen and check their ideas. Stop the recording after each speaker to take feedback on students' answers.

> **Answers**
> Alisha: working with people and helping them
> John: not having to wear a suit or go to many meetings, being his own boss
> Miriam: It's exciting.

Audioscript

ALICIA I love my job … working with people and helping them … but it's often stressful. I have to work long hours including weekends, and I sometimes deal with very serious problems. These days, to become a nurse you have to do well at school – especially in maths, science and English. Then you have to do a nursing degree before you can get a job. You also need to be good at making decisions and working in a team. There are lots of rules to remember. You can't enter a room without washing your hands. You can't lift a patient on your own. When you work with people who are very sick, every decision you make is so important.

JOHN For my job, you need to do two or three years' training – usually while you are working with a company. You can't go to people's houses on your own and start fixing things without a qualification. Now I have my own company, I usually work about 40 to 45 hours a week. It can be tiring. And of course you have to be careful even when you're tired. There are a lot of health and safety rules … for example, you always have to switch off the mains power. I heard of one guy who forgot and nearly died. Anyway … there are good things, too – you don't have to wear a suit or go to many meetings and I enjoy being my own boss.

MIRIAM I'm in investment banking … and to get in I needed a good university degree, and, also, to be a good communicator. You have to enjoy working really hard … I work very long hours, a hundred hours or more a week … And, well … I have to deal with a lot of stress … I look after millions of pounds of other people's money. You also can't relax because if something goes wrong, you lose money – other people's money. I suppose I also like that – it's exciting. But it's not an easy job and sometimes I feel that what I do isn't really that useful.

📖 VOCABULARY SUPPORT

fix (B1) – to repair

investment – (B2) money that you use to make more money

mains power (B1) – the electricity for a building

patient (B1) – a person in hospital who is ill

qualification (B1) – something that you get when you are successful in an exam or course of study

stressful (B1) – making you worried

c ▶ **2.5** Read through the questions with the class and elicit some examples of *qualifications* – e.g. a university degree, a diploma or certificate in something. Then play the recording for students to listen and answer the questions. Ask them to compare their ideas with a partner before you check the answers with the class.

> **Answers**
> Alisha – nursing degree; good at making decisions; dealing with serious problems, lots of rules to remember
> John – two or three years of training, a qualification; tiring, health and safety rules, dangerous
> Miriam – a good university degree; good communicator, enjoy working hard; dealing with stress, can't relax, not an easy job, not useful

💡 EXTRA ACTIVITY

Write: *maths and science, 45–50 hours, 100 hours, millions of pounds* on the board. Ask: *Who said these words and what did they say about them?* (*maths and science:* Alisha, about the subjects you need to do well in at school; *45–50 hours:* John, about the number of hours he needs to work; *100 hours:* Miriam, about the number of hours she works; *millions of pounds:* Miriam, about the amount of money she looks after)

d 💬 Discuss the question with the class. Which is the most popular job?

4 GRAMMAR *must / have to / can*

a Books closed. Read the following sentences to students or write them on the board: *Teachers have to / don't have to wear a suit. Teachers have to / don't have to correct homework. Teachers can / can't be late for a class.* Students choose the correct modal verb in each case. Check answers as a class. Ask concept questions to check understanding of the modal verbs. Open books. Ask students to look at the sentences. Students match the underlined words with the meanings.

> **Answers**
> a don't have to
> b can't
> c have to

LOA TIP CONCEPT CHECKING

Write on the board: *Teachers don't have to wear a suit.* Ask: *Can they wear a suit?* (yes) *Is it necessary?* (no) Summarise: *They can wear a suit if they want to, but it's not necessary.*

Write on the board: *Teachers have to arrive on time for class.* Ask: *Is it ok for teachers to be late for class?* (no) *Is there a rule?* (yes) *Who makes the rule?* (the school) *Did the teacher make the rule?* (no) Summarise: *Teachers have to arrive on time. The school has a rule.*

Write on the board: *Teachers can't take breaks during class.* Ask: *Do teachers take breaks sometimes?* (yes) *Is it ok to take breaks after class?* (yes) *Is it ok to take breaks during lessons?* (no) *Do teacher's need to stay in the class during lessons?* (yes) Summarise: *Teacher can't take breaks during class because they need to stay in the classroom.*

b Read through the written and spoken examples and ask students to complete the rules as a class.

> **Answers**
> must; must not

👁 CAREFUL!

Students often make mistakes by using the *to* infinitive after *must*, e.g ~~We must to go home now.~~ (Correct version = *We **must go** home now.*)

📖 LANGUAGE NOTES

The focus here is straightforward: *must / mustn't* is used for written rules and *have to / can't* for spoken ones. In the positive, the meaning of *must* and *have* to is similar. We use both constructions to express obligation. However, the negative forms – *mustn't* and *don't have to* – have completely different meanings: *mustn't* = not allowed; *don't have to* = not necessary. Also be aware that *must* has no past or future form, so for obligation in the past we use *had to and in the future we use will have to.*

c ▶ Students read the information in Grammar Focus 5A on SB p.150. Play the recording where indicated and ask students to listen and repeat. Students then complete the exercises in Grammar Focus 5A on SB p.151. Check answers as a class. Tell students to go back to SB p.49.

> **Answers (Grammar Focus 5A SB p.151)**
>
> a 1 have to   2 can't wear   3 can't check   4 can't speak
>   5 can talk   6 have to answer   7 have to be   8 have to find
> b 1 must not   2 don't have to   3 don't have to   4 must not
>   5 must not
> c 1 can't   2 can   3 doesn't have to   4 must not   5 must
>   6 has to

> **◉ CAREFUL!**
>
> As well as the differences in meaning, students frequently confuse the negative forms of *must* and *have to*, e.g. *I like shopping online because I don't must go to the shops*. (Correct form = *I **don't have to** go to the shops*.)

d 💬 Read through the question, the list of places and the examples. In pairs, students talk about the rules in the different places. Take feedback and ask students to share their ideas with the class. Make sure students are using the correct forms of *have to* and *can't*.

> **Suggested answers**
>
> office – you have to use a computer/can't work outside
> restaurant – you have to cover your hair/can't be rude to the customers
> bank – you have to be good at maths/can't wear jeans

e In pairs, students write the rules for each workplace, using *must/mustn't*. Circulate and help where necessary.

> **💡 FAST FINISHERS**
>
> Fast finishers can extend this activity by saying and then writing rules for other places, e.g. a hospital, a fire station or a police station.

5 SPEAKING

a 💬 In pairs, students choose five of the jobs and think of advantages and disadvantages of each. Monitor and help with vocabulary as necessary. Take feedback as a class. Go through the different jobs and elicit advantages and disadvantages from the group. Give your own ideas to help where necessary.

b 💬 Discuss the question as a class and see which job most students think is the hardest, and why.

> **ADDITIONAL MATERIAL**
>
> ▶ Workbook 5A
> ▶ Photocopiable activities: Grammar p.212, Vocabulary p.236

5B I might get a job today!

At the end of this lesson, students will be able to:

- use a vocabulary set related to jobs
- use *will* and *might* for predictions
- understand people talking about finding work
- read and understand a text about jobs in the future
- make predictions about jobs in the future

⚲ OPTIONAL LEAD-IN

Books closed. Discuss with students how people choose which job they want to do or which career they want to follow. Ask them to think about: following the example of someone in their family or a friend; celebrity role models; doing what they're good at and/or what they like; the role of a careers advisor at schools.

1 SPEAKING

a Discuss the questions as a class and put some ideas on the board of how people find jobs, e.g. go to a *job centre*, or *careers fair*, answer *job adverts* (*apply for a job*), send your *CV* to different companies, etc. Find an opportunity to introduce *careers fair* because students will need this term for the listening. If you have students in your class who are working, ask them about how they got their jobs.

📖 LANGUAGE NOTES

Students sometimes confuse *job* and *career*. A job is the work you are doing at one particular moment. A career is the series of jobs you do in your working life. *I have a difficult job. I have to start very early and finish very late. I would like to have a career in teaching.*

b In pairs, students match the worries with the situations in the pictures. They can use the captions to help them.

Answers
1 c   2 a   3 b

c 💬 Students discuss the question in pairs. Ask for examples in class feedback. Ask students why they think some people can't get the job they want.

2 LISTENING

a ▶2.9 Tell students that they are going to hear three people talking about finding work. Pre-teach the expression *apply for a job* in the Vocabulary support box. Play the recording for students to listen for general meaning and answer the first question. If you wish, give students information from the Culture notes below. Then play the recording again to choose the most and least positive of the people. First, check students understand the meaning of *positive* by giving two people's comments, e.g. A: *It rained today but I'm sure it will be really nice tomorrow.* B: *It rained today and I think it's going to rain again tomorrow, and be cold.* Elicit which person is positive (A) and which is negative (B). Play the recording again. If necessary, pause after each speaker and ask if that person is positive or negative. Encourage students to justify their answers. Can they remember things that the speakers said that sounded positive or negative?

Answers
They are at a careers fair.
most positive: Marco; least positive: Sara

Audioscript

INTERVIEWER Are you enjoying the careers fair?

SARA It's not bad. It's good to meet people from different companies.

I Are you looking for work at the moment?

S Yes. But it won't be easy to find a job I'll enjoy. There just aren't enough jobs – you have to take what you can find. I applied for a job this week but I don't think I'll get an interview. They won't be interested in me, because I don't have any experience.

I Are you enjoying the fair today?

MARCO Yeah, it's great. I'm sure I'll make some really useful contacts. There are people from some really interesting companies here.

I And are you applying for jobs at the moment?

M Yes. I don't think it'll take long to find work. You never know … I might get a job today! I know someone who found a job at an event like this last year.

I Are you enjoying it today?

KATE Yes it's good. It's useful because I'm not sure what kinds of jobs I'm interested in.

I So are you looking for work at the moment?

K Not yet. I'm still studying and then I'll try to get some work experience when I finish my course. After that I can start looking for a job. I might not get my perfect job, because not many people do, straight out of university.

I And how do you feel about that?

K Well … I just need to pay the bills, you know. I can work my way up. I've got time! I'm sure I'll find some kind of work because I'm happy to do anything they'll pay me for.

📖 VOCABULARY SUPPORT

apply for a job – to present yourself formally, usually in writing, and say you want an employer to give you a job

pay the bills – to pay for electricity/shopping/rent, etc

work experience – work (often unpaid) which people do for a company for a short time to learn about the job

work my way up – to progress through different jobs

🌎 CULTURE NOTES

A careers fair is an event where people can find out more about different companies and the jobs they offer. Employees are available to give information about their company and about career opportunities. These fairs are good for people looking for a job but they are also good for the companies as they can attract new people to work for them.

b ▶ **2.9** Read through the predictions with the class and play the recording again for students to tell you the reasons for each prediction. If necessary, do the first prediction together. Play the relevant section of the recording and ask: *Why does Sara say that it won't be easy to find a job she'll enjoy?* (There aren't enough jobs.) Play the recording for the class to find the other reasons. Pause to allow them time to note down their answers and then check answers as a class. Their answers don't need to be the exact words the speakers used.

> **Answers**
> 1 There just aren't enough jobs – you have to take what you can find.
> 2 They won't be interested in me, because I don't have any experience.
> 3 There are people from some really interesting companies here.
> 4 I know someone who found a job at an event like this last year.
> 5 Not many people do, straight out of university.
> 6 I'm happy to do anything.

c 💬 Discuss the question as a class. If nobody in the group has been to a careers fair, give students two or three minutes to agree with a partner on three things they would do/will do next time they are searching for a job and take feedback from the class.

3 GRAMMAR
will and *might* for predictions

a Books closed. Draw a table with two columns. One column has the heading: *I'm 100% sure* and the other has *Maybe* as the heading. Read Marco's sentences from 2b to students. Say: *I'll make some really useful contacts.* Ask students if Marco was sure about this, (Yes) and which column you should put a tick in (*I'm 100% sure.*) Then read Marco's next sentence: *I might get a job today!* Repeat the process and tick the *Maybe* column. Now read Kate's sentences from 2b: *I might not get my perfect job. (Maybe) I'll find some kind of work (I'm 100% sure).* Open books. Students do the task individually. Check answers as a class.

> **Answers**
> More

b ▶ Students read the information in Grammar Focus 5B on SB p.150. Play the recording where indicated and ask students to listen and repeat. Students then complete the exercises in Grammar Focus 5B on SB p.151. Check answers as a class. Tell students to go back to SB p.50.

> **Answers (Grammar Focus 5B SB p.151)**
> a 1 'll   2 might not   3 will; might   4 won't; might
>   5 might; won't   6 'll; might   7 might; might not
> b 1 might go   2 'll/might   3 I'm sure   4 won't rain
>   5 might buy   6 I'm sure I'll / I think I might
>   7 might not arrive   8 I don't think I'll pass / I might not pass
> c Are you sure you'll enjoy it?   2 Do you think she'll leave?
>   3 ... think it will cost?   4 ... think they'll tell us?
>   5 ... we'll finish on time?   6 ... I'll get an interview?
> d 2   3   4   6

> **📖 LANGUAGE NOTES**
>
> Most modal verbs form their negative by adding *not*, which is then contracted, e.g. *can – can't, must – mustn't*. With *might*, it is possible to use the contraction *mightn't* but it is more common to use the full form – *might not*.

---

c Asks students to look again at the worries in 1b and read through the example with the class. Elicit more possible responses from the group. Write on the board: *You might not find a job you enjoy, but you might …, you will …, you won't …* and ask for possible endings (e.g. *you might make some useful contacts; you might get some ideas; you will see what possibilities there are; you won't miss any opportunities,* etc.). Individually, students write positive responses to other worries and compare their ideas with a partner. Check the answers with the class.

> **Suggested answers**
> You might find a really good job. You might meet someone who can help you. You'll learn a lot, anyway.
> I'm sure you won't. I'm sure you'll be fine. You'll be OK, don't worry.
> I'm sure you'll know all the answers. You might not answer them all, but you'll know most of them. Just take your time and think. You'll be OK.

d Divide the class into pairs and assign A and B roles. If Student A has a job, Student B reads the instructions on SB p.130. If Student A doesn't have a job, Student B reads the instructions on SB p.128. Student B asks Student A the questions about their future. Encourage students to give full answers and to add extra information. Monitor and help where necessary. Don't interrupt fluency unless students make mistakes with the use or forms of *will* or *might*. Then the pairs swap roles and Student A asks the questions to Student B.

4 VOCABULARY   Jobs

a 💬 In pairs students, find the jobs in the pictures. Check answers as a class. Students say if they know anyone who does these jobs and if they enjoy them.

> **Answers**
> computer programmer: c   carer: a   shop assistant: d
> postman: b   builder: e

b ▶ Students complete the exercises in Vocabulary Focus 5B on SB p.136. Play the recording for students to check their answers to Exercise a, and monitor conversations in Exercise c. Tell students to go back to SB p.51.

> **Answers (Vocabulary Focus 5B SB p.136)**
> 1 f   2 k   3 d   4 i   5 a   6 c
> 7 e   8 l   9 g   10 j   11 h   12 b

c ▶ **2.13** **Pronunciation** Play the recording and try to elicit the /ʃ/ sound from the students. Then play it again, stopping after each word for students to repeat.

d ▶ **2.14** Give students a minute to repeat the words to themselves and identify which ones they think have the /ʃ/ sound. Then play the recording for them to check their answers, then listen and repeat the /ʃ/ sound.

> **Answers**
> qualifica**ti**on   informa**ti**on   ma**ch**ine

e Students practise saying the words as a group.

EXTRA ACTIVITY

Play a vocabulary game to practise job vocabulary. Write three jobs on the board with every other letter missing:
_ c _ o _ n _ a _ t/ _ a _ k _ r/ _ l _ c _ r _ c _ a _ .

Students guess the jobs (accountant, banker, electrician). In pairs, they do the same activity with other jobs from Vocabulary Focus 5A on SB p.136.

5 READING

a Ask students to look at the title of the article and predict what the article might be about. (It's about jobs that might or might not disappear in the future.) Then students discuss the two questions in pairs. Ask students to share their ideas with the class and write them on the board.

b Students read the article to check if any of the ideas on the board are mentioned.

> **Answers**
> jobs that might disappear: shop assistant, postman, builder
> jobs there will be more of: computer programmer, carer

VOCABULARY SUPPORT

argue (B1) – to disagree

carer – a person whose job it is to look after people

effect (B1) – result

predict (B1) – say that something will or won't happen in the future

c Students read the article again to find out what will happen because of the things in the list. They should do this individually and then compare answers. Check answers as a class.

> **Answers**
> online shopping: there will be fewer jobs for shop assistants
> sending emails: there will be fewer jobs for postmen and post office staff
> digital photos: there will be fewer jobs for photo processors
> 3D printers: there will be fewer jobs for builders
> environmental problems: there will be a lot of new 'green' jobs
> living longer: we'll need (more) carers
> studying online: there will be jobs for people to create and organise courses

CULTURE NOTES

People in the UK enjoy Internet shopping. In 2014, 6 out of 10 adults used the Internet to buy goods or services. Around 30% of online sales were made from smartphones and tablets.

A 3D printer can make an object of almost any shape from a virtual 3D model. The technology is being used in medicine to make replacement bones. Medical researchers also hope to use the technology to replace skin and organs, such as kidneys. A company in China started printing houses in 2014 using a mixture of cement and construction waste. Most 3D printers make objects out of plastic and it is now possible to buy a 3D printer to make common household objects at home.

Carers care for people who are unable to look after themselves usually because of illness, disability or old age. The UK has an ageing population. The UK government estimates that the numbers of people between the ages of 65 and 84 will increase by 39% by 2032. The current life expectancy in the UK is around 79 years for men and around 83 years for women.

FAST FINISHERS

Fast finishers can think of additional kinds of jobs that might disappear, and why. Check their ideas as part of the feedback.

6 SPEAKING

a In small groups, students discuss the predictions. Encourage them to give reasons. Monitor for any language errors and discuss these with the class after the activity.

b Individually, students write three predictions of their own. To help them think of ideas, write key words such as *food, money, houses, travel, weather, clothes, free time, music* on the board and tell stuents to choose three to make predictions about.

c Ask students for their predictions and let the class say whether they agree or not, and why.

EXTRA ACTIVITY

In pairs, students make predictions about what their partner will do at work or in their studies over the next few days. Tell students to check whether the predictions came true in the next lesson!

ADDITIONAL MATERIAL

▶ Workbook pages 5B

▶ Photocopiable activities: Grammar p.213, Vocabulary p.237 Pronunciation p.273

5C Everyday English
I'll finish things here, if you want

At the end of this lesson, students will be able to:

- understand a conversation where someone is making offers and suggestions
- uses phrases to apologise and offer reassurance
- make offers and suggestions
- understand and pronounce schwa /ə/
- use appropriate language to organise an event

⊛ OPTIONAL LEAD-IN

Books closed. Write the following situations on the board: *on a bus, in a supermarket, at an airport, in the street, in a hospital.* Put students in pairs and ask them to list what kind of help people might need in these places. Give an example: *On a bus, someone might need help with their shopping bags.* Ask students to share ideas with the class and put them on the board as students might refer to these later in the lesson.

1 LISTENING

a 🗨 Tell the class about a time when someone asked you for help (make up a story if necessary), then say: *When was the last time someone asked you for help? What did you do? What did you say?* Ask students to tell their partner. After a minute or two take feedback from the class. Ask individual students what their partner said.

b 🗨 Ask students what has happened in the story so far. Check that they remember that Tina helps Rachel in her shop. Then ask them to look at the picture of Rachel and read the text message. Answer the questions as a class.

> **Answers**
> Rachel is worried/anxious. The text is from Annie. Annie has had some bad news.

c ▶2.15 Read through the questions with the class. Students might be able to guess some of the answers based on the text message. Play Part 1 of the video or play the audio recording for students watch/listen and answer the questions. Check answers as a class.

> **Answers**
> 1 go and see Annie
> 2 finish the work
> 3 Tina will have too much work and won't be able to leave early.
> 4 Rachel will tell Tina what she has to do and Tina will make a list.

Video/audioscript (Part 1)

RACHEL Oh, dear.

TINA Is everything OK?

R I'm not sure really. I've just got a text message from my friend Annie. Do you remember her?

T Yeah, of course.

R Yeah, well she says she's had some bad news and she needs to talk to me.

T Oh dear. I hope she's OK.

R Hmm, I'd better give her a ring. Or maybe I should go and see her.

T Yeah, maybe you should. I'll finish things here, if you want.

R But I can't leave you here on your own.

T I'll be fine! Don't worry about it.

R But we've still got so much to do.

T Oh, it doesn't matter. Honestly, I'll be OK.

R I don't want to leave you with too much work. It doesn't seem very fair. It means you won't be able to leave early today.

T Oh, never mind. Look, why don't you tell me what we still need to do? And I'll write a list. Then you can go and see Annie.

R OK, well if you're sure.

T Of course. It's no problem.

R Well, ...

📖 VOCABULARY SUPPORT

fair (B1) – right

it means (B1) – the result will be

on your own – alone, by yourself

---

d 🗨 Elicit from the class what they would do in Rachel's situation – call or visit? Encourage students to give reasons and justify their answers.

2 CONVERSATION SKILLS Reassurance

a ▶2.15 Ask if anyone in the class can tell you what *reassurance* means. If they can't, don't explain but play the recording again for students to do the matching task and then elicit the meaning. Check answers as a class. Model the reassuring sentences a–d for students to practise the intonation.

↻ LOA TIP ELICITING

To elicit *reassurance*, ask: *What is Tina trying to do when she says these things?* (Answer: make Rachel feel better/stop Rachel worrying) Tell the class: *When we want to tell people not to worry and that things will be OK, we use the verb ...* (reassure) *Do you know the noun from this verb?* (reassurance) Write these examples on the board: *We give reassurance that things will be all right when people are worried or unhappy. Tina reassured Rachel that everything was fine.*

> **Answers**
> 1 c   2 d   3 a   4 b

b ▶2.16 Elicit from the class that Tina uses the expressions to reassure Rachel. Play the recording for students to listen and repeat the reassuring expressions. Explain that intonation and tone of voice is very important to sound reassuring in English and tell students to try to pay special attention to imitating the intonation (voice falls at the end of the sentence).

> **Answer**
> to reassure / to give reassurance to Rachel

c 🗨 Go through the situations to check understanding with the class. Look at the example for the first one and elicit other ways they could apologise in this situation writing suggestions on the board for students to use: *I'm afraid I can't ... I'd love to ... but unfortunately I can't ... It's a shame but it's going to be impossible for me to ...* In pairs, students take turns to apologise and give reassurance. Monitor and give help and ideas where necessary. Nominate students to role play their conversations to the class. If they didn't include an excuse in their original exchanges, ask for examples of excuses now in feedback.

⊛ FAST FINISHERS

Ask fast finishers to choose one of the situations and develop it into a longer conversation, adding detail and extra questions.

---

3 LISTENING

▶ **2.17** Before looking at the task, tell students that in Part 2 of the video Rachel and Tina talk about the jobs Tina will have to do. Ask what they think the jobs will be. Then look through the list of jobs with the class and check their ideas. Play Part 2 of the video or play the audio recording for students to tick the jobs Tina will have to do. Check answers as a class. Ask why Tina doesn't have to do jobs 3 and 5. (They'll have time to do it tomorrow morning. The bag isn't full.)

Answers
1, 2, 4, 6

Video/audioscript (Part 2)

RACHEL Right, and after that …

TINA Shall I finish off those flowers? The ones you were doing?

R OK. That would be great.

T And would you like me to prepare some of the orders for tomorrow?

R Yeah. You could start with that order for Mrs Thompson, because she's picking it up early.

T OK.

R And then maybe you should start on the order for that big birthday party.

T OK.

R Actually, no – we can do that tomorrow morning – we'll have time.

T Yeah, fine.

R OK, I think that's everything. Oh, when you leave, you'll need to put the alarm on. I'll write down the code for you.

T OK. Oh – do you want me to take out the rubbish when I leave?

R Er, no, don't worry. The bag's not full yet. I'll do it tomorrow.

T OK, fine.

R OK, great. I'll text Annie to say I'm coming.

T Oh, how about taking her some flowers? That'll cheer her up.

R Good idea … Oh, hello. How can I help?

CUSTOMER Hi, yeah. Er, I just wanted to make an order for some flowers.

R Of course. What would you like?

C Well, actually, it's for my daughter's wedding. So … er … some red roses …

R Yep.

C Some white roses …

R Hmm hmm.

C Some lilies …

T Rachel – why don't I deal with this?

R Are you sure?

T Yes! Just go!

R OK – bye!

C Oh, bye.

T So, that was some red roses …

C Three dozen, please.

T Three dozen …

C Er, white roses, three dozen.

T OK.

C Lilies, two dozen …

📖 VOCABULARY SUPPORT

alarm (B1) – security/protection for a building

dozen (B1) – twelve

lilies – big white flowers

4 USEFUL LANGUAGE

Offers and suggestions

a ▶ **2.18** Tell students that Tina makes several offers and suggestions about what she can do to help Rachel. Individually, students see which of the offers and suggestions they can complete from memory and compare ideas with a partner. Then play the recording again for students to complete any remaining gaps. Check answers as a class.

📖 LANGUAGE NOTES

We can use *Shall I … ?* for offers, but not *Will I … ?*

Answers
1 I'll 2 don't 3 Shall 4 like 5 could 6 should 7 me
8 about 9 don't

b Ask students which of the sentences they think are offers and which are suggestions.

Answers
1 O 2 S 3 O 4 O 5 S 6 S 7 O 8 S 9 O

c 💬 Put the phrases from the word box in 4c on the board. Tell students to imagine that their friend is having problems remembering new vocabulary from their English class. Elicit some offers and suggestions from the class using the phrases on the board. Make sure that they use the correct verb forms after the phrases, e.g. *Why don't you write down all the new words in a notebook? How about trying to use some of the words when you talk? Maybe you should look at the new words every evening.* In pairs, students think of offers and suggestions to give to people in situations 1–4. Look at the example for the first one with the class. Circulate and prompt where necessary. Ask for examples in class feedback and see how many different suggestions the class found for each situation. Vote on the best suggestions.

Suggested answers:
1 I'll lend you my umbrella, if you like.
2 Why don't I help you? Maybe you should ask your boss for more time.
3 I'll cook something, if you want. Why don't we try a new restaurant?
4 Would you like me to lend you some money? Maybe you should go to the police station.

5 PRONUNCIATION

Sentence stress: vowel sounds

a ▶ **2.19** Ask different students to read sentences 1–4 and identify whether they stress the modal verbs or not. Don't tell them if their pronunciation was correct or not at this point. Play the recording for students to listen to the sentences and answer the question. Model the sentences for students to repeat.

Answers
no

b ▶ **2.19** Students listen again to identify the vowel sound individually. Check the answer as a class. It doesn't matter if students don't know or can't remember *schwa* – accept their answer if they make the appropriate sound.

Answers
/ə/ (schwa)

c Model the sentences for students to practise them, paying attention to *schwa* in the modals.

6 SPEAKING

a 💬 Elicit some examples of things people need to organise, e.g. a meeting, a party, an evening out, a holiday, a day trip. Ask students: *Are you good at organising events?* Tell students that they are going to organise something in small groups. Divide the class into groups of four and read through the two options with them. They need to choose which event to organise. If your class are not in work, the party option will probably be better for them. The groups discuss the options and give you their choice.

b 💬 In pairs (within their groups), students add three more things to the list of things to do for their event.

c 💬 Students discuss their ideas in their groups. The group decides if they should be added to the original list. Then they make offers and suggestions to decide which person in the group will do each job. Tell students that they will have to discuss details such as: *What time shall we start the meeting?* Monitor and note down any common errors to deal with during feedback. Take feedback and ask for examples of what the groups organised.

> ### 💡 EXTRA ACTIVITY
>
> In their groups, students design and write invitations to send out for their event. This can be a party invitation or an email. They can exchange these with students in another group and write replies. If appropriate, put some examples on the classroom wall.

> ### 💡 EXTRA ACTIVITY
>
> Ask students: *When was the last event that you organised? What did you have to do? Was the event a success?* Students discuss the questions in pairs.

ADDITIONAL MATERIAL

▶ Workbook 5C

▶ Photocopiable activities: Pronunciation p.274

▶ Unit Progress Test

▶ Personalised online practice

5D Skills for Writing
I am writing to apply for a job

At the end of this lesson, students will be able to:

- read and understand adverts for jobs
- understand people talking about summer jobs
- read and understand a job application
- organise an email
- write a job application

ⓦ OPTIONAL LEAD-IN

Books closed. Think of a part-time or summer job you have had or imagine one. Describe one or two things you did in that job. Can students guess the job?

1 SPEAKING AND LISTENING

a 💬 In pairs, students tell each other about a summer or part-time job they have had. Ask one or two students to report back to the class. From this feedback, put the names of different part-time and summer jobs on the board. Brainstorm any more that students can add, e.g. *waiter, waitress, newspaper delivery boy/girl, baby-sitting, child minding, shop assistant*. If you wish, give students information from the Culture notes below.

🌍 CULTURE NOTES

Students might have different rules about part-time work for students in their countries. In the UK, the youngest age a child can work part-time is 13.

ⓦ EXTRA ACTIVITY

Tell students that 20% of teenagers in the UK have a Saturday job. Ask students: *Is a part-time job a good thing for students?* In pairs, students think of advantages and disadvantages of a summer or part-time job for teenagers, (e.g. advantages: gaining experience of working life, learning about money; disadvantages: bad for your studies, students should relax or do extra studies in their holidays.) Students decide if they think part-time jobs are a good or bad thing overall. Take a class vote. Multi-lingual classes could also compare their own countries.

b 💬 Ask students to look only at the headings of the job adverts and tell you what jobs they think will be advertised. Students read the adverts quickly to check their ideas. Then ask students to read the adverts more carefully to answer the questions.

Suggested answers
1 barista, assistant at Saveco
2 barista, assistant at Saveco
3 barista, assistant at Saveco
4 all
5 sales assistant at Electrostores
6 barista

📖 VOCABULARY SUPPORT

barista – someone who makes and serves coffee

conditions (B1) – hours/holidays/working environment of a job

situation vacant – a job is available

superstore – very big shop

c 💬 Students talk about the questions in pairs. Check their preferences and answers as a class. See which job is most popular and which is least popular in the class.

d ▶ 2.20 Play the recording for students to listen for general meaning and identify which jobs Penny and John are talking about and what they think about them.

Answers
1 barista, general assistant (at supermarket)
2 John recommends a barista job because you can get tips and training. A supermarket job isn't good because it's tiring with long hours.

Audioscript

PENNY Are you working this summer?

JOHN Yeah, I've got a job in a café, same as last year. How about you?

P I don't know. I usually work in a supermarket, but I don't like it much. It's so tiring and you have to start really early in the morning. I might look for a different job this summer. What's working in a café like?

J Oh, it's good. It gets quite busy, so you need to be good at working really fast. But I like that.

P Well, that's the same as a supermarket.

J Yeah. But it's good fun, too. You're working in a team and you meet lots of people. It's great.

P Is the pay good?

J Not bad and you can sometimes make quite a lot from tips.

P Really? How much do you make in tips?

J It depends. I can sometimes make £20 in one day!

P Wow! That sounds good.

J It's not always that much though. Listen, why don't you apply for a job? I'm sure they'll give you one. They're always looking for new people.

P Yeah, I don't know. I've never worked in a café. I don't know anything about it.

J Oh, that doesn't matter; they'll give you training. You don't need to know anything.

P Really?

J No, you just have to smile a lot and be nice to people. It's easy.

P Hmm, OK. What are they called?

J Cuba Coffee Company, they've got a website.

P OK thanks, I'll have a look tomorrow, update my CV and apply!

J Great – good luck!

e ▶ 2.20 Play the recording again for students to choose the correct alternatives. Check answers as a class.

Answers
1 has   2 likes   3 sometimes   4 hasn't   5 is

ⓦ EXTRA ACTIVITY

Read the conversation and stop at different points to see if students can complete the sentences: *I've got a job in a café, same … .* (as last year) *It's so tiring and you have to … .* (start really early in the morning) Students can also practise this in pairs, taking turns to read parts of sentences from the script.

2 READING

Ask students to imagine that they are applying for the barista's job. In pairs, they should think about what they would include in a job application. Put their ideas on the board and then ask them to read Penny's application and check their ideas. Go through questions 1–4 and the answers as a class.

🌐 CULTURE NOTES

Manchester is a city in north-west England with a population of half a million. The urban area surrounding Manchester has a population of 2.5 million and is the second-largest urban area in the UK. Manchester was the world's first industrial city and is home to the world's first railway station as well as the internationally famous football teams Manchester United and Manchester City. The University of Manchester is one of the largest universities in the UK with around 38,000 students.

Answers
1 F She tells them she has worked in a supermarket before.
2 F She saw it on their website.
3 F She can work in August and September.
4 T

📖 VOCABULARY SUPPORT

attach (B1) – to send something with an email

3 WRITING SKILLS Organising an email

a Ask students to read the email again and match the numbered parts with the points below. Check answers as a class. Students cover the email and tell you phrases Penny used in each section.

Answers
2 says why she's writing
6 asks for more information about the job
5 describes documents she's sending with the email
1 opens the email
7 closes the email
4 says why she wants the job and describes her experience
3 says what she's doing now and when she can work

📖 VOCABULARY SUPPORT

document (B1) – something you've written on a computer

b Read through the task and sentences with the class and ask them for the answers.

Answers
what you are doing now: 3, 4
past jobs: 2
skills: 1, 5

c Students complete the sentences. Check answers as a class.

Answers
1 for, of   2 at   3 of, of, in   4 to

👁 CAREFUL!

Point out the use of the present continuous with *write*: *I **am writing** to apply for a job.* and the present simple with *look forward to*: *I **look forward** to hearing from you.*

📖 LANGUAGE NOTES

To give a more formal style to letters and emails like these, it is better not to use contractions. The ending: *I **look** forward to hearing from you.* is a standard phrase. In formal and semi-formal letters/emails, it is always used in the simple form, e.g. ~~I am looking forward to~~ … (Correct form = *I **look** forward to …*).

d Tell students that now they need to put the paragraphs of another email in the correct order. Allow them to do this in pairs and then check answers as a class.

Answers
Dear Sir/Madam,
I am writing to apply ….
I am currently …
I would like to work for your company …
I attach a copy of my CV.
Could you send me …
I look forward to …

4 WRITING A job application

a Read through the different jobs advertised and ask which jobs students like the sound of, and why. Elicit what kind of experience would be useful for each of the jobs, e.g.

A *You like explaining things to people; you know your area well.*
B *You have done a lot of child-minding; you have lots of brothers and sisters.*
C *You've worked in a restaurant before; you've done delivery work before.*

Go through the checklist of what students need to include in their email. Give students some time to plan their email. Monitor and help where necessary. Students write their emails. They can check through their finished emails with a partner to see if there are any mistakes in grammar, organisation or vocabulary.

b In groups, students read each other's applications and decide which students should get the jobs, and why. Ask for their decisions and reasons in class feedback.

👁 CAREFUL!

training is used in the singular, e.g. ~~I need a lot of trainings for this job.~~ (Correct form = *I need a lot of **training** for this job.*)

💡 FAST FINISHERS

Fast finishers can choose another job to apply for and write that email, too. Or they could add more information to their original email, including some information that is not true. Later during feedback, the class have to guess which information is not true.

⟳ LOA TIP REVIEW AND REFLECT

Close books. In pairs, students talk about what they have learned and can remember about writing a job application. Take feedback and ask if they are more confident about writing emails like this now.

💡 EXTRA ACTIVITY

Students work in pairs or small groups to write an advert for another job. They swap adverts with another group or pair and write the application for that job.

ADDITIONAL MATERIAL

▶ Workbook 5D

UNIT 5
Review and extension

1 GRAMMAR

a Students do the task individually. Check answers as a class.

> **Answers**
> 1 c 2 b 3 a 4 a 5 c

> **EXTRA ACTIVITY**
>
> Write on the board some instructions for students during this lesson: *Don't use dictionaries during the lesson. You're allowed to work with a partner if you want to. You don't need to answer all the questions on the page very quickly.* Ask students to rewrite the sentences using modals from this unit. *(You mustn't use dictionaries. You can work with a partner. You don't have to answer the questions very quickly.)* Check answers and elicit other things you, the teacher, might say to the class during the lesson, using the same forms.

b Students match the sentences and meanings. Check answers as a class.

> **Answers**
> 1 a 2 b 3 c 4 a 5 c

c 💬 Students tell their partners which sentences are true for them. They should then make more predictions about their own future lives over the next five years. Ask students to share their predictions with the class.

> **EXTRA ACTIVITY**
>
> In pairs, ask students to think of rules for an airport. Check their ideas and put suggestions on the board. Ask the class if they think these are good rules for an airport, and why they might be used.

2 VOCABULARY

a Before looking at the task, go round the class and ask each student to name a different job. If a student can't think of one, they drop out. The last student remaining is the winner.

Students complete the sentences. Check answers as a class. Ask students to add another comment for each person, e.g. *vet: I also like science subjects.*

> **Answers**
> 1 vet 2 carer 3 journalist 4 accountant
> 5 hairdresser 6 politician 7 IT worker

b 💬 Ask students to give you their opinions. Encourage them to give reasons as far as possible.

c Students match the sentence halves individually. Check answers as a class.

> **Answers**
> 1 b 2 d 3 a 4 c 5 e

3 WORDPOWER *job* and *work*

a Write the words WORK and JOB on the board and tell students that we use the words in different ways. Ask for some examples from the class of sentences with WORK (as a noun and verb) and others with JOB. If students can't think of examples, put these sentences on the board and ask students to complete them: *My dad isn't at home, he's at ... . (work) Is your new ... easy? (job) No, it's a lot of hard ... . (work) Do you help out round the house? Yes, I do lots of ... at weekends. (jobs) I can't write my emails because my computer isn't ... . (working)*

Ask students the question. Tell them: *We can't say 'a lot of works', but we can say 'a lot of jobs'.*

> **Answers**
> 1 countable 2 uncountable

b Students do the matching task individually. Check answers as a class.

> **Answers**
> 1 b 2 d 3 c 4 a

c Students match the sentences and replies. Check answers. Ask questions and students to reply: *What do you know that isn't working at the moment?* (e.g. my laptop / the drinks machine, etc.) Ask: *What have you tried doing recently that worked?* (e.g. I've found a new shortcut on my computer. It really works!) Ask: *Have you worked out how to do anything difficult recently?* (e.g. I've worked out how to use a new app on my phone.)

> **Answers**
> 1 b 2 c 3 a

d Students complete the sentences. Check answers as a class.

> **Answers**
> 1 work 2 job 3 work 4 job
> 5 work 6 work 7 work 8 work

e Students write their own endings for the sentences.

f 💬 Students compare sentences with a partner. Ask for examples in class feedback.

▶ Photocopiable activities: Wordpower p.256

> 🔄 **LOA REVIEW YOUR PROGRESS**
>
> Students look back through the unit, think about what they've studied and decide how well they did. Students work on weak areas by using the appropriate sections of the Workbook, the Photocopiable activities and the Personalised online practice.

UNIT 6
Problems and advice

UNIT OBJECTIVES

At the end of this unit, students will be able to:
- understand texts and conversations related to problems, experiences and advice
- give advice on common problems
- describe extreme experiences
- ask for and give advice
- write a message giving advice

UNIT CONTENTS

G GRAMMAR
- Imperative; *should/shouldn't*
- Imperatives
- Uses of *to* + infinitive
- Linking: ordering ideas and giving examples

V VOCABULARY
- Verbs with dependent prepositions: *deal with sth, look at sth, concentrate on sth, listen to sth, think about sth, borrow sth from sb, spend sth on sb, pay for sth, wait for sth, ask (sb) for sth, talk to sb, think of (ideas), arrive at sth*
- -ed / -ing adjectives: *amazed, amazing, annoyed, annoying, confused, confusing, disappointed, disappointing, embarrassed, embarrassing, frightened, frightening, relaxed, relaxing, shocked, shocking, surprised, surprising, tired, tiring, exciting, excited, interesting, interested*
- Wordpower: verb + to: *bring, describe, explain, lend, pay, read, sell, write*

P PRONUNCIATION
- Sound and spelling /uː/ /ʊ/
- -ed endings
- Word stress
- Main stress

C COMMUNICATION SKILLS
- Describing extreme experiences
- Asking for and giving advice
- Showing sympathy
- Writing a message giving advice

GETTING STARTED

☼ OPTIONAL LEAD-IN
Books closed. Write the names of three extreme sports on the board, e.g. *mountain biking, skateboarding, paintball*. Ask any students who have tried these sports to describe them. Ask students if they would like to try these sports or if there are any other extreme sports they would like to try.

a Ask students to say what they can see in the picture and what they think the man is doing. Elicit or teach the term *bungee jumping*. Ask students what they know about it. Would they like to try it? Why/ why not? If you wish, give students information from the Culture notes below.

> **Answers**
> bungee jumping

🌎 CULTURE NOTES
The picture is of a bungee jumper falling from a 40-metre-high bridge in Greece. Bungee jumping is when a person jumps from a very high point, like a bridge, crane or helicopter, attached by a strong elastic cord or bungee. The person falls through the air and then gets pulled back by the elastic. It is an exciting sport and is often used to help people overcome a fear of heights. Bungee jumping is considered an extreme experience. Bungee jumping is not as dangerous as it sounds: the risk of death is about 1 in 500,000 – said to be about the same risk as driving 100 miles by car. However, it can cause a number of injuries. Some examples of more dangerous extreme sports are skydiving, base jumping (similar to skydiving, but from a 'base' such as a bridge or building), volcano surfing and highlining (walking on a high rope).

b Ask how the man is feeling. In pairs, students write down words and phrases to explain how they think the man is feeling. Monitor and support students with any vocabulary they may need. Check ideas in feedback.

c Give students a few minutes to discuss the questions in pairs. Monitor and help with vocabulary as necessary. Ask students to share their ideas with the class and extend to a wider discussion if students are interested. Tell them that some therapists or doctors help people with excessive fears (phobias) by exposing them to what they're afraid of.

> **Answers**
> common fears: spiders, snakes, heights, crowds, open spaces, closed spaces, dogs, storms, injections, flying, dirt, bacteria

☼ EXTRA ACTIVITY
Books closed. Tell students briefly about something that you are afraid of, e.g. *spiders, snakes, the dark*. Tell students why you are afraid of this thing and what happens when you are exposed to it in some way. Now ask students to stand up. They should mingle with other students and find someone who is afraid of the same thing(s) as them. Take class feedback and find out what the most common fear was. Ask for ideas on how they might deal with this fear.

6A You should have a break

- read and understand a text giving advice for problems
- use the imperative and *should / shouldn't* accurately
- pronounce long and short vowels /uː/ and /ʊ/ correctly
- use verbs with dependent prepositions
- give advice for small problems

💡 OPTIONAL LEAD-IN

Books closed. Tell students about a problem you have had in the last 24 hours, e.g. *This morning, when I wanted to leave for work, I couldn't find my house keys, the ticket machine at the station was broken, I ran out of milk at breakfast, I forgot homework, I got caught in traffic.* In pairs, students write down the number of minor problems they have had in the last 24 hours. Compare lists during feedback and find out who has dealt with the most problems. Ask what some of the problems were and write them on the board. Ask whether students solved the problems or not. If not, can other students give them advice? Don't worry if students make mistakes with *should* or expressions for giving advice at this stage.

1 READING

a 🗩 Students look at the pictures and captions that go with the article and describe the problems they show. Check they understand the captions and elicit that *addicted* means unable to stop doing something and usually something that's bad for you. Ask them why they think the people have these problems and what the consequences might be. In pairs, students talk about people they know who have any of these problems and ways to solve them. Monitor and help as necessary. Ask students to share their ideas with the class. Put their ideas about solving the problems on the board so that they can compare with the article later.

🌍 CULTURE NOTES

Addiction to your mobile phone has been given a name: *nomophobia* – the fear of being without your mobile phone. The word comes from *no* + *mobile* + *phobia* (fear). Surveys have shown that more than 50 per cent of people with mobile phones become anxious at the thought of being without their phone, losing it, running out of battery or losing signal.

b Read the title of the article and ask: *Do you think the article will be about the problems, the people who have them, or advice for solving them? Why?* (The article is about solving problems because of the phrase *deal with*.) Read through the introduction with the class. Tell students to read the pieces of advice 1–4 in the article and match them with four of the problems. They should then add the four captions as headings to the text. Check answers as a class.

Answers
1 My home is a mess.   2 I'm addicted to my mobile.
3 I can't concentrate on my work.   4 I don't sleep well.

c Encourage students to find and underline the listed words in the text as this will help them to answer the question. They complete the exercise individually then compare their ideas with a partner. Check as a class. You may wish to help students with words in the Vocabulary support box.

Answers
1 music: listen to music while you clean; 15 minutes: clean for 15 minutes only every day
2 rules: give yourself rules for using your phone; a pile: put your phones together in a pile, out of the way
3 breaks: don't work for long periods without a break; rewards: give yourself rewards when you're working
4 screens: don't use bright screens before you go to sleep; milk: drink warm milk before going to bed to help you sleep

📖 VOCABULARY SUPPORT

device (B2) – small (electronic) machine or gadget

enjoy someone's company (B2) – to like being with someone

herbal (B1) – relating to or made from a herb – a plant used in cooking

pile (B1) – a group of things together, one on top of the other

reward (B1) – something you get when you achieve something

d 🗩 Write the four problems the article talks about up on the board. In pairs, students cover the article and give each other advice about each one, using their notes to help them. Ask some of the pairs to give you some examples.

e 🗩 In pairs, students decide if they think each piece of advice is good or not, and why / why not. Can students think of more advice for people with these problems? Take feedback as a class.

💡 FAST FINISHERS

Fast finishers can discuss or write the advice they would give to people with the other problems shown in the pictures. Ask for their ideas during feedback. Put them on the board to refer to later in the lesson.

2 GRAMMAR Imperative; *should*

a Books closed. Give each student in the class a verb: *listen, try, use* or *work*. Read out the sentences from 2a. Students stand up when they hear the sentence their verb comes from. Students then complete the sentences in 2a with the correct verbs and check their answers in the article. Check answers as a class. Elicit other pieces of advice from the article using *should/shouldn't* and the imperative.

Answers
1 listen   2 try   3 work   4 use

b Match the sentences with the rules as a class.

Answers
1 infinitive
4 don't + infinitive
2 subject + should + infinitive
3 subject + shouldn't + infinitive

c ▶ Students read the information in Grammar Focus 6A on SB p.152. Play the recording where indicated and ask students to listen and repeat. Students then complete the exercises in Grammar Focus 6A on SB p.153. Check answers as a class. Tell students to go back to SB p.58.

> **Answers (Grammar Focus 6A SB p.153)**
> a 1 He should get up earlier.   2 He should have breakfast.
>   3 He should drink less coffee.   4 He shouldn't drive to work.
>   5 He shouldn't use his phone in the car.
>   6 He should stop for lunch.   7 He shouldn't eat at his desk.
>   8 He should go to bed earlier.
> b 1 Start   2 Spend   3 wake   4 Set   5 don't go
>   6 get   7 Eat   8 don't drink
> c 1 should bring   2 should I take   3 don't be late
>   4 should be   5 Don't spend   6 shouldn't check
>   7 what do you think

📖 LANGUAGE NOTES

Make sure that students do not try to use the infinitive + *to* after *should/shouldn't*. Also point out the difference between *must* and *should*: **must** is to say that something is necessary, **should** is for when we think something is a good idea.

d ⏵**2.23** **Pronunciation** Model and contrast the long and the short vowels sounds /uː/ and /ʊ/. Say /uː/, /uː/, /uː/, /uː/, /uː/; then /ʊ/, /ʊ/, /ʊ/, /ʊ/, /ʊ/, /ʊ/. Depending on the students' first language, either one sound or the other may be more difficult for them to hear/reproduce in isolation. Then play the recording and elicit from the class which vowel is long and which is short in the sentence.

> **Answers**
> shouldn't: short
> use: long

e ⏵**2.24** In pairs, students look through the sentences and practise reading them aloud to see how they think the vowel sounds are pronounced. Play the recording again. and check the answers as a class.

> **Answers**
> 1 short, long, long
> 2 short, long, long
> 3 short
> 4 long, long
> 5 short

f Model the sentences again for students to repeat.

💡 EXTRA ACTIVITY

Ask students to work in pairs to read the article again and find more examples of words with these vowel sounds. Students share their suggestions with the class.

3 VOCABULARY
Verbs with dependent prepositions

a Ask: *Who spent some money this morning? What did you spend it on?* Write the sentence on the board: *(student's name) spent some money ... a drink this morning.* Elicit the preposition *on* to complete the sentence. Tell students that the verb *spend* must always be followed by *on* when it is used with this meaning (to spend money in a particular way to buy certain things). Tell students *on* is called a dependent preposition. Remind students that when they learn a new verb, they should always record and learn it with its preposition if appropriate. Ask if students can remember any more verbs that are always followed by a preposition and put their (correct) examples on the board.

Students complete the sentences with the prepositions individually. Check answers as a class.

> **Answers**
> 1 with   2 to   3 at   4 on   5 about   6 about

b In pairs, students ask and answer the questions in 3a. Ask students to report their partner's answers to the class.

c Tell students that they are going to read more sentences that give advice about problems and also use verbs with dependent prepositions. They should match the sentence halves. Students do the task individually.

👁 CAREFUL!

Students sometimes use *to* after *arrive*; *at* is used after *arrive* or *in* for very large places, e.g. ~~I arrived to the station~~. (Correct form = *I* **arrived at** *the station at 9.00.*) ~~What time do we arrive to Paris?~~ (Correct form = *What time do we* **arrive in** *Paris?*)

> **Answers**
> 1 d   2 c   3 b   4 a   5 f   6 h   7 e   8 g

d ⏵**2.25** Play the recording for students to check their answers. Ask them which two problems in 1 the advice is for.

> **Answers**
> 1–4 I don't have enough money.   5–8 I feel tired all the time.

💡 EXTRA ACTIVITY

In pairs, students think of advice to give the people with the other problems shown in the pictures, using *should/shouldn't* and some of the verbs with dependent prepositions from 3a and 3c, e.g. *You* **shouldn't spend** *time* **on** *things that aren't necessary.* **Think about** *which of your jobs are most important and prioritise them.* *You* **should ask** *friends* **for** *their help when you need it.* Monitor and help where necessary. Ask students to share some of their ideas with the class.

e Students do the task in pairs. Alternatively, one student in the pair reads the first part of the sentence to his/her partner to elicit the second part. They then swap roles. With books closed, elicit the complete sentences from the class by just giving the verb, e.g. *borrow*. (Don't borrow money from friends because it creates problems.) Ask students if they agree with the advice given. Why / Why not?

4 SPEAKING

a ▶ Ask students if they are usually late for things or punctual / on time. Ask for some examples of times when they have been either very early or very late, and the consequences. Divide the class into pairs and assign A and B roles. Student A reads the text on SB p.130 and Student B reads the text on SB p.132. Tell them that they are going to read some different advice for people who are always late. The pairs read the text and then ask and answer questions. As you monitor, don't interrupt fluency but note any mistakes with the content of this lesson to deal with during class feedback. Ask which piece of advice is the most useful, and why. Do all the pairs agree?

b 💬 In pairs, students write advice for one of the problems in the list. Circulate and help where necessary.

c 💬 Put students in small groups to present their problems and discuss the advice. Take group feedback to see whose advice they found the most useful.

ADDITIONAL MATERIAL

▶ Workbook 6A

▶ Photocopiable activities: Grammar p.214, Vocabulary p.238, Pronunciation p.275

6B I was very frightened

At the end of this lesson, students will be able to:
- use -ed and -ing adjectives correctly
- read and understand a story about a dangerous experience
- understand a person telling the story of a dangerous experience
- use infinitives with to accurately
- talk about dangerous or frightening experiences

OPTIONAL LEAD-IN

Books closed. Ask: *How are you feeling today?* Ask students to mime their feelings, e.g. *relaxed, tired, excited.* Can other students guess how they feel? Write the adjectives on the board as students guess them.

1 VOCABULARY -ed / -ing adjectives

a In pairs, students look at the pictures on the page and say how the people might be feeling. Take feedback from the class and add new adjectives if necessary to the list on the board.

b Students read the sentences and answer the questions.

> **Answers**
> a relaxed b relaxing

c ▶ Students complete the exercises in Vocabulary Focus 6B on SB p.137. Play the recording where indicated for students to check their answers to Exercise a and b and the answers to d and e as a class to ensure that students are making the correct choices about when to use -ed and when to use -ing endings. Tell students to go back to SB p.60.

> **Answers (Vocabulary Focus 6B SB p.137)**
> a 1 a annoyed   b annoying   2 a disappointing
>   b disappointed 3 a confused b confusing   4 a tired
>   b tiring   5 a frightening b frightened   6 a amazing
>   b amazed   7 a embarrassed b embarrassing
>   8 a surprised b surprising   9 a shocking b shocked
> b amazed: 2   excited: 3   annoyed: 2   confused: 2
>   disappointed: 4   embarrassed: 3   frightened: 2
>   interested: 3   shocked: 1   surprised: 2   tired: 1
> c 1 confused/annoyed   2 frightened   3 shocked/amazed
>   4 embarrassed   5 annoyed/surprised   6 tired
>   7 disappointed   8 surprised/amazed/shocked

CAREFUL!

Make sure students use *interested / excited* to describe their feelings and not *interesting / exciting*, e.g. ~~I am interesting in this article.~~ (Correct form = *I am **interested** in this article.*) ~~He's exciting because it's his birthday.~~ (Correct form = *He's **excited** because it's his birthday.*)

EXTRA ACTIVITY

If you used the Optional lead-in at the start of the lesson, look again at the list you have on the board and see how many of the adjectives can be changed using an *-ing* ending.

2 READING AND LISTENING

a Ask students to look at the picture at the top of the page and describe what they can see. Don't worry about any unknown vocabulary at this point – just see how they can manage with the words they already know. Focus on the activity and elicit that the person is scuba diving. Discuss the questions as a class. Ask for examples of the dangers people can face when doing this activity.

b Students match the words with a–f in the pictures. Then ask them to describe the scene again using the new words.

> **Answers**
> a reef b scuba diver c air d breathe e shark
> f the surface

CULTURE NOTES

Scuba diving is a popular water sport. SCUBA stands for Self-contained Underwater Breathing Apparatus: the diver swims with all the equipment he or she needs, including a tank of compressed air, mask, diving suit and flippers. In 2014 Egyptian diver Ahmed Gabr dived to a depth of 332.25 metres and set a new world record, but recreational dives are usually between 30 and 40 metres.

The *bends* is a health problem caused when divers come up to the surface too quickly. Because of the change in pressure, they get bubbles of nitrogen in the blood, which causes severe pain.

There are over 400 known species of shark in the world, but only a few species are considered dangerous to humans. Sharks have an extremely good sense of smell and can detect their prey from miles away. Worldwide, shark populations are going down quickly, due to hunting and fishing.

c Read the title of the article with students and ask them to guess what the article might be about. Students read the article quickly to find which sentence is true and give you their answer in class feedback.

> **Answer**
> 2

d In pairs, students read the text again more carefully to answer the more detailed questions. Check answers as a class.

> **Answers**
> 1 to go scuba diving
> 2 because she didn't have any experience of diving below 30 m
> 3 She was scared because it was very deep.
> 4 because she didn't want to get 'the bends'

EXTRA ACTIVITY

Ask the class to spend another minute reading the article because you are going to give them a short memory test on some words from it. Ask students to cover the article. Read the article to the class but each time you get to an adjective, change it. Students must stop you by saying the correct adjective, e.g. *I started scuba diving because I was **bored with** sharks.* (interested in) *I learnt how to dive in England, but English waters were **confusing**.* (disappointing)

e 🗨 Ask the class to predict what happens next and put some of their ideas on the board.

f ▶2.28 Play the recording for students to hear the end of the story and then check against the ideas on the board to see if any were correct. If necessary, play Caroline's answer to the interviewer's first question and check. (The sharks made her feel relaxed.) Then play the rest to see what happened in the end. (She never goes diving now.)

Audioscript

INTERVIEWER So what did you do?

CAROLINE Well, I was really confused. I thought I was going to die. I didn't really know what to do – I just wanted to get out of the water. But then I saw a shark; then another, and another. And suddenly I stopped feeling frightened. I forgot about dying, and watched those amazing fish moving through the water. Seeing those sharks probably saved my life, because they made me feel relaxed. I started breathing better and – very slowly – I made my way to the top.

I And how did you feel when you got back to the surface?

C Well, once we were back on the fishing boat, I felt a lot of different things. I was happy to be alive, but I was also embarrassed because I used most of my air. And I was shocked and angry with my instructor for taking me down to 40 metres and then disappearing.

I And how has the whole experience changed you?

C After that experience, every time I tried to dive, I got really worried. In the end, I stopped scuba diving. I still love sharks, but I'll never go that deep again to see them.

g ▶2.28 Play the recording again for students to answer the questions. Pause in the appropriate places for students to note down their answers or tell you directly.

Answers
1 She stopped feeling frightened.
2 happy, embarrassed, shocked and angry
3 She got worried every time she dived, and stopped diving.

h 🗨 Discuss the questions as a class. Encourage students to justify their answers as far as possible.

3 GRAMMAR Uses of *to* + infinitive

a Books closed. Ask students to stand up. Read out the sentence with gaps where shown, using expressive gestures/mime to help with the meaning of missing words: *I ___ at my diving watch to see how deep we were.* Students should shout out the missing words. Allow a student who guesses correctly to sit down, then read the next sentence and repeat procedure. *I just ___ to get out of the water. / I didn't really ___ what to do. I am ___ to be alive.* When four students have been allowed to sit down, let everyone sit down and open books. Ask students to complete the sentences from the text and recording.

b ▶2.29 Play the recording to check answers.

Answers
1 to do   2 to get   3 to be   4 to see

c Match the sentences with the rules as a class.

Answers
4 to give a reason
2 after certain verbs
3 after adjectives
1 after question words

d ▶2.28 **Pronunciation** Ask students to predict which part of the infinitive is stressed and then play the sentences for them to check. When you have established that it is the verb which is stressed, point out the pronunciation of unstressed *to* (tə). Give students the opportunity to practise this by modelling the sentences for them to repeat after you.

Answers
the verb

e Students look back at the article on page 60 and underline other examples for the uses of the infinitive + *to*.

Answers
To give a reason: my instructor suggested a trip to the Shaab Shagra reef <u>to swim</u> with the sharks there.
After certain verbs: I decided <u>to try</u> the Red Sea in Egypt. I just wanted <u>to go</u> back up to the surface fast.
After adjectives: I was shocked <u>to see</u> we were at 40 metres!
After question words: I learnt how <u>to dive</u> in England.

f ▶ Students read the information in Grammar Focus 6B on SB p.152. Play the recording where indicated and ask students to listen and repeat. Students then complete the exercises in Grammar Focus 6B on SB p.153. Check answers as a class. Tell students to go back to SB p.61.

Answers (Grammar Focus 6B SB p.153)
a 1e   2f   3b   4c   5a   6g   7d
b 1 what to do   2 how to use   3 where to go   4 how to get
   5 what to watch   6 which to buy   7 who to speak to
c 1 to read   2 to eat   3 not to receive   4 not to listen
   5 not to break   6 to wear   7 to arrive   8 not to go

👁 **CAREFUL!**

Students often confuse *to* + infinitive or *-ing*, e.g. ~~I just wanted getting out of the water~~. (Correct form = *I just wanted **to get out** of the water.*)

---

g Put the class into pairs. Give students some time to read through the pairs of topics and to choose one from each to talk about. They should think about what they are going to say and try to use the infinitive + *to* in these talks. They can make brief notes if they want to.

h 🗨 Students talk about their different topics in pairs. During the activity, students should try to talk continuously for a short time about the topic. If they are hesitant, their partner can help by asking more specific questions. Monitor and point out errors for students to self-correct. When they have finished, ask students to tell the class examples from their discussions/talks and vote on the most interesting experience.

💡 **FAST FINISHERS**

Fast finishers can go back and talk about the topics they did not choose previously.

---

4 LISTENING

a Tell students that they are going to hear about another experience. Ask them to look at the picture and tell you what they can see. Read through the words in the box and elicit or explain the meanings (see Vocabulary support below). Ask students to say what they think happened and put their ideas on the board.

b ▶️ **2.31** Play the recording for students to see if their predictions were similar to what happened or not.

c ▶️ **2.31** Read through the interviewer's questions with the class. Play the recording again for students to make notes on Aaron's answers to the interviewer's questions. Pause after each answer is given in the recording to give students time to make notes. Don't check notes/answers fully at this point, but make sure students have been able to note something for each question. If necessary, play the recording again.

Suggested notes/answers

1 parachute jumping – was pulled along under plane
2 not experienced – went first
3 wind pushed me to side – stuck against plane – hanging from parachute
4 frightened – could die
5 pilot slowed – others (Monica, Ben) freed me
6 no

d 💬 Students use their notes and take turns to retell Aaron's story in pairs. Before the start, elicit ideas for an appropriate sentence or sentences to start the story – e.g. *This happened when I was …, One day, I was ...* and write them on the board. You could also give some phrases for linking ideas together and moving on, e.g. *after that, then, suddenly,* etc. Tell partners to help each other if necessary.

5 SPEAKING

a 💬 Read through the question and the prompts with the class. Be prepared to give an example of your own if students can't think of anything. Tell them your experience (or a friend's) and encourage them to tell the class about something similar. Put students in pairs to think of ideas.

b Read through the questions with students and tell them that they can use their answers to help them describe the experience. Students prepare notes individually about one experience they talked about.

🔄 LOA TIP MONITORING

• When monitoring this activity, your role is to act as a resource: showing that you are available for students to ask questions, and also to prompt and encourage students who are finding it difficult to come up with ideas.

• Make sure that you monitor the stronger students too in order to help them extend their ideas and answers.

c 💬 In new pairs, students use their notes to help them tell their partners about the experience. Monitor and encourage where necessary. Note down mistakes to deal with later. Also listen for interesting stories. During class feedback, ask some students to retell their stories for the class. Vote on the most interesting story.

💡 EXTRA ACTIVITY

Put students into small groups. Give each person in the group a sheet of paper. At the top of the sheet, they should write: *A frightening experience.* Students should write the first sentence of a new story about a frightening experience. Then they pass the paper on to the student on their right. That student then writes the second sentence of the story and passes the paper on. Students read the different stories aloud to their groups. They choose one to read to the class.

ADDITIONAL MATERIAL

▶ Workbook 6B

▶ Photocopiable activities: Grammar p.215, Vocabulary p.239

6C Everyday English
What do you think I should do?

At the end of this lesson, students will be able to:
- understand a conversation involving asking for and giving advice
- use phrases to show sympathy
- use word stress in sentences correctly
- ask for and give advice

ⓦ OPTIONAL LEAD-IN

Books closed. Elicit or input *need / give advice*. In pairs, students brainstorm people or places you can go to if you need advice, e.g. parent, friend, partner, colleague, professional advisor, the Internet, advice phone line, advice service (often a charity). If students are happy to discuss the topic further, they can discuss the following questions in pairs: *If you have a problem, do you prefer to deal with it yourself or do you ask for advice?* Open books.

1 LISTENING

a ⓠ Put the words *money*, *work*, *relationships*, *car*, *clothes*, *health* on the board and ask students to tell their partner who they talk to when they have problems with these things. Take feedback as a class, e.g. *If I have a problem with a girlfriend/boyfriend, I talk to my best friend about it. If I have a problem at work, I might talk to my colleague.*

b ⓠ Ask students what they remember about Annie and Rachel from the video in 5C. (Annie was upset, Rachel decided to visit her.). Then ask them to look at the picture and say what they can see. Read the instructions and the question and ask for students' guesses about what the bad news might be. Put their ideas on the board.

c ▶ 2.32 Play Part 1 of the video or play the audio recording for students to check their ideas.

> **Answers**
> Annie is going to lose her job.

Video/audioscript (Part 1)

RACHEL Hi, Annie.
ANNIE Oh, hi Rachel. Thanks for coming.
R That's OK. Here, I brought you some flowers.
A Oh, thank you. They're lovely.
R Oh, that's OK. What's happened?
A It's work. My boss asked to see me this afternoon. And she told me I'm going to lose my job.

R Oh, how awful! I'm really sorry to hear that. Did she say why?
A She just said the company's having problems.
R That's terrible.
A Yeah ... anyway, I'll make some tea.

2 CONVERSATION SKILLS
Showing sympathy

a ▶ 2.32 Ask students what Rachel said when Annie told her the bad news. Put any phrases they can remember on the board. Then read through the phrases and see if any of these are on the board. Do students want to change add to the list? Play the recording again to check which phrases Rachel used. Tell students that when we use phrases like this, we are showing *sympathy*. Give or elicit the verb: *sympathise (to understand and care about someone's problems)* and adjective: *sympathetic (showing that you understand and care about someone's problems)*. Ask when students last sympathised with someone. If appropriate, ask why.

> **Answers**
> 1, 2, 4

---

b Discuss the question as a class. Ask: *Are 'terrible' and 'awful' words that you use in very bad situations or not very serious situations?* Elicit that they are words used in very bad situations and therefore the other expressions are probably used for less serious problems.

> **Answers**
> a less serious situation

↻ LOA TIP CONCEPT CHECKING

Give examples of some situations and check which phrase in each pair could be used with them, e.g. *My friend has got a bad cold. That's terrible.* (no) / *That's a shame.* (yes)

Someone stole my friend's car: How awful. (yes) / *What a pity.* (no)

My friend missed a good programme on TV: I'm sorry to hear that. (no) / *What a pity.* (yes)

c ▶ 2.33 Play the recording for students to listen and repeat the phrases.

d In pairs, students take turns to give bad news and respond with an appropriate phrase. Ask for examples in class feedback. (The second and fifth situations are probably the most serious.)

3 LISTENING

a ▶ 2.34 Ask students in pairs to think about what advice they would give to Annie about the situation. Put their ideas on the board. Play Part 2 of the video or play the audio recording for them to see what advice Rachel gives about the different points. Check answers as a class.

> **Answers**
> 1 Speak to her because maybe there'll be other jobs there.
> 2 Speak to them and ask them what they're doing.
> 3 Mark works in marketing; Annie and Rachel will speak to him about jobs.
> 4 It could be a good thing – the chance to do something new.

Video/audioscript

RACHEL So, what happened when you talked to your boss? Did you ask when you're going to lose your job? Or if it's completely certain?
ANNIE No, I didn't say much. I was too upset.
R Of course you were.
A I didn't really ask anything. What do you think I should do?
R OK, well, I'd get all the details first.
A Right.
R So I think you should speak to your boss again. Maybe there'll be other jobs there.

A I don't think that's a good idea. I don't know if I want to stay. Lots of people are unhappy there. And I don't think there are any other jobs anyway.
R OK, but I think it's a good idea to ask. You don't know what she'll say.
A I suppose so.
R And why don't you speak to some of the people you work with? Ask them what they're doing?
A Mmm, I don't think I should do that. My boss told me not to talk to anyone else. Because other

people are going to lose their jobs too.

R Mmm. You work in marketing, right?

A Yeah.

R Well, Mark works in marketing, too. His company's often looking for new people.

A Really? Do you think I should speak to him about it?

R Definitely. I'll speak to him, too.

A OK. Great.

R And I wouldn't worry too much – changing jobs could be a good thing. You'll have the chance to do something new.

A Yeah – you're right.

b ▶ 2.34 Play the recording again for students to say which advice Annie disagrees with, and why.

> **Answers**
> 2 She doesn't want to stay; she doesn't think there are any other jobs.
> 3 Her boss told her not to talk to anyone else.

c 💬 Discuss the questions as a class. Encourage students to give reasons for their opinions.

4 PRONUNCIATION Main stress

a ▶ 2.35 Ask students to look at the sentences and remember or guess which word in each sentence carried the most stress. Play the recording for students to underline the words.

> **Answers**
> 1 when   2 other   3 marketing   4 Mark   5 good

b Discuss the question as a class.

> **Answers**
> 3

c ▶ 2.35 Play the sentences again for students to listen and repeat. Remind students that stress can show which words in a sentence are important and helps the speaker get their message across and clarify meaning.

d 💬 In pairs, students practise the dialogues, making sure that they stress the underlined words.

> 💡 **FAST FINISHERS**
>
> Fast finishers can practise dialogues 1 and 4 again but this time substitute different details, e.g. 1 *A: We're going to see a film at 4pm. B: I know. But I don't know which film!* or 4 *A: I don't think it's a good time to buy a house. B: I'm not sure. I think there are lots of cheap houses now.*

5 USEFUL LANGUAGE

Asking for and giving advice

a ▶ 2.36 Tell students about a small problem you have and ask for their advice, e.g. *I can't send emails from my tablet/smartphone. What do you think I should do? Do you think I should … ?* Then ask students to remember what you said to ask for advice and what phrases they used to give advice. Put the phrases on the board. Students listen and complete the phrases. Are the phrases the same as those on the board?

> **Answers**
> 1 What   2 think   3 I'd   4 should   5 good idea   6 wouldn't

b Ask if students can remember how Annie responded to Rachel's advice. Look at the phrases in the exercise and ask which show that Annie doesn't agree. Model the phrases for students to repeat.

> **Answers**
> 1, 3

c ▶ 2.37 Play the recording for students to listen and repeat.

d Students complete the dialogue individually. Check answers as a class. In pairs, students practise reading the dialogue. Monitor and draw students' attention to any sentence stress problems. Nominate a pair to read the dialogue for the class.

> **Answers**
> 1 think   2 hear   3 worry   4 hope   5 should
> 6 Ask   7 that   8 idea   9 right

6 LISTENING

a ▶ 2.38 Tell the class that Annie is worried about Leo and elicit what she might be worried about. Play Part 3 of the video or play the audio recording for students to check their ideas and answer the questions. Check answers as a class.

> **Answers**
> 1 Annie thinks Leo might not be interested in her any more.
> 2 He's probably busy.

> **Video/audioscript**
>
> **RACHEL** Is that everything, Annie? Has something else happened?
>
> **ANNIE** No, it's stupid …
>
> **R** Come on – you can tell me.
>
> **A** Well, it's just – I called Leo to talk about my job but he didn't answer the phone. I sent him a text but he still hasn't replied.
>
> **R** Don't worry. I'm sure he'll call you soon.
>
> **A** Yeah. Maybe he's not interested in me any more. Oh, I don't know.
>
> **R** Oh, you shouldn't worry. He's probably just busy at work!
>
> **A** You're right, you're right.
>
> **R** Everything will be fine. Call Mark tomorrow. I'll tell him what's happened when he comes home tonight.
>
> **A** OK.
>
> **R** And I'm sure Leo will ring you soon!
>
> **A** Thanks, Rachel … for your help.
>
> **R** That's OK! That's what friends are for!

b 💬 Discuss the questions as a class. You can extend this by asking a further question: *Do you think friends should always tell each other the truth? Why / Why not?*

> 💡 **EXTRA ACTIVITY**
>
> Ask students what phrases the speakers said after these words:
> *No, it's stupid.* [Come on – you can tell me.]
> *You're right, you're right.* [Everything will be fine.]
> *Thanks, Rachel … for your help.* [That's OK! That's what friends are for!]

7 SPEAKING

a Divide students into pairs and assign A and B roles. Students choose a problem from the cards, look at the questions and make some notes on what they want to say. Circulate and help with vocabulary as necessary.

b 💬 Student As tell their partners about their problems and Student Bs give advice. Monitor and correct students' pronunciation as appropriate and listen for correct use of the target language from this lesson. Check that students show sympathy when giving advice. Note any interesting points and discuss them with the class at this stage.

c 💬 Students swap roles and repeat the activity.

> ### 💡 FAST FINISHERS
> Fast finishers can describe the other two problems and ask for and give advice.

d 💬 Take feedback and ask for examples of advice students gave for the different problems. Check whether they thought their partner's advice was useful, and why / why not? Also ask if their partners showed sympathy and what phrases they used to do this.

> ### 💡 EXTRA ACTIVITY
> Divide the class into small groups. Students think of a problem they have had recently and write it down on a piece of paper with their name. (The problems can be imaginary.) Take the problems and give them to students in the other groups. They then write advice for the problems on the same paper. Return the problems and advice to the original students. Take feedback and ask students to read out the best advice to the class.

ADDITIONAL MATERIAL

▶ Workbook 6C

▶ Photocopiable activities: Pronunciation p.276

▶ Unit Progress Test

▶ Personalised online practice

6D Skills for Writing
I often worry about tests and exams

At the end of this lesson, students will be able to:
- understand people talking about problems with work and study
- read and understand emails asking for and giving advice
- order ideas and give examples in written work
- write a message giving advice

☺ OPTIONAL LEAD-IN
Books closed. Write on the board: *doing exams, doing a presentation, learning English*. Ask students if they worry about these things. Students discuss in pairs. Encourage students to justify their answers as far as possible. Students share their ideas with the class. If anyone does not worry about these things, ask them to explain why not.

1 LISTENING AND SPEAKING

a Check that students understand the meaning of *presentation* (a short talk about a topic). Ask: *Where do people give presentations?* Elicit: *work, university, school*. Tell students to work in pairs. Students read the list of activities and decide if they are work or study related. Check answers.

> **Answers**
> 1 B 2 B 3 W 4 W 5 B 6 S

b 💬 Elicit ideas about what problems people might have with the different situations. Encourage students to justify their answers by giving reasons for their ideas.

c ▶2.39 Tell students that they are going to listen to some people talking about problems with work and study. Read the first question with the class and emphasise that they are listening for the main problem. Then play the recording for them to complete the first row of the table. Pause after each speaker to give them time to note down their answers. Check answers as a class.

> **Answers**
>
> | | Chloe | Bob | Marisa |
> |---|---|---|---|
> | What's the main problem? | (new) job | learning Polish | exams/not sleeping |

d ▶2.39 Read through the last two questions. Play the recording again for students to complete the rest of the table. You may need to pause the recording after the information has been given. Students complete the exercise individually before comparing notes with a partner. Check answers as a class.

> **Answers**
>
> | Chloe | Bob | Marisa |
> |---|---|---|
> | old boss left (a family problem) and gave her the job; hasn't had any training and doesn't feel ready to be a manager and make decisions | not very good at languages at school not the kind of person who can just listen to a language and learn it | exams/not sleeping didn't do very well in exams last year and was disappointed with results |
> | stressed | excited at first, confused now | really tired |
> | do something relaxing after work, like go for a walk on the beach | 'Don't worry – when we go to Poland you'll really start to learn.' | take more breaks |

Audioscript
CHLOE The problem is that I think about my job even in my free time. I'm so busy during the day I don't have time to think and then when I get home I spend all my time thinking and worrying. You see, my old boss had to leave in a hurry – a family problem – and they gave me his job. But I haven't had any training and I don't feel ready to be a manager and make decisions. Friends tell me I should do something relaxing after work, like go for a walk on the beach. But I still can't stop thinking about meetings I've been to or meetings I will have to go to the next day. And all the reports I have to write! There's so much to do and I just feel so stressed.

BOB At first I was excited about doing something new. I've never done anything like this before. Well, I'm sorry to say I've stopped feeling excited, I'm just generally confused. I don't feel like I'm improving at all. The thing is my wife is Polish and I want to be able to speak to people in her family when we go to Poland. I wasn't very good at languages at school. I mean, I learnt a little bit of French and that was quite hard. But I find Polish really difficult. My wife says 'don't worry – when we go to Poland you'll really start to learn'. But, to be honest, I'm not so sure. I don't think I'm the kind of person who can just listen to a language and learn it.

MARISA I feel really tired, because I haven't been sleeping well for the past week. I stay up late most nights and drink coffee to stay awake. I read the books on my booklist and the notes I've made during the year again and again. And I test myself all the time to help me remember information. My parents tell me I should take more breaks. They forget that I didn't do very well in my exams last year and I was very disappointed with my results. I really want to do well this year, so I need to do all this work. So, I think I'm just going to have to continue like this until I'm sure that I can remember everything.

☺ EXTRA ACTIVITY
Ask students some more detailed questions: *What do Chloe and Marisa do because of the problems?* (Chloe doesn't have time to think / spends time thinking and worrying.) (Marisa doesn't sleep well / stays up late / drinks coffee / tests herself.) *Why is Bob learning Polish?* (His wife is Polish and he wants to be able to talk to her friends and family in Poland.)

e 💬 Students think of advice to give the three people. Go through the example with the class and elicit some more advice before they start. Conduct feedback and ask for ideas from students. Which advice does the class think is best?

2 READING

a Ask students if they often post comments on forums or websites and if so, which kind. Tell them that an English teacher called Eliza encourages her students to write messages asking for and giving advice on a *wiki*. Elicit that a *wiki* is a web application that allows people to contribute to the content at any time. Ask: *Is this a good idea? Why / Why not?* Ask students to read Sevim's message and say what he wants help with.

> **Answers**
> speaking (English)

b In pairs, students talk about what they would advise Sevim to do. Ask students to share their ideas with the class and put some ideas on the board. Students read Eliza's reply to compare with their ideas. Ask how many suggestions she makes and what the suggestions are.

> **Answers**
> 5 1 don't worry about making mistakes;   2 remember that the only way to learn to speak a second language is by speaking;   3 try practising new vocabulary and grammar we learn in class by repeating it at home;   4 think about extra speaking practice outside the classroom;   5 practise speaking online

c Ask students to read Eliza's reply again and do the task. Check answers as a class.

> **Answers**
> 1 F Eliza felt embarrassed about speaking Turkish.
> 2 F Eliza thinks language learners shouldn't worry about making mistakes.
> 3 T
> 4 F The chat groups at the study centre are free to join.
> 5 T

3 WRITING SKILLS

Linking: ordering ideas and giving examples

a Ask students to look at, but not read, Eliza's reply again and say how the reply is organised. (It's divided into clear paragraphs. The first is a short introduction, then there are three paragraphs that are quite long – these have information in them. The last is very short and finishes off the message politely.) Ask students to cover the message. Put the first words of each paragraph on the board to show how the information is introduced and elicit what follows.

Thanks ... (for the message)
I remember ... (personal information about learning)
First of all ... (initial advice)
Next ... (continued advice)
I hope ... (general wish)

Point out the importance of ordering information clearly so that the reader knows what to expect. Look at the underlined example with students and ask them to underline three more words used in the reply to order the information. Check answers as a class.

> **Answers**
> Secondly, Next, Finally

b Students read the advice on studying vocabulary and insert the words and phrases. Check answers as a class.

> **Answers**
> First of all, Secondly, Next, Finally

c Give instructions for the next activity. Say: *First of all, I want you to read the text in 2b again. Secondly, I want you to notice the expressions that Eliza uses to give examples. Next, I'd like you to cover the text. Finally, I'd like you to complete the sentences.* Ask students if they can repeat the instructions you have just given them. Then they do the task. Check answers as a class.

> **Answers**
> 1 For example   2 such as   3 For instance

d Students match the sentence halves. Check answers and ask how useful this advice is, and why.

> **Answers**
> 1 c   2 a   3 b

 EXTRA ACTIVITY

Put students in pairs. Tell them to think of something they know how to do that their partner doesn't, e.g. a hobby, a sport or a game. They then tell their partner about this using the phrases for ordering and giving some examples, e.g. *I play a word game called Scrabble. First of all, you choose seven letters. Next, ...* Take feedback and ask for instructions and examples from some of the talks.

4 WRITING

a Tell students that Sevim also wants to improve her writing and they are going to write a message giving some advice to her. In pairs, students read the ideas and add three more to the list. Check ideas in feedback and write some of them on the board.

b Students work in pairs to write the message to Sevim. Remind them to plan the message by grouping their ideas into paragraphs and to use phrases from this lesson to order ideas and give examples.

c Put students into groups of four to compare their messages and decide if the ideas are ordered clearly and whether there are examples. Take feedback and ask some students from the different groups to read out their messages for the class. Discuss whose advice is the best.

 LOA TIP REVIEW AND REFLECT

Close books. In pairs, students discuss which new linking phrases they learnt in this lesson or which linking phrases they will try to use again in their writing.

 FAST FINISHERS

Fast finishers can write a message to give advice about improving a student's listening skills. Check these during feedback, too.

ADDITIONAL MATERIAL

▶ Workbook 6D

UNIT 6
Review and extension

1 GRAMMAR

a Students complete the exchanges. Check answers as a class.

> **Answers**
> 1 shouldn't 2 should 3 shouldn't
> 4 should 5 should 6 should

b Students change the advice in 1a into imperatives. Look at the example together. Check answers as a class.

> **Answers**
> 1 Don't drink coffee in the afternoon.
> 2 Tidy it at the end of every day.
> 3 Don't watch more than two hours a day.
> 4 Try to walk for ten minutes every day.
> 5 Don't buy so many clothes.
> 6 Join a club or a sports team.

c Students do the exercise individually. Before they begin, remind them to think about whether the verb should be the infinitive with or without *to*. Check answers as a class.

> **Answers**
> 1 do 2 to find 3 to go 4 learn 5 to meet 6 to drive

d 💬 Students ask and answer the questions in 1c in pairs.

2 VOCABULARY

a Students complete the sentences with the correct forms of the verbs. Check answers together.

> **Answers**
> 1 concentrate 2 arrive 3 asked
> 4 borrowed 5 spent 6 deal

b Students choose the correct alternatives to complete the sentences. Check answers as a class.

> **Answers**
> 1 relaxed 2 shocking 3 tiring
> 4 amazing 5 annoying 6 embarrassed

> 💡 **EXTRA ACTIVITY**
>
> Ask students to change the sentences to use the other form of the adjective.   (1 My holiday was very relaxing.   2 I was shocked by the news.   3 I was tired after a long day.   4 I was amazed by the things I did and saw in the city.   5 I'm annoyed when I have to queue.   6 It was embarrassing when I fell over.)

c 💬 Ask students to tell the class when the situations in 2b have been true for them.

3 WORDPOWER verb + *to*

a Books closed. Write these verbs on the board: *lend, explain, pay, write, sell, read, describe, bring*. Ask students to think about what they all have in common. Tell them that if they think of a couple of examples using the verbs, it will help them to answer the question. (They can all be followed by object + *to*, e.g. *I lent my dictionary to my friend.*) Students match sentences 1–2 with the replies a–b. Check answers as a class.

> **Answers**
> 1 b 2 a

b Elicit which verb + *to* combination is related to giving and which to communicating. Check answers as a class.

> **Answers**
> giving: lend to
> communicating: explain to

c Tell students to add the verb + *to* combinations to the table. Check answers together.

> **Answers**
> communicating: explain to / write to / read to / describe to
> giving: lend to / pay to / sell to / bring to

d Students answer the question together.

> **Answer**
> 2

e Ask students to put *to* in the correct place in the sentences. Students compare answers with a partner.

> **Answers**
> 1 They sold their house to some friends …
> 2 When Steve described his holiday to his friends …
> 3 Please bring something to drink to the party.
> 4 I read the joke to my friend …
> 5 Tara lent an umbrella to her neighbour …
> 6 Did you write the letter to the bank …
> 7 I explained the problem to the company …
> 8 I paid the money for my course to the school …

f Students write five sentences about their lives using the verbs from the table. Students compare answers in pairs. Ask students to share some of their sentences with the class.

> 💡 **EXTRA ACTIVITY**
>
> In pairs, students write three more sentences using the verbs from the table and then jumble the words. Students give their sentences to another pair who put them in order.

> 💡 **EXTRA ACTIVITY**
>
> Ask students what advice they can give other students after studying this unit. List the ideas on the board, e.g. *You should always learn a verb with its preposition. You should use the infinitive + to after certain adjectives.*

▶ Photocopiable activities: Wordpower p.257

> **LOA REVIEW YOUR PROGRESS**
>
> Students look back through the unit, think about what they've studied and decide how well they did. Students work on weak areas by using the appropriate sections of the Workbook, the Photocopiable activities and the Personalised online practice.

UNIT 7

Changes

UNIT OBJECTIVES

At the end of this unit, students will be able to:
- understand texts and conversations about changes in their lives
- talk about life-changing events
- describe health and lifestyle changes
- talk to the doctor
- write a blog about an achievement

UNIT CONTENTS

G GRAMMAR
- Comparatives and superlatives
- *used to/didn't used to*
- Linking: ordering events

V VOCABULARY
- *get* collocations: *get together* (= start a relationship), *get engaged, get divorced, get on well (with sb), get to know, get a place at, get in touch (with sb), get an offer, get paid, get rich, get a job, get ill, get better* (= recover)
- Health collocations: *eat a healthy diet, be overweight, keep in shape, (go/be) on (a) diet, lose weight, get fit, put on weight, be a regular smoker, give up (smoking), have an allergy*
- Medical problems and treatments: *backache, a cold, a temperature, a broken leg, a stomachache, the flu, a rash, get a prescription from a doctor, take pills or other medicine, have some tests, go to the hospital, go to the chemists, have an operation, put on cream*
- Wordpower: different meanings of *change*: *change* (noun): 1 = coins; 2 *the right / wrong change* = money a shop assistant returns to you; 3 *for a change* = for a new experience. *change* (verb): 1 *change* (on transport) = get off one and get on another; 2 *change* sth (in a shop) = return something and get a new one; 3 *change* sb's *mind* = make an alternative decision / opinion; 4 *change* (money) = exchange money for different notes or coins; 5 *change into* (an outfit) = put on different clothes

P PRONUNCIATION
- Sound and spelling: *used to/ didn't used to*
- Tones for asking questions

C COMMUNICATION SKILLS
- Talking about life-changing events
- Describing health and lifestyle changes
- Talking to the doctor
- Writing a blog about an achievement

GETTING STARTED

💡 OPTIONAL LEAD-IN

Books closed. Ask students to work in pairs and write down five things that children can learn from their grandparents and five things grandparents can learn from their grandchildren. Circulate and encourage with prompts and questions. Take feedback and see how many pairs had the same ideas. Ask the class which is the most important thing grandparents and children can learn from each other.

a 💬 Ask students to look at the picture and say what they can see. Give students one minute to think about their answers to the questions before talking about the picture as a class. If students don't know where the old man and the girl are, say: *Look at what they are sitting on. Where do you often see chairs like this?* (on the beach) If you wish, give students information from the Culture notes below.

🌍 CULTURE NOTES

The British seaside is a popular place for families to spend holidays in the summer or to visit for the weekend. The seaside became very popular in Victorian times (the second half of the nineteenth century) when the railways were built and families could travel from big cities to towns on the coast like Blackpool and Brighton. Many traditions that are related to days out at the seaside started then and continue today, such as:
- sitting on deckchairs on the beach, as in the picture
- eating ice cream or fish and chips
- paddling in the sea (walking in the water up to your ankles)
- building sandcastles
- riding donkeys (animals similar to horses, but smaller and with long ears) along the sand
- walking along a pier (a structure built over and into the water)

b Students discuss the questions in pairs. Monitor and support students with any vocabulary they may need. You could introduce the expression *to be proud of* (B1 – feel pleased and satisfied about something you have or have done). Students share their ideas with the class.

💡 EXTRA ACTIVITY

In pairs, students make a list of ways in which the seaside in their countries has changed in the last 50 years (or since their grandparents were young). Ask students to share their ideas with the class and ask: *Do you think these changes have been good? Why / Why not?*

7A I'm the happiest I've ever been

At the end of this lesson, students will be able to:

- use comparatives and superlatives correctly
- read and understand texts about famous people's life-changing events
- understand people talking about their achievements
- use collocations with *get*
- discuss their own and other people's life-changing events

💡 OPTIONAL LEAD-IN

Books closed. Play a guessing game: *Who am I?* Choose a famous person from SB pp.68–69 that students will know. Students guess the person by asking yes/no questions, e.g. *Are you a man? Yes, I am. Are you young? No, I'm not.* Monitor and suggest questions if necessary. Encourage students to use short answers (e.g. *No, I'm not. Yes, I have*) rather than saying just yes or no. Students play the game in pairs selecting famous people of their choice.

1 READING

a 💬 In pairs, students look at the pictures and discuss who the people are, why they're famous and what they know about them. In feedback, ask for as much information about each person as students can give you. If you wish, give students information from the Culture notes below.

🌍 CULTURE NOTES

Nelson Mandela was a world-famous political leader who was imprisoned for many years in South Africa but led the fight against black/white separation and became South Africa's first black leader. He died in 2013.

Brad Pitt is a famous American actor who is married to actress Angelina Jolie. Together they have adopted several children from different countries.

Jane Goodall is a British scientist who specialises in monkeys and apes. She spent 45 years studying wild chimps in Tanzania and is considered the world's greatest expert on them.

Beyoncé is a famous singer. She used to belong to a group called Destiny's Child but left to become a solo singer. She is married to the rapper Jay-Z and their daughter, Blue Ivy Carter, was born in January 2012. Two days later Jay-Z released a song called *Glory* on which the baby's cries can be heard.

Rupert Grint is an actor who played one of the main characters in the *Harry Potter* film series. He was only 11 when he starred in the first film.

PSY is the Korean musician who performed the pop hit *Gangnam Style*. The video, released July 2012, became the most popular video ever on YouTube. People all over the world copied the singer's dance moves and posted their own videos to YouTube. As of August 2014, the video is one of only two videos to exceed 1 billion views and the only video ever to exceed 2 billion views.

b Students read the quotes and match the people to the topics 1–6. Check answers as a class and ask students to tell you what words or pieces of text helped them choose the answer. Alternatively, with books closed, put the names of the people on the board. Read the quotes one by one for students to tell you which person they think you're quoting, and why.

Answers
1 b d   2 c   3 f   4 e   5 a

📖 VOCABULARY SUPPORT

chimps – kind of clever monkey (short for *chimpanzee*)
give birth – have a child
a handful of (B2) – a small number of
independent (B1) – not taking/needing help or money from other people
informed (C1) – having knowledge/information about something
motherhood – being a mother
power (of doing something) – ability or skill
primatologist – a scientist who studies primates, e.g. monkeys and chimps
self-control (C2) – the ability to control your emotions, especially when you are angry or upset

c Ask the class to read the quotes again and tell the class how the events changed each person's life. You may wish to help students with words in the Vocabulary support box at this point. Ask them to find out and tell the class.

Answers
Nelson Mandela – reading the book – helped him to improve his thinking and self-control and also improved his relationships
Brad Pitt – having a big family – he only has a few close friends now but he's happier than he's ever been
Jane Goodall – getting older – difficult to climb the mountain to see the chimps
Beyoncé – motherhood – braver, more secure, sees things differently
Rupert Grint – making films – grew up more quickly, but less independent
PSY – becoming a celebrity – has made parents proud, especially his father

💡 EXTRA ACTIVITY

In pairs, students think of other famous people. Ask if they know of any interesting life-changing events that they experienced. Students share their information with the class.

d Discuss which quote students liked most, and why.

2 GRAMMAR
Comparatives and superlatives

a Books closed. Write the following adjectives and adverb on the board: *brave, happy, quickly*. Read out the quotes from the texts below, missing out the comparative or superlative forms. Stop after each quote and ask students if they can complete the quote using the adjective/adverb in the correct form. Can they remember who said each quote? *You grow up … than other teenagers.* (more quickly; Rupert Grint) *I'm the … I've ever been.* (happiest; Brad Pitt) *I'm a lot … and more secure.* (braver; Beyoncé). Ask students to complete the table with the correct comparative and superlative forms. Check answers as a class.

Answers

1 braver 2 the biggest 3 the happiest
4 more famous 5 the most famous 6 more quickly

b In pairs, students read the quote from Jane Goodall again to answer the question. Check answers together as a class.

Answers

1 b 2 a

c ▶ Students read the information in Grammar Focus 7A on SB p.154. Play the recording where indicated and ask students to listen and repeat. Students then complete the exercises in Grammar Focus 7A on SB p.155. Tell them that there is more than one possible answer in some cases. Check answers as a class, making sure students are using the definite article in the superlative. Tell students to go back to SB p.68.

Answers (Grammar Focus 7A SB p.155)

a 1 better: the best
  2 fitter: the fittest
  3 further than: the furthest
  4 friendlier than: the most friendly: the friendliest
  5 drives more carefully than Alex: drives the most carefully
  6 Eric works faster than Alex: works the fastest
  7 Eric is more fashionable than Alex: is the most fashionable
b 1 c 2 a 3 c
c 1 worse than I do / worse than me 2 the best movie
  3 as friendly as 4 the fastest 5 as cold as
  6 the most beautiful 7 less 8 as well as

d Students complete the sentences individually and compare with a partner before you check answers as a class.

e Play the recording for students to listen and check their answers. Then play the recording again for students to listen and repeat, paying attention to the sentence stress and the weak form of *than*. Point out the weak form of *than* /ðən/ and model this clearly.

Answers

1 better 2 most confident 3 more slowly
4 busy 5 largest 6 tidier 7 harder 8 better

⊙ **CAREFUL!**

A common mistake students make when forming comparatives is that they use *that* instead of *than*. ~~The city was bigger that I thought~~. (Correct form = *The city was bigger* **than** *I thought*.)

f 💬 In pairs, students discuss whether the sentences in 2d are true for them or not. Look at the examples with the class and encourage them to give similar examples. Ask students to share some examples with the class. Be prepared to give your own examples, too.

⊙ **CAREFUL!**

• Monitor to check students are not using a double comparative form, e.g. ~~He's more older than me~~. (Correct form = *He's* **older** *than me*.) ~~I think the countryside is more better than the city~~. (Correct form = *I think the countryside is* **better** *than the city*.)

• Also make sure students include *the* with superlative forms, e.g. ~~It was happiest day of my life~~ (Correct form = *It was* **the** *happiest day of my life*.)

③ LISTENING

a 💬 Ask students to cover the page. Write the anagrams on the board: IDVRLAO / LTRESYEVS NOTSLELA. Tell students that one is a famous footballer and one is a famous actor. How quickly can they find the names? Students uncover the page to check the answers. (Rivaldo and Sylvester Stallone) Ask students what they know about these two people and put their ideas on the board. Then ask them to read the biographies to check if their information is included. In pairs, students discuss how they think these people's lives were different before they became famous. Ask students to share their ideas with the class. Put some ideas on the board.

b ▶2.42 Tell students that they are going to hear more about the two people. Play the recording and students listen to see which of the ideas/information on the board is mentioned. You can pause after each section and ask students to summarise points they heard. Take feedback as a class. Elicit any new facts that the students learned about each person.

Audioscript

The subject of this week's one-minute inspiration is Brazilian footballer, Rivaldo. Rivaldo came from a very poor family. They didn't have enough to eat and so, growing up, he had some serious health problems. As a teenager, he spent his days on the beach, he sold souvenirs to tourists in the morning and played football in the evening.

Rivaldo got on very well with his father, who was sure that one of his three sons would become a professional footballer. But when Rivaldo was only 16, his father died in a car crash. Rivaldo wanted to give up football and didn't play for a month, but his mother told him he should make his father's dream come true.

Later that year, he got an offer to join Paulistano, a small football club in his home town. He didn't get paid much and he sometimes had to walk 15 kilometres to go to training, because he did not have enough money for the bus. He worked very hard at the club but, because of his health problems, his coach did not believe he could get fit enough to be a star.

But Rivaldo proved the coach wrong and became one of the best footballers in the world. He played for Brazil, and helped them to win the 2002 World Cup. He also played for Barcelona, who paid a 26-million-dollar transfer fee for him. Rivaldo dedicates his success to his father who he says was always with him.

One-minute inspiration this week comes straight from Hollywood. Sylvester Stallone grew up in a poor neighbourhood in New York. He had a difficult childhood and, after his parents got divorced, he got into trouble at school. When he left school, he managed to get a degree before looking for work in films.

But Stallone couldn't get regular work as an actor. In 1975, he was at his poorest. He had got married and his wife was going to have a baby. He got a job at a cinema and another at a zoo to pay the bills, but he didn't even have enough money to feed his dog. Instead, he sold his dog for $50 to a man outside a shop and walked away crying.

Two weeks later, he was watching a boxing match and he had an idea. In just 20 hours he wrote the script for *Rocky*. Then he tried to sell it. Amazingly, he got an offer of $325,000 from a film studio but he said no! He told the studio he wanted to play Rocky in the movie, but the studio didn't think the film would be successful if he did.

In the end, the studio agreed to let him star, but they only paid him $35,000 for the script. As soon as he got paid, Stallone went to see the man he sold his dog to and gave him $3,000 to get it back!

The rest is movie history. *Rocky* was a big hit. It was nominated for ten Oscars and Stallone got rich and became a star.

c ▶️**2.42** Read through the sentences with the class. Look at the first sentence and then play the first part of the recording which gives the information. Stop and check the answer. Then play the whole recording for students to listen and answer the remaining questions. They complete the exercise individually and then check their answers in pairs before you take feedback as a class.

> **Answers**
> 1 B – Rivaldo – health; Stallone – divorced parents, trouble at school
> 2 B – Rivaldo – didn't have enough to eat; Stallone – not enough money to feed dog
> 3 S – his dog
> 4 R – his father died
> 5 R – had to walk to work
> 6 B – Rivaldo – his coach did not believe he could get fit enough to be a star; Stallone – studio didn't think he'd be a success
> 7 S – when he appeared in his own film
> 8 B – The answer is debatable. Rivaldo wanted to succeed for his father, not the money. Stallone paid $3,000 to get his dog back.

d 💬 Students discuss the questions in pairs. Monitor and help with vocabulary as necessary. Take feedback as a class and ask for the names of any other examples of famous people who started life poor and became rich and famous.

4 VOCABULARY *get* collocations

a ▶️**2.44** Tell the class that the verb *get* is one of the most common in the English language and has many different possible meanings. In pairs, students complete the sentences with the different phrases containing *get* before listening to check their answers.

> **Answers**
> 1 get a job   2 got rich   3 got an offer   4 get paid

b ▶️**2.45** Students complete the exercises in Vocabulary Focus 7A on SB p.138. Play the recording where indicated for students to check their answers to Exercises a and c. Monitor the pairwork in Exercise d and point out any errors for students to self-correct. Check the definitions for Exercise e as a class or ask students to use dictionaries. Tell students to go back to SB p.69.

Answers (Vocabulary Focus 7A SB p.138)

a 1 get a job   2 get an offer   3 get ill   4 get better
   5 get on well   6 get paid

c 1 got a place   2 got to know   3 get in touch   4 got together
   5 got engaged   6 got divorced

d get divorced – when husband and wife separate; get on well – have a good relationship (with); get together – start a relationship (with); get engaged – when two people agree to marry; get in touch – make contact (with); get to know – find out more about a person after meeting them

5 SPEAKING

a Explain that students are going to write a timeline about the important events in a person's life. Ask them to think of someone they know well. Elicit some examples of people they could think about, e.g. a very good friend, a member of their family, someone they know about at work or school, a famous person. Look at the timeline in the book with the class. Give some examples to clarify if necessary, e.g. *When he was five, my brother started learning to play the piano. So, on the timeline I write 'play the piano'.* Give students some time to choose their person and complete the timeline. Encourage them to use expressions with *get* where possible. Monitor and give help where necessary.

b 💬 In pairs, students tell their partner about the person they chose. Monitor and make notes of any common errors to deal with during feedback. Take class feedback and ask for interesting comments and information students learned.

c 💬 Students ask and answer the questions in pairs. Go through the prompts in the box to give them some ideas before they start the activity. Monitor and listen to the discussions. Take feedback as a class and see if students agree with each other's decisions for question 2.

LOA TIP REVIEW AND REFLECT

• Have a brief class discussion and ask students what new information they found out in this lesson. What was the most interesting thing? e.g. *I learned some interesting information about Rivaldo.*

• Ask what students learned in English that they didn't know at the beginning of the lesson, e.g. *I learned some new meanings of the verb **get**.*

 FAST FINISHERS

Fast finishers should think of some other important life-changing events and discuss their impact on people's future lives, e.g. get promotion at work, win a lot of money, move to a new country. Discuss their ideas as part of the class feedback.

ADDITIONAL MATERIAL

▶ Workbook 7A

▶ Photocopiable activities: Grammar p.216, Vocabulary p.240

7B I didn't use to eat healthy food

At the end of this lesson, students will be able to:

- read and understand an article about health in the past
- use *used to* to talk about the past
- use health collocations
- pronounce /juːs tə/ correctly
- talk about things that have changed in their lives

⦿ OPTIONAL LEAD-IN

Books closed. Put students into pairs. Ask them to list five kinds of food that are healthy and five kinds of food that are unhealthy. Ask the class for their suggestions and list them on the board. See if students agree on what is healthy and unhealthy, and why. Ask students if any of these kinds of food can be considered both healthy and unhealthy and why. (e.g. milk and milk products – healthy because good for bones and teeth, unhealthy because can contain a lot of fat.) Agree on a separate list with students.

1 READING

a 💬 Ask students to look at the photos and say how we can tell they are from the 1950s. You may want to point out that the photos are from the USA. Encourage students to think about fashion (e.g. *The people are smart / smartly dressed. She's wearing a turtle neck top / high heels. He's wearing a suit and tie.*) and lifestyle (e.g. *She's a housewife. Home / Family life is very important. The family are going shopping.*) Ask students to think about family life and how it has changed, e.g. *Women did more housework. Children played outside more.* If you wish, give students information from the Culture notes below.

🌍 CULTURE NOTES

Many new houses were built in suburbs around American cities in the 1950s, giving young couples the chance to own their own homes. Television was new and advertising created a consumer culture for the first time. People were encouraged to buy new household appliances. Many women stayed at home while their husbands went out to work. In 1950, around 29% of the workforce were women compared with around 50% in 2012.

b 💬 Read the title of the article and the introduction with the class. If you wish, give students information from the Culture notes below. Ask students if they think we are any healthier today than 70 years ago. Put their ideas and reasons on the board. Leave these on the board to refer back to later. Students read the sentences and decide whether they think they are true or false and then compare answers with a partner.

🌍 CULTURE NOTES

Mad Men is a popular American TV series about a group of people who work in an advertising agency. It is set in the 1960s and has won many awards.

James Dean was an American actor who played Jim Stark in the iconic film *Rebel Without A Cause* (1955). He died in a car accident that year at the age of 24.

Audrey Hepburn (1929–1993) was a British actress who starred in a number of famous Hollywood films in the 1950s, such as *Roman Holiday*, *Funny Face* and *Sabrina*. One of her most popular roles was Holly Golightly in *Breakfast at Tiffany's* (1961).

c Students read the article quickly to check their answers from 1b. Ask them to correct the false statements (2 they spent less time; 3 they lived shorter lives).

Answers
1 T   2 F   3 F   4 T

📖 VOCABULARY SUPPORT

calorie – unit of heat energy used as a measurement of the amount of energy that food provides

common (B1) – usual

housework (B1) – the work of keeping a house clean and tidy

illegal (B2) – not allowed by law

recommend (B2) – advise

d For the more detailed reading task, look through the questions first with the class before they start the activity. You may also wish to help students with words in the Vocabulary support box. Ask students to read the article again to answer the questions individually and then check with a partner.

Answers
1 two glasses of milk a day
2 They say we should eat more vegetables and less meat, cheese and butter.
3 31 years
4 by doing housework
5 Inventions have made our lives easier.
6 when they were seriously ill
7 allergies to food, diabetes
8 They didn't know how dangerous it was.
9 in public places like offices, schools and restaurants

e 💬 Refer to the ideas that you wrote on the board earlier in the lesson about being healthier now or in the 1950s. Discuss the question as a class. Have students' ideas changed?

2 VOCABULARY Health collocations

a In pairs, students discuss which of the highlighted phrases are good or bad for our health. You might want to teach the expression *underweight* as the opposite of *overweight* and the construction *to be allergic to*. (Point out the difference in word stress between **allergy** and **allergic**). Check answers as a class.

Answers
1 good – eat a healthy diet (eat healthy food), (be) on a diet (eat healthy food), keep in shape (stay fit), lose weight (become less fat), get fit (become fit), give up smoking (stop smoking)
2 bad – put on weight (become fatter), have allergies (have a medical problem which starts because of a particular substance), be overweight (be heavier than the correct weight for your height), (be) regular smokers
Note that losing weight and dieting can also be bad for health if done to excess.

b ▶ **2.46** Students complete the sentences with the correct phrases from the article individually and then compare answers with a partner. Play the recording to check.

> **Answers**
> 1 lost weight   2 give up   3 overweight   4 put on weight
> 5 keep in shape   6 (regular) smoker   7 eat a healthy diet
> 8 on a diet   9 have; allergies

c 💬 Students discuss the questions in small groups. If you have a multilingual group, try to put groups of different nationalities together to encourage a good discussion. If your class is monolingual, students should discuss this country and possibly make comments about any other country they know something about. Monitor.

d Put students into pairs. They read through and underline words and phrases related to health and add them to the good/bad lists. Check their ideas as a class.

> **Answers**
> 1 good – get enough exercise (do enough physical activity), hospital operations (when a special doctor cuts your body to make you better), go to the doctor (see the doctor when you're ill)
> 2 bad – seriously ill (badly ill), health problems, have diabetes (have an illness where you have to be careful about the amount of sugar you eat)

💡 **EXTRA ACTIVITY**

Write these discussion points on the board:

1 *Would you like to live to 100?*

2 *Who should be responsible for helping children to be healthier – the government or families? Why?*

3 *Do you think the 1950s were a good time to live? Why / Why not?*

Put students into small groups to discuss the points and then bring their ideas into a full class discussion.

---

3 GRAMMAR *used to*

a Write the example sentences from 3a on the board but leave out the verbs, e.g. *Smoking ... very popular.* Students try to gap-fill the sentences in pairs before opening their books to check their answers. Ask the class whether these things are the same or different now? Explain that we use the construction *used to* to talk about things that happened in the past but don't happen now.

> **Answer**
> different

b Ask students to complete the rules for the formation of *used to* and check answers with the class. Ask: *What is the difference between the meanings of past simple and used to?* Remind them that *used to* means that something was different in the past; the past simple doesn't tell us about a difference, just that something happened.

> **Answers**
> used to   didn't use to

 LOA TIP CONCEPT CHECKING

Write the sentence on the board: *I used to play tennis.* Then ask: *Do I play now?* (no) *Do you know when I stopped playing tennis?* (no) *Did I play tennis regularly?* (yes) *Has my sport or interest changed?* (yes) Encourage students to write similar concept questions for their partners. Monitor and help, then ask students to share some examples with the class.

👁 **CAREFUL!**

The verb following *used to* is not in the past simple form, e.g. ~~They used to lived in the city~~. (Correct form =*They **used to live** in the city*.)

---

c ▶ **2.47** **Pronunciation** Play the recording for the class to compare the pronunciation. Ask them to focus on the pronunciation /juːstə/ and to say whether the pronunciation changes in negative sentences.

> **Answer**
> no

d ▶ **2.48** Students read the information in Grammar Focus 7B on SB p.154. Play the recording where indicated and ask students to listen and repeat. Focus on the tip about *used to* and the past simple. Students then complete the exercises in Grammar Focus 7B on SB p.155. Check answers as a class. Tell students to go back to SB p.71.

> **Answers (Grammar Focus 7B SB p.155)**
> a 1 People didn't use to work in IT.
>   2 People used to work on farms.
>   3 People didn't use to live as long as they do now.
>   4 Children's education didn't use to be free.
>   5 Cities used to be smaller than today.
>   6 People used to travel by horse.
>   7 People didn't use to use microwaves to cook food.
> b 1 used to eat
>   2 used to write
>   3 did you use to live
>   4 used to be
>   5 Did your parents use to read
>   6 didn't use to like
>   7 Did you use to be
>   8 didn't use to be
> c 1 Mary used to have long hair.
>   2 Jeff used to be thinner.
>   3 Jeff didn't use to wear suits.
>   4 They didn't use to look after the garden.
>   5 They used to ride a motorbike.
>   6 They didn't use to own a car.

e Students complete the sentences with the correct form of *used to* individually and then compare their answers with a partner. Check answers as a class.

> **Answers**
> 1 used to walk   2 used to think   3 didn't use to suffer
> 4 didn't use to eat   5 used to spend   6 used to be

f 💬 Read through the question and the examples. Students change the sentences so that they are true for them and compare their answers with a partner. Encourage them to respond as in the example in the book.

4 SPEAKING

▶ Divide the class into pairs. Ask them to turn to SB p.129. Students do the quiz individually and then compare and discuss their answers with their partner. Ask pairs to report their results to the rest of the class and see how healthy the class is.

ADDITIONAL MATERIAL

▶ Workbook 7B

▶ Photocopiable activities: Grammar p.217, Vocabulary p.241, Pronunciation p.277

7C Everyday English
It hurts all the time

At the end of this lesson, students will be able to:

- use phrases to describe symptoms of an illness
- use phrases to show concern and relief
- understand a doctor's questions
- understand a conversation with a doctor about an illness
- use tones for asking questions
- explain a health problem and give advice

⊙ OPTIONAL LEAD-IN

Books closed. Put students into pairs. Tell students that they are going to play a game – one pair against another pair. They have to think of parts of the body. One pair must say how many parts they think they can name. The other pair either agrees to name more or asks the original pair to name them. If a pair manages to name the number they say, they win the game. If not, the other pair wins. Take feedback and list as many parts of the body on the board as students can name.

1 VOCABULARY At the doctor's

a 💬 Before looking at the task, elicit the names of different sorts of health problems, e.g. *headache*, *a cold* and put them on the board. Read through the words in the box with the class, eliciting or explaining the meanings and giving examples as necessary. Ask students which of these they have had in the last six months. Write the following words on the board, too, and ask students in pairs to teach each other the meaning of any words they know: *symptom* (signs of an illness), *treatment* (what to do to get better), *prescription* (an official note the doctor gives you for tablets or medicine). Confirm or correct the meanings as a class. Elicit examples of symptoms and treatments for the health problems on the board.

b 💬 Go through the list and check that students understand the different options. Note that *pill* is a synonym for *tablet*. In pairs, students tell each other what people in their country/countries do when they have these health problems. If you have a multilingual group, put different nationalities together if possible. Circulate and listen to the discussions. Take feedback and compare different treatments in different countries.

📖 LANGUAGE NOTES

We can use 's to talk about shops, e.g. *the baker's*. We can also say *the doctor's* and *the dentist's*.

2 LISTENING

a ▶️ **2.49** Ask students to describe what's happening in the picture and guess why Leo has gone to the doctor's. Play Part 1 of the video or play the audio recording for students to answer the two questions. Check answers as a class.

> **Answers**
> 1 His back hurts. / He has backache.
> 2 three/four days ago

Video/audioscript (Part 1)

RECEPTIONIST Mr Seymour?
LEO Yes.
R Dr Evans is ready to see you.
L Thank you.
DOCTOR Come in . . . Please, take a seat. So, what's the problem?
L Well, my back hurts. It's very painful. And I can't get to sleep.
D I see. And when did this problem start?
L About three or four days ago.
D Hmm. And where does it hurt? Could you show me?
L Here. This area.

D Can I have a look?
L Sure.
D So, does it hurt here? And here?
L Yes. Not so much.
D And here?
L Yes!
D And here?
L Yes!
D OK. You can sit down again.

VIDEO ONLY

D Have you had any accidents recently?
L No.
D And you haven't hurt your back in any way? Playing sport, that kind of thing.
L No, no. Nothing.
D OK.
L I'm quite worried about it. It hurts all the time – when I walk, when I sit down. I've spent the last few days in bed. And I feel exhausted.
D OK. Well, I don't think it's anything to worry about.
L Phew. That's good to hear.

⊙ EXTRA ACTIVITY

Ask students to remember the questions the doctor asked Leo: *What's the problem? When did this problem start? Where does it hurt? Could you show me? Can I have a look? Have you had any accidents recently?*

b ▶️ **2.49** Play Part 1 of the video again or play the audio recording for students to note other information the doctor finds out from Leo. Pause after the first piece of additional information (*It's very painful.*) and elicit the information. Then play the whole recording and let students discuss their answers in pairs before taking feedback as a class.

> **Answers**
> it's very painful
> he can't get to sleep
> where it hurts
> he hasn't had an accident
> he hasn't hurt it playing sport
> it hurts all the time
> he's spent the last few days in bed
> he feels exhausted

c 💬 Students discuss the questions in pairs. Monitor and help with vocabulary as necessary. Take feedback and ask students if their partner is healthy or not. Put suggested treatments on the board.

> **Suggested answers**
> 2 an accident/playing sport/sitting at a computer for too long
> 3 rest/heat/ice/visit a physiotherapist or chiropractor/stop sport

3 USEFUL LANGUAGE
Describing symptoms

a ⏵**2.50** Ask students if they can remember what Leo said about his bad back. Then ask them to use the words in the box to complete the sentences. Check answers by playing the recording.

> **Answers**
> 1 back   2 painful   3 get to sleep   4 all the time   5 exhausted

b ⏵**2.50** Play the recording again for students to listen and repeat.

c Read through the words in the box and explain *itchy*. Say and mime: *I have a rash and it's itchy*. Individually, students make eight more phrases using the phrases and words in the box with 1–5 from 3a. Ask students to share some examples with the class.

> **Suggested answers**
> 1 My arm hurts.   2 It's very itchy/uncomfortable.   3 I can't run/concentrate.   4 It hurts when I walk.   5 I feel terrible/sick.

d 💬 In pairs, students discuss when people get the symptoms in 3a and 3c. Tell them that they must give at least one detail about each symptom, as in the examples in the book. Ask students to share examples and details with the class.

4 LISTENING

a ⏵**2.51** Ask students to predict what treatments the doctor will suggest for Leo. Read through the list of possibilities with the class and ask them to put a tick or a cross against the different options. Play Part 2 of the video or play the audio recording for students to check their ideas.

> **Video/audioscript (Part 2)**
> **DOCTOR** OK. Well, I don't think it's anything to worry about.
> **LEO** Phew. That's good to hear.
> **D** But you shouldn't stay in bed – that's not going to help.
> **L** Oh dear. Really?
> **D** No – try to do all the things you normally do, but gently. Don't stay in the same position for a long time. Maybe go for a short walk.
> **L** OK. That sounds fine.
> **D** Do you do any exercise?
> **L** Well, I usually go to the gym, but I haven't been recently. I'm very busy at work at the moment and I just don't have the time.
> **D** I see. And do you spend a lot of time sitting down at work?
> **L** Yes, I do. I work in an office, so I spend a lot of time at my computer.
> **D** Right. It's really important, if you spend a lot of time at a desk in an office, to take regular breaks. And you'll need to start doing exercise again. When you feel ready.
> **L** OK. Breaks, exercise. Fine.
> **D** Are you taking anything for the pain?
> **L** Yes, I've taken some aspirin.
> **D** OK, good. And do you have any allergies?
> **L** No, I don't think so.
> **D** Good. Well, I'll give you a prescription for something a bit stronger.
> **L** OK, that's great.
> **D** Take these, but only when you need them, after food. No more than two every four hours.
> **L** Right.
> **D** And don't take any more than eight in a 24-hour period.
> **L** Fine.
> **D** And come back again in a week's time if it doesn't improve. I expect you'll feel a lot better by then anyway.
> **L** OK, thanks very much.
> **D** I really don't think it's anything to worry about.
> **L** What a relief! Bye.
> **D** Bye now.

> **Answers**
> 1 ✗   2 ✓   3 ✗   4 ✓   5 ✓

📖 VOCABULARY SUPPORT
aspirin (B1) – a pill/tablet you can take for pain
expect (B1) – to think/believe something will happen
period (B1) – length of time
position (B1) – place
prescription (B1) – a piece of paper from a doctor with some medicine you can get from the chemist's
relief (B2) – a good feeling when you thought something bad was going to happen

b ⏵**2.51** Before you play Part 2 of the video or play the audio recording again, you may wish to help students with the words in the Vocabulary support box. Give the class a minute to read through the true/false statements, then play the recording for them to listen and complete the exercise. In feedback, ask students to correct the false sentences.

> **Answers**
> 1 F (Leo is busy, so he hasn't been recently.)
> 2 T
> 3 F (Leo is taking some aspirin.)
> 4 F (Leo should take the pills only when he needs them.)
> 5 F (Leo shouldn't take more than eight pills in a day.)
> 6 T

💡 EXTRA ACTIVITY
Read some phrases from the dialogue for students to complete, e.g. *I don't think it's anything to ...* (worry about). *But you shouldn't ...* (stay in bed). *Don't stay in the same ...* (position for a long time). *Do you spend a lot of time ...* (sitting down at work)? *You'll need to start ...* (doing exercise again).

5 CONVERSATION SKILLS
Showing concern and relief

a Write the words *concern* (when you are worried about something) and *relief* (when you were worried about something and now it's OK) on the board and explain the meanings. Ask students for examples of situations when someone might experience these different feelings, e.g. you are worried you have a serious illness, the doctor tells you you are fine. Ask for recent examples of occasions when students have been concerned or relieved in the last few days. Students read the conversations and choose option 1 or 2.

> **Answers**
> 1 Phew. That's good to hear. What a relief!   2 Oh dear. Really?

b ⏵**2.52** Ask if students can remember how Leo pronounced *Phew*. Play the recording and ask students to repeat the phrase. Model the pronunciation for students to practise.

> **Answer**
> /fjuː/

c 💬 In pairs, students take turns to give information and respond appropriately. Choose one or two students to repeat for the class.

> **Answers**
> respond showing concern: A2, B1
> respond showing relief: A1, A3; B2, B3

6 USEFUL LANGUAGE Doctors' questions

a **2.53** Ask students to match the questions and answers individually and then to compare with a partner. Play the recording for them to check.

> **Answers**
> 1 g 2 a 3 b 4 e 5 f 6 c 7 d

b **2.54** Tell students that they are going to hear some more doctors' questions. They need to listen to each question and choose the best answer. Play the recording, pausing between questions to allow students time to think and choose an answer. Check answers as a class.

> **Answers**
> 1 a 2 b 3 a 4 b 5 a 6 b 7 b

Audioscript

1 Are you taking anything for the pain?
2 Can I have a look?
3 Do you do any exercise?
4 Do you have any allergies?
5 So, what's the problem?
6 When did this problem start?
7 Where does it hurt?

> **⚬ EXTRA ACTIVITY**
>
> In pairs, students write three more questions and answers between a doctor and a patient. They should then swap partners and give their new partner the answers for him/her to guess the questions. Monitor and point out errors for students to self-correct.

7 PRONUNCIATION
Tones for asking questions

a **2.55** Ask students to listen to the questions and note whether they go up or down at the end. Play the recording and then check answers.

> **Answers**
> 1, 2, 3 down; 4 up

b Students use their answers to 7a to complete the rule. Check as a class.

> **Answers**
> down; up

c Students practise by repeating the sentences.

> **↻ LOA TIP DRILLING**
>
> • Intonation patterns are difficult for students to learn. It is therefore important to give them as much opportunity to repeat correct patterns as possible.
>
> • Model the sentences yourself and ask the class to repeat together. You can vary this by making it a transformation drill: Say: *When did this problem start?* Then extend by giving prompts, e.g. *When did this problem/illness/ symptom/cold start? Where does it hurt/the bus go/your friend live/your dad work? Can I have a look/a cup of coffee/ a break/ a sandwich?*

8 SPEAKING

a 💬 Set up the speaking activity by putting students into pairs and choosing Students A and B. They take it in turns to be the patient and the doctor. The patient chooses a health problem and describes it to the doctor. The doctor must give advice. Monitor and correct students' pronunciation as appropriate and listen for correct usage of the target language from this lesson. Note any errors to deal with later in feedback.

b 💬 Students swap roles and act out the conversation again. This time Student A chooses a health problem.

> **⚬ FAST FINISHERS**
>
> Fast finishers can repeat the role play with another problem.

> **⚬ EXTRA ACTIVITY**
>
> Organise a rotating role play. Divide the class into patients and doctors. Give the patients some time to think of a new health problem. The doctors can brainstorm a range of kinds of advice to give patients. Students can work in pairs at this stage. Then ask the patients to patients sit on one side of a row of desks and the doctors sit on the other. Individually, the patients talk about their problem with their doctor and get advice. After a short time say: *All change!* and the patients move to the next doctor (the doctors stay where they are). The patients take the same problem to this new doctor and see what advice he/she gives. This continues until all the patients have seen several doctors. Take feedback to compare the different advice given. Have a vote on the best advice given for each problem.

> **ADDITIONAL MATERIAL**
>
> ▶ Workbook 7C
> ▶ Photocopiable activities: Pronunciation p.278
> ▶ Unit Progress Test
> ▶ Personalised online practice

7D Skills for Writing
After that, I decided to make a change

At the end of this lesson, students will be able to:

- understand people talking about changes they have made to their lives
- read and understand a text about a person who made a big change to his life
- use linking words and phrases to order events
- write an article for a blog
- talk about changes

💡 OPTIONAL LEAD-IN

Books closed. Write on the board: *later starting time, smaller classes, longer holidays, less homework, no uniforms, mobile phones allowed.* Elicit from students what these are (a list of changes children often request at school). In pairs or small groups, students say whether they agree with these changes, and why or why not. Monitor and listen to the discussions. Take feedback and compare views across the groups.

1 LISTENING AND SPEAKING

a 💬 Tell students about one change you would like to make in your life, e.g. *I live a long way from the school and I'd like to live nearer so that I don't have to spend so much time travelling.* Ask for examples from the class of one change they would like to make, and why. Ask what other kinds of things people sometimes want to change about themselves and put students' ideas on the board, e.g. *diet, bad habits, job, appearance.* Then compare the ideas in the book with the list on the board. Students suggest about one example for each kind of thing.

b ▶ 2.56 Tell students that they are going to listen to three people who have tried to make some changes in their lives. They should first listen to tell you what the changes were and whether they were successful or not. You may need to play the recording twice and/or pause after each speaker to get feedback. Check answers as a class.

> **Suggested answers**
> Jeff: stop spending so much money; yes   Silvia: do exercise / get fit; yes   Lucas: get/stay in touch with old friends; yes

Audioscript

PRESENTER My name's Jenny Jackson and today we're talking about how to change your life. In the studio with us today, we have three people who have made changes in their lives: Jeff, Silvia, and Lucas. Hi guys, welcome to the show.

GUESTS Hi

P So first of all, Jeff. Can you tell us what your problem was? Why did you need to make a change?

JEFF Well ... one day I suddenly realised that if I wanted to buy a new car or my own apartment, I needed to save some money.

P I see. Why didn't you have any money?

J Well. I used to spend a lot of money on things that I didn't really need. So, for example, I used to go out for dinner at a restaurant at least four times a week. I loved getting new things – like, you know, the latest phone, clothes ... One weekend I sat down and added up the money I had spent in a month ... I was shocked.

P I can imagine. So what have you changed?

J Well, now I eat at home most of the time. And I think 'do I need this?' before I buy something new. I've saved almost £5,000. I'm really pleased with myself.

P Cool. That's great. Next up we have Silvia. Silvia, tell us about your change.

SILVIA Hi, Jenny. Well, my story began when one day I had to walk up a hill. When I got to the top, it was difficult to breathe. I was so unfit! The problem is I really hate most kinds of exercise – you know, running, cycling, swimming ... Then this friend said, 'Why don't you come to a dance class?' The first time was so hard, I had to sit down and rest. But ... but I enjoyed it ... So I went back again ... and again. And very slowly I'm getting fitter and losing weight. I climbed that hill again last week – easy!

P That's great, Silvia. I really need to get fit myself! Anyhow, last up we have Lucas. Hi, Lucas.

LUCAS Hi.

P So, Lucas, what did you need to change?

L Well, about six months ago I realised that I had a very small number of friends. But if I thought back ... well, seven, eight years ago I used to have a lot of friends. And I asked myself, why is that? Well, some of them got married and had children and their lives sort of went in another direction. And a couple of friends got job offers overseas. But when I thought about it a bit more, well, another answer was I'm a bit lazy – lazy about keeping in touch with people.

P I see. So what did you do about it?

L So, I started to get in touch with my old friends. And then, after that, I had to stay in contact and arrange to meet them again. Now I find that people call me! And the great thing is we still enjoy the things that we used to.

P Well, thanks so much, guys, for sharing your story with us. It just shows that we can all make that change if we decide to do it!

📖 VOCABULARY SUPPORT

add up (B1) – put two numbers together

overseas (B2) –in another country/abroad

c ▶ 2.56 Read through the questions in the table. You may wish to help students with the words in the Vocabulary support box at this point. Then play the recording again for students to note down the answers. Play the recording all the way through and ask students to complete the table afterwards. If students need more support, you could pause the recording after each person has finished speaking to give students time to make their notes. Check answers as a class. Ask: *Are you similar to any of the three people? How?*

> **Answers**
> 1 Jeff – needed to save some money ; Silvia – was unfit; Lucas – didn't have many friends
> 2 Jeff – spent too much, going out for dinner, buying clothes and the latest phone; Silvia – didn't do enough exercise; Lucas – friends got married or moved overseas, he was lazy about keeping in touch
> 3 Jeff – eats at home, asks himself if needs something before buying it; Silvia – started going to a dance class; Lucas – started to get in touch with old friends
> 4 Jeff – saved almost £5,000; Silvia – fitter, lost weight; Lucas – now people call him

d Ask students to think of a specific change they would like to make in their own lives. They make notes in answer to the questions. If necessary, give an example of your own, saying why you want to make the change, how you could make the change and what you hope the result will be.

e 💬 In pairs, students tell their partners about the thing they would like to change. Encourage them to interact and ask each other for more details, as in the example in the book. Take feedback and ask for examples from their conversations.

2 READING

a Ask students to look at the pictures of Simon with his blog and guess the answers to the questions. They read the article quickly to check their ideas. Check answers as a class.

> **Answers**
> 1 very unfit   2 running
> 3 He can now run a long way easily and he has lost weight.

b Students read the blog again to do the true/false task, correcting the false sentences. Check answers as a class.

> **Answers**
> 2 F – He started afterwards.
> 5 F – He missed it, for two weeks after he'd fallen over.

3 WRITING SKILLS
Linking: ordering events

a Tell students that when we write, we need to pay attention to putting events in a logical order because this helps the reader to follow the story. Read through the first few events from Simon's story from the board using just the word *then*, e.g. *Simon was overweight. Then he gave up smoking. Then he started to put on weight. Then he decided to do more exercise.* Elicit what was wrong with your story (the use of *then* is repetitive and boring). Explain that we can and should use a variety of expressions to order events and indicate the beginning and the end of a story. Read through the words and phrases in the box and ask students to complete the rules. Check answers as a class.

> **Answers**
> to begin with; at first
> After that; after a while; soon; then
> In the end

b Answer the questions as a class.

> **Answers**
> 1 soon   2 after a while

c Ask students to complete the text with the correct words and phrases. Check answers as a class.

> **Suggested answers**
> 1 To begin with / At first
> 2 After that / Then
> 3 Soon
> 4 After a while
> 5 After that / Then
> 6 In the end

 **EXTRA ACTIVITY**

In pairs, students note down five or six facts from Simon's story, e.g. 1 *couldn't run so went for walks* 2 *started to run and walk* 3 *fell over and stopped for two weeks* 4 *started again and didn't need to walk* 5 *ran 10 km with no problems*. Books closed. In pairs, students retell the story, using their notes and the linkers from this lesson. Monitor and point out errors for students to self-correct. Choose a pair to retell the story for the class.

d Ask students to look at the picture and predict what change the young woman made to her life, and why. After they have read through the text to check their

predictions, take feedback by eliciting a brief summary of the story in a couple of sentences. Then ask students to complete the text with the words and phrases in the box. Check answers as a class.

> **Answers**
> 1 At first / To begin with   2 Soon / After that / Then / After a while
> 3 At first / To begin with   4 Soon / After that / Then / After a while
> 5 After a while / Soon   6 In the end

 FAST FINISHERS

Fast finishers can retell the swimming story in their own words, using correct linkers.

4 WRITING

a Explain that students are going to write an article for the blog about a difficult change that they have made or something difficult they have tried to do. They can use one of the topics or their own idea. Give them a short time to think of an idea. If this is difficult, they can discuss it with a partner to give each other ideas.

b Students use the questions to help them plan their article. Remind them that it is always important to make notes about what they want to say before writing as it helps to organise their ideas logically and group them into paragraphs. Monitor and help with vocabulary as necessary.

> **LOA TIP MONITORING**
>
> • Students need a lot of support when preparing for a writing activity. Monitor and encourage students to note down ideas in groups. This will help them plan their paragraphs.
>
> • In a class with students of different abilities, you will need to adapt your monitoring to take into account the different levels of ability. Some will need help with ideas whereas others will need language advice. Take this opportunity to correct students' language in a more private situation. Remember that some students lose confidence if they are corrected a lot in front of the group.

c Give students time to write their articles. Remind them to use the time linkers to show the order of events. Monitor carefully offering help and suggestions as necessary but also encouraging self-correction. If time is short, this activity can be done for homework.

 FAST FINISHERS

Fast finishers can tell each other about another change that they have made, with details.

d In pairs, students read each other's articles. Take feedback and ask some students to read their articles to the class. Award one point for each time linker they used. Find out which students have the most points.

ADDITIONAL MATERIAL

▶ Workbook 7D

UNIT 7
Review and extension

1 GRAMMAR

a Students do the task individually. Check answers as a class.

> **Answers**
> 1 faster than, the fastest
> 2 more expensive than, the most expensive
> 3 better than, the best
> 4 less popular than, the least popular

> **EXTRA ACTIVITY**
> Put students into small groups and give them a minute to write down as many adjectives as they can. Then ask them to play the comparative/superlative game: the groups take turns to say an adjective. The first person from another group to give the comparative and superlative for that adjective gains a point for their group. If they can make a sentence using them both correctly, they gain an extra point. The group with the most points at the end wins.

b Students complete the text individually. Check answers as a class.

> **Answers**
> 1 didn't use to have   2 used to buy   3 used to see
> 4 didn't use to be   5 didn't use to open   6 used to plan

> **EXTRA ACTIVITY**
> In pairs, ask students to talk about changes in this area or their home town that have happened in the last few years. Ask the class to share their comments with the class. Ask:
> *Have these changes been good or bad, in your opinion? Why?*

2 VOCABULARY

a Students complete the sentences with the correct words or phrases. Check answers as a class.

> **Answers**
> 1 in touch   2 paid   3 a place   4 on well   5 to know

b Students match the sentence halves. Check answers together.

> **Answers**
> 1 c   2 a   3 b   4 e   5 d

3 WORDPOWER *change*

a Ask students to work in pairs and think of as many words that go with the verb *change* as they can in a minute, e.g. *change your mind, change something you've bought, change your plans*. Ask for ideas in feedback and put them on the board to refer to later. Look at the sentences with the class and ask whether the word *change* is a verb or noun.

> **Answers**
> 1 verb   2 verb   3 noun   4 verb   5 verb   6 noun
> 7 noun   8 verb

b Students match the words and meanings individually. Check answers as a class.

> **Answers**
> a 2   b 5   c 1   d 8   e 4   f 7   g 6   h 3

> **EXTRA ACTIVITY**
> Ask students some extra questions using *change*, e.g.
> *When did you last change your mind?*
> *How much change do you have in your pocket?*
> *When did you last change an item in a shop? Why?*
> *What would you like to do in the next lesson for a change?*

c Students complete the sentences with the words or phrases in the box. Check answers as a class. Refer back to the board and the collocations you wrote up earlier. How many have been included in Exercises a–c?

> **Answers**
> 1 keep some change   2 change into   3 change trains
> 4 for a change   5 change some money   6 change my mind
> 7 change   8 the right change

d 💬 Ask students which sentences in 3c are true for them.

▶ Photocopiable activities: Wordpower p.258

> **LOA   REVIEW YOUR PROGRESS**
>
> Students look back through the unit, think about what they've studied and decide how well they did. Students work on weak areas by using the appropriate sections of the Workbook, the Photocopiable activities and the Personalised online practice.

UNIT 8
Culture

UNIT OBJECTIVES

At the end of this unit, students will be able to:
- understand texts and conversations related to culture and cultural events
- talk about music, art and literature
- talk about sports and leisure activities
- apologise, make and accept excuses
- write a book review

UNIT CONTENTS

G GRAMMAR
- The passive: present and past simple
- Present perfect with *for* and *since*
- Linking using *although* and *however*

V VOCABULARY
- Art and music: *architecture, novel, photograph, poem, sculpture, TV series, painting, album, classical music, film*
- Common verbs in the passive: *base on, design, direct, perform, play, write, paint*
- Sports and activities: *athletics, (scuba) diving, golf, gymnastics, ice hockey, ice skating, jogging, rock climbing, skateboarding, snowboarding, squash, surfing, volleyball, windsurfing, yoga*
- Wordpower: different meanings of *by: created/written, near / next to, not later than, using*; phrases: *by far, by hand, by heart, by mistake*

P PRONUNCIATION
- Tones for continuing or finishing

C COMMUNICATION SKILLS
- Talking about music, art and literature
- Talking about sports and activities
- Apologise, make and accept excuses
- Writing a book review
- Making positive and negative comments

GETTING STARTED

💡 OPTIONAL LEAD-IN
Bring a few postcards of paintings into the class. These could be paintings by artists from your own country, paintings by British artists or paintings you particularly like. Students discuss each painting in small groups. Encourage the discussion by asking questions: *Which painting do you like / not like? Why / Why not? What does it remind you of? How would you describe the colours?* (e.g. *bright, happy, dull, pale*) *Who is the painting by? Would you like to see more works by this artist?* Students share their ideas with the class. Are any of the paintings popular with the class as a whole?

a 🗨 Ask students to tell you what they can see in the painting. Monitor and support students with any new vocabulary they may need, e.g. *cave art/paintings, clean (off), pressure washer*.

b 🗨 Ask: *What style of painting is this? Who did it and how?* Elicit or input: *graffiti, graffiti artist, spray paint / spray can (n), spray (on) (v), stencil*. Students may want to mention famous graffiti artists at this stage such as Banksy (from the UK), Blek le Rat (France), Zephyr (New York). Students discuss the questions in pairs. Ask students to share their ideas and comments with the class.

c Play the recording for students to compare their ideas about the painting with the speaker's. Discuss the similarities and differences as a class. Ask some detailed questions, e.g. *Which city is the festival in?* (London) *Where exactly can you see the paintings?* (in an old underground station) *Who organises the festival?* (Banksy) If you wish, give students information from the Culture notes below.

Audioscript
I saw this painting at The Cans Festival in London. It's a graffiti festival and it takes place in an old London Underground tunnel. The festival is organised by Banksy, the famous graffiti artist. He painted this piece for the event. For me, the painting makes me think about how every time somebody cleans graffiti off a building, it's like they're removing history, like they're cleaning away the future history of art. It definitely gives you something to think about, so I think it's a really clever piece of art.

d 🗨 Students discuss the questions in pairs. Check ideas in feedback. Elicit or input: *art gallery, exhibition*.

🌍 CULTURE NOTES
Banksy is a very famous graffiti artist from the UK. People know very little about him because he never shows his face or gives interviews. Banksy's work is controversial – some people think it is great art, but others think it is criminal. They say it encourages people to paint on walls and buildings illegally. Banksy does most of his paintings at night and in cities, especially in poorer areas. His work sometimes has a political message, is sometimes funny and sometimes beautiful. Once (in disguise, so no one would recognise him), he sold 25 original paintings, signed by himself, to tourists in New York for $60 each. These are now worth up to $31,000 each.

💡 EXTRA ACTIVITY
Write on the board. *Graffiti should not be allowed*. Divide the class into groups of around six students and divide each group into two teams. Ask one team to agree with the sentence and one team to disagree. The teams prepare their ideas for a debate. Ask each group to debate the sentence. Set a fixed amount of time for the debate, e.g. ten minutes. Monitor but don't interrupt fluency. Note down any common mistakes or errors to deal with during feedback. Ask if any students were persuaded to change their point of view!

8A My favourite book is based on a true story

At the end of this lesson, students will be able to:

- use the passive (present and past simple) correctly
- talk about art and music using related vocabulary
- read and understand a text about the most popular works of art
- understand and use common verbs related to the arts in the passive

1 VOCABULARY Art and music

a 💬 Ask students to cover the article and the pictures on the page. Read through the words in the box and check understanding of each term by eliciting examples of it from the class, e.g. ask individual students *Tell me a novel/painting/film that you like.* Then elicit what we call the people who create these things (*producer, director, novelist, writer, poet, sculptor, architect, photographer, painter, artist, singer, composer*). Students match the pictures with the words in the box. Check answers as a class. If you wish, give students information from the Culture notes below.

> **Answers**
> 1 photograph 2 album 3 classical music 4 painting
> 5 architecture 6 poem 7 sculpture 8 novel 9 film
> 10 TV series

b ▶ 2.58 Ask students to read the words aloud and guess which syllables are stressed. Then play the recording for them to underline the correct stressed syllables and compare with their guesses. How many students got the correct answers? Model the words again for students to repeat.

> **Answers and audioscript**
> <u>pho</u>tograph <u>al</u>bum <u>class</u>ical <u>mus</u>ic <u>pain</u>ting <u>arch</u>itecture
> <u>po</u>em <u>sculp</u>ture <u>nov</u>el <u>film</u> <u>TV</u> series

📖 **LANGUAGE NOTES**

If students try to use the noun *photographer* during the lesson, note that the stress moves to the second syllable: <u>pho</u>tograph – pho<u>tog</u>rapher.

c 💬 In pairs, students discuss with their partner which kinds of art and music they are interested in. Encourage them to ask about their partner's favourite music at the moment and compare their tastes. Take feedback as a class on what students found out about their partner's tastes in music and art and anything that surprised them.

💡 **EXTRA ACTIVITY**

In pairs, students think of three questions for another pair, asking them to name an artist from a particular country, e.g. *Can you name a painter from Italy? Can you name a writer from the USA?* Students then swap questions with another pair and try to answer the questions. Ask one or two students to share their ideas with the class.

2 READING

a 💬 Ask students to look at the pictures and titles in the article and tell you which of the things they have read, seen or listened to. Encourage students to give more details, e.g. when and where they saw them. Ask: *Did you like/enjoy them? Why / Why not?* Be prepared to give your own opinion.

🌍 **CULTURE NOTES**

1 *The Lord of the Rings* is a best-selling trilogy of fantasy novels by English author J. R.R. Tolkien. The novels were published in 1954 and are set in the magical world of Middle-earth. The novels were made into a highly successful series of films between 2001 and 2003. The films, which starred Elijah Wood as the hero, Frodo Baggins (pictured), cost around $280 million dollars to make. They won a number of Oscars, including Best Film for the third film in the series, *The Return of the King*.

2 Michael Jackson lived from 1958 to 2009. He was first a member of a family group with his brothers, The Jackson Five, and then was extremely successful as a solo singer. His 1982 album *Thriller* is the best-selling album of all time.

3 Beethoven was a German composer who lived from 1770 to 1827. He lived at the same time as Mozart and Haydn. In his later life, Beethoven became deaf but continued to compose, and some of his most popular work is from this period. Beethoven's Fifth Symphony written at the beginning of the nineteenth century is probably now his most famous work.

4 Leonardo da Vinci was a famous artist, sculptor, architect, engineer and inventor. He was Italian and lived from 1452 to 1519. He is most famous for his paintings, in particular *La Gioconda* (*Mona Lisa*).

5 Rupert Brooke was an English war poet who wrote during the First World War. He wrote about patriotism rather than the horrors of war as later war poets did. His most famous poem is *The Soldier*.

6 Charles Dickens wrote novels and short stories about Victorian England. He lived from 1812 to 1870. In particular, his books describe the life of poor people in big cities like London. However, he is also famous for the funny characters he created.

7 Michelangelo (1475–1564) was an artist from Florence, Italy. A sculptor, architect and painter, he is considered the most influential artist of the Italian Renaissance. The statue of David (pictured) was completed when he was still in his twenties.

8 Stephen King is a famous American writer and has written many frightening horror and fantasy stories. Many of these, such as *The Shining*, *Carrie* and *The Green Mile* have been made into successful films.

9 *Game of Thrones* is an American TV fantasy series and computer game. It has one of the largest casts ever used in a series. It has an enormous number of fans.

b Tell students that some sentences have been taken out of the article. Ask them to ignore the gaps and read the article to answer the questions. You may wish to help students with the words in the Vocabulary support box at this point. Encourage them to underline the key words or terms in the questions (*many years, sold, crime*) and then scan the texts for words/ideas that are related to them. Check answers as a class.

> **Answers**
> took many years to become popular: Beethoven's *Fifth Symphony*, *La Gioconda* (Mona Lisa), *The Shawshank Redemption*
> has sold more than any other: *Thriller* by Michael Jackson, *A Tale of Two Cities* by Charles Dickens
> people have committed a crime to see: *La Gioconda*, *Game of Thrones*

> 📖 **VOCABULARY SUPPORT**
>
> *best-selling* – very popular / has sold in large numbers
>
> *currently* (B2) – at the moment
>
> *electro dance* – energetic form of street dance
>
> *previous* (B1) – one before
>
> *surf rock* – music from 1960s famous band: The Beach Boys
>
> *track* (B2) – song (on an album)

c Read through the sentences with students to check understanding. Students do the task individually. Check answers as a class and ask students to say how and why they chose their answers. Go through the sentences and elicit or point out the clues (a *a single novel*, b *It's/named Khaleesi*, c *da da da dah introduction*, d *ten million more*, e *the story*, f *taken/return/Italy*).

> **Answers**
> 1d 2c 3f 4a 5e 6b

d In pairs, students look at the highlighted words and phrases and discuss what they mean. Encourage students to look carefully at the context of a word – the sentence and the sentences before and after – to work out its meaning. Check answers as a class.

> **Answers**
> *copies:* individual (albums)
> *notes:* tones made by music
> *well-known:* known by lots of people, famous
> *best-selling:* very popular; selling lots of copies
> *voted:* chosen in a vote (formal way of choosing between things)
> *illegally downloaded:* copied from the Internet without permission or payment

> 📖 **LANGUAGE NOTES**
>
> Compound adjectives placed before the noun are usually formed with a hyphen, e.g. *best-selling, well-known*.

> 💡 **EXTRA ACTIVITY**
>
> Ask the following questions to practise the some of the words and phrases from 2d: *Have you bought a copy of a music album or book recently? What was it? Do many people you know illegally download things, like films or music? Is this a big problem? Do you ever vote in reality TV shows? Why / Why not? Who is the most well-known American actor or singer in your country at the moment?*

e 💬 Discuss the question briefly as a class. Ask the class to compile a list of their own most popular things by giving suggestions and then voting.

3 GRAMMAR
The passive: present and past simple

a Books closed. Ask: *Who wrote A Tale of Two Cities?* On the board write *Charles Dickens wrote A Tale of Two Cities*. Highlight *Charles Dickens* by writing it in a different colour or circling it. Now write *A Tales of Two Cities* on the board and highlight it. Can students tell you the rest of the sentence? (*A Tale of Two Cities was written by Charles Dickens.*) Ask students to use the example sentences to answer the questions. Check answers as a class.

> **Answers**
> 1 the same
> 2 the second, the first
> 3 be + past participle (the third part of the verb, e.g. *go/went/gone*)

> 💡 **EXTRA ACTIVITY**
>
> Revise the past participles of irregular verbs with a quickfire test. Give the infinitive and ask the whole class to respond with the past simple and past participle. Students can test each other by using the list on SB p.176.

> 🔄 **LOA TIP CONCEPT CHECKING**
>
> Check understanding of the passive by asking concept questions for the following sentences from the Grammar Focus:
>
> 1 *This house was built in the 1960s.* Ask: *What is the subject of this sentence?* (the house) *Do we know who built it?* (no) *Is it important for us to know who built it?* (no) *What do we find out from the sentence?* (the date) Summarise: *We are interested in the date the house was built, not who built it.*
>
> 2 *The picture was stolen last night.* Ask: *What is the subject of this sentence?* (the picture) *What happened?* (It was stolen.) *Do we know who stole it?* (no)

b ▶ ⏵**2.59** Students read the information in Grammar Focus 8A on SB p.156. Play the recording where indicated and ask students to listen and repeat. Students then complete the exercises Grammar Focus 8A on SB p.157. Check answers as a class, making sure students are using the correct word order and correct form of the verb *be*. Tell students to go back to SB p.79.

> 🔄 **LOA TIP CONCEPT CHECKING**
>
> • Point to something in the room, e.g. a notice on the wall or board.
>
> • Then ask questions about it using the passive: *When was the notice put on the board?* (yesterday) *Why was the notice put on the board?* (to advertise a trip) Write the answers up: *The notice was put on the board yesterday. It was put on the board to advertise a trip.*
>
> • Use concept questions to check that we don't know WHO put up the notice:
>
> Ask: *Do we know who put the notice on the board?* (no)
>
> Ask: *Is it important for us to know who put up the notice?* (no)
>
> Ask: *Is the information in the notice important?* (yes)

Answers (Grammar Focus 8A SB p.157)

a
1 The story was written two hundred years ago.
2 My car was made in Germany.
3 That book isn't sold in your country.
4 Sushi is eaten all over the world.
5 In the UK, the number 1 song is played on the radio every hour.
6 A window was broken in the night.
7 India wasn't described very well in the article.
b
1 The Guggenheim in Bilbao was designed by Frank Gehry.
2 Chanel No. 5 perfume was worn by Marilyn Monroe.
3 The Taj Mahal is visited by 3 million people every year.
4 Many parts of London were destroyed by a fire in 1666.
5 Pluto was discovered by Clyde Tombaugh in 1930.
c
1 Where was the film made?
2 When was the book written?
3 How is cheese made?
4 When was your bike stolen?
5 Was the statue made in France?
6 Who was her wedding dress designed by?

📖 LANGUAGE NOTES

- It is important that students work out the correct tense they want and then make sure that the verb *be* is in that form when using the passive, e.g. ~~The book is written in 1975.~~ (Correct form = *The book **was written** in 1975*.)

- Also remember that the passive is most often used in written work, such as newspaper articles, essays, etc, or more formal speech. Do not encourage students to overuse the form.

---

c Ask students to work in pairs to find and underline five more examples of the passive in the article. Explain that there are seven more altogether, but they only need to find five. Check answers together.

💡 FAST FINISHERS

Ask fast finishers who have found five passive verb forms to find the remaining two passive verb forms.

Answers
1 … around 130,000 copies are sold in the USA …
2 … the first four notes were used by other musicians …
3 … which is called the *Mona Lisa* …
4 … it was stolen from the Louvre …
5 The painting was found two years later …
6 The film … was based on a book …
7 … the programme as soon as it was shown.

4 VOCABULARY
Common verbs in the passive

a Read through the verbs in the box and ask students to complete the sentences using the past participles of the verbs. First, read the example with the class and ask which other verb in the box is irregular (*set*). Point out that some of the sentences are not true. Check answers as a class.

Answers
1 written   2 performed   3 painted   4 based
5 played   6 directed   7 set   8 designed

---

b Students tell their partners which sentences they think are true and, if possible, correct the ones that aren't. Play the recording to check their ideas. Ask if students were surprised by any of the answers, and discuss any of the details of interest in the recording.

Answers and audioscript
Number one is false. Only four of the songs on *Thriller* were written by Michael Jackson.
Number two is true. The performance wasn't very successful. The orchestra made a mistake. It was also a very cold day and the audience was cold and tired at the end of the performance.
Number three is false. The *Mona Lisa* was painted by Leonardo Da Vinci.
Number four is true. *The Dark Knight Rises* contains many of the ideas in *A Tale of Two Cities*.
Number five is false. Morgan Freeman is in the film, but the main character is played by Tim Robbins.
Number six is false. *Game of Thrones* is directed by many different people, but not Peter Jackson.
Number seven is true, although, of course, none of the magical places are real places.
Number eight is false. The building was designed by Antoni Gaudí.

💡 EXTRA ACTIVITY

Ask students what information people like to know about a new film before they go to see it. Elicit the ideas: language, actors, director, the story, costumes, soundtrack. Then ask students if they can talk about a film they have seen recently using some of the passive forms of the verbs they have learned, e.g. *The film was set in Spain. The main character was played by George Clooney. The songs were written by Adele.*

👁 CAREFUL!

Students may miss out the verb *be* when using a present passive form, and they may use the verb in the present simple instead of the present passive, e.g. ~~It's a great film which calls The Return of the King.~~ (Correct form = *It's a great film which **is called** The Return of the King*.)

5 SPEAKING

a Individually, students complete the sentences so that they are true for themselves. Monitor and help as necessary.

b 💬 In small groups, students tell each other about their sentences. Ask for examples during feedback. Ask some students to give clues for the class to guess their sentences. For example, they can hum the song, recite the first line of the poem, describe the sculpture, start the story of the book, say what we can see in the painting, etc. Give an example yourself for them to guess. See which student in the group is the first to guess each item.

ADDITIONAL MATERIAL

▶ Workbook 8A

▶ Photocopiable activities: Grammar p.218, Vocabulary p.242

8B I've hated rugby since I was at school

- use present perfect with *for* and *since*
- understand people talking about record breakers
- use vocabulary related to sports and activities
- talk about their own attitudes to sports

💡 OPTIONAL LEAD-IN

Books closed. Put students into small groups. Ask them to write down a sport that begins with each letter of the alphabet, e.g. A = athletics, B = baseball, etc. If they can't think of a sport for a particular letter, they move on to the next one. After a few minutes, tell them to stop. Then ask each group in turn for a sport beginning with A, then B and so on. Each group to give a different sport gets a point.

Some suggestions: *athletics, basketball, cricket, diving, equestrian sports, football, golf, horse racing, ice skating, judo, karate, lacrosse, mountain biking, netball, off-road motorcycle racing, polo, quoits, rugby, skiing, tennis, underwater hockey, volleyball, windsurfing, xare (a racquet sport from the north of Spain), yoga, zumba.*

1 SPEAKING

a 💬 Tell students about some things you did related to sport – one of which is a lie, e.g. *I won a lot of swimming competitions when I was at school.* Ask students which was a lie and why they thought this. Ask them to talk about the question with their partner. Monitor and help where necessary. Ask students to share their ideas with the class.

b 💬 Discuss the question as a class. Students may mention card games such as *Cheat* where you have to lie about the cards you have or haven't got, or some TV game shows.

2 LISTENING

a ▶️ 2.61 Tell students they are going to listen to a radio show called *I can't believe it!* and ask them to guess what the show is about. Play the recording for students to check their ideas and answer the two questions. Check answers.

Answers
1 (famous) world record breakers   2 two

Audioscript

HOST Welcome to *I can't believe it!* Today's topic is famous world record breakers, and, as usual, we have three players: Michael, Alice and Neil. Each player is going to talk about one record breaker. While they're talking, they'll tell two lies. The other players are going to guess which information is not true. Michael. we'll start with you … Who are you going to talk about today?
MICHAEL Yes. I'm going to talk about …

📖 VOCABULARY SUPPORT

record (B1) – the best someone has ever done
record breaker – someone who beats a record

📖 LANGUAGE NOTES

We talk about *telling lies* or *to tell a lie*, but to express the opposite idea we use a construction with the noun **truth**, e.g. ~~She always tells the true.~~ (Correct form = *She always tells* **the truth**.)

---

b Tell students that Michael is going to talk about Usain Bolt. Ask students what they know about him – they may use the picture to help. Don't say whether they're right or wrong.

c ▶️ 2.62 Read through the sentences with the class. Play the recording. Ask students to look at the sentences again and decide which they think are Michael's two lies. They then compare their ideas with a partner. Don't check answers at this point.

Audioscript

H Michael. We'll start with you … Who are you going to talk about today?
M Yes. I'm going to talk about the fastest man in the world – Usain Bolt from Jamaica. Well, Bolt has been in the Jamaican Olympic team since 2004. He was only 17 when he was chosen. He's 1.95m tall – that's a lot taller than most runners. And because of this, his team mates call him 'Giraffe'. Runners as tall as Usain don't usually win races. So it's amazing that he's held both the 100 metres and 200 metres world records since 2008. And we all know that, in 2012, he became the first person ever to win those races in two Olympics. In the 100 metres in 2012 he forgot to tie his shoes and he also slowed down at the end of the race. But amazingly he still won!
H Thank you, Michael. Alice and Neil, can you guess what Michael's lies were?

📖 VOCABULARY SUPPORT

giraffe (B1) – animal with a very long neck
hold a record (B1) – officially be the best at something
tie your shoes (B1) – to fasten shoes

d ▶️ 2.63 Before playing the recording for students to check their answers, you may wish to help them with the words in the Vocabulary support box. Afterwards take feedback from the class and find out how many students managed to correctly identify the lies.

Answers
2 His team mates don't call him 'Giraffe'.
6 He didn't tie one of his shoes in 2008.

Audioscript

H Thank you, Michael. Alice and Neil, can you guess what Michael's lies were?
ALICE I don't think it's true that he slowed down at the end of the race.
H Michael – is that true?
M It is true, actually!
H Bad luck, Alice! Neil …
NEIL Well, I think he forgot to tie his shoes.
M You're right. He did run with one shoe untied, but it was in 2008 not in 2012!
H Well done on that one, Neil. What was lie number 2?
N Hmmm. Is it true that tall runners don't usually win races?
M Yes, that one's also true.
H So, what was the lie, Michael?
M Well, he is very tall but his team mates don't call him 'Giraffe'.

e 💬 Ask students to look at the other two men and discuss the questions with a partner. Take feedback from the class on their ideas but don't check answers at this point.

f ▶ **2.64** Play the recording for students to check their answers. Emphasise that they are not listening for details at this point, just to find out where each person is from, their sports and their world records. Pause after each speaker, to let students note their answers. Check answers as a class – and remind them that this information may not all be true!

> **Answers**
> Konishiki is from Hawaii. His sport is sumo wrestling. He is the heaviest professional (sumo) wrestler ever (287 kilos).
> Kittinger is from the USA. He is getting ready to jump out of a plane from a great height. He made the highest jump ever; made the longest free fall ever; travelled through the air fastest.

Audioscript

H Alice – what are you going to talk about?

A Well, I'm going to talk about Konishiki Yasokichi, the sumo wrestler. He's actually from Hawaii, but he's lived in Japan for most of his life. He is famous, because he was the heaviest professional sumo wrestler ever. He weighed an incredible 287 kilos. Konishiki used his huge weight to help him win fights – he usually sat on people until he won. As Konishiki got older he started to lose against smaller, faster wrestlers. But in Japan, sumo wrestlers are as famous as film stars and the Japanese people loved him even when he lost, because he was so big. He has been really successful since he stopped fighting. He's a musician, he's acted in films and he's had his own radio show for many years now. He even had his own TV cookery show for a while – he showed people how to cook sumo meals.

H And finally, let's hear from Neil.

N Thank you. I'm going to talk about a captain in the US Air Force, Joseph Kittinger. In 1960, he broke three world records when he jumped to earth from the stratosphere – that's the edge of space, 31 kilometres above the earth. He travelled up there by balloon and when he jumped he broke the record for the highest jump ever. He fell for more than four minutes – the longest free fall ever. He fell at a speed of 988 kilometres per hour, and got the record for travelling through the air faster than any other human. He actually fell faster than the speed of sound. He later wrote a song about the experience, called 'Jump into Space', which is quite good! But Kittinger's story doesn't end there. In 2012, a man called Felix Baumgartner tried to break his three records. Kittinger helped him because he was the only person who had ever jumped from space before. But Baumgartner didn't break all of Kittinger's records, he only broke two. He opened his parachute early and so Kittinger has held his amazing record of longest free fall for over 50 years!

📖 VOCABULARY SUPPORT

captain (B2) – person in charge of a plane or a ship

free fall – a jump from a plane or another high point with a parachute. The free fall is how far the person falls before opening the parachute.

professional (B1) – able to earn money for playing a sport

stratosphere – very high above the surface of the earth, on the edge of space

wrestle – to fight with someone (especially as a sport) by holding them and trying to throw them to the ground

---

g ▶ **2.64** Check students understand what information they have to listen for this time. You may wish to help them with the words in the Vocabulary support box. Play the recording for students to note answers. Students will probably benefit from listening twice to each speaker and having longer to note down answers. You may also need to pause after an answer has been given.

> **Answers**
> Konishiki: 1 heaviest professional sumo wrestler 2 has been a musician, has acted in films, has had own radio show and TV cookery show
> Kittinger: 1 broke three world records when he jumped to earth from stratosphere 2 has written a song, has helped Felix Baumgartner try to break his records

h 💬 Students compare their notes in pairs and discuss which pieces of information they think are lies.

i ▶ **2.65** Play the recording for students to check their ideas.

> **Answers**
> Konishiki Yasokichi
> Lie 1: sat on people in his fights
> Lie 2: had a cookery show
> Captain Joseph Kittinger:
> Lie 1: fell faster than the speed of sound
> Lie 2: wrote a song

Audioscript

H Thank you, Alice. Right – Neil and Michael. What do you think the lies were about Konishiki Yasokichi?

N Hmm. I don't know … I don't think he sat on people in his fights. That sounds too dangerous.

H Alice?

A You're right. That isn't true. He won his fights by pushing the other man out of the ring, not by sitting on him.

H Well done, Neil! Anything else?

N Hmm. I don't think he acted in films.

A No, that was true. He was in a couple of films.

H How about you, Michael?

M I don't think he's originally from Hawaii.

A Sorry, that's true.

H Tell us the lie then, Alice.

A The lie was the cookery show. He didn't have one.

H Interesting story about Captain Kittinger, Neil. What do you think, Michael and Alice?

M What about the balloon? Was that really how he got up there?

N Yes, it was. Sorry.

H Alice?

A Well, I'm not sure he was the person who helped Felix Baumgartner.

N Actually, he was. And he was there on the ground when Baumgartner landed.

H So, what were the lies?

N Well, he didn't fall faster than the speed of sound. And he didn't write a song about his parachute jump. He wrote a book about it.

H Well done, Neil! Alice and Michael believed both of your lies! You're today's winner on *I can't believe it!*

j 💬 Discuss the question as a class and encourage students to give their reasons. Ask: *Would you like to do any of the things they did? Why / Why not?*

💡 EXTRA ACTIVITY

Put students into pairs to think of a famous person they both know some information about. They write three sentences about the famous person – one which is true, and two lies. Each pair reads out their sentences to another pair who guess which sentence is true.

---

3 GRAMMAR
Present perfect with *for* and *since*

a Books closed. Read out the following sentences from the listenings in this lesson. Can students remember the time expressions? *Konishiki Yasokichi has had his own radio show …* (for many years). *Joseph Kittinger has held his record …* (for over 50 years). *Usain Bolt has been in the Jamaican Olympic team …* (since 2004). Don't worry if students get the time expressions wrong at this stage but give them the opportunity to correct their ideas during the following activity. Students look at the sentence and answer the question.

> **Answer**
> yes

b Students complete the rule with the correct words. Check answers together.

> **Answers**
> past; present

c Ask students to complete the rules and the sentences in pairs. Check answers as a class.

> **Answers**
> 1 for   2 since
> for; since

LOA TIP ELICITING

* To establish the concept of: period + *for* and point of time + *since*, say: *We've been in this classroom today **since** …* (invite a response with a gesture perhaps pointing to the clock, e.g. *9.30*). Ask: *Is 9.30 a period of time or a point in time?* Elicit that it's a point in time.

* Then, say: *We've been in this classroom **for** (25) minutes.* Ask: *Is 25 minutes a period of time or a point in time?* Elicit that it's a period of time.

* Write *since* and *for* on the board. Elicit examples of different periods and points of time to list under each, e.g. *for: seconds, minutes, hours, days, weeks, months, years, ages, a long time; since: 10 o'clock, Monday, April, 24th May, 2014.*

---

d ▶ ⓟ 2.66 Students read the information in Grammar Focus 8B on SB p.156. Play the recording where indicated and ask students to listen and repeat. Students then complete the exercises Grammar Focus 8B on SB p.157. Check answers as a class, making sure students are using *has/had* and past participles correctly. Tell students to go back to SB p.81.

> **Answers (Grammar Focus 8B SB p.157)**
> a 1 since   2 for   3 for   4 since   5 for   6 since   7 since
>   8 for   9 since   10 for   11 for   12 since
> b 1 I've worked here since January.
>   2 I've lived here for three months.
>   3 He's held the record since the last Olympics.
>   4 She's owned the car since 2011.
>   5 They've been married for two days.
>   6 I haven't listened to pop music for a long time.
>   7 We haven't been friends since we had a fight.
>   8 I haven't had a TV in my home for a few years.
>   9 He hasn't eaten meat since New Year's Day.
> c 1 have you studied   2 has she lived   3 has Mr Bell taught
>   4 have we had   5 has he been
> d 1 She's worked   2 She started   3 did you buy
>   4 have you had   5 We haven't seen   6 We didn't see
>   7 I loved   8 I've loved

👁 CAREFUL!

Remember that to talk about a finished period in the past, we use the past simple, and not present perfect or past continuous: e.g. ~~I have studied / I was studying in Madrid for a year when I was a student~~. (Correct form = *I **studied** in Madrid for a year when I was a student.*)

---

e Ask students to complete the sentences individually. They should write four true sentences and two lies. Check for correct use of *for* and *since*. To extend, you can ask them to write an additional sentence in the past simple to give extra detail, e.g. *I've owned my car for six months. My parents gave it to me for my birthday.*

f 💬 In pairs, students take turns to read their sentences and guess which were lies. Take feedback and ask students to share their ideas with the class.

4 VOCABULARY   Sports and activities

a In pairs, students look at the pictures at the bottom of the page and make a list of the sports and activities. Check their ideas as a class.

> **Answers**
> ice skating   jogging   surfing   snowboarding

b 💬 Discuss the question as a class. Encourage students to give reasons for wanting / not wanting to try the sports.

c ▶ ⓟ 2.67 Students complete the exercises in Vocabulary Focus 8B on SB p.138. Check their answers to Exercise a and play the recording for them to underline the stressed syllables, and then to listen and repeat. Monitor the conversations in Exercise e and correct students' pronunciation as appropriate. Tell students to go back to SB p.81

> **Answers (Vocabulary Focus 8B SB p.138)**
> **a/b**
> 1b sur<u>f</u>ing   2d <u>s</u>nowboarding   3j golf   4c <u>v</u>olleyball
> 5f <u>s</u>kateboarding   6k <u>rock</u> climbing   7l gym<u>n</u>astics
> 8m <u>s</u>cuba diving   9h <u>y</u>oga   10g <u>j</u>ogging   11o <u>wind</u>surfing
> 12a ath<u>le</u>tics   13i <u>ice</u> hockey   14e squash   15n <u>ice</u> skating

5 SPEAKING

a Students read through the different points 1–4 and make some notes about them.

b 💬 Put students into small groups to compare their interests and experiences. Ask them to find the person who is most similar to them in the group. Read through the examples before they start. Listen for correct usage of the target language in this lesson. Point out errors for students to self corrrect. After the activity, ask students to say who they are most similar to in their group, and why.

ADDITIONAL MATERIAL

▶ Workbook 8B

▶ Photocopiable activities: Grammar p.219, Vocabulary p.243, Pronunciation p.279

8C Everyday English
I'm really sorry I haven't called

At the end of this lesson, students will be able to:

- use phrases to make apologies and to make and accept excuses
- understand a conversation where someone apologises and makes excuses
- recognise and use tones to indicate they are continuing or finishing a sentence

---

💡 OPTIONAL LEAD-IN

Write on the board: *a) arrive late b) phone the dentist and say you will be late c) phone the dentist and see if you can arrange the appointment for another day d) don't go.* Say: *You have an appointment at the dentist. You don't want to go! On the way to the dentist you get stuck in traffic. What do you do?* Point to the board and ask students what they would do. Encourage them to explain why.

1 LISTENING

a 💬 In pairs, students look at the list and discuss whether these things are annoying. Encourage them to justify their answers as far as possible. Ask one or two students to share their ideas with the class. Ask students if the discussion has made them think of any other annoying situations.

b ▶️ 2.68 Ask students what has happened in the story so far. Then ask them to look at the pictures and say how Annie and Leo seem and what they think is happening. Play Part 1 of the video or play the audio recording for them to check their ideas.

> **Answer**
> Leo is explaining to Annie why he hasn't called. Annie doesn't believe him.

Video/Audioscript (Part 1)

LEO Hi, Annie.

ANNIE Oh, hi.

L Are you busy? Can I come in?

A Er, yeah – come in …Do you want anything to drink? A coffee?

L No, no, I'm fine.

A So, how are you?

L I'm …well, I'm OK. Look, I'm really sorry I haven't called you.

A It doesn't matter.

L No, look – let me explain. I couldn't call or send you a message. I've had a really bad back. I was in bed for days.

A What do you mean you couldn't call? Did your arms stop working? How hard is it to call someone?

L No, no – you don't understand. I was going to call you, but I couldn't find my mobile.

A I don't know, Leo. How can I believe you?

L It's true!

A I thought you were avoiding me.

L No, of course not.

A So, what happened? Did you have an accident?

L No, nothing. I just woke up one day and it was hurting. And then every day it got worse.

A Oh.

L So, in the end, I went to the doctor.

A And what did the doctor say?

L Well, he said it was because I'm always behind my desk, in the office.

A I was worried, you know?

L I'm sorry. I didn't mean to make you worry. And then I meant to call you after I went to the doctor, but I was working so much.

A Well, it's not your fault. But why were you working so much?

L Well, because I missed so much work. Because of my back.

A Leo, the doctor said you had a bad back because of your work. And then you work even more?

L I know, I know. I had to work that much. I didn't have a choice.

A Oh, Leo.

L I'm sorry, Annie.

A Don't worry about it.

L No, there's no excuse.

A No really, it's fine. Are you sure you don't want that coffee?

L Oh, that would be great – thanks.

c ▶️ 2.68 Read through the questions with the class and check understanding. Teach or elicit the meaning of *avoid* – to deliberately stay away from someone. Then play Part 1 of the video or play the audio recording again for students to answer the questions. Check answers as a class.

> **Answers**
> 1 He had a bad back and was in bed.
> 2 No. Did your arms stop working? 3 He couldn't find his mobile.
> 4 She thought Leo was avoiding her.
> 5 because he missed so much / a lot of work 6 no

d 💬 Students talk about the questions in pairs. Circulate and encourage students to give reasons for their answers. During group feedback, build up a list on the board of things that the class agree you should always or don't have to apologise for.

2 USEFUL LANGUAGE
Apologies and excuses

a ▶️ 2.69 Read through the sentences. With the class and give students the opportunity to complete the sentences before hearing the recording again. Then play the recording to check answers. If necessary, you could play the recording for students to listen and complete the sentences.

> **Answers**
> 1 really sorry 2 couldn't 3 was going 4 didn't mean
> 5 meant 6 had to 7 there's

b Elicit from the class the difference between to *apologise* and to *make an excuse*. Write on the board the sentence from the optional activity at the beginning of the lesson – *I'm sorry I haven't got my homework, but I was walking beside the river and my bag fell into the water* and ask students to tell you which part is an apology and which is an excuse. Establish that an apology is when you say you are sorry for something and an excuse is when you try to justify or give reasons for your actions. Then ask students to classify Leo's phrases in 2a as either apologies or excuses.

> **Answers**
> 1 1, 4, 5, 7   2 2, 3, 6

c ▶️ 2.69 Play the recording for students to repeat. Encourage students to try and imitate the 'rhythm' of the sentences – the word stress and intonation.

d Students complete the sentences individually, and compare with a partner before you check as a class.

> **Answers**
> 1 was 2 meant 3 had to 4 didn't mean 5 couldn't

e ▶️ 2.70 Before playing the recording, ask if students can remember what Annie said to accept Leo's apologies. They look at the sentences and see if they can complete them before you play the recording for them to check.

> **Answers**
> 1 matter 2 fault 3 worry 4 fine

f ▶ **2.70** Play the recording for students to listen and repeat. Tell the class that to sound apologetic in English, your voice should go down at the end of the sentence rather than up and encourage them to try to achieve this.

g 💬 Tell students that they are going to apologise and give excuses in different situations. First, look at the situations with the class and then suggest that they may want to use the possible excuses given. However, they can think of their own if they wish. Model one of the situations with a student as an example. In pairs, students take turns to apologise, give an excuse and respond appropriately. Monitor and prompt if necessary. During feedback, ask for examples of excuses students gave.

3 PRONUNCIATION
Tones for continuing or finishing

a ▶ **2.71** Read through the instructions with the class and play the recording. Model the sentences and get the students to repeat after you and then elicit whether students think the speaker's voice goes up or down.

> **Answers**
> 1, 3 down then up   2, 4 down

b Students complete the rule. Check answers.

> **Answers**
> down then up; down

c ▶ **2.72** Play the recording for students to answer the question.

> **Answers**
> 1 more to say   2 finished   3 finished   4 more to say

💡 **EXTRA ACTIVITY**

Model the sentences in 3c and ask students to repeat them with the same intonation. Then elicit what they might say next, e.g. 1 *because he wasn't there*, 4 *because I couldn't find my phone*. They should join the information together with the correct intonation. Model this first if it's hard for the class. Write the sentence parts on the board. Divide the class in half and ask one group to say the first parts and the second group to say the second parts. Swap roles and repeat for practice. Make sure they are using the correct intonation.

---

4 LISTENING

a ▶ **2.73** Tell students that they are going to listen to the next part of the story. Ask for examples from the class about what Annie and Leo might talk about next. Read the question and play Part 2 of the video or play the audio recording for students to answer the question. Check answer as a class.

> **Answer**
> go to the gym (with Mark)

Video/audioscript (Part 2)

ANNIE Oh, is it hurting now?

LEO A bit.

A Did the doctor give you anything?

L Yeah, he gave me some pills. They're helping, but not much.

A Ooh, I know! Lie down and I'll walk on your back.

L What?

A I saw it on a TV programme! It'll help.

L Annie, I don't really think that's for serious back problems.

A No, of course not – sorry.

L No, it's fine – it's just, you know – I think I should do what the doctor says.

A Well, you could come to my yoga class! I think yoga's really good for your back.

L Hmm, yoga … I'm not sure.

A Come on – you'll love it!

L Do any other men go?

A Well, no, but you could be the first.

L It's not really my kind of thing.

A They do water aerobics too … in the swimming pool …

L Annie, that sounds worse than yoga.

A Well, what about the gym? I know … you can go with Mark! He asked you, remember. You should call him! What do you think?

L Yeah, I suppose.

A Call him! It'll be fun!

L OK, OK – I will. I promise.

📖 **VOCABULARY SUPPORT**

water aerobics – exercise in water

yoga (B1) – exercises for the mind and body

---

b ▶ **2.73** Play Part 2 of the video or play the audio recording again for students to find the other three suggestions that Annie makes and say why Leo doesn't like them. Check answers as a class.

> **Answers**
> 1 walk on Leo's back; I don't really think that's for serious back problems.
> 2 come to Annie's yoga class; It's not really my kind of thing.
> 3 go to a water aerobics class; That sounds worse than yoga.

c 💬 Discuss the questions as a class. Encourage students to use the phrases for making suggestions where appropriate, e.g. *be careful when you pick something up, go to a chiropractor, do gentle exercise.*

5 SPEAKING

a 💬 In pairs, students talk about who might say each of the things. Encourage them to take turns to read the phrases aloud to each other with correct stress and intonation. Check answers as a class.

> **Suggested answers**
> boss, policeman, friend on phone, waiter, ticket inspector, friend, wife/husband, parking attendant, people waiting in a shop / at an airport / at a bus stop

b 💬 Individually, students think of excuses to use in the different situations. Then ask them to compare their ideas with a partner and make sure they have at least two excuses prepared for each situation.

c 💬 Students swap partners and role play the situations, taking it in turns to give excuses. Encourage them to put expression into their voices. Ask for students' examples in class feedback and see which excuses were the best.

💡 **FAST FINISHERS**

Working with the same partners, students discuss whether they themselves have been in situations like the ones in 5a and what happened.

ADDITIONAL MATERIAL

▶ Workbook 8C

▶ Photocopiable activities: Pronunciation p.280

▶ Unit Progress Test

▶ Personalised online practice

8D Skills for Writing
I couldn't put the book down

At the end of this lesson, students will be able to:

- understand people talking about books they have read
- read and understand online reviews
- write negative and positive comments
- link sentences with *although* and *however*
- write a review

OPTIONAL LEAD-IN

Books closed. Write some questions on the board: *What book are you reading now? What was the last book you finished? Can you name a book that you started but didn't finish? Can you name a book from your country that you would recommend to other people? Can you name the first book you remember reading as a child? Can you name a book you have read that has been made into a film?* Give students two minutes to think about their answers and then talk about their ideas with a partner. Take feedback and ask students to share some examples with the class. Encourage students to justify their opinions as far as possible.

1 LISTENING AND SPEAKING

a Ask students to look at the book covers and describe what they can see. Then they give suggestions for what they think the stories are about. Ask for comments during feedback but don't check answers at this point.

b In pairs, students read the summaries and match them with the book covers. Check answers as a class.

> **Answers**
> 1 *Two Lives* 2 *Eye of the Storm* 3 *A Puzzle for Logan*

VOCABULARY SUPPORT

fall in love (B1) – to start to love someone

hurricane – a big storm with very strong winds

murder (B1) – to kill someone (person = *murderer*)

LANGUAGE NOTES

When we talk about the story of a film or book, we generally use the present tense. Focus students' attention on this. Ask: *What tense is mainly used in the summaries?*

c Play the recording for students to answer the two questions. Tell students not to worry about details at this stage. Check answers together.

> **Answers**
> 1 Speaker 3 has finished the book; 1 and 2 are still reading.
> 2 They all think the stories are good.

VOCABULARY SUPPORT

escape (B1) – to get away

fiction (B1) – stories

LANGUAGE NOTES

The *eye of the storm* is the centre of the storm and is quiet and calm.

Audioscript

1 I'm reading a book called *Two Lives*. I've had this book for about a year, but I only started reading it last week. It's about a man and a woman who fall in love, but then something happens in the family and the man has to leave. He goes abroad and lives there, but then

he comes back and they meet again years later. The man still loves her, but of course he's been away for years and now she's found another man and she's going to marry him. I don't know what's going to happen, but I hope they'll be happy in the end! I'm really enjoying it. I usually read it on the way to work.

2 I'm reading a very good book at the moment. It's fiction, but I think it's based on a true story. It's called *Eye of the Storm*, and it's about a hurricane – a very strong storm – which is coming towards the coast of Florida, in the USA. The main characters in the story are a man and his daughter, and her friend. And the man is out in his fishing boat and he hasn't heard about the hurricane. So, his daughter and her friend have to go out to sea and try to tell him before it's too late. It's very exciting. I can't stop reading it!

3 I'm not reading anything at the moment, but I've just finished a book called *A Puzzle for Logan*. It's a crime story and it happens in Edinburgh, in Scotland. It's a murder mystery. The police have found a woman who was murdered, and at the same time a man has just escaped from prison. He's been in prison for six years and he knows the woman, so of course everyone thinks that he murdered her. But the police officer, Inspector Logan, doesn't believe it. So, he tries to find out who really murdered the woman. It's a good story, I liked it.

d ▶ 2.74 Read through the questions with the class. Give students the opportunity to answer before hearing the recording again. Play the recording for them to check anything they aren't sure about. Pause after each speaker and elicit answers from the class.

> **Answers**
> 1 Something happens in the family.
> 2 The woman has found another man and she's going to marry him.
> 3 Yes, it's based on a true story.
> 4 She goes out to sea, with her friend, to try to tell him about the storm.
> 5 He's just escaped from prison and he knows the woman.
> 6 He tries to find out who really murdered the woman.

e Students make notes about a book they are reading, or have read. Explain that *kind of story* relates to the kind of topic, e.g. a romantic book, a crime story. Monitor and help with vocabulary as necessary.

f Put students into small groups. They should talk to the group about their book and discuss if they enjoyed it and if they would recommend their book to other readers. Listen and note down any interesting points to mention during feedback. Find out which of the books that has been discussed most students would now like to read, and why.

LOA TIP MONITORING

When monitoring, the purpose is not always to note things students are doing wrong. It is also to note things they are doing right. In this case, note down interesting points they mention and tell the rest of the class about them in full group feedback. Also note examples of good language and draw attention to these.

2 READING

a Ask students how they usually find out about new books or films to read or see. Elicit different ways we can find out and put these on the board, e.g. articles in magazines, newspapers, online. Students might also suggest TV programmes where people and/or critics talk about new books and films. We can also learn about them from friends. Tell students that these are called *reviews*. Ask: *Have you read an online review recently? Was it useful? Why / Why not?* Students read the online reviews and match them with the books in the pictures. Check answers together.

> **Answers**
> 1 *A Puzzle for Logan*
> 2 *Two Lives*
> 3 *Eye of the Storm*
> 4 *A Puzzle for Logan*

b Discuss the question as a class. Ask: *Which book would you most like to read? Why?*

> **Suggested answers**
> 2 five stars   3 one or two stars   4 four or five stars

3 WRITING SKILLS

Positive and negative comments; Linking: *although, however*

a Ask students to categorise the comments in pairs. Check answers as a class and put two lists on the board. Brainstorm other words or phrases they could add to the list, e.g. Positive: *fantastic, informative, easy to follow, amazing, imaginative, educational.* Negative: *confusing, boring, scary, very slow.*

> **Answers**
> Positive: well written, realistic, wonderful, couldn't put the book down
> Negative: hard to follow, not brilliant, not very exciting, a bit dull, quite complicated

b Remind students that when writing, it is important not to have lots of short sentences but to link sentences and ideas. Students look at the examples and answer the questions.

> **Answers**
> 1 b
> 2 a However
>   b although

c Students underline four more examples in the texts. Check as a class.

> **Answers**
> 1 However, the story is quite hard to follow, because …
> 2 It's a beautiful story, although it's also very sad …
> 3 However, it's not very exciting, because …
> 4 Although the story is quite complicated, you should …

d Ask students about the position of *although* in a sentence.

⊙ CAREFUL!

Make sure that students are clear that *however* usually goes at the beginning of a sentence to link back to the previous sentence. Students may try to use it in the middle to join two parts, but this is likely to result in clumsy over-long sentences. *Although* can be placed either at the beginning or middle of a sentence.

> **Answer**
> 2

e Students join the sentences individually. Check answers as a class.

> **Answers**
> 1 I can recommend the book. However, it's difficult to read. / Although I can recommend the book, it's difficult to read. / I can recommend the book, although it's difficult to read.
> 2 The story is a bit boring. However, the characters are interesting. / Although the characters are interesting, the story is a bit boring. / The characters are interesting, although the story is a bit boring.
> 3 It's an exciting story. However, it's not the best story I've ever read. / Although it's an exciting story, it's not the best story I've ever read. / It's an exciting story, although it's not the best story I've ever read.
> 4 It's fiction. However, it's based on a true story. / Although it's fiction, it's based on a true story. / It's fiction, although it's based on a true story.

EXTRA ACTIVITY

Ask students to work in pairs. They take it in turns to start a sentence which uses *although* in the middle. Their partner has to complete the sentence so that it makes sense. They could also start a new sentence with *However* and ask their partner to continue, e.g. *I watched a reality TV show last night, although … (I don't really enjoy them!) I watched a good film last night on television. However, … (I didn't see the end because my friend phoned me.)* Ask students to share examples during feedback.

4 WRITING

a Tell students that they are going to write a book review. Go through the points they need to think about with the class. Give students some time to note down their ideas for 1 and 2, and remind them to use *although* and *however* for linking. Monitor and help with vocabulary and ideas as necessary.

b Students write their reviews and give their star rating. Monitor and answer questions. Point out errors for students to self-correct. or encourage self-correction if you see mistakes.

⚑ FAST FINISHERS

Fast finishers can add another paragraph about other reasons why a reader might like / not like the book, e.g. length, setting, style, kind of book, etc.

c Students read their partner's review and check for the points mentioned in the task. Monitor and find something to praise in all the reviews.

d Pass students' reviews around the group or choose some to read aloud to the class. Ask students to choose which book they would like to read from these reviews and to give their reasons.

ADDITIONAL MATERIAL

▶ Workbook 8D

UNIT 8
Review and extension

1 GRAMMAR

a Ask students to read and complete the text with the passive forms of the verbs in the box. Check answers as a class. Ask students what they think should be top of the DVD popularity list.

> **Answers**
> 1 were sold   2 weren't performed   3 were/are loved
> 4 was directed   5 was filmed   6 is shown   7 were written

b 💬 Students tell their partner about a film that they like. If students have already discussed this at some stage during the unit, ask them to start describing a film and their partner has to guess the film as quickly as possible.

c Students complete the sentences. Point out there is more than one possible answer for some. Check answers as a class.

> **Answers**
> 1 was created   2 took / has taken   3 is/was based
> 4 directed   5 wrote   6 is/was designed

d Students correct the sentences. Check answers.

> **Answers**
> 1 We've lived   2 for two years   3 since 2010
> 4 They've been   5 since 2012   6 I've loved

> ### 💡 EXTRA ACTIVITY
> Individually, students write down the names of a favourite book, film and song. Now put students into small groups. Each group in turn says one of the names they have written down. The other groups try to make a correct passive sentence about it. The first group to say a sentence which is correct both grammatically and factually wins a point.

2 VOCABULARY

a Students complete the sentences. Check answers together.

> **Answers**
> 1 sculpture   2 concert   3 series   4 poem   5 architecture

b 💬 Students tell the class which sentences are true for them.

c Students complete the sports and activities. Tell students that one is two words. Check answers together.

> **Answers**
> 1 snowboarding   2 gymnastics   3 windsurfing   4 scuba diving
> 5 jogging   6 athletics   7 golf   8 yoga

> ### 💡 EXTRA ACTIVITY
> In pairs, students can mime a sport from this task or Vocabulary Focus 8B on SB p.138 for their partners to guess.

3 WORDPOWER by

a Write the word *by* on the board. Ask students in pairs to write down some sentences using *by* in different ways. Check their ideas in feedback and put some examples on the board.

Students match the sentences and meanings. Check answers. See if these meanings match any of the sentences on the board.

> **Answers**
> 1 c   2 b   3 d   4 a

b Tell students that there are several useful expressions that include the word *by*. Students match the questions and replies. Check answers as a class.

> **Answers**
> 1 b   2 c   3 e   4 a   5 d

c Elicit the answer to the question (*by the way*).

d Students match the meanings with the phrases in 3b. Check answers.

> **Answers**
> 1 by mistake   2 by hand   3 by far   4 by heart

e Students complete the sentences with expressions from 3b. Check answers as a class.

> **Answers**
> 1 by the way   2 by mistake   3 by hand   4 by far   5 by heart

f 💬 Have a full group discussion about what things students know by heart and do by hand/mistake.

▶ Photocopiable activities: Wordpower p.259

> ### 🔄 LOA REVIEW YOUR PROGRESS
>
> Students look back through the unit, think about what they've studied and decide how well they did. Students work on weak areas by using the appropriate sections of the Workbook, the Photocopiable activities and the Personalised online practice.

UNIT 9
Achievements

UNIT OBJECTIVES

At the end of this unit, students will be able to:
- understand texts and conversations related to achievements in careers and education
- talk about future possibilities using conditional sentences
- describe actions and feelings
- make telephone calls
- write a personal profile

UNIT CONTENTS

G GRAMMAR
- First conditional
- Verb patterns

V VOCABULARY
- Degree subjects: *art, drama, education, engineering, law, medicine, business management, psychology*
- Education collocations: *do a degree in (a subject), get a place at university, hand (work / an essay) in, revise (for an exam), write an essay, get into university, take notes, get good/bad marks*
- Verbs followed by *to* + infinitive / verb + *-ing*: *agree, arrange, avoid, dislike, imagine, manage, miss, recommend, refuse, regret, seem, forget*
- Wordpower: multi-word verbs with *put*: *put back, put down, put off, put on, put (someone) through, put up*

P PRONUNCIATION
- Word groups
- Main stress: contrastive

C COMMUNICATION SKILLS
- Talking about future possibilities
- Describing actions and feelings
- Making and receiving telephone calls
- Writing a personal profile

GETTING STARTED

♀ OPTIONAL LEAD-IN

Books closed. Ask students: *What have you read today?* Give some examples of things you have read, e.g. *bus timetable, email, Facebook update, staff notice board*. Put students in pairs to think of different things that we read every day. After two minutes, ask the class to tell you their ideas and build up a list on the board. Ask students if they are surprised by how much they read every day. Tell them to think about the list of ideas on the board, e.g. You would need to ask other people what time the buses came. Elicit ideas for each text type on the board.

a 🗩 In pairs, students look at the picture and talk about the questions. Take feedback as a class and write students' ideas on the board. Elicit which country students think the picture was taken in.

b ▶3.2 Play the recording for students to check their ideas from Exercise a. Then discuss the questions as a

class. Elicit from students what kind of difficulties they think Kimani might have beginning school so late in life and also what he might have particularly enjoyed. If you wish, give students information from the Culture notes below.

> **Answers**
> 1 Kimani is 84. The children are eight years old.
> 2 He is studying because he didn't go to school when he was young.

Audioscript

Kimani Maruge became the world's oldest primary student in 2006. He was 84 when he first went to school with his eight-year-old classmates at a primary school near Nairobi, in Kenya. Mr Maruge never had the chance to go to school when he was younger, but he believed education was important and wanted it for himself; it didn't matter to him how old he was. He was thankful for the opportunity to go to school and he hardly ever missed a day. He wanted to improve his maths and reading ability. Sadly, Mr Maruge died in 2009. A film was made about his life in 2011, called *The First Grader*.

🌍 CULTURE NOTES

Kimani Maruge was the subject of an interesting film in 2011, *The First Grader*. (In the USA the first class children go into at school is called *first grade*.) Kimani was born in Kenya in about 1920. He never got the chance to go to school and grew up unable to read or write. In 2003, Kenya introduced free education for all primary school children. Kimani decided to go to school and finally learn the basic skills. When he was asked why he decided to go to school at such an age, Kimani said that he wanted to be able to read so that he could do business and read letters from family and friends. In 2005, he was invited to New York to address the UN on the importance of education in Africa.

c 🗩 In pairs, students predict three things they will find out about Kimani in the film (for example, Kimani's childhood and early life, why he couldn't go to school, how he managed in his adult life, why he thinks learning to read and write is important, the progress he made in his studies). Check ideas as a class and see if all students thought the same.

♀ EXTRA ACTIVITY

Put students into pairs. Ask them to imagine that one is Kimani and the other is his wife. They should write the conversation when Kimani tells his wife that he is going to go to school. When they have finished, ask one or two pairs to act out their conversations. The class votes on the best one.

At the end of this lesson, students will be able to:

- use the first conditional correctly
- use vocabulary related to degree subjects
- use education collocations
- read and understand a text about unusual degree subjects
- understand people talking about their study habits
- talk about plans for the future

💡 OPTIONAL LEAD-IN

Books closed. Individually, students think of their favourite subject at school and write three reasons why they like or liked it, e.g. *I learned about other countries. I loved drawing diagrams. My teacher was really interesting.* (geography) In pairs, students read each other their reasons. Their partner tries to guess the subject. Take a class vote. Which school subjects are popular?

1 VOCABULARY Degree subjects

a 💬 Students discuss the questions and give their opinions. If your class is multilingual, put different nationalities together if possible.

🌍 CULTURE NOTES

Statistics for the percentage of young people in further education in the UK vary, but in 2013 it was reported that around 40% of school leavers had entered some form of higher education by the age of 19. Popular degree subjects in the UK are Business Studies, Law, IT, Social Studies, Art and Design, any form of Medical studies, and Biosciences.

b Ask students to cover their books. Ask: *What other subjects can people study at university today?* Elicit any more ideas that students can think of for subjects that can be studied at university and add them to the list on the board. Then let the class read the list of subjects and match them with the pictures. Play the recording to check answers. Pay special attention to the pronunciation and stress pattern on *engineering, psychology, medicine* and *management*.

Answers
1 drama 2 law 3 engineering 4 psychology
5 education 6 medicine 7 business management 8 art

📖 LANGUAGE NOTES

The *p* at the beginning of *psychology* is silent. Students may try to pronounce it.

👁 CAREFUL!

Check for the correct spelling of *business*, e.g. *I'm going to study ~~bussiness~~ or ~~bussines~~.* (Correct form = *business*.). Also look out for the spelling of *management* e.g. He wants to work in ~~managment~~. (Correct form = *management*.).

💡 EXTRA ACTIVITY

In pairs, students choose one of the subjects from 1b and say something that a student of that subject might need to do. Their partner guesses the subject, e.g. *check your temperature* (medicine), *learn lines* (drama).

c 💬 Students discuss the questions in pairs. Take feedback as a class. Elicit any other degree subjects which are popular in students' home countries – e.g. degrees related to computer science. Ask students: *Which subjects do you think are the most popular? Why?*

2 READING AND SPEAKING

a 💬 Tell students that they are going to read an article about unusual degrees that people can do at university today. Ask if they have heard of any unusual degrees themselves. Students read the introduction, and look at the pictures and the names of the unusual degrees. Discuss the questions briefly as a class.

📖 VOCABULARY SUPPORT

bakery (B2) – place where bread is made or sold

ceramics – plates, dishes, vases

citrus – fruits like oranges, lemons

b Ask students to read the article to check their ideas. While reading, they should underline the words which say what students study. You could clarify by saying the students should underline words that tell you what exactly the students learn about or do on the course.

Answers
Football Studies: business, society, the media, sports injuries, coaching
Citrus Studies: grow, chemistry, biology
Toy Design: design toys, child psychology, 3D design, mechanical engineering
Bakery Science: chemistry, manage production
Popular Music: science of sound, production, engineering
Ceramics: produce ceramics

c 💬 In pairs, students discuss the meaning of any new words. In feedback, check the meanings and see if the rest of the class can explain any words the other students don't know.

📖 VOCABULARY SUPPORT

ceramics – the art of making objects by shaping pieces of clay and baking them

coach (B2) – to teach someone so that they improve at sport, skill or school subject

design (B1) – the art of making plans or drawings for something which show how it will be made

exhibition (B1) – when objects such as paintings are shown to the public

injury (B2) – when you hurt a part of your body in an accident

lecture (B1) – a talk by an expert

lime – a small green citrus fruit, which is not sweet

mechanical engineering (B2) – the study of the design and production of machines

psychology (B2) – the study of the mind and how people behave

society (B1) – large group of people who live in the same country or area and have the same laws, traditions, etc.

d 💬 Read through the questions with the class. If possible, put different nationalities together in pairs for them to discuss the questions. Monitor and help with vocabulary as necessary. Ask for ideas during full group feedback.

3 VOCABULARY Education collocations

a Put students in pairs and ask them to note down things that good students do and things that bad students do in class or while learning. Give an example: *arrive on time / be late for class.* Ask for ideas during feedback and put them on the board in two lists. Point out which list is longer! Read through the words and phrases in the box with the class and check them against the lists. If they are not included, ask students which list they should go in.

> **Answers**
> G: pass your exams, take notes, revise
> B: fail your exams, get low grades, hand an essay in late

> 📖 **LANGUAGE NOTES**
>
> A *grade* (B2) or a *mark* (B1) means a number or letter that is written on a piece of work, saying how good the work is. *Grade* is the term commonly used in the US; in the UK, *mark* is more common.

b ▶ ⏺ 3.4 Students complete the exercises in Vocabulary Focus 9A on SB p.139. Play the recording where indicated for students to check their answers to Exercise b. Check answers to Exercises a and d as a class. Tell students to go back to SB p.88.

> **Answers (Vocabulary Focus 9A SB p.139)**
> **a** 1 e 2 c 3 a 4 b 5 d 6 g 7 f
> **b** 1 get into 2 do 3 get 4 write
>   5 took 6 handed 7 got 8 failed
> **d** 1 degree 2 essay 3 exam 4 mark
>   5 notes 6 place 7 university

4 LISTENING

a ⏺ 3.5 Ask the class: Remind me: *what do successful students do, those who have good study habits? For example, they hand in their essays ...* Elicit on time from the class. Continue revising the collocations from 3a by eliciting other examples of what good students do - *they take notes, they revise,* etc. and getting students to add more ideas, e.g. *they ask questions in class, they go to bed early and get enough sleep,* etc. Then play the recording for students to listen and decide which of the speakers have good or bad study habits. Check ideas as a class.

> **Answers**
> good habits: B, C, D revising a lot/studied hard/hours in the library
> bad habits: A, E late starting an essay/no revising

Audioscript

A I'm writing an essay at the moment. But I'm a bit worried, because I only started today and I have to hand it in on Friday. I really need to speak to my lecturer. I might fail the year if she doesn't give me more time.

B I can't believe it's all over – the last exam was yesterday. Now I just have to wait for the results. I studied hard, so I'm quite confident. If I pass, I'm going to have a big party! If I don't, well ... I'm not going to think about that ...

C So I've got my results and ... I'm really happy with my marks. All those hours in the library paid off! The problem now is that I have to choose which course to do at which university. I've got three places to choose from and they're all really good, but they're slightly different. I have to be quick – if I don't decide soon, I'll miss the deadline.

D Well, my exams start next week, so I'm revising a lot at the moment. I really want to do an economics degree but it won't be easy to get a place – there are a lot of people who want one. But I'm sure I'll get the grades I need if I work hard.

E The exam's in a couple of hours. I'm not really ready, because I went to a few parties this week and I haven't had time to revise. If the questions aren't too hard, I might be OK. But this lecturer normally gives us difficult exam papers, so I think I'm in trouble!

> 📖 **VOCABULARY SUPPORT**
>
> *deadline* (B2) – the latest time to do something by
>
> *fail the year* – fail a whole year of studying and need to repeat
>
> *it's all over* – it's completely finished
>
> *paid off* (B2) – produced good results
>
> be in *trouble* (B2) – be in a difficult, unpleasant or dangerous situation

> 📖 **LANGUAGE NOTES**
>
> When we use *deadline*, the verbs that collocate with this are *meet a deadline* (to do the work by the time) and *miss a deadline* – not to do the work by the time).

b ⏺ 3.5 Encourage the class to underline the key words in the list of factors they have to match with the speakers (e.g. *finished, worried, decision*). Explain that if they can identify these key words as they listen, this will help them with the matching. You may also wish to help students with the words and expressions in the Vocabulary support box. Play the recording again for students to answer the questions, pausing after each speaker if appropriate. Check answers as a class at the end of the recording.

> **Answers**
> 1 B 2 E 3 C 4 A 5 D

c 💬 Students discuss the question in pairs. and feed back as a class. Which of the speakers 1–5 do students identify with the most?

5 GRAMMAR First conditional

a ⏺ 3.6 Books closed. Ask individual students: *What will you do / are you going to do if you pass your exam(s)?* Don't correct students if they make a mistake with the first conditional form at this stage, but note down their errors. Ask students: *Can you remember what Speaker B said he was going to if he passed his exams.* Students open books to check. Play the recording for students to complete the sentences. Check answers as a class. Give the students the opportunity to correct their sentences after they have completed 5c Grammar Focus, by writing the sentences on the board.

> **Answers**
> 1 pass 2 don't decide 3 doesn't give 4 aren't 5 work

Write sentence 1 from 5a on the board: *If I pass my exam, I'm going to have a big party!* Ask concept questions to reinforce the idea that the first conditional refers to something that may happen in the future. Ask: *Has the speaker taken the exam?* (no) *Is he going to pass?* (we don't know) *Is it possible?* (yes)

b Ask students to answer the questions and complete the rules.

> **Answers**
> 1 future   2 possible   3 present tense

c ▶ ⊙**3.7** Students read the information in Grammar Focus 9A on SB p.158. Play the recording where indicated and ask students to listen and repeat. Students then complete the exercises in Grammar Focus 9A on SB p.159. Check answers as a class, making sure students are using the present simple for the *if*-clause. Tell students to go back to SB p.89.

> **Answers (Grammar Focus 9A SB p.159)**
> **a** 1 g   2 c   3 e   4 a   5 h   6 d   7 b   8 f
> **b** 1 pay/I'll pay   2 don't /I'll   3 isn't going to/doesn't
>   4 will/there is   5 like/might stay   6 won't/don't
>   7 Are you going to/get
> **c** 1 will you do   2 it breaks   3 I'll ask   4 it's   5 I'll take
>   6 I have   7 I'll make   8 you don't   9 we'll be
>   10 I won't finish   11 the cat doesn't get   12 I push
>   13 he'll jump

> 📖 **LANGUAGE NOTES**
> • The two clauses of a conditional sentence can come in either order. The *if*-clause can come first or second. However, if it comes first, we use a comma after it.
> • Remember that the result clause can also use *might* to give less certainty.

d ⊙**3.8** **Pronunciation** Choose a sentence from 5a or Grammar Focus 9A and say it to students, e.g. *If I pass, I'm going to have a big party*. Then say the sentence without a pause. Ask the class what was different between the way you said the sentence the first time and the second time. Then ask students to look at the sentences. Play the recording for students to listen to examples of where to pause between the two parts of a conditional sentence. The sign // means there is a pause.

e ⊙**3.8** Play the recording again and pause after each sentence for students to repeat.

f Give students two or three minutes to change the second half of the sentences so that they are true for them. Then they compare their sentences with their partners. Ask students to share some examples with the class.

g 💬 Tell students about a plan: *I'm going to meet my friend in the park.* Write *And if it rains?* on the board. Tell them: *If it rains, we're going to meet in the café.* Elicit another possibility, e.g. *And if the café is full? If the café is full, we'll go to the café in the shopping centre.* Read through the examples in bubbles with the class and ask them to work in pairs to make as many exchanges for each sentence in 5d as they can. Ask one or two pairs to act out their best/longest exchanges.

> 💡 **FAST FINISHERS**
> Fast finishers can write two new sentences like the ones in 5d and 5f and think of further exchanges. Check these during feedback.

6 SPEAKING

a Tell students that they are going to talk to each other about their own long-term future. Read through the topics and ask students to note down their plans regarding these topics individually. Monitor and give encouragement and ideas where necessary.

b 💬 Put students into small groups. Read through the examples with the class. Students should tell their group about their plans. Other students should ask first conditional about these plans. Monitor but don't interrupt fluency unless students make mistakes with first conditional structures. Point out the errors for students to self correct. When the groups have finished, ask them to share examples of different plans and their questions with the class. Point out any language problems at this point, remembering to praise good use of language as well.

> **ADDITIONAL MATERIAL**
>
> ▶ Workbook 9A
> ▶ Photocopiable activities: Grammar p.220, Vocabulary p.244, Pronunciation p.283

9B I managed to stop feeling shy

At the end of this lesson, students will be able to:

- use verbs followed by *to* + infinitive / verb + *-ing* correctly
- read and understand a text about difficulties in celebrities' lives
- understand someone talking about shyness

💡 OPTIONAL LEAD-IN

Books closed. Think of a celebrity students will all know. Write down five facts about the celebrity's life. Make sure some of the facts focus on the personal life of the celebrity. Write the facts on the board, one sentence at a time, and see how quickly the class can guess the name of the person. Ask students to do the same in pairs. Ask one or two students to play the game with the whole class.

1 SPEAKING AND LISTENING

a 💬 Ask students to look at the pictures. Ask: *Where are the people? What are they doing? How do you think they are feeling?* Elicit adjectives, e.g. *shy, worried, nervous, anxious, happy, confident.* Then ask: *Why are they feeling like this?* Ask the class if they find the situations in the pictures easy or not, and why / why not. Elicit examples of when students have been in these situations recently. Find out how many people in the class feel shy in these situations.

b 💬 In pairs, students discuss their reactions to the statements before you take feedback as a class. Encourage students to justify their opinions as far as possible.

c ▶3.9 Tell the class that they are going to listen to an interview about shyness. Tell them not to worry if they don't understand everything they hear, but encourage them to focus on listening for the specific information they need to a check their answers for 1b. You may need to play the recording twice and/or pause it after the information is given.

Answers
1 T 2 F 3 F 4 T

Audioscript

PRESENTER So, let's have a look at another story in the news today. A study reported in the newspapers this week has found that 50% of people in the USA say they are shy. And also that this is an increase, and shyness is becoming more common. Well, here to talk about this is Dr Lamb, from the University of South London. Dr Lamb, good morning.

DR LAMB Good morning. Thanks for inviting me here.

P Let's talk first about shyness in general. Obviously we all feel shy sometimes. When does it become a problem?

L Well, it becomes a problem when it stops you doing what you want to do. Shy people normally want to communicate with other people. They don't want to be on their own. But they find it difficult when they need to talk to other people. Or when people talk to them.

P OK, and is it true that people are becoming shyer? Is shyness becoming more common in the world?

L That's a difficult question to answer. But some people say that modern technology is making us shyer.

P Yes, in fact the study mentions technology. What is the relationship between technology and shyness?

L Yes, well, the idea is basically that we speak to other people much less now … because of technology. The Internet has changed things a lot. We maybe use email or Facebook more than we talk on the phone or meet our friends. We check our bank account online. We don't go to the bank much anymore and speak to someone. We book our holidays online, not at a travel agent's. So there are all of these things. We just speak to other people less than in the past. So when we do speak to someone, it's more difficult for us.

P So tell us – what makes shy people feel the way they do? What's going on in a shy person's head?

L Well, first it's important to say – everyone is different so there's no single answer. But in general, shy people worry a lot and they expect things to go wrong. Let's imagine a shy person wants to go to a party. He or she will probably make lots of predictions about the party, normally bad ones. So they'll say, 'If I go to the party, I won't know anyone and it will be difficult. I won't enjoy it.' And so on. Or often they imagine terrible situations – 'Everyone will laugh when I speak', 'Everyone will hate me', that kind of thing.

P These are, I think, the kinds of feelings we all get sometimes. But you're saying that very shy people get more of them.

L Yes, yes – absolutely.

P And what can you do to help shy people?

L Well, when I work with shy people, I ask them to talk about these feelings. I tell them to make a list of all the things they worry about. Then I can ask, 'Well, do you think these things will really happen?' At the beginning they say, 'yes'. But I work with them and I hope in the end they'll realise the things probably won't happen. That's important. And after this training, I ask the shy person to go out and speak to people, to see what happens. And normally nothing bad happens. Then they can compare this real experience they've had to the list of fears they wrote on Day 1. There's normally a big difference and this really helps them to deal with their shyness.

P OK, Dr Lamb, we have to finish there. Thanks for coming to speak to us.

L Thank you.

📖 VOCABULARY SUPPORT

basically (B2) – simply

becoming more common (B1) – happening more often

on their own (B1) – alone

report (B1) – to say/tell the results of something

study (B2) – a survey / some research

📖 LANGUAGE NOTES

The verbs *increase* and *study* both have a countable noun which is the same form, e.g.

*There is **an increase** in the number of students at this school.*
*There has been **a study** about people's social habits.*

d ▶3.9 Read through the questions with the class. You may wish to help students with the words in the Vocabulary support box at this point. Encourage them to underline the key words in the question (problem, technology, worries, problem) and listen out for those in particular. Play the recording again for students to answer the questions. If students need more support, you can play the recording twice and pause for them to answer. Check answers as a class.

Answers
1 Shyness becomes a problem when it stops you doing what you want to do.
2 Because of technology / the Internet, we speak to other people much less now.
3 They worry a lot and they expect things to go wrong.
4 She asks them to talk about their feelings and make a list of all their fears; then she asks if things will really happen and they say 'yes'; she works with them and in the end they say 'no'; they go out and speak to people and see what happens – normally nothing bad.

e 💬 In pairs, students discuss what they think of Dr Lamb's advice. Take feedback as a class and elicit tips from the group for what people can do if they feel nervous or shy.

2 READING

a Elicit from the class the different kinds of celebrities there are – e.g. film stars, singers, sports celebrities, politicians and people in power, reality TV celebrities etc. – and also elicit and write on the board examples from each group. Ask for a show of hands for people who are interested in celebrities' lives and those who are not. Nominate students from each group to explain the reasons for their answer.

b Ask students to look at the pictures of the celebrities in the article. Ask: *Do you know the celebrities? What are they famous for?* Then read through the list of problems with the class and check students understand *bullying* (C1) – hurting or making fun of people who are weaker/ less powerful than you. In pairs, students try to match the celebrities with the problems.

🌍 CULTURE NOTES

Lady Gaga is from Manhattan in the USA. She is one of the best-selling musicians of all time. Her debut album *The Fame* has sold 15 million copies worldwide.

Michael Phelps has won more Olympic medals than any other Olympic athlete. The American swimmer won eight gold medals in the Beijing Olympics. After the 2012 Olympics in London, he had won 22 Olympic medals.

Salma Hayek was born in Mexico, but now lives in the USA. She has starred in over 40 films and also produces both film and TV shows. She was nominated for an Oscar™ for her role as artist Frida Kahlo in the film *Frida*.

Johnny Depp is probably most famous for his role as Captain Jack Sparrow in the *Pirates of the Caribbean* films. He has been nominated for an Oscar™ for this role as well as for his roles in *Finding Neverland* and *Sweeney Todd: The Demon Barber of Fleet Street*.

Sir Peter Jackson is a film director and producer from New Zealand. He directed the very successful *The Lord of the Rings* film trilogy as well as *The Hobbit*.

Benecio del Toro is from Puerto Rico. He won an Oscar™ for his role in *Traffic* (2000). Other film credits include *The Usual Suspects, Fear and Loathing in Las Vegas, Sin City* and he played Che Guevara in *Che* (2008).

c Ask students to read the article to check their ideas from 2b. You may wish to help them with the words in the Vocabulary support box at this point. Check answers as a class.

📖 VOCABULARY SUPPORT

budget (B2) – the money you have to do something

bullying (C1) – when children hurt or are unkind to weaker or less popular children

champion (B1) – a winner who beats everyone else

dyslexia – problem with reading words and writing

give up (B1) – to stop doing something

remade – made a new version of a film

Answers
family disagreements – Benicio Del Toro
language problems – Salma Hayek
shyness – Lady Gaga, Johnny Depp
not finishing school – Peter Jackson
bullying – Michael Phelps

📖 LANGUAGE NOTES

• The word *celebrity* is often abbreviated to *celeb*.

• Michael Phelps says: *I kind of laugh … We use *kind of* to mean, a little bit, or almost, e.g. *I laugh a little bit / I almost laugh about it.*

d Ask students to cover the article. Read out the sentences for students to try to remember and write down who the sentences refer to. Then they read the text again to check. Finally, check answers as a class.

Answers
1 Johnny Depp 2 Benicio Del Toro 3 Peter Jackson
4 Michael Phelps 5 Salma Hayek 6 Lady Gaga

e 💬 Students answer the questions in pairs. Check answers as a class.

Answers
1 people she doesn't know
2 no (because people who read fast forget it)
3 It made him stronger.
4 no (he's done everything he can to avoid it)
5 so he could get a job and save money for film equipment
6 be(come) a lawyer

f 💬 Discuss the questions as a class. Take a vote on which celebrity the group think had the most difficult time and which celebrity (if any) they admire the most.

💡 EXTRA ACTIVITY

Ask students in small groups to discuss the question: *Do you think celebrities have an easy life?* Put some ideas on the board to help them, e.g. *money, friends, photographers, travelling*. Monitor and support students with any vocabulary they may need. Encourage students to justify their opinions as far as possible.

3 GRAMMAR Verb patterns

a Ask: *Who decided to leave university to study acting?* (Benicio Del Toro). Write *Who loved using the family video camera?* (Peter Jackson) Elicit the different verb patterns after each main verb: verb + -*ing* and *to infinitive*. Then students look at the sentences and answer the question.

Answer
1 *to* + infinitive   2 verb + -*ing*

Verb patterns are complex in English and students need to learn that different verbs take different patterns. Establish the need to learn these patterns in this way: Ask students: *Which celebrity did you enjoy reading about most? Which celebrity – NOT in the article – would you like to know more about?* Put some of their answers on the board in full form, e.g. *I **enjoyed reading** about Johnny Depp. I **would like to know** more about Robert Pattinson.* Underline *reading* and *to know* and ask what these forms are: *to* + infinitive and verb + *-ing*.

b Remind students that it is important to know which form follows a main verb. Tell them that we need to learn this when we learn the main verb. Advise them to record new words in sentences so they remember this, e.g. *give up – I gave up running because I had an injury.*

Students complete the table with verbs from the texts. Check answers as a class. In feedback, ask for more example sentences from students for each verb, to practise using the correct form.

> **Answers**
> Verbs followed by *to* + infinitive: decide, learn, want
> Verbs followed by verb + *-ing*: love, enjoy, think about, start

⊙ **CAREFUL!**

Students may omit *to* before the infinitive, e.g. ~~We want see the new movie.~~ (Correct form = *We **want to** see the new movie.*)

c ▶ ⊙ **3.10** Students read the information in Grammar Focus 9B on SB p.158. Play the recording where indicated and ask students to listen and repeat. Students then complete the exercises Grammar Focus 9B on SB p.159. Check answers as a class. Tell students to go back to SB p.91.

> **Answers (Grammar Focus 9B SB p.159)**
> **a** 1 to leave 2 playing 3 working 4 starting 5 to visit
>   6 to live 7 talking 8 to help 9 to go 10 to save
> **b** both OK 2 not doing 3 to make 4 both OK
>   5 to start 6 to become 7 both OK 8 both OK
>   9 having 10 both OK
> **c** 1 to pass 2 not to be 3 getting 4 not putting 5 to speak
>   6 doing 7 to visit 8 not to play
> **d** 1 hates 2 thinks of 3 didn't expect 4 started 5 hated
>   6 continued 7 needed 8 discussed 9 preferred

4 VOCABULARY

Verbs followed by *to* + infinitive / verb + *-ing*

a Ask students to find four more verbs in the text followed by either form and add them to the table. Check answers together. Point out the use of a verb with a different pattern: *help* + object + *to* + infinitive (Phelps).

> **Answers**
> verb + *to* + infinitive: refuse (Hayek), manage (Jackson)
> verb + *-ing*: avoid (Gaga), regret (Del Toro)

b ⊙ In pairs, students discuss the meanings of the verbs in 4a before you check answers as a class. Elicit any other verbs the class knows which follow the patterns, e.g. + **-ing** – verbs of liking and disliking: *like, love,*

enjoy, fancy, dislike, detest, hate, can't stand; phrases with mind: *would mind, don't mind;* verbs of saying and thinking: *admit, consider, deny, imagine, intend, remember, suggest;* verbs of stopping and starting: *start, begin, stop, finish;* other common verbs: *avoid, miss, practise.*

+ **to** + **infinitive** – *afford, agree, allow, ask, choose, decide, encourage, expect, forget, hope, learn, manage, mean, need, offer prepare, pretend, promise, refuse, teach, want, would like.*

Tell students that they need to learn what verb pattern the verb takes when they learn the verb; there aren't any short cuts. However, as their English improves they will start using the most common patterns automatically.

> **Answers**
> *refuse:* say no
> *manage:* do but with difficulty
> *avoid:* stay away from
> *regret:* feel sad about something that happened in the past

c ▶ ⊙ **3.11** Students complete the exercises in Vocabulary Focus 9B on SB p.139. Tell students to use infinitive forms for the table in Exercise b. Play the recording where indicated for students to underline the stressed syllables in Exercise a and to practise saying the sentences. Tell students to go back to SB p.91.

> **Answers (Vocabulary Focus 9B SB p.139)**
> **a** 2, 10, 3, 4, 6, 1, 7, 5, 8, 11, 9, 12
> **b** *to* + infinitive: refuse, arrange, forget, seem, agree, manage
>   + verb + *-ing*: recommend, imagine, miss, dislike, regret, avoid
> **c** 1 re<u>fused</u> 2 ar<u>ranged</u> 3 for<u>got</u> 4 recom<u>mend</u>ed
>   5 im<u>agined</u> 6 <u>missed</u> 7 dis<u>liked</u> 8 <u>seemed</u> 9 a<u>greed</u>
>   10 <u>managed</u> 11 re<u>gretted</u> 12 a<u>voids</u>
> **d** 1 regretted 2 dislikes 3 forgot 4 imagined 5 refused
>   6 agreed/arranged 7 avoids 8 recommended 9 misses
>   10 agreed 11 managed 12 seemed

5 SPEAKING

a Put students into pairs. Tell them that they are going to take turns to make and guess phrases using the verb patterns. Look at the example in the book and give another example of your own for students to guess, e.g. *clean fridge.* Elicit guesses, e.g. *Are you avoiding cleaning your fridge? No. My fridge is beautifully clean. I'm very proud of it. Did you manage to clean your fridge recently? Yes, that's right. It was really dirty, but I had been so busy at work I hadn't had time to clean it!* Students choose five topics each and then prepare their sentences. They put their key words in the boxes.

b In pairs, students guess their partner's sentences from the key words. Monitor and help with question forms. Take feedback and ask students to tell their partner's most interesting or surprising sentence to the class.

> ⊙ **FAST FINISHERS**
>
> Fast finishers can write sentences and key words for two more topics.

ADDITIONAL MATERIAL

▶ Workbook 9B

▶ Photocopiable activities: Grammar p.221, Vocabulary p.245

9C Everyday English
Who's calling, please?

💡 OPTIONAL LEAD-IN

Books closed. Ask students in pairs to think of as many reasons why people might call this school as they can in two minutes. Give examples, e.g. *to give a message to someone who works or studies here or to ask for information about course prices.* Ask students to share some examples with the class.

1 SPEAKING AND LISTENING

a 💬 Look at the questions with the class and tell students about your own phone use, whom you call often, how long you spend on the phone, your experiences of using the phone in a foreign language. Students work in pairs and discuss the questions with a partner before you take feedback as a class.

b ▶️**3.12** Ask students to tell you the story so far. Tell the class that they are going to hear Annie making a phone call. Play Part 1 of the video or play the audio recording for students to listen and find out who Annie wants to speak to and if she is going to call back later. Check answers as a class.

Answers
Mark (Riley)
No, Mark will call her back.

Video/audioscript (Part 1)

RECEPTIONIST Good morning, Turner and Collins.
ANNIE Oh, good morning. Is it possible to speak to Mark Riley in Marketing?
R I'll just put you through.
COLLEAGUE Hello, Mark Riley's phone?
A Oh, hello. Is Mark there?
C I'm afraid he's not available – he's in a meeting. Can I take a message?
A Umm, can you just tell him that I called?
C And who's calling, please?

A This is Annie Morton speaking.
C OK. And shall I ask him to call you back?
A Ah, yes please.
C Did you say your name was Annie Morgan?
A No, sorry, Annie Morton. That's M-O-R-T-O-N.
C OK. And has he got your number?
A Yes, he has.
C Fine, I'll ask him to call you.
A Thanks very much.
C No problem. Bye.
A Goodbye.

c ▶️**3.12** Read through the detailed questions with the class and check students understand the meaning of *colleague* – a person you work with. Play Part 1 of the video or play the audio recording again for students to answer the questions. Check answers as a class.

Answers
1 Mark's in a meeting.
2 Annie asks him to tell Mark that she called.
3 He offers to ask Mark to call Annie back.
4 Annie's name; if Mark has Annie's number

2 USEFUL LANGUAGE
Telephoning people you don't know

a ▶️**3.13** Tell students that there are a lot of short set phrases that are commonly used in phone calls and these (taken from the recording) are some common examples. Students complete the missing words in pairs before you play the recording again for them to check their answers.

Answers
1 possible 2 put 3 there 4 available 5 take
6 calling 7 speaking 8 back 9 got

b Elicit from the class which phrases are used by the person who is making the call and which by the person receiving the call.

Answers
1 1, 3, 7
2 2, 4, 5, 6, 8, 9

c Answer the questions together. In pairs, students match the phrases to the functions. Check the answers as a class.

Answers
1 2   2 4   3 6   4 8

💡 EXTRA ACTIVITY

Books closed. Write sentences from 2a on the board, but leave out key words, e.g. *Is it ... speak to Mark Riley?* (possible to).

d 💬 Put students into groups of three and ask them to have a similar conversation to the one they've just heard. If you used the Optional lead-in, refer back to the ideas students gave then. If not, elicit some reasons for phoning someone at work. As the receptionist only has one thing to say, ask this student to listen to the rest of the conversation and give feedback. Students can then swap roles and do the role play again. Monitor the role plays and point out errors for students to self-correct. After the activity, ask students to tell the class examples from the conversations and if appropriate, choose a group to act out their conversation for the class.

3 LISTENING

a ▶️**3.14** Tell students that they are going to hear some more conversations. Play Part 2 of the video or play the audio recording for students to say when Mark and Annie arrange to meet. Then ask how many different conversations they heard (Three: Annie and Rachel, Mark and Annie, Rachel and Mark). Check answers together.

Answers
at 2.30 tomorrow / the next day

Video/audioscript (Part 2)

RACHEL So, how are you doing? Are you feeling better about finding a new job?

ANNIE Yeah, definitely. I'm sure I'll find something.

R Good … thank you, Tina.

A And I called Mark this morning. He wasn't there, but I left a message for him.

R Great. And did you speak to your boss? Did you ask about other jobs at your company?

A Yeah, I did. But she said there won't be anything else there.

R Oh dear. Well, it was still a good idea to ask.

A Yes, definitely. It was good to get everything clear. I understand the situation now.

R Exactly. And what happened with Leo in the end? Is everything OK?

A I met him just now for lunch actually. But yeah, everything's fine. He wasn't very well – that was all.

R Oh dear.

A Anyway, what about you? How are things here at the shop?

R Fine. Actually, it's been quite quiet this week.

A Oh, this could be Mark now.

R Answer it!

A Hello?

MARK Hi, is that Annie?

A Yes?

M Hi, it's Mark here.

A Oh hi, Mark!

M Is now a good time?

A Yes, it's fine.

M Well, I got your message. And Rachel explained you're looking for a new job.

A Sorry, Mark, I didn't catch that.

M Yeah, I was just saying, Rachel explained you're looking for a job.

A Yes, that's right.

M Well, look, why don't you come in to the office some time? We're always looking for new people here. Come in and we can have a chat.

A OK, that sounds great. How about two thirty tomorrow?

M Sorry, was that three thirty tomorrow?

A No, two thirty.

M Er … OK, that's fine.

A Great. Well, see you tomorrow then. Oh, I'm with Rachel and she wants to speak to you.

R Hi, Mark.

M Yep.

R Yes, I just wanted to ask you if you could buy a few things on your way home.

M Er …

R We need some milk, some orange juice …

M Sorry, can I call you back? I've got a meeting now, so I've got to go.

R OK …

M I'll call you in about an hour.

R All right. Speak to you soon. Bye.

M Bye.

📖 **VOCABULARY SUPPORT**

How are you doing?/How are things? – How are you?

leave/get/give/take – all collocate with *a message*

👁 **CAREFUL!**

Students sometimes confuse *quite* and *quiet*. In the dialogue, you can point out *quite quiet* and the pronunciation and spelling.

---

b ▶**3.14** Read through the questions with the class. Play Part 2 of the video or play the audio recording again. Students answer the questions. If necessary, pause after the information is given so that they can note answers. Check answers as a class.

> **Answers**
> 1 Annie's feeling better and she's sure she'll find something.
> 2 She's called Mark. She's spoken to her boss.
> 3 so they can have a chat (because they're [the company is] always looking for new people in Mark's office)
> 4 Rachel wants to ask Mark to buy a few things on his way home.

---

4 USEFUL LANGUAGE
Telephoning people you know

a ▶**3.15** In pairs, students complete the sentences. See if students are able to do this from memory, then play the recording for them to check their answers. Model the sentences for students to repeat, paying particular attention to intonation and word stress.

> **Answers**
> 1 is that   2 it's   3 good time   4 call you   5 got to   6 to you

b ▶**3.16** Ask students to find and correct the mistakes in pairs. Point out that there aren't mistakes in every line, but there is a case where there are two mistakes in one line. Play the recording for them to check their answers.

> **Answers**
> A Oh hi, is that Bernice?
> A Is now a good time?
> B Well, I'm a bit busy. Can I call you back?
> B Yeah, fine. But I've got to go. Speak to you soon.

c 💬 Students practise the conversation in pairs using their own names.

---

5 CONVERSATION SKILLS
Dealing with problems on the phone

a ▶**3.17** Elicit from the class what kind of problems you can have when you're talking on the phone – for example, technical problems – you can't hear the person you're speaking to, it's too noisy; language problems – you can't understand the person you are speaking to, etc. Build up a list on the board. See if students are able to complete the exchanges from memory and play the recording for them to check their answers. If necessary, play the recording again and pause so that students can complete the sentences. Check as a class.

> **Answers**
> 1 I didn't catch that
> 2 was that

b In pairs, students match the phrases with the situations. Check answers as a class.

> **Answers**
> 1 to say that you didn't hear what someone said
> 2 to check that you heard what someone said correctly

---

6 PRONUNCIATION
Main stress: contrastive

a ▶**3.18** Students listen to the exchange and answer the question. To consolidate the idea of corrective stress ask a student: *What time did you get up this morning?* Then make an obvious mistake: *Was that **five** thirty?* The student may make the correct emphasis in his/her reply: *No, **six** thirty.* Then ask the class: *Did he/she say **four** thirty?* This should elicit the correct emphasis.

> **Answer**
> two

b Answer the question as a class. Tell students that when you are correcting something, you can repeat the false information with the stress on the mistake, before giving the correct version with the stress on the correct word – *No, not _three_ thirty, _two_ thirty.*

Answer
2

 LOA TIP ELICITING

- Tell students that they have to correct things you say.
  Say: *I'm going home at four thirty.*
  Students repeat: *I'm going home at four thirty.*
  Say: *Did you say **five** thirty?*
  Students reply: *No, we said **four** thirty.*
- Repeat the drill with these sentences:
  My favourite subject is Maths. (English)
  I have a black car. (red)
  I live in Jackson Road. (Clarkson Road)
  My son is 15. (14)

---

c Students do the task in pairs, but they don't look at each other's ideas. They complete the sentences about their partner, guessing any information they don't know.

d To model the activity, ask for two volunteers to read the example with the correct contrastive stress (on *Valencia*). Students then ask their partners the questions for them to say *Yes, …* or *No, …* and correct their partner's error. Monitor the activity and encourage self-correction if students get the contrastive stress wrong.

7 SPEAKING

a Tell students that they are going to practise the phrases they have learned in this lesson by role playing some more phone conversations. Read through the situations with them. Then ask them to choose one of the situations and have the telephone conversation.

b Students swap roles and choose another situation. Monitor and correct students' pronunciation as appropriate. Listen for correct usage of target language from this lesson and note any errors to deal with later, but do not interrupt fluency.

FAST FINISHERS
Fast finishers can choose another situation to role play.

ADDITIONAL MATERIAL

▶ Workbook 9C
▶ Photocopiable activities: Pronunciation p.282
▶ Unit Progress Test
▶ Personalised online practice

Skills for Writing
Online courses are new to me

At the end of this lesson, students will be able to:
- write a personal profile
- talk about ways of learning
- read and understand a text about learning experiences
- avoid repetition when writing

☀ OPTIONAL LEAD-IN

Books closed. If you have a multilingual class, put students in pairs to find out the differences between the education systems in their countries. Put some ideas on the board to guide them, e.g. ages for different school stages, size of classes, school times, technology in the classroom.

If the class is monolingual, ask them to talk about the differences between ways of learning English at state schools and other places, e.g. universities, private language schools. Monitor and contribute to the conversations. Take feedback and ask pairs for comments.

1 LISTENING AND SPEAKING

a 💬 Read through the ideas and the questions with the class and ask for some examples of when we might use some of these different ways of learning, e.g. reading – for an essay; online or with an app – for languages in the classroom; – for all secondary school subjects; one-to-one – for music lessons, driving lessons. Ask students to talk about the questions, and allow the discussion to continue if they're interested.

b ▶ 3.19 Tell the class that they are going to hear two women talking about online learning. Read the question and play the recording for students to listen and answer. Check answers together.

> **Answer**
> Janina; her IT skills aren't very good

Audioscript

ROBERTA Hi Janina. What are you reading?

JANINA I'm just looking at the course information for next year.

R Oh, OK.

J It says that one of the psychology courses I have to do is going to be online.

R That's good.

J You think so? I've never done an online course.

R I did one this year – it was great. I wouldn't mind doing my whole degree online.

J Really, Roberta? What's so good about it?

R Well, we only had about two classes on the whole course. And they recorded them and put them online anyway. I was free to study whenever I wanted. Good for people like me who are always late for classes!

J Yeah, I don't have a problem with that but it sounds good.

R I mean, you still have to write essays and hand things in on time and all that kind of thing.

J Of course.

R And I got good grades on that course.

J But did you ... I mean, didn't you miss asking your teachers questions? And what about meeting other students?

R Well, we could go and meet the teachers if we wanted to ... you know, make an appointment and ask about something one-to-one. And at the beginning of the course, we had to write an online profile. We had students from all round the world in our class, so the profiles were really interesting.

J How many international students were there?

R About 15, I think. And from all kinds of different places – Colombia, China, Morocco, Turkey, Oman – all over the place.

J And did they talk about their countries a lot?

R Yeah, that's what I really enjoyed.

J The only thing I'm not sure of ... well, you know that my IT skills aren't very good. Like, I'm OK making documents and using the Internet. But this could be a bit more ... I don't know ... difficult?

R Not really. You don't need any special skills. It's quite easy. And there's an introduction course you can do.

J Yeah, I was just reading about that. At least it's free.

R Yeah, you should do it, Janina. It's only two weeks long and you can do it any time. It really helped me.

J OK – sounds like a good idea.

c ▶ 3.19 Read through the sentences with the class and encourage them to underline the key words. Play the recording again for students to choose true or false and to correct the false sentences. Check answers as a class.

> **Answers**
> 1 T
> 2 F – She thinks online courses are great.
> 3 T
> 4 F – She could meet teachers if she wanted to.
> 5 T
> 6 F – She doesn't need any special skills.
> 7 F – She can do it any time.

📖 LANGUAGE NOTES

- Make sure students understand the meaning of an *online profile* (a short description of yourself for other people you communicate with online).
- In the conversation, there are some good examples of words we use to make our speaking more natural or to give us more thinking time, e.g. *I mean ... You know ... Well ... Like ...*
- We sometimes miss out words when we're speaking, e.g. *(It's) Good for people like me!*

d 💬 Individually, students make lists of the good and bad points of learning with a teacher and learning online, as shown in the book. Monitor and help with vocabulary as necessary.

e 💬 In small groups, students discuss their ideas and which they prefer, and why. Take feedback and build up a list on the board of the good and bad points of each method of learning. (Suggested answers: in class: the teacher can correct you; you can ask questions; you can talk to other students; however, you can't work at your own pace, you can be distracted by other students. Online: you can choose when to work; you can do it when you've got the time; you don't have to travel; however, you can't ask questions, you have no contact with people.) Take a vote on which way of learning the class prefers overall.

Finish this stage by asking: *Do you think online learning will ever completely replace learning in a classroom with a teacher? Why / Why not?*

2 READING

a Elicit from students when they last wrote a profile of themselves, and why, e.g. for a social media site, for a company website, etc. Ask them to read the two profiles and find out what is similar about the two people. Check answers as a class.

> **Answers**
> They both speak two languages. They are both studying in their second languages.

> 🌍 **CULTURE NOTES**
> With over a million people, Birmingham is the second largest UK city outside London. Birmingham has six universities and 40% of the population are under the age of 25.

b Students read the profiles again to complete the table individually, and then compare notes with a partner. Check answers as a class.

> **Answers**
> Degree subjects: Janina – psychology; Gonzalo – sports science, business
> Languages: J – Polish, English; G – Spanish, English
> Reason: J – improve IT skills; G – get a place on a business degree programme, own a gym
> Work/free time: J – part-time job in restaurant, doesn't have a lot of time; G – manager of a gym, watch sport, football

> 📖 **LANGUAGE NOTES**
> The adjective *poor*, as well as meaning *not rich*, can also refer to something that is weak, e.g. *poor memory, poor skills.*

3 WRITING SKILLS Avoiding repetition

a Ask students to read the first paragraph of Janina's profile again and then cover it. Then ask them to look at the sentences in 3a and try to do the task from memory. They can then uncover the paragraph to do the task. Check answers as a class. Elicit that Janina replaced certain words with pronouns in order to avoid repeating them. This makes her text shorter and easier to read and digest.

> **Answers**
> <u>My psychology degree</u> is a great course and I'm really enjoying the course, although the course is hard work.
> The sentence above is longer, repetitive and unnatural.

b In pairs, students look at the highlighted words in the profiles and in pairs find and underline the information the pronouns replace. Check answers together.

> **Answers**
> 1 My psychology degree course   2 year
> 3 online courses   4 my IT skills
> 5 work(ing) one night in the week and all day on Saturday
> 6 the degree   7 Spanish   8 studying with people in the UK
> 9 a gym   10 Claudia

c Students look at the sentences and tell you the difference between *it* and *one*.

> **Answers**
> *it*: definite pronoun; refers to the gym where Gonzalo works (definite means specific)
> *one*: indefinite pronoun; refers to any gym (indefinite means unspecific)

d In pairs, students select appropriate pronouns to replace the highlighted words in the text about Muneera. Remind them to think about whether the word they are replacing is singular or plural and whether it refers to one specific thing or a general category of things. Check answers as a class.

> **Answers**
> 1 It   2 it   3 They   4 it   5 This/It   6 them   7 them   8 her

4 WRITING

a Tell students that they are going to write a similar student profile about themselves. Give them time to prepare by making notes under the headings. Monitor and help with vocabulary as neccessary.

b Students write their profiles. Remind them to use pronouns to avoid repetition. Monitor and point out errors for students to self-correct.

c Students swap profiles with a partner to read and check for use of pronouns.

> 💡 **EXTRA ACTIVITY**
> Give each student in the class a new identity, e.g. Tom from Scotland, Katya from Russia. They should take a few minutes to invent the following information about this person: studies, how they feel about their studies, languages spoken, one or two interests. Then in pairs they interview each other to find out information about their new partner. Elicit interview questions students could ask, e.g. *What are you studying? Do you like the course? Why is that? How many languages do you speak? What do you do in your free time?*. With the information they write a profile for this person, e.g. *Tom is from Scotland and he's a psychology student. He loves his subject and thinks it will be very important in his future life because …*

> 🔄 **LOA TIP REVIEW AND REFLECT**
>
> • Put students into pairs and ask them to write down three things they've learned to do this lesson. Take feedback and put a list on the board.
>
> • Ask the class to rank the importance of these different things they have learned and also to say which they need to practise more to feel confident.

> **ADDITIONAL MATERIAL**
> ▶ Workbook 9D

UNIT 9
Review and extension

1 GRAMMAR

a Ask students to choose the correct forms to complete the sentences. Check answers as a class.

> **Answers**
> 1 study   2 'm going to go   3 don't
> 4 work   5 might buy   6 can't

b Students complete the conversation individually. Point out that both options may be correct. Check answers as a class.

> **Answers**
> 1 to leave   2 to do   3 to think / thinking   4 working
> 5 to be / being   6 to use / using   7 to talk   8 to bring

c Model the conversation for students to repeat. In pairs, they can practise again.

> ### 💡 EXTRA ACTIVITY
> Ask students to work in pairs and write five *if*-clauses for conditional sentences, e.g. *If I miss the train at 4.30, …* Then students swap partners. They take turns to give their partner an *if*-clause to complete. However, their partner only has 10 seconds to finish the sentence. If they do it inside 10 seconds, they win a point. Monitor to check accuracy as far as possible. Tell students to ask you if they are unsure about their partner's sentence. Take feedback and ask students to share some of their sentences with the class.

2 VOCABULARY

a Students complete the words individually or in pairs. Check answers.

> **Answers**
> 1 drama   2 education   3 medicine
> 4 business management   5 engineering   6 psychology

> ### 💡 EXTRA ACTIVITY
> Ask students to look back through the unit and find six words to revise. They should write them down as in 2a with just the first and last letters and a clue. They swap these with a partner who tries to solve them. Ask students to tell some of their clues to the class.

b Students complete the sentences with the verbs in the box. Check answers together.

> **Answers**
> 1 get   2 take   3 fail   4 get   5 revise   6 hand in

c Discuss the question as a class and encourage students to justify their answers as far as possible.

3 WORDPOWER
Multi-word verbs with *put*

a Write the word *put* on the board and ask for a sentence using the verb. Write it on the board. Ask students to tell you different prepositions we can use after *put*, with examples, e.g. *I put **on** a scarf this morning because it was cold.* Put the prepositions on the board. Look at the words in bold in the replies in 3a with the class. See how many you have already got on the board. Ask students to match the sentences 1–7 with the replies a–g. Check answers as a class.

> **Answers**
> 1 d   2 a   3 g   4 b   5 f   6 c   7 e

b Do the matching task as a class. Ask for an example from students for each multi-word verb. Extend by asking: *What have you put off recently? What's the last thing you put down? What prices have been put up recently? Do you always put things back if you borrow them?*

> **Answers**
> 1 put off   2 put on   3 put on   4 put down
> 5 put through   6 put up   7 put back

c Students complete the sentences individually. Check answers as a class.

> **Answers**
> 1 puts, down   2 put(s) up   3 put, off   4 put on
> 5 put, through   6 put on   7 put, back

d 💬 In pairs, students talk about which sentences in 3c are true for them or which they agree with.

▶ Photocopiable activities: Wordpower p.260

> ### 🔄 LOA REVIEW YOUR PROGRESS
> Students look back through the unit, think about what they've studied and decide how well they did. Students work on weak areas by using the appropriate sections of the Workbook, the Photocopiable activities and the Personalised online practice.

UNIT 10

Values

GETTING STARTED

💡 OPTIONAL LEAD-IN

Books closed. Write the words *crime* and *criminal* on the board and ask for an example of each. Put students in pairs to brainstorm as many words related to the two words as they can in two minutes. Collate their ideas and put them on the board. Suggested words: *to steal, to rob, to break into, to burgle, to vandalise, to shoplift, thief, robber, burglar, vandal, shoplifter, police, prison, detective, killer, to kill.*

a 💬 Ask students to tell you what is happening in the picture. Write some phrases for speculation on the board which they can use to help them express their ideas, e.g. *It looks like … , It/He might be …, It seems as if … .* If you wish, give students information from the Culture notes below.

UNIT OBJECTIVES

At the end of this unit, students will be able to:
- understand texts and conversations about moral issues and complaining
- discuss moral dilemmas, including attitudes to criminal behaviour
- describe problems with goods and services
- return goods and make complaints
- write an (informal) apology email

🌍 CULTURE NOTES

This picture is from a book by Professor Joseph Giacomin called *Thermal – Seeing the World Through 21st Century Eyes*. It contains thermal images, i.e. images produced by recording the temperature of people and things, using an infra-red camera. People can be seen in complete darkness as the thermal camera picks up their body temperature. The book includes pictures that show the effects of global warming, pollution, and how houses lose energy. It also gives an interesting picture of everyday events around us. This particular picture is of someone breaking into a car at night and shows how, with modern technology and recording devices, no one is protected by darkness.

b 💬 Students speculate what happens next. Write some expressions for making predictions on the board they can use to help them express their ideas. e.g. *I think he'll…, I think someone will …, He'll probably run away …, He might …*

c 💬 Students discuss the questions in pairs. The questions use the second conditional, which students will look at in this unit. Don't spend time explaining the language point at this stage, but encourage students to express their ideas, using the structure *I'd …,* and justifying their answers as far as possible. Monitor but don't interrupt fluency unless students make mistakes in their choice of vocabulary. Take feedback and see if the class agree on their answers. Ask for reasons and examples.

💡 EXTRA ACTIVITY

Ask students to tell their partners about a recent news story about a crime. They should try to say what happened, when and where. Circulate and give help where necessary. Ask some students to share their stories with the class.

10A Would you do the right thing?

At the end of this lesson, students will be able to:

- talk about a moral dilemma
- use the second conditional correctly
- understand people talking about illegal downloading
- understand and use multi-word verbs

⚙ OPTIONAL LEAD-IN

Books closed. Put students in pairs. Give them a few minutes to write down as many rules that they have followed so far today as they can. e.g. keeping to the speed limit, not playing loud music on public transport, not smoking in the corridor, etc. Ask them to say which rule on their list is the most and least important.

1 SPEAKING

a Write the words *legal* versus *illegal* (B2) on the board and elicit from the students or explain that when something is *legal* it is allowed or permitted by the law; *illegal* means the opposite. Ask students to look at the pictures and match the activities a–e with the pictures 1–5. Check answers as a class.

> **Answers**
> a 2 b 5 c 1 d 4 e 3

b 💬 In pairs, students put the activities in order from worst to least bad. Take a vote on which activity the group thinks is the worst.

c 💬 Discuss the question as a class. Ask students under what circumstances doing some of these things might be justified. Ask: *Is it ever OK to park illegally / drive too fast on the motorway / download a film from the internet, etc.?* (For example in a medical emergency; if you have already bought the film, etc.)

2 LISTENING

a 💬 Elicit from the class what kinds of things people download illegally (songs, films, books, etc.). Students read the text about illegal downloading individually and discuss their opinions as a class. If you wish, give students information from the Culture notes below.

🌐 CULTURE NOTES

Philip Pullman wrote a famous trilogy of fantasy books for children called *His Dark Materials*. *Northern Lights*, the first book in the trilogy, was made into a popular film called *The Golden Compass*, starring Nicole Kidman and Daniel Craig, in 2007.

b ▶3.20 Tell students that they are going to hear five people being asked about downloading. For each speaker, students need to establish the person's attitude towards downloading from the Internet (tell students to write 'yes', 'no' or 'maybe') and what kind of things they would download. Play the recording. Students make notes as they are listening or at the end. Check answers as a class.

> **Answers**
> Speaker 1: yes, TV programme; Speaker 2: maybe, TV programme (not if small company); Speaker 3: no, it's illegal; Speaker 4: yes, TV programme, music (not if charity album); Speaker 5: no, can't, may ask granddaughter

c ▶3.20 Play the recording again for students to note down the reasons the speakers give for their answers. If necessary, pause the recording after each piece of information is given. Check answers together.

> **Answers**
> 1 doesn't hurt anyone 2 big companies, actors are rich enough
> 3 it's illegal 4 everyone does it
> 5 doesn't know how, worried about police

Audioscript

PRESENTER Downloading is in the news again, with the news that more people downloaded the hit show *Game of Thrones* than actually watched it on TV. We're often told that downloading illegally from the Internet is the same as stealing from a shop. But do people really believe this? We asked the people of Camden Town: *If you wanted to watch a TV programme but it wasn't available in your country, would you download it illegally?*

1 Ah … maybe. I don't know … Yeah, if the programme wasn't available, I'd download it!

P What if it *was* on TV in your country, but not for another month?

1 Yeah, I would still download it. What's the difference? Downloading doesn't hurt anyone and no one ever gets into trouble. It would just mean I didn't need to wait a month!

2 Maybe it depends who made the programme. I don't think the big companies that make these TV programmes are poor. All the actors are rich enough … But if it was a film made by a small company, it would be a bit different. I'd prefer to pay a company like that because they need the money.

3 No, I wouldn't. I just watch what's on TV. No need to download things.

P And how about a book? Would you download a book?

3 Well, no. It would be illegal, I think.

P But what if it was a book that you knew was in your local library. But you didn't have time to go to the library.

3 Well … I suppose … if it was in the library … but, no. It's illegal. I wouldn't do it.

4 A TV programme? Of course, why not? It's easy. Everyone does it!

P And what about music? Would you download an album?

4 An album …? Yeah, maybe. But I'm one of those strange people who still buys CDs. So if I liked the album I'd buy it afterwards – because I like to own something I can hold in my hands.

P And what if it was a charity album? Would you download that?

4 No, I wouldn't download an album if it was for charity. That wouldn't be right.

5 I'd have no idea how to download a TV programme! But I'd ask my granddaughter to download it for me if I really wanted to see it, although I'd probably be worried about the police knocking at my door the next day.

📖 LANGUAGE NOTES

Some students confuse the word *library* and *bookshop*. Make sure they are clear about the difference: *library* – a place where you borrow books; *bookshop* – a place where you can buy books.

d 💬 Discuss the questions briefly as a class. Encourage students to give reasons for their opinions.

3 GRAMMAR Second conditional

a ⏺**3.21** Play the recording for students to complete the sentences. Check answers as a class and elicit that the pattern of verb forms exemplified in all these sentences (*if* + *would* + verb in one clause + simple past tense in the other clause) is called the second conditional.

> **Answers**
> 1 wanted 2 wasn't 3 liked 4 was 5 wanted

b Individually, students choose the correct options to complete the sentences about the form and usage of the second conditional. They compare their ideas with a partner before you check the answers as a class.

> **Answers**
> 1 b 2 b 3 a

LOA TIP CONCEPT CHECKING

• Ask: *If your friend stole something from a shop, would you tell someone?* and write it on the board. Ask these questions to reinforce the idea of an imaginary situation.
Are we asking about a real situation? (no)
Are we asking about an unreal or imagined situation? (yes)
Are we asking about an imagined past action? (no)
Are we asking about imagined present or future action? (yes)

---

c ⏺**3.22** Students read the information in Grammar Focus 10A on SB p.160. Play the recording where indicated and ask students to listen and repeat. Students then complete the exercises in Grammar Focus 10A on SB p.161. Check answers as a class. Tell students to go back to SB p.99.

> **Answers (Grammar Focus 10A SB p.161)**
> **a** 1 e 2 h 3 a 4 g 5 f 6 b 7 c 8 d
> **b** 1 were; I'd give 2 would be; wasn't 3 I had; I'd read
>   4 would; you saw 5 didn't smoke; you'd save
>   6 wouldn't; didn't like 7 found; would you
> **c** 1 I were/was you 2 I wouldn't eat 3 I didn't eat them
>   4 they would throw 5 would you do 6 a shop assistant saw
>   7 I would promise 8 they didn't believe 9 they called
>   10 You would go 11 the police came
>   12 they wouldn't send 13 it would be

📖 LANGUAGE NOTES

As with the first conditional, the clauses can be in either order but when the *if*-clause comes first, we use a comma.

◉ CAREFUL!

Though mixed conditional sentences are possible, students sometimes use *will* when *would* is more appropriate, e.g. ~~If I were you, I'll download it~~. (Correct form = *If I were you, I'd download it.*)

---

d ⏺**3.21** Pronunciation Play the recording for students to listen and notice the two different possible pronunciations of the vowel sound in *would*: /wʊd/ (when stressed) and /wəd/ (when unstressed). Point out that the *l* is always silent. Model the sentences again for students to repeat.

e ⏺**3.23** Play the recording again for students to work out the rules. Check answers as a class.

> **Answers**
> 1 silent 2 questions 3 /wʊd/

---

f Read the sentence parts with the class (the first has an example) and elicit some answers. Students complete the sentences individually with two different ideas.

g 💬 Students compare their sentences with a partner. Encourage them to expand on their answers and ask their partner questions as in the examples in the speech bubbles. Take feedback and ask students to tell you the most surprising or interesting thing they learned about their partner.

4 VOCABULARY Multi-word verbs

a 💬 Ask students to look at the pictures and say what is happening in each one. Ask: *What's the best thing to do next?* for each situation. You may wish to help them with the words in the Vocabulary support box.

📖 VOCABULARY SUPPORT

crash (B1) – to have an accident with another vehicle
damage (B1) – the result of hitting a car
notes (B1) – paper money
pavement (B1) – place beside the road that we walk on

---

b Remind students that in English there are a lot of verbs composed of a main verb and a preposition (or sometimes two prepositions) and the meaning is sometimes quite literal and easy to guess, e.g. *put on* (clothes) or sometimes more abstract, e.g. *put off* (meaning to postpone or cancel). Students match the multi-word verbs in bold with the definitions. Check answers as a class.

> **Answers**
> 1 look after 2 put off 3 carry on 4 hand in

c Students complete the exercises in Vocabulary Focus 10A on SB p.140. Check answers to the exercises and go through the Tip with the class to check understanding. Tell students to go back to SB p.99.

> **Answers (Vocabulary Focus 10A SB p.140)**
> **a** 1 carried on 2 felt like 3 came round 4 looked after
>   5 broke up 6 turned down 7 joined in 8 put off
>   9 handed in 10 passed on
> **b** 1 came round 2 put off 3 pass on 4 broke up 5 joined in
>   6 handed in 7 turned down 8 feel like 9 looking after
>   10 carry on

5 SPEAKING

a 💬 In pairs, students discuss the questions. Take feedback as a class and ask students what they learned about their partner.

b ▶ Tell students that they are going to do a quiz to find out how honest their partner is. Divide the class into pairs and assign A and B roles. Student As read the surveys on SB p.129 and Student Bs read the surveys on SB p.131. They take turns to ask each other the quiz questions. When they have finished, ask students to look at the results on SB p.127 to find out how honest they are.

ADDITIONAL MATERIAL

▶ Workbook 10A
▶ Photocopiable activities: Grammar p.222, Vocabulary p.246, Pronunciation p.283

10B I'm too embarrassed to complain

At the end of this lesson, students will be able to:

- read and understand a text about a shopping survey
- use quantifiers and *too / not enough* correctly
- understand people talking about a shopping survey
- understand an expert talking about complaining
- make nouns from different verbs
- talk about complaining in general

💡 OPTIONAL LEAD-IN

Books closed. Tell students about somebody you know who complains a lot, e.g. *My father always complains about other people's driving (it's too fast, dangerous); he complains about the treatment the doctor gives him (it doesn't work, makes him sleepy).* Ask students if they can think of a person among their family or friends (not in the class) who enjoys complaining. Students share their ideas with the class. (If students come from a culture where describing somebody they know as a complainer would be disrespectful, you could ask them about characters in comedies/dramas who complain a lot.)

1 READING AND SPEAKING

a 💬 Point out the title of the lesson *I'm too embarrassed to complain* and teach or elicit from the class the meaning of *embarrassed* (B1) – feeling shy or ashamed about something. Ask: *Is it OK to complain about things in your country or are most people usually too embarrassed to complain?* Elicit examples of the kind of things people complain about.

🔄 LOA TIP ELICITING

Say: *I went shopping yesterday and when I got to the checkout, I found I didn't have enough money. How did I feel?* (embarrassed) Ask: *When have you felt embarrassed?* Ask one or two students to give you an example.

b In pairs students match the complaints and what people are complaining about. Check answers as a class. Elicit or explain the meaning of *rug* (B1) – a small carpet. Each time a student gives you the right answer, ask them to explain the meaning of the word – e.g. *the price is how much something costs, the quality is how good it is,* etc.

> **Answers**
> 1 price   2 quality   3 delivery   4 service

c 💬 In pairs, students discuss their recent experience of the situations in 1b. Take feedback as a class. Encourage students to expand their answers by saying where, why and when.

d Before students look at the title of the article, ask them if they think the British complain a lot or not. Then ask them to look at the title. Ask: *Are you surprised by this? Why / Why not?*

e Individually, students scan the article and underline the key information the task asks them to locate. Encourage them to compare their answers with a partner then check as a class.

> **Answers**
> 1 Britain (the British), Germany (the Germans), Italy (the Italians), Sweden (the Swedish).
> 2 What do the British complain about? Why do some choose not to complain?
> 3 the service is not good enough
> 4 five minutes
> 5 don't have time

📖 LANGUAGE NOTES

verb: *complain* noun: *complaint* person: *complainer*

f 💬 Ask students read the text again and list all the things that the British complain about. Take feedback from the class and write the things mentioned on the board (poor service, not enough shop assistants, slow queues, bad quality products, rude staff, delivery problems). Ask if there any things in this list which people wouldn't complain about in students' home countries and why.

2 GRAMMAR Quantifiers; *too / not enough*

a Books closed. Tell students you are not having a very good day and they are going to guess your complaints. Think of three complaints about your day, using *too, too much* or *too many*, e.g. *It's too hot in here. There are too many chairs. There was too much sugar in my coffee.* Say the beginning of each complaint and clues to the rest of the sentences by miming, e.g. *It's too ….* (mime *hot*). *There are too many …* (point to chairs). *There was too much ….* (pretend to drink coffee and make face). Can they guess what your complaints are? Write the words up they give you (*hot, chairs, sugar in my coffee*). Now try to elicit the rest of the complaint from the students and write the full sentences on the board. Elicit or correct mistakes with forms with *too / not enough*. Books open. Students look at the complaints in 2a and answer the questions. Remind them about countable and uncountable nouns by eliciting examples, or putting *person/salt* on the board and asking which is countable (person) and which is uncountable (salt). Check answers as a class.

> **Answers**
> 1 a too b not enough   2 a after, b after, c before   3 a many, b much

📖 LANGUAGE NOTES

Students may have a problem with pronunciation and spelling of *enough* /ɪˈnʌf/.

b ▶ 🔊 3.24–3.25 Students read the information in Grammar Focus 10B on SB p.160. Play the recording where indicated and ask students to listen and repeat. Students then complete the exercises in Grammar Focus 10B on SB p.161. Check answers as a class, making sure students are checking for countable and uncountable nouns and negative and positive sentences. Point out that in Exercise d, 1–3 can be past or present. Tell students to go back to SB p.100.

Answers (Grammar Focus 10B on SB p.161)

a 1 c 2 a 3 d 4 a 5 c 6 d
b Correct: 2, 3, 5, 7
c 1 There aren't many 4 A few of 6 I love hot / very hot
   8 too difficult
d 1 There were too many people on the beach.
   2 The soup was too hot.
   3 She wasn't tall enough to reach the top shelf.
   4 The waiter spoke too quickly.
   5 The service here is too slow.
   6 Sorry, I don't have enough money.

c Students choose the correct options individually. Check answers as a class.

> **Answers**
> 1 too 2 too many 3 warm enough 4 too much
> 5 enough seats 6 long enough

d 💬 In pairs, students talk about possible situations for each complaint in 2c. Take feedback as a class. How many possible different contexts can students find for each complaint?

> **Suggested answers**
> 1 swimming pool/holiday 2 restaurant/hotel
> 3 hotel/school/work 4 cinema/theatre/lecture
> 5 restaurant/classroom/lecture 6 holiday tour

3 LISTENING

a 💬 Ask students to cover the *TOP TEN* and *BOTTOM TEN* lists and to read the title and introduction to the survey. Ask students to guess where their country would be on the list of the most complaining countries. Then they look at the survey results to check if their country is named and if they were right. Ask: *What is the difference between this survey and the survey on p.100?* (This survey is international, not just Europe. The survey question was different: *Have you made a complaint in the last 12 months?*) Have a brief discussion about why students think the countries at the top complain a lot and why the countries at the bottom of the list don't. After reading about the survey, ask students to cover the text. Ask them what these numbers refer to:

30,000 (the number of people asked), 30 (the number of different countries), 12 (months: the period of time the survey was for).

b ▶ 3.26 Tell students that they are going to listen to a radio programme about the survey. Read through the two questions and play the recording for students to listen and answer. Check answers as a class.

> **Answers**
> 1 Brazil, China 2 yes (Clara); no (Feng)

Audioscript

PRESENTER Now, a new survey has shown the countries in the world where people complain the most. And to discuss the results we've got two guests – Clara Gomes from Brazil, which is in the top ten of countries that like to complain, and Zhang Feng, from China, from the bottom ten on the list.
CLARA Good morning.
FENG Good morning.
P So let's start with you, Clara – what do you think of the survey results?
C Well, I'm surprised we're in the top ten, but I'm not shocked because things are slowly changing in Brazil. Many Brazilians have got more money these days. So they buy more and also expect better quality – if something's not good enough, they'll complain.

And another thing is education. I think people know more now about the law than they used to. They know what the companies have to do, like replace things if they break easily, or giving customers their money back if the bill is wrong ... so they're asking companies to play by the rules.
P OK, and what about China, Feng? You're very low down the list. Do you think that's surprising?
F Not really, not these days. In China, people don't really believe everything a company says. Because of this they always like to check the products carefully before they pay for them. When you buy something online in China, you can contact the company first to check all the details of the product – it's very quick and easy to do. And then, you don't have to pay when you order, you don't even have to pay when the product arrives – you **only** pay if **you** think the product is the same as the product that the company promised. So in the end, there isn't much to complain about.

📖 **LANGUAGE NOTES**

The phrase *play by the rules* may be unfamiliar to your students. It means *to follow the rules, to not break the rules*. It comes from sport and games where the rules must be followed.

---

c ▶ 3.26 Read through the questions with the class. Play the recording again for students to answer the questions. If necessary, play the recording twice and/or pause after the information to give students time to answer. Check answers together. Ask students: *Do you think what companies do in China is a good thing? Should companies in other countries do the same? Why / Why not?*

> **Answers**
> 1 Brazilians have got more money these days and expect better quality. People know more now about the law than they used to.
> 2 You can contact the company first to check all the details of the product. You don't have to pay when you order or when the product arrives. You only pay if you think the product is the same as the product that the company promised.

d 💬 Discuss the question as a class. Ask students if they are surprised by where their country is on the list. If their country is not on the list, ask where they think it might appear – between 11 and 29 – and why.

e 💬 In pairs, students complete the advice about complaining. Give them a few minutes to try and fill the gaps, then the answers on the board in jumbled order for them to choose from. Check answers as a class. Accept any alternative answers offered by the students as long as they are grammatically correct and make sense.

> **Answers**
> 1 the same day 2 shout 3 description 4 decision
> 5 manager, director 6 explain, angry 7 felt, enjoyment

f ▶ 3.27 Tell students that in the next part of the programme, an expert on complaining joins the discussion. Play the recording for students to compare their advice from 3e with the expert's.

📖 VOCABULARY SUPPORT

choose your words – be careful when you decide what to say

go to the top – ask to speak to a superior

in detail (B1) – with all the facts

spoil (B1) – to make something bad

---

g 💬 Students discuss the questions in pairs. Monitor and help with vocabulary as necessary. Take feedback as a class. Ask students if their partners had any interesting or original advice on how to complain.

4 VOCABULARY Noun formation

a Tell students that in the last activity you asked them to discuss a question. Write the word *discuss* on the board. Then say: *You had interesting discussions about the question* and write *discussion* on the board, too. Ask students to say which word is a verb (discuss) and which is a noun (discussion). Ask if they know any other common noun endings, e.g. *-ation, -er, -ist*, and write them on the board.

Students complete the table with a partner. Check answers as a class. Ask students if they can remember the contexts in which the words appeared in the lesson.

> **Answers**
> Verb: choose, explain, queue
> Noun: complaint, delivery, decision, description, enjoyment

b ▶ 3.28 Before you play the recording, ask students to take turns saying the verb/noun pairs aloud and to underline the stressed syllables. Then play the recording for them to compare. Check answers as a class.

Answers

Verb	Noun
choose	choice
com<u>plain</u>	com<u>plaint</u>
de<u>liver</u>	de<u>livery</u>
ex<u>plain</u>	expla<u>nation</u>
de<u>cide</u>	de<u>cision</u>
des<u>cribe</u>	des<u>cription</u>
en<u>joy</u>	en<u>joyment</u>
queue	queue

c ▶ 3.28 Tell students that although there are distinguishable patterns in verb to noun changes, there are lots of exceptions. For instance, sometimes the vowel sound changes, as in the example *choose/choice*. (The others which change are *explain/explanation, decide/decision, describe/description*.) Play the recording again for students to notice these changes. Play it again or model the words for students to repeat.

d Students complete the sentences with the correct words from the table. Check answers as a class.

> **Answers**
> 1 choice   2 complaint   3 queue
> 4 description   5 delivery   6 decision

e 💬 In pairs, students ask and answer the questions in 4d. Monitor and point out errors in pronunciation for students to self-correct. You can do this by echoing the incorrect pronunciation a student has given. Ask for examples during group feedback. Take feedback as a class on the most interesting item their partners talked about.

5 SPEAKING

💬 In pairs, students discuss if they would complain in the situations, how they would complain, and what they would say. Take feedback and ask for examples. Write the best ones up on the board (or nominate a student to do so). Find the biggest complainer in the class.

💡 EXTRA ACTIVITY

In pairs, students write an email making a complaint. First, they must decide what they are complaining about and who they are writing to. Remind them to be polite, but they are allowed to complain about as many things as they wish. When they have finished, they can read their complaints to the class. Take a vote on the best, funniest and the one most likely / least likely to get a good response.

ADDITIONAL MATERIAL

▶ Workbook 10B

▶ Photocopiable activities: Grammar p.223, Vocabulary p.247, Pronunciation p.284

10C Everyday English
Can I exchange it for something else?

At the end of this lesson, students will be able to:

- understand a conversation about returning something to a shop
- use phrases to return goods and make complaints
- use correct sentence stress
- use *not very / a bit* to sound polite

💡 OPTIONAL LEAD-IN

Books closed. In pairs, students write down one or two things they have returned to shops. Put the items on the board and see which is the most common item to be returned.

1 LISTENING

a 💬 In pairs, students discuss the possible reasons for complaining about the different items.Take feedback as a class and write students' ideas on the board. Check ideas in group feedback.

> **Suggested answers**
>
> jeans – wrong size, wrong colour, have got a hole in them
> sandwich – past its sell-by date, tastes odd, not fresh, has got something in it you can't eat
> DVD – poor picture, sound quality, wrong DVD in box
> present – you've already got one, doesn't work, don't like it, wrong colour, shape, size etc.

b Ask students what a shop can do if a customer complains about an item. Elicit the idea that the shop can either give the customer's money back or give the customer a different item in exchange. Then ask students to read the notice and do the matching. Check answers as a class.

> **Answers**
>
> 1 receipt 2 exchange 3 refund 4 goods, products

📖 LANGUAGE NOTES

Students may have problems with pronunciation and spelling of *receipt* /rɪˈsiːt/. Model the word for them to repeat, and point out the silent *p*.

c 💬 Discuss the any differences between the rules in students' home countries and in Britain as as a class. If you wish, give students information from the Culture notes below.

d ▶️3.29 Ask students to look at the picture and tell you who the person is (Leo) and what they can remember about him from the story so far. Ask them where he is and what he's doing. *Leo is in a shop. He's talking to a shop assistant.* They might or might not realise that the object in Leo's hand is the football clock he got for his birthday and he's trying to return it. Play Part 1 of the video or play the audio recording for students to answer the questions. Check answers as a class.

> **Answers**
>
> the football clock
> He doesn't like football.
> He doesn't have the receipt.

Video/audioscript (Part 1)

LEO Hi. Could you help me, please?

SALES ASSISTANT Yes, of course. How can I help?

L Er, I'd like to return this clock, please.

SA Would you like to exchange it for something?

L No. I'd like a refund, please.

SA Do you have a receipt?

L No, I don't. It was a present, you see.

SA Well, I'm terribly sorry, but we can't give you a refund without a receipt.

L But … it came from this shop. Look – you've got the same clock there.

SA Yes, but without a receipt, I can't give you a refund. I'm very sorry. Is there anything wrong with it?

L No. It was a present, but I don't really like it.

SA Well, I'm sorry, but there's nothing I can do then.

L Right. Could I speak to the manager, please?

SA Of course.

MANAGER Hello. What seems to be the problem?

L Yes, I'd like to make a complaint.

2 USEFUL LANGUAGE
Returning goods and making complaints

a ▶️3.29 Read through the phrases for returning goods and making complaints with the class. Ask students to choose which phrases they heard in Part 1. Play Part 1 of the video or play the audio recording again for them to check their answers. Model the phrases for students to repeat paying special attention to correct word stress and intonation.

> **Answers**
>
> Could you help me, please?
> I'd like to return this clock, please.
> Could I speak to the manager, please?
> I'd like to make a complaint. (Please note that this final answer only applies to the audio-only version.)

b 💬 In pairs, students talk about the situations when the other phrases from 2a could be used.

c ▶️3.30 Read through the gapped sentences and play the recording for students to complete. Check answers as a class.

> **Answers**
>
> 1 exchange 2 receipt 3 sorry
> 4 right away 5 replace 6 refund

d Students work in pairs to complete the conversations. Check answers as a class.

> **Answers**
>
> 1 phone/electronics shop: 1 a complaint 2 work
> 3 terribly 4 look at
> 2 clothes shop: 5 fit 6 receipt
> 3 café/restaurant: 7 here 8 manager

e 💬 Give students a few minutes to practise the conversations in their pairs. As a follow-up ask students to cover the conversations. Read alternate lines and ask students to give the next lines.

3 LISTENING

a ⏯3.31 Ask students what they think will happen when Leo speaks to the manager. Play Part 2 of the video or play the audio recording for them to check their ideas.

> **Answer**
> Leo doesn't get a refund, but the manager offers him an exchange.

Video/audioscript (Part 2)

MANAGER What seems to be the problem?

LEO Yes, I'd like to make a complaint. I have this clock. It was bought in this shop. Your sales assistant hasn't been very helpful. She won't give me a refund.

SALES ASSISTANT He doesn't have a receipt.

L No, I don't have a receipt.

M Well, I'm sorry, but we don't do refunds without a receipt.

L Yes, that's what she said. OK, then. Can I exchange it for something else?

M Is there anything wrong with it?

L No, there's nothing wrong with it.

M Can I just ask – why do you want a refund if it works OK?

L Well, I just … It was a present and I'm not a big football fan.

And it's a bit ugly. Well, not ugly, but it's not very … adult. You know, it's more for children.

SA I have one. I love it!

M Look, as it was a present, I'll let you exchange it for something else in the shop. But normally we wouldn't do this.

L That's very kind.

SA So, what would you like to exchange it for?

L Actually, I've decided that I'll keep it. It might be useful.

M Well, OK then, if that's what you prefer.

L Yes, yes, it's fine. Thanks very much for your help.

M Thank you.

L Bye

M Goodbye.

SA Bye.

b ⏯3.31 Play the recording again for students to answer the questions. Check answers as a class. Ask students: *Why do you think Leo has decided to keep the clock?*

> **Answers**
> 1 seems to be the problem; wrong with it; want a refund
> 2 It was a present and he's not a big football fan; it's ugly; it's not very adult / more for children.
> 3 because it was a present
> 4 He decides to keep the clock.
> 5 He says, 'It might be useful'

c 💬 In pairs, students tell their partner about the last time they took something back to the shop, why and what happened. If they can't think of a time when they did this, ask them to talk about an article they wished they had returned (and why they didn't). Take feedback as a class. Nominate students to tell the class their own on their partner's story.

4 PRONUNCIATION Sentence stress

a ⏯3.32 Play the recording for students to tell you which of the highlighted words are stressed. If students find this very challenging, pause the recording after each phrase and repeat it, exaggerating the stressed words. Check answers as a class.

> **Answers**
> 1 have   2 help   3 speak   4 Why, want
> 5 What, like   6 How, help

b In pairs, students choose the correct options to describe the rules for sentence stress. Check answers as a class. Remind students that the words that are most important for getting the message across that are more heavily stressed.

> **Answers**
> auxiliary verbs, pronouns

c ⏯3.32 Play the recording again for students to repeat the questions. Focus on sentence stress.

5 CONVERSATION SKILLS Sounding polite

a Ask students to choose the more polite options. Elicit or tell the class that the option a sentences 'soften' the negative impression of the b variant by using a modifying adverb (*a bit, not very*) and/or the opposite positive adjective.

> **Answers**
> 1a   2a
> Leo used the more polite sentences.

b As a class, students choose the correct words to complete the rule. Explain that this kind of 'softening' is important in Anglophone culture if you want to sound polite.

> **Answers**
> *a bit* + negative adjective
> *not very* + opposite positive adjective

c Students do the task in pairs. Check answers as a class.

> **Answers**
> 1 dirty, clean   2 quick, slow   3 polite, rude   4 cold, hot/warm

d 💬 Ask students if they can remember the complaints they wrote in the last lesson. Put some of them on the board. Can they change these complaints to something more polite? e.g. *The water was too cold. – The water wasn't very hot.* Give students a minute or two to make four or five polite sentences and take feedback as a class.

6 SPEAKING

a 💬 Put students in pairs and tell them that they are going to role play a situation where one of them complains to the other. Read through the task and give students time to prepare and then a few minutes to role play the situation.

b 💬 Students swap roles and find a different thing to complain about. Monitor and correct students' pronunciation as appropriate.

> **LOA TIP MONITORING**
>
> Monitoring a role play gives you the chance to stretch the faster students and prompt slower ones. To stretch faster learners, you can enter the role play as a manager or another customer with the same complaint. With slower learners, you can prompt by supplying language items or by giving simple definitions to help elicit forgotten items.

> **ADDITIONAL MATERIAL**
>
> ▶ Workbook 10C
> ▶ Unit Progress Test
> ▶ Personalised online practice

At the end of this lesson, students will be able to:

- understand people talking about complaining
- read and understand apology emails
- use formal and informal language in apology emails
- write an apology email

💡 OPTIONAL LEAD-IN

Books closed. Write some or all of the following on the board: *waiter, barista, shop assistant, railway booking clerk* (someone who sells train tickets), *bus driver, customer service advisor, salesperson*. In pairs, ask students to say which of these people they meet/talk to regularly and how they would describe the attitude of the people in these roles. Elicit useful adjectives, e.g. *very/really (un)helpful, (un) friendly, rude, polite, bored, kind*. Ask one or two students to share any interesting stories with the class.

1 LISTENING AND SPEAKING

a Read through the situations with the class. Individually, students think about how they would react. Encourage them to note down what they would say in each case.

b 💬 Students tell their partner what they would do and say. Take feedback as a class. Elicit phrases that students could say to the shop assistants/people who hadn't replied to the invitation – e.g. *Excuse me, I'm waiting to be served, I sent you an invitation X weeks ago. Did you get it?*

c ▶️ 3.33 Tell the class that they are going to listen to three people talking about and their task is to match the speakers with situations in 1a. Point out that one talks about a different situation. Play the recording for students to do the matching and identify the third situation. Check answers as a class.

> **Answers**
> Tim: 2
> Vicki: (complaining about) buying something online
> Rebecca: 1

Audioscript

TIM I went to buy a new pair of jeans the other day. I was the only customer in the shop and there were two shop assistants. They were chatting about what they did at the weekend and, when I asked for assistance, they just carried on talking. It was so rude. All I wanted to know was the price of some jeans. In the end, I decided to just leave the shop. I don't think they even noticed I was there. I felt like writing an email to the shop manager to complain, but then I forgot to.

VICKI One thing that I think is rude is when shops or companies don't reply when someone makes a complaint. I remember once I bought an MP3 player online. It took ages to arrive – like, about a month. So, I wrote an email to complain, but I didn't hear anything from them. I mean, is it too hard just to send an email saying sorry? If I were the manager of a company, I'd make sure I replied to every customer. I know it's not easy to run a business. But if you want to keep your customers happy, you should answer their emails. Well, I won't use that company again. I'll go to a local shop instead.

REBECCA Look, if I invited you to my party, you'd let me know if you could come or not, wouldn't you? You'd think so. But last month I had a party and invited about 40 people and about half of them didn't say if they were coming or not. Most of them didn't come in the end and, in my invitation, I did ask them to let me know. I think that kind of behaviour is incredibly rude, don't you? I mean, I needed to know how many people were coming, so I had enough food and drink. But then I made too much food and it was embarrassing. All they needed to do was send a text or email – which is not very difficult. There are some people I invited to that party who I'll never get in touch with again.

📖 LANGUAGE NOTES

There are several useful collocations in the script – you might wish to point these out to students:

chat about – talk about something that is not very serious

ask for assistance – ask for help (formal)

feel like – want to, e.g. *I felt like shouting*

run a business – organise everything for a business

make sure that – be certain that

let someone know – tell someone

Practise the collocations by asking questions, e.g. *What were you chatting about before the lesson started? When did you last ask for assistance in a shop? What do you feel like doing now? When did you last hear from an old friend? Do you know anyone who runs their own business? What must you make sure that you do this evening? Do you need to let anyone know something soon?* Ask students to answer with full sentences so they use the collocations.

d ▶️ 3.33 Read through the questions with the class. Play the recording again for students to answer. Encourage students to compare their ideas with a partner before checking answers as a class.

> **Answers**
> 1 the price of some jeans 2 left the shop
> 3 reply to every customer 4 use the company again
> 5 so she'd have enough food and drink
> 6 she made too much food

e Ask students to think about an experience where someone was rude and make notes individually. They can use the questions to help them give details. Monitor and help with vocabulary as necessary.

f Students tell a partner about their experience. Take feedback as a class and find out whose situation was the worst.

2 READING

a Ask students how they would apologise if they arrived late for a class or an appointment. Write these examples on the board and ask which is more formal (the second).

I'm sorry I'm late. / I'm really sorry I'm late. I got held up.

Ask the class to read the salutation and the subject line of the three apology emails and elicit guesses from the class as to which topic they match with. Then give students some more time to read through in detail and see if they were right. Check answers with the class.

> **Answers**
> 1 b 2 c 3 a

b Students read the emails again to answer the questions. Check answers as a class.

c Discuss the questions as a class. Elicit that email b is the most formal and ask students to tell you what they think makes it formal than the others (writer doesn't use the first name of the person he's writing to, use of *apologise* for rather than *say sorry*, the ending is formal – *Yours sincerely*). Ask students if they think the apology emails would have the desired effect on the readers i.e. make them feel better, less angry, etc. and why / why not.

③ WRITING SKILLS
Formal and informal language

a Individually, students look at the sentences from the emails and match them with their functions a–d. Check answers as a class.

b Discuss the question as a class.

c In pairs, students try to rewrite the email so that it is more informal. Monitor and give help as necessary. Encourage students to look at the other two emails to find examples of less formal expressions that they could use or adapt.

d Give the students a few minutes to read through the emails again and look at how they are organised. Then take feedback as a class.

④ WRITING

a Tell students that they are going to write an apology email to Rebecca in 1a. Read through her situation again with the class. and elicit ideas for possible explanations/excuses as to why students didn't respond to her invitation – e.g. they were away/ill/had lots of problems/lost the message, etc. Then give them some time to plan and structure their email using the notes to help them. Monitor and help as necessary.

b Students write their emails. Remind them to use informal language. Monitor and encourage self-correction by pointing out errors for students to self-correct.

c Students swap emails with other students in the class to read and evaluate by answering the questions. Ask students if they think their partner's apology would make Rebecca feel better. If not, what improvements they would suggest? Take feedback and ask for comments and opinions.

UNIT 10
Review and extension

1 GRAMMAR

a Students complete the conversation with the correct words individually. Check answers as a class.

Answers
1 would; do   2 were   3 was   4 'd keep   5 saw   6 'd get
7 handed   8 would give   9 'd expect   10 gave back

b 💬 Students practise the conversation in pairs. If appropriate, choose a pair to repeat their conversation for the class.

c Students choose the correct options individually. Check answers as a class.

Answers
1 much   2 warm enough   3 a bit of   4 a lot of
5 enough money   6 many

💡 EXTRA ACTIVITY

Write the following situations on the board: *I saw a classmate cheating in an exam.*

I heard someone opening the bathroom window in our house at night. I saw someone taking an old lady's handbag in the street. I saw someone shoplifting in the supermarket.

Ask students to write down what they would do in these situations. Then, in pairs, they cover what they've written and have to guess what their partner would do. In feedback, see how many students guessed correctly.

2 VOCABULARY

a Students choose the correct answers individually. Check answers together.

Answers
1 choice   2 complain   3 decision   4 descriptions   5 enjoy

b 💬 Ask students which of the sentences in 2a are true for them.

c Students complete the sentences with the correct form of the verbs in the box. Check the forms as a class.

Answers
1 look   2 broken   3 feel   4 turned
5 pass   6 join   7 carried   8 Come

3 WORDPOWER
multi-word verbs with *on*

a Ask students to tell you any verbs they know that can be followed by *on*. Conduct feedback and write examples of different verbs they have thought of on the board. Only write one example of each use. Students decide which category the expressions in bold fall into. Check answers together.

Answers
continuing: 1, 2, 4, 6
wearing: 3, 5, 7

b Read through the definitions with students and ask them to complete the sentences.

Answers
1 keeps on   2 get   3 went, carried, kept

c Students do the task individually. Check answers as a class.

Answers
1 c   2 a   3 b

d Students match the sentence halves individually. Check answers together.

Answers
1 c   2 a   3 e   4 b   5 d

e 💬 Students talk about which sentences in 3d are true for them.

💡 EXTRA ACTIVITY

Ask students to write down five verbs with *on* from this section, but in a jumbled order. They should give each verb a number but not show their partner. In pairs, they take turns to choose a number from their partner's list. The partner then says this verb, and the first student must make up a sentence using this verb + *on*. In feedback, ask for example sentences from each pair.

💡 FAST FINISHERS

Fast finishers can try to write a short text or story using as many of the verbs + *on* as they can. Check through these during feedback.

▶ Photocopiable activities: Wordpower p.261

 LOA REVIEW YOUR PROGRESS

Students look back through the unit, think about what they've studied and decide how well they did. Students work on weak areas by using the appropriate sections of the Workbook, the Photocopiable activities and the Personalised online practice.

UNIT 11
Discovery and invention

GETTING STARTED

💡 OPTIONAL LEAD-IN

Books closed. Write *robot* on the board. Say: *Robots can say words, but they can't have a conversation.* In pairs, students think of other things that robots can or can't do, e.g. *Robots can walk, pick up something, take messages, clean floors, rescue people at sea, travel into space, explore inside volcanoes. Robots can't feel emotion, take care of someone, breathe, think, learn new skills.* Ask students to share their ideas with the class. Encourage them to give examples if they know of any.

🧭 UNIT OBJECTIVES

At the end of this unit, students will be able to:
- understand texts and conversations about discoveries and inventions
- discuss attitudes to discoveries and inventions
- describe how discoveries were made
- ask for and give directions in a building
- write a post (for a website) expressing an opinion

a Ask students to look at the picture and tell you what they can see. In pairs, students read and discuss the questions. Monitor and help students with any vocabulary they may need, e.g. *bark, wag its tail, fetch, dog hairs, take the dog for a walk, feed, vet, charge up batteries.* Ask students to share their ideas with the class. If you wish, give students information from the Culture notes below.

Suggested answers
1 playing with a ball
2 to let him have some fun / for company
3 perhaps – it would be warm and friendly; perhaps not – have to feed it, it makes a mess, it needs walks
4 nothing; it can't lick you, communicate

🌍 CULTURE NOTES

The picture shows the AIBO, an artificial intelligence robot. Several models of the robot dog were produced by Sony between 1999 and 2006. The AIBO had many abilities, including understanding commands, reacting to touch, chasing a ball, barking, dancing and even walking to a docking station to charge its own batteries. The AIBO was the first consumer robot to be offered to the public and the first model cost around $2000.

b Students discuss the questions in pairs and report back to the class. Write the best ideas on the board. Ask the class to vote for their favourite 'new robot' from the descriptions on the board.

💡 EXTRA ACTIVITY

Ask the class: *Do you think robots will be good for family life? Why / Why not?* Divide the class into two groups. Ask one group to think of reasons why robots will be good, and the other group to think of reasons why they won't. Ask for reasons from both groups in full group feedback.

11A It's a robot that looks like a human

At the end of this lesson, students will be able to:

• use defining relative clauses
• read and understand a text about inventions from science fiction
• understand a person talking about inventions
• use compound nouns
• talk about new technology

⚲ OPTIONAL LEAD-IN

Books closed. Ask students if they have been to see a film at the cinema recently and find out from them what films are currently on. Ask students to tell you the names of the films, but also the genre, e.g. *comedy, drama, animated film, thriller, documentary, science fiction film*. Find out if any students have a particular film genre they enjoy.

🌍 CULTURE NOTES

Books and films in the science fiction genre speculate about future events and technology, and their effects on the human race, but the stories are not fantasy. The stories always show a good understanding of scientific principles. Some of the most popular science fiction authors are Aldous Huxley (*Brave New World*), H.G. Wells (*The Invisible Man*), and Arthur C. Clarke (*2001: a Space Odyssey*). *Return from the Stars* by Polish author Stanislaw Lem tells the story of an astronaut returning to Earth to find it completely changed. It was translated into English in 1980, 19 years after it was first published.

Fahrenheit 451 by American author Ray Bradbury tells the story of a future society where reading or even owning books is illegal. The title refers to the temperature that paper catches fire. There were many ideas in this book which have later become reality including large-screen TVs, in-ear wireless headphones, electronic surveillance and more. The novel has won many awards.

Back to the Future is an extremely successful trilogy of films directed by Robert Zemeckis and produced by Steven Spielberg. The first film was released in 1985 and used state-of-the-art special effects which are now common in action adventure movies. The films starred Michael J. Fox (pictured on SB p.109, top right) who travels in time both to the past and to the future in a car which is adapted into a time machine.

A.I. stands for Artificial Intelligence. The film of this name was released in 2001 and was written, directed and produced by Steven Spielberg. It was based on a 1969 short story *Super-Toys Last All Summer Long* by British author Brian Aldiss. The film starred Jude Law and child actor Haley Joel Osment (pictured on SB p.109, top left). Haley Joel Osment plays a child-like robot called David who is the result of a scientist's experiment to make a robot who can love and be loved.

The *Iron Man* films are based on the Marvel comicbook superhero (pictured on SB p.109, bottom) who first appeared in comicbooks in 1963. *Iron Man 3* (2013) is one of the highest-grossing films of all time. In the films, Robert Downey Jr plays engineer Tony Stark who creates a suit of armour which gives him superhuman strength and the ability to fly. In time the armour becomes part of Stark's body, turning him into a cyborg.

The film *Minority Report* (2002) is a science fiction thriller based on a short story by Philip K. Dick of the same name, starring Tom Cruise, Colin Farrell and Samantha Morton. Directed by Steven Spielberg, this film was one of the first to make extensive use of digital production. The story features *precogs*, mutated humans who can see into the future. Special *precrime* police officers try to use this information to prevent crimes being committed.

1 READING AND LISTENING

a 💬 In pairs, students look at the pictures and the film and book titles on this page and tell their partner what they know about each one. Take feedback and find out which students have read the books or seen the films. Elicit what they know about them and ask if anyone has both read the book and seen the film. Ask: *Did you prefer the book or the film? Why?*

> **Answer**
> science-fiction stories

b Ask students to read the title of the article and guess what it is about (some inventions were first thought of by science fiction writers, but went on to become a reality). They then read the introduction to check their ideas and to answer the question.

> **Answer**
> Both cash machines and e-book readers appeared in stories about thirty to forty years before they were invented.

c Ask students who have seen all or some of the films featured in the article to tell the class what they think were the most interesting technological inventions and gadgets featured in these films. Put these on the board and then ask students to read the article to check if they are mentioned. If not, they should write down the other inventions that are talked about. Check answers as a class.

> **Answers**
> *Back to the Future II*: flying cars
> *AI*: androids / robot children
> *Iron Man*: cyborgs
> *Minority Report*: predicting crimes before they happen; personalised advertising

📖 VOCABULARY SUPPORT

android – a robot that is made to look like a person
billboard – a very large board on which advertisements are shown, especially by the side of the road
break the law (B2) – do something against the law
personalised – make something suitable for the needs of a particular person
psychic – a person who has the ability to predict the future
robotic – adjective from *robot*

📖 LANGUAGE NOTES

Sci fi is a common abbreviation of *science fiction*. It can also be abbreviated to *SF*.

d ▶3.34 List the technologies from c on the board and ask the class if they think they exist in real life yet. Elicit a 'yes' or 'no' answer for each. Then play the recording for students to find out whether they were right.

Answers

flying cars – yes
androids – no
cyborgs – yes, almost
predicting crimes – yes
personalised advertising – yes

e ▶ **3.34** Students listen to the recording and note down the differences between the real technology and the book/film version. Encourage them to compare their ideas with a partner before you check answers as a class.

Answers

There are flying cars (but very expensive and you need a licence). There aren't robots that can love their owners yet, but there are robots that appear friendly.
There are cyborgs – doctors often give people robotic hands and arms. There is even an 'Iron Man' suit which allows people who can't use their legs to stand, walk and climb stairs and also makes people ten times stronger – only for use in hospitals but possibly in development for rescue workers.
Police can't exactly predict crimes but a computer program can say where and what kinds of crime might occur.
Personalised advertising is possible: it recognises the age and sex of a person and when you look at one, it chooses an advert for something it thinks you will like. It also records how long you look at the advert and how close you stand.

Audioscript

There aren't any road signs in the sky yet, but just like in *Back to the Future II*, flying cars are real. The Terrafugia Transition is a car which can fly for 800 kilometres at a speed of 185 kilometres an hour. It has two seats and wings that fold up, so it can be driven on a road, too. But it isn't cheap – it costs about €220,000. And to fly the Terrafugia, you have to have a pilot's licence.
People who have seen *AI* might be happy to hear that no one can make robots that love their human owner yet. But scientists are trying to make friendly robots: One example is Kirobo – a Japanese robot that was designed as a friend for astronauts. Kirobo goes with the astronauts into space. It recognises their faces and says "hello" in Japanese when it sees them. It also gives them messages from people on Earth.
You might not know it, but there are already many cyborgs – doctors give people robotic hands and arms every week. And, these days, 'Iron Man' suits are also available … well, almost. In Japan, Cyberdyne have created a suit which allows people who can't use their legs to stand, walk and climb stairs. The suit also makes the person who wears it five to ten times stronger. At the moment, the suit is produced for use in hospitals, but Cyberdyne also want it to be used by rescue workers to lift heavy objects and get to injured or trapped people more quickly after an accident or disaster.
In the United States, the Memphis Police Department is trying to predict the future, just like in the film *Minority Report*. They don't have psychics, but they do have a computer program called *Blue CRUSH*. The program can't tell the police exactly who will break the law, but it can tell the police where it might happen and even what kind of crime it might be. Crime has gone down by 30% since they started using the program. …
The Japanese company NEC has invented billboards which are similar to the ones in *Minority Report*. The billboards know how old you are and if you are male or female. And when you look at one, it chooses an advert for something it thinks you will like. It also records how long you look at the advert and how close you stand. This measures your interest in the advert. The billboards are already used in train stations in Tokyo.

f ▶ **3.34** Read through the sentences and play the recording again for students to do the true/false task. Check answers as a class. You may wish to help students with words in the Vocabulary support box.

Answers

1 T
2 F – You have to have a pilot's licence.
3 F – It was designed as a friend for astronauts.
4 T
5 T
6 T
7 F – Crime has gone down by 30%.
8 T

📖 **VOCABULARY SUPPORT**

fold up (B1) – you can bend it to take up a smaller space
recognise (B1) – know someone / something because you have seen them before
rescue (worker) (B1) – person who saves others
trapped (B2) – unable to move, get out of a place

g Students discuss the questions in pairs. Monitor and help with vocabulary as needed. Point out errors for students to self-correct. Take feedback as a class and ask students to give examples of the most interesting or extraordinary new technologies they have heard/read about.

💡 **EXTRA ACTIVITY**

In pairs, students choose a science-fiction film that has not been discussed so far in class. They write a summary of the film like the ones described in the article, pointing out the interesting technology in the film. Students read out their summaries or circulate them in the class. The rest of the students try to guess which film they are describing.

2 GRAMMAR Defining relative clauses

a Books closed. Ask: *What do you call robots that look like humans?* (androids) *What do you call the place where astronauts go?* (space) Ask students to look at the words and complete the definitions, using what they remember from the reading and listening to help them. Check answers as a class.

Answers

1 Psychics 2 Androids 3 Cyborgs 4 Billboards 5 Space

b Draw students attention to the underlined words in the definitions. Elicit or explain that the function of these words is to refer/*relate* back to the word you are defining and that they are called *relative* pronouns. Students complete the rules individually and compare their ideas with a partner before you check answers as a class.

Answers

who; that   which; that   where

🔄 **LOA TIP ELICITING**

Ask students to look at the completed sentences in 2a. Ask: *Are the underlined words giving more information about the subject or the object of the sentence?* (the subject) Ask: *If we take out these words, do the sentences still make sense?* (no) Ask: *What do we call these words?* (relative pronouns)

c Answer the questions as a class.

Answers

1 which 2 who 3 where

d ▶ ⏵**3.35** Students read the information in Grammar Focus 11A on SB p.162. Play the recording where indicated and ask students to listen and repeat. Students then complete the exercises in Grammar Focus 11A on SB p.163. Check answers as a class. Tell students to go back to SB p.109.

> **Answers (Grammar Focus 11A SB p.163)**
> a 1 which   2 who   3 where   4 who   5 which
>   6 where   7 which   8 who
> b 1 where   2 who, which, that   3 which, where
>   4 who, which, that   5 which, where   6 who, which, that
>   7 who, where
> c 1 the actor who   2 the shoes that/which   3 a shop where
>   4 a device that/which   5 The man who
>   6 camera that/which broke

> 👁 **CAREFUL!**
>
> Students sometimes use *what* instead of *that/which* in relative clauses, e.g. ~~This is one of the best films what stars Brad Pitt.~~ (Correct form = *This is one of the best films* **which/ that** *stars Brad Pitt.*).

e Read through the examples with the class and elicit what they are describing. Write: *It's a person who ... It's a thing which ...* on the board and say that these are very useful phrases for defining and explaining. Give the beginning of some definitions and elicit different possible endings from the class, e.g. *a teacher is a person who ...* (helps students to learn); *a dictionary is a book that* (you can look up new words in).

> **Suggested answers**
> A doctor, nurse   B bed, (sofa)

f ▶ Divide students into pairs and assign A and B roles. Student A turns to SB p. 129. Student B turns to SB p.131. Explain that they need to describe the words for their partners to guess, using relative clauses. Allow two minutes for each student's descriptions. Monitor and point out errors for students to self-correct. Ask some students to tell you some of their descriptions. Who described most things? Ask students to describe any remaining words as a class.

> 💡 **EXTRA ACTIVITY**
>
> In pairs, students role play a conversation between a teenager and a great-grandparent. The great-grandparent asks the teenager to explain some modern technology, e.g. *What's an email? How does a smartphone work?*. The teenager describes the item for their great-grandparent. They then swap roles. Choose a pair to role play a conversation for the class.

3 VOCABULARY Compound nouns

a Write the word *driving licence* on the board and ask whether it is a noun or a verb (a noun). Explain that nouns that are made up of two words like this are called *compound nouns*. Ask students to do the matching task and check answers as a class.

> **Answers**
> science fiction   cash machines   street lights
> television programme   road sign

b Go through the words with the class and elicit whether each one is singular or plural. Establish that they are all in the singular form.

> **Answers**
> singular

c ▶ ⏵**3.36** Students complete the exercises in Vocabulary Focus 11A on SB p.140. Go through the two points in the Tip with the class and check understanding. Check answers to Exercise a. Play the recording where indicated for students to decide on the stressed syllables in Exercise b and repeat. Check answers to Exercises d and e and monitor the conversations in Exercise f. Then tell students to go back to SB p.109.

> **Answers (Vocabulary Focus 11A SB p.140)**
> a 1 shoe shop   2 address book   3 bookshelf   4 ticket office
>   5 key ring   6 television programme
>   7 street lights / streetlights   8 road sign   9 cash machine
>   10 science fiction
> b 1 shoe shop   2 address book   3 bookshelf   4 ticket office
>   5 key ring   6 television programme   7 street lights
>   8 road sign   9 cash machine   10 science fiction
> 1 the first one   2 science fiction
> d mountain top, mountain climbing, mountain centre; TV star,
>   TV screen, TV game; bread knife; coffee cup; shopping bag,
>   shopping centre; city park, city centre; kitchen knife, kitchen
>   door; computer screen, computer game; tea bag, teacup; rock
>   climbing, rock star; car park, car door; bottle top
> e 1 computer games   2 TV screen / computer screen
>   3 rock climbing / mountain climbing   4 rock star / TV star
>   5 rock star / TV star
>   6 shopping centre / city park / computer game

4 SPEAKING

a 💬 Ask the class if anyone has recently bought or started used a new piece of technology and elicit more information about it. Ask individual students what was the last piece of technological equipment they bought and why they bought it.

b 💬 Individually, students think about the inventions in the pictures and then compare answers with a partner.

c Take feedback as a class and compare different suggestions from the pairs about the gadgets. (top left) Smoke detectors are fitted to the ceiling inside a building. A smoke detector sounds an alarm when smoke is present. The alarm allows people to either prevent or escape a fire. Deaths due to fire have been reduced by 50% since smoke detectors became easily available. This smoke detector is in the shape of a bird which 'chirps' to warn you of smoke. (top right) This is an induction hob. Electromagnets in the hob are used to heat pans by induction. This means only the pan heats up and not the hob, which is energy-efficient and safer. (bottom) This is a charging station. Phone chargers are put inside the box and covered with artificial grass. This keeps a number of different phone chargers in one place and looks more natural.

> **Answers**
> top left: smoke detector   top right: induction hob
> bottom: charging station

> **ADDITIONAL MATERIAL**
>
> ▶ Workbook 11A
> ▶ Photocopiable activities: Grammar p.224, Vocabulary p.248

11B I think they discovered it by chance

At the end of this lesson, students will be able to:

- read and understand texts about discoveries
- use articles correctly
- use adverbials related to luck and chance accurately
- talk about discoveries and inventions
- relate experiences about unexpected events

💡 OPTIONAL LEAD-IN

Books closed. Play *Backs to the board*. Split the class into two teams. One student from each team sits with their back to the board. Write a word on the board. The students who can see the board must explain the word to their teammate who cannot see the board. They may not use their own language. The person who guesses the word from their team's clues wins a point for their team. Use these words in this game: *statue, stone, metal, soldier, diamond, cave, painting, microwave, farmer, popcorn, climber.*

1 READING

a 💬 Students match the headlines with the stories and pictures. Check answers as a class and ask which story they would like to read most, and why.

Answers
1 second story   2 third story   3 first story

b Ask students to read the stories and answer the questions about each one. You may wish to help students with words in the Vocabulary support box at this point. Check answers as a class. If you wish, give students information from the Culture notes below.

Answers

Scientist discovers how to cook food in seconds
1 Percy LeBaron Spencer
2 working on radar for the army
3 the microwave oven

5,000-year-old body found in the Alps
1 Helmut and Erika Simon
2 hiking in the mountains in Italy
3 one of the oldest, most complete human bodies

Farmers uncover ancient army in the fields
1 local farmers
2 digging and looking for water
3 thousands of clay/terracotta soldiers buried underground

📖 LANGUAGE NOTES

Point out the difference between *inventions* and *discoveries*. *Inventions* are things that people create/imagine/build. *Discoveries* are things that already existed but we find out about them.

📖 VOCABULARY SUPPORT

archaeologist (C1) – someone who studies ancient cultures by looking for and examining their buildings, tools, and other objects

bury (B1) – to put something into a hole in the ground and cover it

clay – a kind of heavy, sticky earth, soft when wet and hard when dry or baked, which is used for making pots and other objects

curious (B1) – wanting to know or learn about something

dig (B1) – to make a hole in the ground by moving some of the earth away

hike – to walk a long distance especially in the countryside

melt (B2) – go from solid to liquid because of heat

pop (C2) – sudden loud, short sound like a small explosion

popcorn (B1) – seeds of corn that have been cooked to break open into soft, light balls and are eaten as a snack

radar – a system that uses radio waves to detect objects you cannot see

terracotta – a hard, baked, red-brown clay

📖 LANGUAGE NOTES

Some students confuse *hope* and *expect*. Explain that we use *hope* when we want something to happen and *expect* when we think it will happen. Elicit some examples to show the meanings: *I hope I pass the exam. (I'm not sure.) I expect I'll pass the exam. (I think I will.)*

👁 CAREFUL!

- When we use a compound noun as an adjective like this, all nouns remain in the singular form singular, e.g *a multi-words verb* (Correct form = *a multi-**word** verb*); *a 5,000-years-old body* (Correct form = *a 5,000-**year**-old body*); *a ten years old boy* (Correct form = *a ten-**year**-old boy*, BUT *The boy was ten **years** old*); a five **pages**-story (Correct form = *a five-**page**-story*).

- In headlines, articles (and auxiliaries) are often left out, e.g. *5,000-year-old body discovered in Alps!* = *A 5,000-year-old body has been discovered in the Alps.*

🌐 CULTURE NOTES

Percy LeBaron Spencer created the first microwave oven in 1947. It was about two metres tall and weighed 340 kilograms. It cost between $2,000 and $3,000. It wasn't until 1967 that an affordable microwave was on sale for $495. Spencer didn't profit from his invention – he was paid a fee of $2.00 by his company!

Ötzi the Iceman is thought to have been 1.65 metres tall, about 50 kilograms in weight and about 45 years old. Scientific tests have shown where he lived and what his last meals were – red deer, herb bread, grain and fruits. They also show that he looked old for his age, had been quite ill just before his death and that he had tattoos. He was wearing a coat, leggings and well-made shoes.

The Terracotta Army includes soldiers and horses and are representations of Qin Shi Huang, the first Emperor of China. It is believed that the army is a kind of funeral art and that it was buried with the Emperor to protect him after death.

c Students read the texts again and answer the questions individually. Check answers as a class.

> **Answers**
> 1 He put a small bowl of popcorn in front of the machine.
> 2 They thought that it was the body of an unlucky mountain climber. They tore the clothes and broke one arm.
> 3 They believe most of them are still buried underground.

💡 EXTRA ACTIVITY

Write on the board: 700,000 / 6,000 / 1991 / 5,000 / 2,200 and ask students what the numbers refer to in the text.

(700,000 people who helped make the army; 6,000 – approximate number of figures; 2,200 – the terracotta army was made 2,200 years ago; 1991 – 5,000 – age of body when the body of the Iceman was discovered)

d 💬 In pairs, students discuss the questions before you take feedback as a class. Take a class vote on the order of the importance of the discoveries and elicit some ideas from the group about important discoveries in their lifetimes.

2 GRAMMAR Articles

a Books closed. Read the first sentence, leaving out some of the articles: *He put … small bowl in front of the machine. It started popping and jumping out of … bowl.* Ask students what words are missing (*a, the*) and what we call this kind of word (articles). Read through the sentences and rules and ask students to match them individually. Check answers as a class.

> **Answers**
> a 6 b 3,4 c 1 d 2,5 e 7

b ▶ ⏵3.37 Students read the information in Grammar Focus 11B on SB p.162. Play the recording where indicated and ask students to listen and repeat. Students then complete the exercises in Grammar Focus 11B on SB p.163. Check answers as a class. Tell students to go back to SB p.111.

> **Answers (Grammar Focus 11B SB p.163)**
> a 1 A 2 Ø 3 the 4 A 5 An 6 a 7 a 8 Ø 9 the 10 An
> b 1 D 2 D 3 S 4 S 5 D 6 S
> c 1 Ø 2 Ø 3 a 4 the 5 a 6 a 7 The 8 Ø 9 a 10 The 11 a 12 the 13 the/Ø

c Ask students to look at the picture and title and tell you what the picture shows. Ask: *What do you think the article will be about?* Students read the article to check their ideas. Ask: *Which articles could we add to the title?* (**a** new species, on **the** menu). Ask: *Which auxiliary could we add?* (**was** discovered) Students then read the text and complete it with the correct articles. They do this individually and then compare answers with a partner.

d ⏵3.38 Play the recording for students to check their answers.

> **Answers**
> 1 the 2 a 3 a 4 a 5 a 6 the 7 the
> 8 the 9 the 10 a 11 no article 12 a
> 13 the 14 the 15 the 16 the 17 a

📖 VOCABULARY SUPPORT

bench (B2) – long seat for two or more people

nearby (B1) – not far away

e Students answer the questions in pairs. Take feedback and check answers.

> **Answers**
> 1 Ngo Van Tri
> 2 he thought they looked unusual; to send to a biologist in America
> 3 by plane
> 4 The lizards were cooked and eaten.
> 5 in a nearby restaurant

f 💬 Students work in pairs. Ask them to take turns covering the story and using the prompts to retell it. Monitor and correct students' pronunciation as appropriate and listen for appropriate usage of articles. Point out errors for students to self-correct where necessary.

💡 EXTRA ACTIVITY

Ask students if they have ever eaten lizards. What other unusual things do students eat in their countries? What would they never eat? Why?

3 VOCABULARY
Adverbials: luck and chance

a Write the highlighted adverbials from the four stories on the board. In pairs, students discuss the meanings. Check their ideas as a class. Use some of the adverbials in sentences and concept check. Keep the adverbials on the board to refer to later.

> **LOA TIP CONCEPT CHECKING**
>
> Use concept questions to check the understanding of the adverbials in the sentences you have on the board. For example, to check the meaning of *by chance* in the sentence *I met James by chance in the station*, ask: *Did I arrange to meet James?* (no) *Was it a surprise to meet James?* (yes)

> **Answers**
> *as expected* – this was something we thought was going to happen
> *by chance* – it wasn't planned
> *accidentally* – it wasn't planned
> *amazingly* – it was a real surprise
> *fortunately* – it was a good/lucky thing
> *surprisingly* – it was a surprise
> *on purpose* – it was planned
> *unfortunately* – it was a bad / an unlucky thing
> *luckily* – it was a lucky thing

> 👁 **CAREFUL!**
> Watch out for mistakes: ~~unfortunatly~~ or ~~unfortunatelly~~.
> (Correct spelling = **unfortunately**.)

b Individually, students search the texts for the opposites of the words and phrases in the table. They compare their answers with a partner before you check as a class.

> **Answers**
> 1 fortunately   2 luckily   3 by chance
> 4 accidentally   5 amazingly   6 surprisingly

c ▶3.39 In pairs, students take turns to practise pronouncing the words out loud. They underline where they think the main stress falls. Play the recording for them to listen, check their answers and repeat.

> **Answers**
> <u>luck</u>ily, <u>for</u>tunately, acc<u>i</u>dentally, by <u>chance</u>, un<u>for</u>tunately, sur<u>pri</u>singly, a<u>ma</u>zingly, on <u>pur</u>pose, as ex<u>pec</u>ted

d Read through the task with the class and give students a couple of minutes to prepare their sentences using three of the phrases from c. Monitor and help with vocabulary as necessary.

e 💬 Take feedback and ask students to share some of their examples with the class. Find out which student has written about the most interesting/amusing/ frightening occasion.

> 💡 **EXTRA ACTIVITY**
> In pairs, students take turns to make up a sentence and give an adverbial to begin the next sentence for their partner to complete, e.g. *I opened the classroom door. Surprisingly ...* (the room was empty). Take feedback and ask students to share some examples with the class.

4 SPEAKING

a ▶ Divide the class into pairs and assign A and B roles. Student As read the texts on SB p.128 and Student Bs read the texts on SB p.132. Explain that they are each going to read about three different accidental discoveries. They can use their dictionaries to check the meaning of any unfamiliar words. Monitor and help with vocabulary as necessary. Students tell their partners their three stories. One of the stories is not true and the pairs decide together which one it is. Take feedback as a class and ask students to share their ideas and say why they think the stories they have chosen are untrue. Give the answers from SB p.131.

> **Answers**
> Car keys were not invented by an American businessman called Spencer.
> The exercise bike was not invented by Hans Weger.

> **ADDITIONAL MATERIAL**
>
> ▶ Workbook 11B
> ▶ Photocopiable activities: Grammar p.225, Vocabulary p.249

11C Everyday English
It's straight ahead

At the end of this lesson, students will be able to:
- use phrases to ask for and give directions in a building
- check information
- differentiate between /ɜː/ and /ɔː/
- understand someone asking for and being given directions

OPTIONAL LEAD-IN

Write *sat nav* on the board. Ask students if they have a sat nav in their car. Ask: *Is a sat nav an essential invention? Should you have one in your car?* Divide the class into small groups. Some of the groups think of reasons why sat navs are essential, e.g. *You can find new places. You don't need to stop to look at a map.* Some of the groups think of reasons why the sat nav is not a good invention, e.g. *You can look at road signs instead. It is dangerous to take your eyes off the road. Sat navs are always out-of-date.* Set up short debates between the groups. Now take a class vote on students' real opinions.

1 LISTENING

a Ask the class if they are good at knowing where they are and elicit examples from individual students of what they would do if they got lost in a town or city. In pairs, students ask and answer the questions. Encourage them to give details and extend their answers. Take feedback as a class on the most interesting items their partners talked about. Extend by asking how many students have apps on their phones to find the way and how useful these are.

b ▶ 3.40 Ask students to tell you what has happened to Annie in the story so far and the reason why she has come to visit Mark at his office. Play Part 1 of the video or play the audio recording for the class to find out why she gets lost. Check the answer together.

> **Answer**
> Annie can't remember the receptionist's directions to Mark's office.

Video/audioscript (Part 1)

ANNIE Excuse me. Can you tell me where the reception is?
PERSON It's over there, by the trees. Can you see the doors? And the sign that says reception.
A Oh, yes. Thanks very much.
P You're welcome.
RECEPTIONIST Good afternoon.
A Hello. I'm here to see Mark Riley.
R What's your name, please?
A It's Annie Morton.
R OK, I'll let him know you're here. Oh, hello Mark, it's Sandra here at reception. I've got Annie Morton here to see you. OK, thanks. Bye. Yes, he's

expecting you. He said you can go up to see him. Have you been to his office before?
A No.
R OK. It's on the first floor. So, go up the stairs and turn left. Go through the door and turn right. Then go down the corridor and it's the first door on the right.
A Fine. Thank you.

AUDIO ONLY
A Sorry, I got lost. Could you tell me where the office is again, please?
R Yes, of course. So, first go up the …

c ▶ 3.40 Elicit from students what they can remember about the directions that the receptionist gives Annie. Write any phrases they manage to produce on the board. Then play Part 1 of the video or play the audio recording again for the class to complete the directions in 1c. Check answers as a class.

> **Answers**
> 1 first 2 up 3 left 4 door 5 right 6 down
> 7 first 8 right

LANGUAGE NOTES

Make sure that students know the words and phrases:

first floor   *ground floor*   *top floor*   *corridor*

In many countries, *first floor* is the same as *ground floor* in the UK.

EXTRA ACTIVITY

Give students two minutes to memorise the directions in 1c. Students role play the conversation between Annie and the receptionist. The receptionist gives instructions and Annie mimes following them. Then students swap roles. Monitor and point out errors for students to self-correct.

2 USEFUL LANGUAGE
Asking for and giving directions in a building

a 3.41 Ask students to complete the question, and then play the recording to check. Check the answer as a class and focus on the position of the verb (*is*) at the end of the sentence.

> **Answer**
> Excuse me, can you tell me where the reception is?

↻ LOA TIP DRILLING

Give a short transformation drill to practise the structure, e.g.

Say: *Reception. Can you tell me where the reception is?* (Gesture for students to repeat.)

Students: *Can you tell me where the reception is?*

Say: *Mark's office*

Students: *Can you tell me where Mark's office is?*

Say: *the language lab*

Students: *Can you tell me where the language lab is?*

Say: *the cafeteria*

Students: *Can you tell me where the cafeteria is?*

b 3.42 Individually, students match the phrases with the pictures. Play the recording for them to check their answers. Play it again or model the phrases yourself for students to repeat. Ask them to underline the stressed word or words in each sentence and to pay attention to correct sentence stress and intonation.

> **Answers**
> 1 b 2 f 3 c 4 g 5 h 6 d 7 a 8 i 9 j 10 e

c In pairs, students take turns to cover the phrases and remember the directions for each picture. Uncover and check.

3 CONVERSATION SKILLS
Checking information

a ▶3.43 Ask the class what they think Annie does next after she gets lost and elicit some ideas – e.g. she goes home, she goes into another office to ask directions, she goes back to reception, etc. Then play Part 2 of the video or play the audio recording for them to check their ideas.

> **Answer**
> She goes back to (the) reception (and asks again).

Video/audioscript (Part 2)

ANNIE Sorry, I got lost. Could you tell me where the office is again, please?
RECEPTIONIST Yes, of course. So, first go up the stairs to the first floor and turn left. Then go through the door and turn right.
A So go up the stairs to the first floor and turn left. Then go through the door and turn right.
R Yes. Then go down the corridor and it's the first office on the right.
A Sorry, the fourth office?
R No, the first.
A Right, I think I've got that.
R Good.
A So can I just check? Go up the stairs and turn right …
R No, turn left.
A Left! Then go through the door and turn left … no … right.
R That's it.
A Thanks very much

b ▶3.44 Students read and listen to the three exchanges based on the conversation and match the underlined phrases with their uses. Check answers as a class. Then play Part 2 of the video or play the audio recording again for students to listen and repeat the conversations.

> **Answers**
> to check information by repeating it: 1, 2, 4
> to show we understand: 3

c 💬 Choose a place in the building you are in and direct students to it. e.g. *Go out of the classroom and turn right. Go down the corridor and turn left. Go down the stairs and through the big glass doors at the bottom. Where are you?* Elicit the correct answer, then tell the class that you are going to direct them again, but this time you want them to check the information and show they understand, using the phrases in b. Repeat the directions, pausing where appropriate to elicit the checking or confirming phrases from the class. Then give students a couple of minutes to prepare their own directions. They take turns to read their phrases to their partner who listens and repeats the information to check it's correct. Monitor and correct students' pronunciation as appropriate and listen for correct use of the target phrases.

d ▶3.45 Tell students that now they're going to hear the conversation between Mark and Annie. Look at the question and play Part 3 of the video or play the audio recording for students to answer. Check the answer as a class.

> **Answer**
> Mark thinks Annie has a good chance.

Video/audioscript (Part 3)

MARK Obviously, I can't promise anything. But I think you've a really good chance of getting a job here.
ANNIE Thanks, Mark! That's great. You've helped me so much.
M Not at all. You've got a really good CV and lots of experience. I'm sure my boss will be very impressed.
A I hope so! Anyway, I'll let you get back to your work now.
M OK.
A Oh, and have fun at the gym with Leo tomorrow!
M Thanks. I'm sure it'll be good. Do you want me to walk down with you or …?
A No, it's OK – I know the way out. Thanks again.
M Not a problem. See you soon.
A Bye.
M Bye.

> 📖 **VOCABULARY SUPPORT**
>
> *a good chance of* – quite likely that
>
> *CV* (B1) – document that describes your education and experience
>
> *impressed* (B2) – think something is very good

e 💬 Ask the class whether they would give Annie a job at their company and elicit reasons as to why or why not.

4 PRONUNCIATION
Sound and spelling: /ɜː/ and /ɔː/

a ▶3.46 Tell the class that they are going to hear two words with different vowel sounds. Play the recording for students to listen and repeat. Contrast the two sounds /ɜː/ and /ɔː/ for students to repeat after you in chorus. Do this several times to give them practice in producing as well as hearing the sounds.

b In pairs, students take turns to say the pairs of words, circling the word with the /ɜː/ sound. Check answers as class. Model the word pairs for students to repeat after you.

> **Answers**
> 1 third 2 Thursday 3 thirty 4 work 5 bird

c ▶3.47 Play the recording for students to circle the words they hear. Check answers as a class.

> **Answers**
> 1 fourth 2 Thursday 3 thirty 4 work 5 board

5 SPEAKING

Ask the class to look at the plan of the building and go through the key with them. Check understanding of any words they do not know. Students work in pairs and take turns to ask for and give directions from the entrance of the school. Remind them to check and confirm information. Monitor and correct students' pronunciation as appropriate and listen for correct usage of the target language from this lesson.

> **ADDITIONAL MATERIAL**
>
> ▶ Workbook 11C
> ▶ Photocopiable activities: Pronunciation p.285, 286
> ▶ Unit Progress Test
> ▶ Personalised online practice

11D Skills for Writing
In my opinion, it's because of the Internet

At the end of this lesson, students will be able to:

- understand people talking about inventions
- read and understand a text about inventions
- use phrases to give opinions, results and reasons
- write a web post giving an opinion

💡 OPTIONAL LEAD-IN

Books closed. Individually, students write down an invention that they have used today and think about how their lives would be different without it. Students share their ideas with the class, e.g. *My alarm clock is an excellent invention. Without it, I might still be in bed! Or my mum would need to wake me up every day.*

1 LISTENING AND SPEAKING

a 🗨 Ask students: *Is there one new invention that would have helped you today?* Students can talk about this in pairs and then tell the class in feedback, e.g. *a time machine to get them to school faster.* Ask students to look at the pictures and talk about what they can see and what kinds of inventions they might be. Elicit or point out that the man is saying *Hello! How are you?* in Spanish. Take feedback as a class and write on the board students' different ideas about what the three inventions might be.

b ▶️ 3.48 Tell students that they are going to hear people on a radio programme talking about the inventions in the pictures. Play the recording for the class to listen for general meaning and to complete the first row of the table with the invention each person talks about. Check answers as a class.

> **Answers**
> Amir – new kind of car engine
> Utta – artificial meat
> Pierre – device to put in ear to translate languages

Audioscript

HOST Hi, welcome to the show. Today we're looking at great inventions for the future. What really useful inventions do you think we need? People have called in to the show to tell us their ideas. First up we have Amir. Hi, Amir.

AMIR Hi.

H So Amir, tell us about what invention you'd like to see.

A I think the most important invention we need is a new kind of car engine that doesn't need petrol. There are too many cars in the world already, and as countries become richer, more and more people will want a car. That will be terrible news for the environment. But imagine a world with clean cars and no more pollution to worry about! I'm sure it will be invented soon. We already have electric cars, but I think it will be something different, maybe something like a car that runs on air. I'm sure someone will invent something to solve the problem. I hope so, anyway.

H Thanks, Amir. That's a great invention. Next on the line we have Utta. Utta, tell us about your invention.

UTTA Hi, well, one really useful invention would be artificial meat that's cheap and tastes good and which doesn't need cows, sheep or chickens to produce it. It sounds like science fiction, but in fact they've already invented it in a way. Amazingly, they've produced beef in a laboratory, but it cost thousands of pounds to make. But that's the same with all new inventions; they're always expensive at the start. So, I think it will happen and it'll be really good, because all the fields we use to grow food for cows could be used for something else – to grow vegetables or plant trees, for example.

H Thanks, Utta. Artificial meat! Wow, that sounds scary … Anyhow, last up we have Pierre. Hi, Pierre.

PIERRE Hi.

H So Pierre, tell us about your idea for a great invention.

P Well, a really useful invention I read about was a device that you could put in your ear and it would translate languages for you. You wouldn't need to study for hours and hours to learn a foreign language. You could just put it in your ear when you went on holiday to foreign countries and you'd understand everything everyone was saying to you. It would help people to communicate and would be very useful for business people or for politicians. But it wouldn't be very good news for teachers. Fortunately, for them, it's probably impossible to make such a device, or at least it will take many years.

H Cool. I'd love that invention! Thanks for those great ideas. Who knows which of them will happen! We can only wait and see!

📖 VOCABULARY SUPPORT

artificial (B2) – not natural or real

device (B2) – a piece of equipment that is used for a particular purpose

laboratory (B1) – a room used for scientific work

pollution (B1) – damage caused to water, air, etc. by harmful substances or waste

run (on) (C1) – uses a supply of power to work

📖 LANGUAGE NOTES

The host uses idiomatic phrases to sequence the people he talks to: *First up (Firstly)* and *Last up (Lastly/Finally).*

c ▶️ 3.48 Read through the remaining two questions in the table. You may wish to help students with the items in the Vocabulary support box at this point. Then play the recording again for students to complete the rest of the table. You may need to play the recording more than once. Check answers as a class.

> **Answers**
> Amir – clean cars so no more pollution; yes (someone will invent something to solve the problem)
> Utta – cheap, tastes good, fields used for growing food for cows can be used for something else; yes (I think it will happen and it'll be really good)
> Pierre – no need to study, would help people to communicate; no (it's probably impossible or will take many years)

d Individually, students decide if they think the inventions are a good idea or not and why and any other ways they might be able to think of to solve the same problem. Give them a couple of minutes to do this and tell them to make notes about their ideas – at least two or three lines for each invention.

e 🗨 In small groups, students compare their ideas from d. Monitor and help with vocabulary as necessary. Take feedback as a class and ask different groups to summarise their ideas and suggestions regarding each invention. If you wish, give students information from the Culture notes below.

CULTURE NOTES

Meat has been grown in a laboratory, and in March 2013 the first lab-grown burger was eaten in London. It was produced in the Netherlands and the cost of the project was €250,000. The critic who ate the burger said that it tasted similar to meat but was drier and not as tasty as real meat. At the moment, it is far too expensive to grow a lot of meat in this way, but this proves that it is possible and it may be produced more cheaply in the future.

2 READING

a Ask students to tell you what they think was the most important invention of the last 2,000 years. Put their suggestions on the board. Then tell them they are going to read some web posts where people answer the same question. Ask the class to read the posts quickly in order to find the names of the inventions and write them in the list. Check their answers as a class.

> **Answers**
> 1 the Internet   3 Hindu-Arabic number system
> 2 paper   4 reading glasses

b Students read the posts again to match the inventions and the results. Check answers as a class.

> **Answers**
> a 4   b 3   c 1   d 2

 VOCABULARY SUPPORT

active (B1) – busy, moving around

essential (B1) – very important

c Individually, students read the web posts again and note down their answers to the questions. Encourage them to compare their ideas with a partner before checking answers as a class.

> **Answers**
> 1 earliest: paper, latest: the Internet
> 2 We might/will do everything from home.
> 3 People were able to write down information, keep it and send it over long distances.
> 4 There might be no science, engineering or computers.
> 5 He can do lots of things (that he couldn't do without them).

EXTRA ACTIVITY

Have a brief open discussion about which of the inventions the class think is most important and why. Make a note of any errors students make when giving their opinions so that they can self-correct after the class has studied the language for giving opinions in the next section.

3 WRITING SKILLS

Giving opinions; Expressing results and reasons

a Students underline the phrase *I think* in the sentence. Ask the class if they know any other phrases for giving opinions and write any suggestions on the board. Say that there are four more phrases for giving opinions in the texts and give students a minute or two to find and underline them. Then check answers as a class.

> **Answers**
> I think
> it seems to me that (2), I believe (3), In my opinion, In my view (4)

b Read through and correct the sentences as a class.

> **Answers**
> 1 In my view   2 In my opinion   3 I believe   4 It seems to me

c Write *cause* and *result* on the board. Underneath write a sentence such as *Pablo speaks better English than he did last year.* Elicit possible causes for this from students (e.g. he did an English course last summer, he's got an English girlfriend) and then possible results (e.g. he gets better marks for his homework, he feels more confident, etc.). When you are sure students understand cause and result, ask them to look at the sentences and elicit the cause and result for each one. Check answers as a class.

> **Answers**
> 1 cause/reason: invention of numbers; result: science could develop
> 2 cause/reason: invention of paper; result: send messages long-distance
> 3 cause/reason: do everything online at home; result: stop using shops and offices
> 4 cause/reason: invention of reading glasses; result: stay active when older

d Individually, students match the phrases and the different possible structures. Check answers as a class.

> **Answers**
> noun / noun phrase / pronoun + comma: because of, as a result of
> join two clauses: as, because

EXTRA ACTIVITY

Give students some extra practice by writing this sentence on the board:

The computer was broken, so we couldn't finish our work.

Ask students in pairs to rewrite the sentence in as many ways as they can using *as / because / as a result of / because of*. Suggested answers: *As/Because the computer was broken, we couldn't finish our work. We couldn't finish our work as/ because the computer was broken. The computer was broken. As a result of this, we couldn't finish our work. Because of the broken computer, we couldn't finish our work.*

e Students complete the sentences individually. Check answers as a class.

> **Answers**
> 1 Because; As   2 Because of; As a result of
> 3 Because of; As a result of

f Say: *Let's revise: tell me some possible phrases for giving your opinion.* Elicit three or four from the class (they should be able to produce the phrases from 3b). *Tell me some phrases for connecting causes and results.* Elicit the phrases from 3c from the class. Then give students a minute or two to write the sentences about the telephone using this language. Check answers as a class.

> **Suggested answers**
> In my opinion, the telephone is the most important invention of the 19th century. Because we can talk to people in other places, we can communicate more quickly.

g Students write an additional sentence. Ask for examples in feedback.

4 WRITING

a Tell students that they are going to write a web post like the ones in the reading text. This time, they have to choose one of the inventions in the list or think of another important invention. Ask students to note down the ideas they're going to write about, using the questions to help them. Then give them some time to do research by asking other students in the class for their responses to the questions. They can either simply talk to the students on either side of them or you can encourage them to walk round the class and ask more people. Monitor and help students with ideas if they need them.

LOA TIP MONITORING

When monitoring, be aware of differences of ability and personality. Ensure that shyer students have a chance to contribute by encouraging them to speak. Prevent the more confident students from dominating with a gesture or by saying 'one moment'.

b Students write their posts. Remind them to use words and phrases to explain reasons and results. Monitor and help with vocabulary as necessary.

c Students swap their posts with another student and reply to it. They should give comments including whether they agree or disagree, and why. Monitor and point out errors for students to self-correct.

d Students return their posts and replies. They should read the replies and check them according to the points given. Ask some students to read their posts and replies to the class.

FAST FINISHERS

Fast finishers can return to 3f and write a post about the invention of the telephone. Remember to look at these posts, too, during feedback.

ADDITIONAL MATERIAL

▶ Workbook 11D

UNIT 11
Review and extension

1 GRAMMAR

a Students do the task individually. Point out that there may be more than one possible answer. Check answers as a class.

> **Answers**
> 1 He was the man who/that invented the colour TV.
> 2 These are the mobile phones that/which work under water.
> 3 That is the machine that/which makes the screens for the computers.
> 4 This is the place where they found the statue.
> 5 These are the people who/that discovered the ancient city.
> 6 This is the shop where they sell that delicious bread.

b Students complete the conversation with the correct articles. Check answers together.

> **Answers**
> 1 a   2 the   3 a   4 the   5 a   6 the   7 a   8 a   9 a
> 10 The   11 the   12 an

c 💬 Students practise the conversation in 1b. If necessary, model it first with a student for the class to repeat.

> ### 💡 EXTRA ACTIVITY
>
> Write some sentences from the web posts in 11D on the board but leave a space where the articles should or shouldn't be. Ask students to tell you which (if any) articles should fill the gaps, e.g. *I believe … (the) … most important invention is … (the) … Hindu-Arabic number system, which was invented around … (the) … sixth century in … (no article) … India.*
>
> Students then work in pairs. Each looks back at a different unit in the book so far and writes down two or three sentences from a text but takes out the articles. Their partner has to fill the gaps. To make this more fun, they can read out the sentences but make a 'beep' sound instead of the gap. Ask for examples in feedback.

---

2 VOCABULARY

a Remind students that a compound noun combines two words and elicit examples that they remember from the unit. Then they make compound nouns for the definitions. Check answers as a class. Say each compound noun in turn and ask individual students to make a sentence with it.

> **Answers**
> 1 cash machine   2 rock star   3 ticket office   4 road signs
> 5 street lights (or one word)   6 shopping bag   7 kitchen knife
> 8 bottle top

b Students choose the correct alternatives to complete the sentences. Check answers together.

> **Answers**
> 1 accidentally   2 as expected   3 by chance   4 luckily
> 5 on purpose   6 Surprisingly

3 WORDPOWER: preposition + noun

a Write these sentences on the board: *My printer's not working properly. It can't print anything in colour at the moment.* Underline *in colour* and tell students that this is an example of a phrase with preposition + noun. Explain that we can't guess the preposition in phrases like this. We need to learn them as complete phrases. Ask students to work in pairs to match the phrases in bold in the sentences with their meanings. Check answers together.

> ### 💡 FAST FINISHERS
>
> Fast finishers can think of more sentences using the different phrases.

> **Answers**
> 1 f   2 d   3 a   4 e   5 g   6 c   7 b

b 💬 In pairs, students discuss which sentences are true for them or which they agree with.

c Read the explanation and the example with the class. Then ask them to match the sentences with the pictures. Check answers.

> **Answers**
> 1 b   2 c   3 d   4 a

d Students underline the preposition + noun combinations in the sentences in 3c. Ask them to write a sentence about somebody they know (of) who is in each place. Check answers and ask students to give you some example sentences.

> **Answers**
> 1 in hospital   2 at university
> 3 in school   4 in prison

> ### 📖 LANGUAGE NOTES
>
> *In school* is used in the USA; *at school* is more common in the UK.

▶ Photocopiable activities: Wordpower p.262

> ### 🔄 LOA REVIEW YOUR PROGRESS
>
> Students look back through the unit, think about what they've studied and decide how well they did. Students work on weak areas by using the appropriate sections of the Workbook, the Photocopiable activities and the Personalised online practice.

UNIT 12
Characters

↻ UNIT OBJECTIVES

At the end of this unit, students will be able to:
- understand written and spoken stories
- understand the links between different parts of a story
- tell a story
- talk about family relationships
- agree and disagree in discussions
- write a short story, using time linkers

UNIT CONTENTS

Ⓖ GRAMMAR
- Past perfect
- Reported speech
- Using past time linkers

Ⓥ VOCABULARY
- Animals: *bee, camel, gorilla, mosquito, parrot, spider, tiger, whale*
- Personality adjectives: *anxious, confident, creative, easy-going, fair, fun, generous, honest, patient, reliable, selfish, sensible, serious, shy, sociable, strict, careless, funny*
- Wordpower: *age: about my age, (three years) apart in age, at an early age, at your age, in old age, middle-aged, of a similar age*

Ⓟ PRONUNCIATION
- Sound and spelling: /ʌ/, /ɔː/ and /əʊ/
- Sentence stress: *that*
- Word stress
- Main stress: contrastive

Ⓒ COMMUNICATION SKILLS
- Talking about family relationships
- Agreeing and disagreeing
- Telling and writing a story

GETTING STARTED

💡 OPTIONAL LEAD-IN

Books closed. Ask a student to name an animal. The next student must repeat the previous animal and then name another one. This continues round the class until a student forgets an animal or cannot name another one. This student drops out. The winner is the last student to name a new animal as well as remember all the previous ones.

Elicit *orang-utan* by saying: *It has red hair. It's very clever. It lives in Borneo and Sumatra. It's a bit like us.* Write the word on the board.

a Students look at the picture and say what they can see. They then read and discuss the questions in pairs. Monitor and support students with any vocabulary they may need, e.g. *animal care/rescue centre, wildlife reserve; vet, keeper, volunteer; feed, look after itself, find food, how to survive.* Check and discuss answers in feedback. If you wish, give students information from the Culture notes below.

🌍 CULTURE NOTES

Orang-utans are a kind of ape that live in Borneo and Sumatra. They spend most of their lives in trees and live on fruit and vegetation. These apes are highly intelligent and can use tools to get what they need. Orang-utans live up to 30 years old and form strong social bonds. However, this species of ape is in danger. The numbers of orang-utans have gone down by 55% in the last 20 years. This is because their habitat has been destroyed and also because of illegal hunting. Sadly, many orang-utans have been taken to be sold as pets because they have such lovely characters. This is particularly sad because in the wild, young orang-utans stay with their mothers until they are about eight years old. If the mothers are killed or taken away, the young orang-utan is unable to survive by itself. There are several care centres for rescued young orang-utans to teach them the skills they need before they can go back to the wild, e.g. what food to eat, how to use tools, how to move through the trees. This photograph was taken at the Orang-utan Care Center in Borneo, Indonesia.

b Students write down three words to describe the orang-utan in the picture and then compare them with their partner's words. Take feedback as a class and ask students to share their words with the class.

> **Suggested answers**
> small, naughty, cuddly (good to hold), wet, energetic, uncomfortable, lovable, dependent

c 💬 Discuss the question about the orang-utan's future as a class. Encourage students to justify their answers by explaining and giving reasons.

💡 EXTRA ACTIVITY

Ask each pair to choose an animal that is in danger of extinction. Students think of ideas to raise awareness about this animal's situation. Monitor and help with suggestions and vocabulary. Take feedback and encourage the pairs to explain their ideas to the group. Vote on the best idea.

12A I had always thought they were dangerous

At the end of this lesson, students will be able to:
- use the past perfect
- read and understand a story about a frightening experience
- tell a story involving an animal
- use vocabulary related to animals

💡 OPTIONAL LEAD-IN

Books closed. Ask students: *What is the most dangerous animal in the world?* Write all the suggestions on the board and encourage students to justify their answers. Tell or confirm the answer: *the mosquito.* (The mosquito is found everywhere in the world except Antarctica. More than 700,000 people die every year from diseases spread by mosquitoes, most significantly malaria which kills around 600,000 people every year.) Can students find the picture of the mosquito in lesson 12A?

1 VOCABULARY Animals

a 💬 Ask the students to think of the names of as many different types of animals as they can. Write all the correct suggestions they come up with on the board. Then write the words for different categories of animals e.g. *mammals (animals that feed babies with milk from their body), fish, birds, insects, reptiles (animals that produce eggs and use heat from the sun to keep warm).* Ask students to categorise the animals they have named.

In pairs, students match the pictures of animals with the names. Don't check answers at this point.

b ▶️ **3.49** Play the recording for students to check their answers. Play it again for them to practise the pronunciation of the names of the animals. Ask them to cover the words and spell them for you to write on the board. Ask students to tell you which category – mammals, insects, reptiles, etc. – each animal belongs to and also give you any other information they know about it, e.g. where it lives, what it eats, any particular behaviour it is well known for, etc.

> **Answers**
> 1 bee   2 mosquito   3 spider   4 parrot
> 5 gorilla   6 camel   7 tiger   8 whale

c 💬 Read through the questions about students' own experience of these animals and look at the examples. Then discuss the questions as a class and ask for details and reasons. During the discussion, ask students where we can see animals these days. Elicit: *in zoos, in safari parks, in the wild, in our homes, in rescue centres* and ask for examples of animals for each place.

2 READING

a 💬 Ask students what they know about gorillas – e.g. where they live, what they eat, etc. – and if they think they are dangerous.

b Tell students that they are going to read a story about a gorilla. Give the class a couple of minutes to read the introduction and answer the questions. Check answers as a class.

> **Answers**
> 1 a frightening event involving a gorilla and a boy
> 2 The video changed people's opinions of gorillas forever.

c 💬 Read through the words in the box with the class and tell them that these are from Jambo's story. Elicit or explain the meaning of *enclosure* and *stroke*. In pairs, students discuss what they think the story is about. Monitor and help with vocabulary as necessary. Take feedback and encourage students to justify their answers as far as possible, but don't say if they're right or not. Compare students' stories.

d Explain that the story is in different sections and that they are not in order. Ask students to read the story in pairs. They should start at square 1 and then discuss the question together. They then follow the directions to the next section and so on until they reach the end. Monitor and check that the pairs are discussing the questions before moving on to the next section. You may wish to help students with words in the Vocabulary support box. When they have finished, conduct feedback and ask whether they guessed the answers to the questions correctly. Check the story against their ideas for the story in 2c and see which pair (if any) predicted the story accurately.

📖 VOCABULARY SUPPORT

alive (B1) – living

disappear (B1) – to go out of view

enclosure – an area in a zoo where animals are kept

hero (B1) – someone who does something brave or good, which people respect or admire them for

ran away (B2) – secretly leave a place because you are unhappy there

seriously (B1) – badly or severely

straight away (B1) – immediately

stroke (B2) – to move your hand gently over an animal or a person

zookeeper – person who looks after animals in a zoo

e 💬 Discuss the questions as a class. If you wish, give students information from the Culture notes below.

🌍 CULTURE NOTES

In the past, gorillas were captured from the wild to be put in zoos so that people could see these amazing animals. Today, our attitude to taking animals from the wild has changed.

Gorillas are an endangered species. They are suffering from the loss of their habitat in the forests of Central Africa, and from poaching and disease. Mountain gorillas are critically endangered and it is thought there are fewer than 800 alive today. Gorillas live in groups of up to 30 individuals and are led by an older adult male. They live for around 35 years in the wild.

It is often thought that we humans are the only animals to feel emotions like sadness and love and empathy (an understanding of how others are feeling), but research has shown that gorillas feel emotions, too.

3 GRAMMAR Past perfect

a Books closed. Elicit these verbs and write them on the board: *break, disappear, rescue, turn back.* Read the following pairs of gapped sentences to students who write them in their books: *a) The father … to his son. Levan … . b) Zookeepers … Levan. He … several bones.* In pairs, students see if they can remember which verb goes in which gap and write it in the correct form (past simple or past perfect). Check as a class, but don't offer any explanation at this point. Open books. Ask students to look at the sentences in 3a. Students look at the verbs in bold and write which actions happened first and second. Check answers as a class.

> **Answers**
> 1 turned back (2), had disappeared (1)
> 2 rescued (2), had broken (1)

b Give students one minute to read through the rules and complete them with the words in the box. Check the answer as a class.

> **Answer**
> perfect; simple; participle

> 📖 **LANGUAGE NOTES**
>
> Point out that the contraction for the past perfect *I had = I'd* is the same as for *I would = I'd.*

c Students read Jambo's story (in correct order) again and underline more examples of the past perfect. Tell the class there are six examples of the past perfect in the text and turn the activity into a race to see which student can find all six examples first. Check answers as a class.

> **Answers**
> had fallen (3), had come (5), had come (4), had (seriously) hurt, had filmed (6), had (always) thought (2)

d ▶ 🔊 3.50 Students read the information in Grammar Focus 12A on SB p.164. Play the recording where indicated and ask students to listen and repeat. Students then complete the exercises in Grammar Focus 12A on SB p.165. They complete the tasks individually, but compare their ideas with a partner before you take feedback as a class. Tell students to go back to SB p.119.

> **Answers (Grammar Focus 12A SB p.165)**
> a 1 had gone 2 had broken 3 hadn't gone 4 had forgotten
>   5 had made 6 had found 7 had eaten 8 had finished
>   9 had escaped; had left
> b 1f 2e 3b 4a 5d 6c
> c 1 came; had forgotten 2 arrived; had broken
>   3 hadn't gone; were 4 hadn't done; asked 5 found; had sold
>   6 was; hadn't had 7 had never flown; felt
>   8 Had the match finished; got

> 💡 **FAST FINISHERS**
>
> Ask students to think of alternative endings to the sentence beginnings in Exercise b of Grammar Focus 12A.

> • Say or write on the board: *When we'd seen the film, we went for a meal at a restaurant.*
> Ask: *Did we have the meal first?* (no)
> Ask: *Did we see the film first?* (yes)
> Say: *The meal happened in the past, but we saw the film before the meal, so we use the past perfect – 'had seen'.*
> • Give another example. Say or write on the board: *I hadn't phoned my sister before I left the house.*
> Ask: *Did I phone my sister first?* (no)
> Ask: *Did I leave the house first?* (yes)
> Say: *Leaving the house happened in the past, but not phoning the sister happened before the person left, so we use the past perfect – 'hadn't phoned'.*
> • Write an example from the Grammar Focus on the board and ask concept questions to check understanding of the use of the past perfect. For example, write: *When I got home, my goldfish had disappeared.*
> Ask: *Did the goldfish disappear after I got home?* (no)
> *Did the goldfish disappear before I got home?* (yes).

> 💡 **EXTRA ACTIVITY**
>
> If students need additional practice in forming the past perfect, ask them to complete these sentences in their own words. *I arrived at school/work late because …, My teacher/boss was angry because …, When I got home last night, I found that …*

e ▶ 3.51 **Pronunciation** Ask students to look at the past participles in the box and focus on the vowels in bold: *drunk* /ʌ/, *brought* /ɔː/, *chosen* /əʊ/. Model first the words and then the individual vowel sounds /ʌ/, /ɔː/ and /əʊ/, for students to repeat in chorus after you. Depending on the students' first language, they may find the difference between the sounds difficult to hear and/or reproduce so don't hesitate to exaggerate the pronunciation and the different positioning of the lips for each sound. In pairs, students take turns to pronounce the past participles aloud and put them into the correct column according to the vowel sounds. Play the recording for them to check their answers.

> **Answers**
> drunk, become, swum, won
> brought, bought, caught, thought
> chosen, flown, stolen, thrown

f ▶ 3.52 Let students practise pronouncing the sentences in pairs before you take feedback as a class. Nominate individual students to say the sentences with the correct vowel sounds. Check by playing the recording after each sentence.

g 💬 Read through the problems 1–5. Check understanding of *skin* – the outer layer of a person or an animal's body, *itchy* – you have an uncomfortable feeling on your skin and you need to *scratch* (gesture, and see if students remember from Unit 7), *mouse* – small animal that lives in the walls of our houses and in fields. Students tell you what kind of animal they think caused the problems, giving reasons for their ideas.

Suggested answers

1 mosquito 2 cat 3 spider, bee, wasp 4 dog, cat
5 spider, mouse, gorilla, large dog (pretty much anything!)

h Students complete the sentences in 3g using verbs in the past perfect. Before they start, elicit or provide verbs they might need, e.g. *bite/bit/bitten, sting/stung/ stung, rub against.* Take feedback and ask for examples. Put some correct sentences on the board. Elicit other possible endings for the sentences.

Suggested answers

1 because a mosquito had bitten me.
2 because my cat had killed it during the night.
3 because a bee had stung me.
4 because my dog had rubbed against me.
5 because she had seen a mouse/spider.

i 💬 Discuss the question as a class. Encourage students to expand their answers by giving details about when/ where/why/what was happening at the time, what had happened and what happened next.

4 SPEAKING AND LISTENING

a 💬 Tell students that they are going to make a story using the pictures in the book in the correct order. In pairs, students write down any words they think will be useful when talking about each picture. Elicit ideas from the class and write all suggestions on the board to create a vocabulary resource for students when they're making their stories. Then students work in pairs to make the story. Monitor and help with vocabulary as necessary. Take feedback by asking for volunteer pairs to tell their stories. Ask the class if they agree with the order of events/pictures each pair has chosen, but don't check answers at this point.

b ▶️ **3.53** Play the recording for the class to check their answers.

Audioscript

A parrot in Denver, USA, became a hero when it helped to save the life of a two-year-old girl. Megan Howard – the parrot's owner – was looking after two-year-old Hannah. It was morning and Hannah was eating her breakfast on her own, because Megan had gone to the bathroom. While Megan was in the bathroom, the parrot, Willie, started to make a very strange noise. Megan realised something bad had happened. Willie started screaming the words "Mama! Baby!" again and again. Megan said she had never heard the parrot scream like that before. She came out of the bathroom to see what was happening. And when she looked at Hannah, she saw that her face had gone blue. Some of Hannah's breakfast had got stuck in her throat. She couldn't breathe because the food was still there. Luckily for Hannah, Megan had learned what to do in this situation. She immediately ran over to her and performed the Heimlich manoeuvre. Hannah started to breathe again normally. And once Willie saw that Hannah was OK, he stopped screaming. Willie the parrot was given a prize by the Red Cross for his actions. He was named 'animal hero of the year' and they gave him a box of cereal with his picture on it. Hannah's mum thanked both Megan and Willie and said she thought they had both saved Hannah.

Answers

3 2
6 5
4 1

📖 VOCABULARY SUPPORT

breathe (B1) – take air into and out of your lungs

go blue (B1) – become blue in colour

Heimlich manoeuvre – a way of unblocking the windpipe when food is stuck in it

stuck (B2) – not able to move anywhere

throat (B1) – the space inside the neck down which food and air can go

c 💬 In pairs, students tell the story of Willie the Parrot, taking it in turns to tell the story for each picture. Remind students to use the past perfect when possible. Monitor but don't interrupt fluency unless students make mistakes with the past perfect. Point out errors for students to self-correct. In feedback, ask for examples of the past perfect from the stories and put them on the board.

d 💬 Ask students to tell the class any stories they know about animals and humans helping each other.

ADDITIONAL MATERIAL

▶ Workbook 12A

▶ Photocopiable activities: Grammar p.226, Vocabulary p.250, Pronunciation p.288

12B He said I was selfish!

At the end of this lesson, students will be able to:

- use reported speech correctly
- understand stories about family relationships
- use personality adjectives
- talk about members of their family
- read and understand a survey about brothers and sisters' relationships

OPTIONAL LEAD-IN

Books closed. Tell the class three facts about people in your family, using two sentences for each. The follow-up sentence must give more detailed information to support the first sentence. Two facts should be true and one false. Write them on the board if necessary, e.g.

1 *My brother is a film actor. He was in the film 'Thor'.*

2 *My cousin is a good swimmer. He won the southern area competition.*

3 *My uncle loves rats. He has kept pet rats since he was a teenager.*

Ask students to guess which facts are true and which is false. Students then do the same activity in pairs.

1 LISTENING

a In pairs, students discuss how well they used to get on with other children and their brothers and sisters when they were children. Elicit/Remind them of how we use *used to* (from Unit 7). Take feedback as a class. Encourage students to tell the class the most interesting thing their partner talked about.

LOA TIP ELICITING

Eliciting can also be used to establish a concept or establish awareness of the activity that is coming up. In this case, students will be listening to stories about brothers and sisters.

Ask: *How big is your family?*

Ask: *Do you have a good relationship with everyone?*

Ask: *What kinds of problems can brothers and sisters have?*

b In pairs, students look at the pictures and say what they can see. They then guess what is happening in each. Take feedback as a class and write students' ideas on the board, but don't say if they're right or not.

c ▶ 3.54 Tell students that they are going to hear three people talking about the pictures. Play the recording for students to match the stories with the pictures. Pause after each story to let students check the pictures and decide. Check answers as a class and compare the stories with students' previous ideas. Some of the new vocabulary can be explained by using the pictures, e.g. *fence, kettle*.

Answers

Story 1: the picture with the cow, bottom left; Story 2: the picture with the two boys and the kettle, middle right; Story 3: the picture with the girl with lots of books, top left

Audioscript

CLAIRE My little sister and I have always had our fights. I think the funniest time was when I made her ride a cow. We lived in a house with a field of cows on one side and I told my sister that they were horses. I went into the field and stood behind the cows making horse noises. When the cows were right next to our garden fence, I said she could ride one of the horses … just like a cowboy! I still can't believe she listened to me! She just jumped off the fence onto a cow's back! The cow was very surprised. It ran away with my sister holding on to its back. I couldn't stop laughing. In the end, my sister fell off. Her clothes were really dirty and she was crying. Then I felt bad and helped her back home. When we got back, I told my mum my sister had tried to ride a cow and I had saved her. She believed me … I still feel guilty.

JEREMY I often used to play with my younger brother, but we did fight a lot, too. I remember one time when I was really mean to him. That day my parents had burnt some leaves in the garden and the fire was still a bit hot. So I had an idea for a joke to play on my brother. We had an old kettle in the garden. It was really dirty. I told my brother I was going to make 'grass soup'. So I took some grass and put it in the dirty old kettle with some water. I put it on the fire for a minute. Then I poured some into a cup and gave it to my brother. It was a horrible brown-orange colour with green bits of grass in it. He didn't look very sure about drinking it, so I put the cup near my mouth and told him I had drunk some and it was delicious. I hadn't even tasted it, of course. I gave him the cup and he drank all of it. Later that evening, my brother said he wasn't feeling very well. My parents wanted to know why … so, really, I had to tell them about my 'soup'.

TANYA My sister's a year and a half older than me and we always got on well. When we were little, we were very similar and did everything together. But then she started to read a lot, and she was very strong for her age. I didn't mind, but I didn't like the attention she got from my parents. One day some of my parents' friends came to visit us. My dad told them he was very proud of my sister because she could read so well. I got really angry, so I went to the bookcase in the hall and chose five of the biggest, thickest books I could see. Then I went back to my parents and their friends and said I had just finished reading the books. My dad asked me to describe the stories. I had no idea, so I just looked at the front of the books and guessed. So I talked about a happy king with lots of rings – that was Lord of the Rings – and also lots of stories about people with names beginning with N. That was volume 12 of an encyclopedia. I could hear my sister laughing in the other room the whole time …

d ▶ 3.54 Read through the questions with the class. Ask students to decide if the sentences are true or false and to correct the false ones. Play the recording again for them to do this. If appropriate, pause the recording after each story. Give them some time to check their answers with a partner. Check answers as a class.

📖 VOCABULARY SUPPORT

cowboy – a man who rides a horse to look after cows, typically in western USA

delicious (B1) – good to eat or drink

fence (B2) – made of wood, it separates gardens and fields

get attention from (B1) – make people notice you

guilty (B1) – feel you've done something wrong

kettle (B1) – people boil water in these

leaves (B1) – these drop from a tree every year

mean (B2) – unkind

play a joke on (B2) – do sth to sb that makes other people laugh

pour (B1) – to transfer liquid from one thing into another

📖 LANGUAGE NOTES

Some nouns have irregular plurals, e.g. leaf (from a tree) = leaves; shelf (from a book case) = shelves.

> **Answers**
> Claire: 1 T   2 T   3 F Claire helped her sister back home.
> 4 F She told her mother that she'd saved her sister.
> Jeremy: 1 F He wanted to play a joke on him.
> 2 F He didn't want to drink it.
> 3 F He pretended to drink some of it.   4 T
> Tanya: 1 T   2 T   3 F He asked her to describe the stories.
> 4 F She guessed the stories by looking at the covers.

e 💬 Put students into small groups to discuss the two questions. Monitor and help with vocabulary as necessary. Take feedback as a class. Encourage students to share the most interesting stories they heard in their groups.

2 GRAMMAR Reported speech

a Books closed. Ask students: *Can you remember what Claire told her sister about the cow?* Note down the answers they give you verbatim. Don't correct any mistakes with information or direct or reported speech. Do punctuate direct speech if students say: *Claire/She said "Those are/were horses."* However, do not punctuate if they say: *She said / told her the cows are/were horses.* Repeat the process with two more questions. *Can you remember what Tanya told the guests 'The Lord of the Rings' was about?* (She told them it was about a happy king with lots of rings.) *Can you remember what Jeremy told his brother he was going to make?* (He said he was going to make grass soup.) Open books and check information. Write the sentences you noted on the board and ask students to correct any grammar mistakes using the 2d Grammar Focus for reference. Students then do task 2a and match the examples of reported speech with the direct speech. They can do this in pairs. Check answers as a class.

> **Answers**
> 1 d 2 e 3 a 4 c 5 g 6 b 7 f

b Give students one minute to read through the rules and complete them. Check answers as a class.

> **Answers**
> present simple ➜ past simple
> present continuous ➜ past continuous
> present perfect ➜ past perfect
> past simple ➜ past perfect
> am/is/are going to ➜ was/were going to
> can ➜ could

📖 LANGUAGE NOTES

We can use *that* to introduce reported speech, but it is not essential and can be left out, e.g. *He said that he wanted to go to the cinema. / He said he wanted to go to the cinema.*

c Ask students to complete the two sentences. Check answers and elicit the reason: we need an object with *tell* but *say* can't be followed by an object.

> **Answers**
> 1 told   2 said

d ▶ ⏵3.55 Students read the information in Grammar Focus 12B on SB p.164. Play the recording where indicated and ask students to listen and repeat. Students then complete the exercises in Grammar Focus 12B on SB p.165. Check answers as a class, making sure students are changing the tenses correctly. Tell students to go back to SB p.120.

> **Answers (Grammar Focus 12B SB p.165)**
> a 1 could 2 wasn't going 3 would; got 4 we'd seen 5 she'd go 6 told them; liked 7 could come 8 had been
> b 1 she; me 2 his 3 we; we; our 4 she; her 5 they; their 6 they; me; I

👁 CAREFUL!

Students often confuse the use of *say* and *tell*, e.g. ~~The man told that the film was boring~~ (Correct form = *The man **said** that the film was boring.*) *Tell* is usually followed by a personal object, unlike *say*. However, we can use *say* with a personal object if we add *to*, e.g. ~~The nurses said me that I was in hospital~~ (Correct form = *The nurses **told me / said to me** that I was in hospital.*)

e ⏵3.56 **Pronunciation** Play the recording to focus students on the different pronunciation of *that*: /ðæt/ (strong) and /ðət/ (weak). After they have listened once, model and contrast the two different pronunciations /ðæt/ and /ðət/ for the students to repeat in chorus. Answer the questions as a class.

> **Answers**
> 1 that /**ðæt**/ = strong form; refers to the previous sentence and needs emphasis / can't be in weak form
> 2 that /**ðət**/ = weak form; as used in reported speech

f ⏵3.57 Students do the task of writing the sentences as reported speech individually. Play the recording for them to check answers. Remind them *that* is possible in all cases, but not essential. In spoken English *that* is often omitted.

> **Answers**
> 1 I told her (that) she couldn't read my diary.
> 2 She said (that) she was going to tell Dad.
> 3 I told him (that) I wasn't talking to him.
> 4 She said (that) she didn't want to play with me.
> 5 He told me (that) it wasn't fair.
> 6 I said (that) he had broken my toy.

g Model the sentences in 2f, or play the recording again, pausing after each reported sentence, for students to repeat.

h 💬 Read through the examples in bubbles with the class. Elicit similar examples of what students remember from when they were younger and write them on the board.

i Give students a minute or so to find examples of the things people told them and to make some brief notes.

j 💬 In pairs, students use their notes to talk about the things they remembered. Monitor and check they are using reported speech correctly. Point out errors for students to self-correct. Take feedback as a class and elicit examples from students of what people said to their partner in order to encourage use of third-person pronouns – e.g. *Pablo's teacher told him ...*

3 VOCABULARY Personality adjectives

a 💬 Write the name of a member of your family on the board and tell students one thing about him/her, e.g. *Jack is my brother. He's very calm. He never gets worried about things.* Ask students to tell their partners about four members of their family. If you used the Optional lead-in, remind students that this time it has to be the truth! Ask for examples during feedback, and write any personality adjectives that students mention on the board.

b ▶ ⏵**3.58** Students complete the exercises in Vocabulary Focus 12B on SB p.141. Check the answers to Exercises a and b. Use the pictures to help understanding. Play the recording where indicated for students to underline the stressed syllables in Exercise c. Ask them to do d and then check answers for Exercises c and d at the same time. Monitor the conversations in Exercise e. Tell students to go back to SB p.121.

> **Answers (Vocabulary Focus 12B SB p.141)**
> a 1d 2b 3a 4c
> b 1 sensible   2 confident   3 reliable   4 strict   5 careless
>   6 patient   7 generous   8 fair   9 creative   10 honest
>   11 funny
> c anxious, careless, confident, creative, easy going, fair, fun, funny, generous, honest, patient, reliable, selfish, sensible, shy, sociable, strict
> d Suggested answers: careless, selfish

> 💡 **EXTRA ACTIVITY**
>
> To practise the adjectives in pairs, students take turns to describe people that they both know using the adjectives and a detail. Their partner has to guess who it is.

4 READING AND SPEAKING

a 💬 Read through the questions and examples in bubbles with the class. Students discuss their families in pairs. Monitor and help as necessary. Encourage students to use the personality adjectives from the preceding exercise. Take feedback as a class. Ask students to tell the class the most interesting thing that they learned about their partner's family.

b 💬 Students cover the words and phrases in the box. Ask students to work in pairs and read through the information about brothers and sisters. Can they guess the information that is missing? Check ideas in feedback. Then ask them to look at the word box and confirm or change their answers. Don't check their ideas at this point.

c ▶ Students turn to SB p.131 and check their answers with the complete text. In pairs they discuss whether they agree with the statements, giving examples from their own experience. For task c, ask students to discuss their opinions with the class and take a vote to see how many students agree with each fact.

> **ADDITIONAL MATERIAL**
>
> ▶ Workbook 12B
> ▶ Photocopiable activities: Grammar p.227, Vocabulary p.251, Pronunciation p.288

12C Everyday English
I'm pretty sure it's Japanese

At the end of this lesson, students will be able to:
- use phrases to agree and disagree
- use contrastive stress
- understand conversations where the speakers disagree

OPTIONAL LEAD-IN

Books closed. Ask students in pairs to write down the names of as many makes of cars as they can in three minutes, e.g. *Ford, Renault, Kia*. Find out which pair has the most. Ask if students know the logos for the cars, too. If so, they can draw one or two of the logos on the board. Do other students recognise which logo they are drawing?

1 LISTENING

a 💬 In pairs, students discuss the questions. When you feed back as a class, ask for examples of what students say they talk and argue about and build up a list of topics on the board. What are the most common subjects of conversation and of arguments? Ask students if they notice any differences between women and men.

b Ask students if they recognise the logos. They are all logos from large car companies. Try not to get into a discussion of what country the companies are from at this stage.

c ▶️**3.59** Students look at the pictures. Ask them what is happening and elicit that Leo and Mark arranged to go to the gym together. Read through the questions with the class. Play Part 1 of the video or play the audio recording for students to answer the questions. Tell them not to worry about who is correct at this stage. You may need to play the recording twice. Check answers as a class.

> **Answers**
> It's making a strange noise. It's a Nissan. Because they don't agree whether Nissan is Japanese or not.

Video/audioscript (Part 1)

MARK So, any plans for the rest of the week?

LEO No, not really. Oh, tomorrow I've got to take the car to the garage. It's making a strange noise – must be the engine.

M Oh, what a pain! What kind of car have you got?

L It's a Nissan. It's strange. Normally these Japanese cars are very reliable.

M That's true – Japanese cars are normally reliable.

L Yeah.

M But I'm afraid Nissan is actually Korean.

L Er ... I don't think so ... I'm pretty sure it's Japanese.

M I'm sorry, but it's definitely Korean. I remember reading an article about the factories in South Korea.

L Well, maybe Nissan have factories in Korea, but that doesn't mean it's a Korean company. I think they just make some of them in Korea.

M Maybe you're thinking of Toyota? That's a Japanese company.

L That's right. Toyota is the biggest Japanese car company.

M Exactly.

L Yes, but the second biggest is Nissan, then Honda, probably. Or maybe Suzuki.

M Oh, I'm sorry but firstly, Nissan isn't a Japanese company – like I said. And then, Mazda is a much bigger company than Suzuki or Honda.

L I'm not sure about that. I think they're all a very similar size. And Nissan is Japanese.

M No, I really think ...

L Oh, never mind. It's not important.

M Maybe you're thinking of Mitsubishi? They're a big Japanese company.

L No, I have a Nissan. That's what I'm talking about.

M In Korea, there's Kia, and I'm sure Nissan.

VIDEO ONLY

L Mark ...

M Or ... maybe I was thinking of Hyundai.

L Mark!

M Oh sorry.

📖 VOCABULARY SUPPORT

reliable (B1) – able to be trusted or believed

second biggest – not the biggest, but the next biggest

What a pain! (B2) – You can say this when sb or sth annoys you

d ▶️**3.59** Tell students that this time they need to listen for who agrees with each statement. Read through the statements. You may wish to help students with the words in the Vocabulary support box. Then play Part 1 of the video or play the audio recording again for students to decide on their answers.

> **Answers**
> 1 B   2 B   3 B   4 M

e ▶️**3.60** Play Part 2 of the video or play the audio recording for students to say how Mark ends the argument. Check the answer. Ask the class if they know who is right. (Nissan is a Japanese company.) If you wish, give students information from the Culture notes below.

> **Answers**
> He says he can check on his phone.

Video/audioscript (Part 2)

RACHEL So, when you do start the new job?

ANNIE Next month. I'm a bit nervous, actually ...

R Oh, don't worry, you'll be fine. Just remember ...

MARK Maybe you were right. I don't know now ... but no, I'm sure it's not Japanese.

LEO Really, it doesn't matter.

M I know – I can check on my phone!

L Hi.

M Or Chinese? Maybe it's Chinese.

A What's he talking about?

M Do they make cars in China? I think they do.

R Mark ... be quiet.

🌍 CULTURE NOTES

The largest car manufacturers in Japan are Toyota, Nissan, Honda, Suzuki, Mazda, Daihatsu, Subaru and Mitsubishi. Toyota is the largest car manufacturer in Japan and in the world. The most well-known automobile manufacturers in South Korea are Hyundai, Kia and Daewoo.

EXTRA ACTIVITY

Read out the following phrases from the dialogue. Students listen and tell you which were said by Leo (L) and which were said by Mark (M): *I've got to take my car to the garage. (L); What kind of car have you got? (M); I'm afraid Nissan is actually Korean. (M); I'm pretty sure it's Japanese. (L); Oh, never mind. It's not important. (L); Do they make cars in China? I think they do. (M); I know – I can check on my phone! (M)*

2 USEFUL LANGUAGE Agreeing and disagreeing

a ▶ 3.59 Ask students if they can remember what language Leo and Mark use to agree or disagree with each other. Put ideas on the board. Students may only remember one or two phrases at this stage. Then direct students' attention to the list of phrases for agreeing and disagreeing. Did they mention any of the phrases on the list? Play Part 1 of the video or the audio recording again for students to tick the phrases they hear. Check answers as a class. Ask if students can remember the context for these phrases – i.e. what was said before and after.

Answers
✓ That's true.
✓ I'm afraid …
✓ Exactly.
✓ I don't think so.
✓ I'm sorry, but …
✗ You're absolutely right.
✗ Definitely.
✓ That's right.
✗ Oh, please.
✓ I'm not sure about that.

b In pairs, students match the phrases with the functions. Check answers as a class.

Answers
1 Agree: That's true, Exactly, You're absolutely right, Definitely, That's right
2 Disagree: I'm afraid …, I don't think so, I'm sorry, but …, Oh, please, I'm not sure about that
3 Strongly agree: Exactly, You're absolutely right , Definitely
4 Strongly disagree: Oh, please

c ▶ 3.61 Play the recording for students to listen and repeat the phrases. Pause after each phrase for students to repeat. Focus on the stressed words and syllables and on the intonation for strong dis/agreement.

d ▶ 3.62 Individually, students complete the conversations with phrases from 2a. Play the recording for them to check answers. Divide students into pairs. They take it in turns to be Student A and Student B and read out the conversations. Monitor and check use of stress and intonation.

Answers
1 sure about   2 That's   3 absolutely   4 please   5 sorry

e Students complete the sentences with their own ideas. Monitor and help with examples if necessary.

f 🗨 In pairs, students agree or disagree with each other's statements. Monitor but don't interrupt fluency. Point out errors for students to self-correct. Take feedback as a class and ask for examples of things students agreed with their partners about and things where they disagreed strongly.

3 PRONUNCIATION Main stress: contrastive

a ▶ 3.63 Play the recording for students to see how the underlined words in the exchange have extra stress.

b Complete the rule as a class. Remind students that English is a stress-timed language and that stressing particular words in a sentence is one of the ways of conveying meaning.

Answer
extra

↻ LOA TIP DRILLING

Elicit the names of some famous celebrities and their nationalities, e.g. Rafael Nadal – Spanish, Brad Pitt – American, Nicole Kidman – Australian. Then drill the sentences so that students use contrastive stress. Do this initially as a group and then ask individual students.
Say: *Brad Pitt is English.*
Students say: *No, Brad Pitt is* <u>American.</u>

c 🗨 Give the students a minute to look at the statements and underline the words that they will need to stress when they make dialogues. Model the example with a student. Emphasise that in the first statement, the adjective *bad* isn't stressed. *Good* and *bad* are stressed in the following exchange in order to make a particular point.

Students practise the exchanges in pairs. Monitor and focus on good use of stress.

d In pairs, students discuss whether they really agree or disagree with the statements. Ask for comments in feedback.

4 SPEAKING

a Read through the statements with the class and check they understand the meaning of *celebrity magazines* (magazines with a lot of information about the lives of famous people, such as film stars and singers) – give (or elicit) some examples, e.g. *OK, Hello.* Give students two or three minutes to note down their opinions about the statements and also to think of two or three reasons to support their opinion in each case.

b Students discuss the statements in pairs and give their opinions in pairs. Encourage them to expand their ideas by giving reasons and examples. Take feedback and ask students to tell the class what they agreed and disagreed about. Find out the majority opinions in the class.

ADDITIONAL MATERIAL

▶ Workbook 12C
▶ Unit Progress Test
▶ Personalised online practice

12D Skills for Writing
About an hour later, the rain stopped

At the end of this lesson, students will be able to:
- understand a person telling a story
- read and understand a story
- use linkers to show sequencing in past time
- write a story

💡 OPTIONAL LEAD-IN

Books closed. Give the names of one or two places that are famous locally or nationally for being haunted (i.e. it is believed that a ghost visits there). Can students guess what these places have in common? Do they know any more information about the ghosts who are believed to visit these places? Or do they know any more places which are said to have ghosts?

1 LISTENING AND SPEAKING

a 💬 In pairs, students discuss the questions. Emphasise that 'stories' needn't just mean fictional stories from books. It could also be stories about real-life interesting events. Students might have favourite Internet websites or chat rooms where they find out about things. In feedback ask students to share their ideas about stories with the class.

b ▶3.64 Tell the class that they are going to hear someone telling a story about when she was a child. Ask them to look at the picture and say what they can see. Elicit that the building in the picture is a summer house. Ask what might happen in the story. Read through the questions and play the recording for students to answer the questions. Check answers as a class.

Answers
1 her sister
2 in the summer house, at the end of the garden
3 an old lady

Audioscript

When I was a child, we went to live in an old house in the country with a big garden. And at the end of the garden there was a summer house, it was a little house with just one room and windows, and my sister and I often played in this summer house. When I was about five – my sister was eight – we were playing one day in the summer house, and suddenly I looked up and I saw an old lady in black. She was wearing a hat and she was reading a book. I said to my sister, 'Who's that old lady?' and my sister said, 'What old lady?' She couldn't see her. So we ran back to the house and I told my mother that I'd seen this old lady, but, of course, she didn't believe me.

Then, a few months later, my mother was talking to the neighbours. And they told her about the person who had lived in the house before us. They told her that a rather strange old lady had lived there. She had always worn black clothes and a hat – and she had died in the summer house.

c ▶3.64 Students order the events from the story individually. Encourage them to compare their ideas with a partner before you play the recording again to check answers.

Answers
3 Olga saw an old lady.
5 Olga's mother spoke to the neighbour.
2 Olga was playing with her sister.
4 Olga told her mother.
6 Olga found out the old lady was dead.
1 Olga's family went to live in the country.

d 💬 Read the opinions with the class – you could nominate a different student to read each one aloud. Ask for a show of hands for who agrees with each one and find out the majority opinion for the class.

e ▶3.64 Ask students to cover exercise 1c and practise retelling the story in pairs. Ask them to cover exercise 1c. If appropriate, put some words to prompt them on the board, e.g. *child – old house – country – summer house – playing with sister – old lady – hat – book – sister – mother – neighbours – died.* Play the recording again for them to check whether they included all the details.

💡 FAST FINISHERS

Ask fast finishers to do the activity again, but this time they must add some more details of their own. Monitor and prompt or give help. In feedback, ask the class for examples of interesting details.

2 READING

a 💬 Students cover the story text and look at the picture. Elicit their ideas about the answers to the questions and write them on the board, but don't say if they are right or not.

b Give students a few minutes to read the story to see how similar their ideas were. Elicit answers to the questions to check their general understanding. The two people in the story are on holiday and they get lost going for a walk. They don't know the man but they take shelter in his house from the rain.

c Students read the text again to answer the questions. You may wish to help them with the words in the Vocabulary support box at this point. Check answers as a class.

Answers
1 They had been careless; Mary said she knew the way.
2 They heard a dog barking.
3 because they were lost and wet
4 ever since he was a chid
5 The man gave them directions to the village.
6 Plants were growing across it.
7 There was no old man (or cottage).

📖 VOCABULARY SUPPORT

cottage (B1) – a small country house

feel sorry for yourself (B1) – to pity (have sympathy for) yourself

the following day (B1) – the next day

know the way – to know the correct direction

d 💬 Students discuss the questions in small groups.

3 WRITING SKILLS Linkers: past time

a Write these sentences on the board: *We sat down under a tree. We felt sorry for ourselves. We heard a sound.* Ask the class what we need to do to make this set of sentences sound more like a story. Elicit that we need to add linking phrases. Students complete the task individually, choosing the correct linking phrases from the box and then check their answers by finding the sentences in the story.

> **Answers**
> 1 Suddenly   2 A minute later   3 About an hour later
> 4 The following day   5 later that week   6 After a while

b Students answer the questions as a class.

> **Answers**
> 1 suddenly   2 after a while

c Read through the information about moments in time and time between events with the class. Then give students a couple of minutes to do the classification exercise in pairs. Check answers as a class.

> **Answers**
> 1 evening, year, morning, night
> 2 five minutes, a short time, about a month, many years, a few days

d In pairs, students correct the mistakes in the sentences. Remind them to refer to the lists of expressions in 2c to check how certain time phrases are formed and which words can be used together. Check answers together.

> **Answers**
> 1 two years later   2 Suddenly, the plane   3 A week later
> 4 Later that morning   5 The following morning

4 WRITING

a Put the class into small groups of three or four students. Each group should elect a 'secretary' who does the writing. Give the groups a minute to choose which sentence they want to begin their story with and write it at the top of the page.

b Each group writes the first paragraph of their story following the instructions in step 1. The groups then exchange papers and continue with step 2 and so on up until step 5 when each group writes the last paragraph of their story. The papers are exchanged so that they go back to the group who wrote the first sentence.

c When the story returns to the group that started it, they should check it for correct use of time linkers.

d Ask one student from each group to read their story for the class. Point out the good use (or lack) of time linkers. Ask the class to vote on the best story and the story with the best use of linkers.

UNIT 12
Review and extension

1 GRAMMAR

a Students do the task individually. Check answers together. To extend, you can ask students to suggest follow-up sentences for each sentence.

> **Answers**
> 1 2 1
> 2 1 2
> 3 2 1
> 4 1 2
> 5 2 1

b Students choose the correct alternatives individually. Check answers together.

> **Answers**
> 1 Did you read   2 happened   3 saw   4 hit   5 hadn't seen
> 6 read   7 looked after   8 had fallen

c Students do the task individually. Check answers as a class.

> **Answers**
> 1 He said (that) we couldn't leave the party.
> 2 She told me (that) Marc had moved to a new flat.
> 3 He said (that) he was seeing Sarah later.
> 4 She said (that) she would help me with the shopping.
> 5 He told me (that) Michele had got a great new job.
> 6 He said (that) he was going to get a new car.
> 7 She told me (that) she didn't like the hotel.

> ### 🔅 EXTRA ACTIVITY
>
> Ask students to write a text or email message to their partner. They can write about anything they like – but warn them that their messages will be read out! Give some examples:
>
> *an arrangement for later, some interesting information or gossip, something interesting they have done or did yesterday.*
>
> Students swap their messages with their partner and read them. Ask one or two students to tell the class what their partner said in the message, e.g. *José texted me earlier and he told me that ...*

2 VOCABULARY

a Students complete the words individually. Check answers together.

> **Answers**
> 1 whale   2 spider   3 gorilla   4 tiger   5 mosquito   6 parrot

> ### 🔅 EXTRA ACTIVITY
>
> In pairs, students choose six other animals and write the words with gapped letters for their partners to complete.

b Students complete the task individually. Check answers together.

> **Answers**
> 1 funny   2 selfish   3 honest   4 anxious   5 reliable
> 6 careless   7 generous   8 sensible

3 WORDPOWER *age*

a Tell the class the age of someone you know who is a similar age to you, e.g. *My sister Agnes is 38; I'm 36.* Ask them if they can describe her age in another way. Elicit: *We're about the same age. / We are of a similar age.* Then put the word *age* on the board and ask students if they know or can remember any more phrases with this word, e.g. *old age, middle-aged* etc. Put any examples on the board, too. Read the task together and students answer the question.

> **Answer**
> 1: children who are different ages
> 2: children who are almost the same age

b Students do the matching task in pairs. Check answers together.

> **Answers**
> 1d   2b   3a   4c

c Students complete the sentences individually. Check answers as a class.

> **Answers**
> 1 of a similar age   2 at an early age   3 At your age
> 4 early twenties   5 apart in age   6 old age   7 about my age
> 8 middle-aged

d 💬 Students do the task in pairs. Ask for examples in group feedback.

▶ Photocopiable activities: Wordpower p.263

> ### ⟳ LOA REVIEW YOUR PROGRESS
>
> Students look back through the unit, think about what they've studied and decide how well they did. Students work on weak areas by using the appropriate sections of the Workbook, the Photocopiable activities and the Personalised online practice.

Teaching plus

Ideas for pre-teaching vocabulary

Before reading and listening tasks, it's often necessary to make sure students understand a few key words. This is called 'pre-teaching'. There are a number of ways to do this. Here are some ideas:

Give a definition: Use a short sentence to explain the meaning of a word. If you wish, use the defi nitions given in the Vocabulary support boxes throughout the Teacher's Notes. You could also use a learner dictionary to find onlevel definitions, e.g. *dive – to swim under water, usually with breathing equipment.* (from *Cambridge Essential English Dictionary*, Second Edition).

Draw/Show a picture or object: One of the easiest ways to teach students new words is to draw a picture on the board, or show a picture on an interactive whiteboard or a computer or tablet. Using (or drawing) funny and/ or interesting pictures is a good way to ensure students remember the new words, e.g. to teach the word *dive* you could find a picture of a diver with a big shark behind him.

Act it out: With lower-level students it can be useful to show the word by acting it out, rather than giving definitions which may use above-level vocabulary.

Elicit it: Elicitation allows you to check which words students may already know. Don't tell them the word you want to teach. Elicit it by asking questions or saying openended sentences, e.g. *What is the activity when we swim under the sea and look at fish?* or *When we swim under water and look at fish, we … ?* (dive).

Gapped sentences: It's useful for students to see the word in a sentence to understand the context. Write a gapped sentence(s) on the board (this can be one from the text), e.g. *Cristina in the Mediterranean Sea every summer. She loves to see the beautiful fish under the water.* (dives) Allow students to guess what word goes in the gap, but don't confirm if they're right or wrong. After they read the text, they can guess again. Then confi rm their answer.

Discussion questions: With stronger students you can write discussion questions containing the new words on the board. Then give students one or two example answers to these questions. Students try to guess the meaning. Give more example answers, if necessary. You may then wish to allow students to ask and answer these questions for themselves.

Pre-teaching for listening: You can use any of the above ideas, or others you may have, to teach new words before students listen. It may also be useful to model the pronunciation of the words so students are used to hearing how it sounds. This is particularly useful when a word has an unfamiliar spelling rule. If you don't want to model the word, it can be useful to write the word in IPA on the board (you can fi nd this in all dictionaries).

Extra activities – how to …

Class survey
Use: to revise tenses, verb patterns, verb collocations, conversational language
Dynamic: whole class
Procedure:
- Write a list of questions which practise the target language. Ideally, each student will have a different question, but if this is difficult, aim to have one question per two students.
- Photocopy the list and cut up into strips to hand out. Make sure each student has a question, even if the question is the same as another student's. OR Dictate each question to one (or two) student(s) in turn.
- Ask students a question as an example and elicit a response which uses the target structure. Write the response on the board.
- Set a time limit for the activity, e.g. ten minutes. Students move around the class and ask their question to as many different other students as they can. They write down the responses in their notebooks.
- When the time is up, divide students into smaller groups and ask them to compare their most interesting responses.

Running dictation
Use: to practise using all four skills in a collaborative way to review all kinds of lexis
Dynamic: whole class
Procedure:
- Choose a short text or a list of sentences/questions which you wish to revise. Around six to ten sentences should be adequate, depending on how confident your students are. Choose a text of the right level for your students and which does not contain unfamiliar words.
- You will need one sheet per pair of students, plus a few extra sheets.
  Put the extra sheets on a far wall of the classroom or just outside the classroom door. Mark the halfway point on the text.
- Divide the class into pairs: Student A is a reader and Student B is a writer. A has to go to the text/list and memorise as much as he/she can. Encourage students to remember a few words accurately rather than try to memorise too much. Student A goes back to Student B and dictates what he/she can remember. Student A must walk over to Student B before dictating and not shout the text out! Student A is not allowed to do any writing at this stage. The dictation continues until Student A has reached the halfway point on the text.
- The students swap roles with Student B dictating and Student A writing.
- As each pair finishes, hand them one of the copies and allow them to check their text against the original. Students should correct their mistakes. Monitor and help students to decide whether any differences are grammatically correct or not.

Grammar auction

Use: to revise a specific grammar area or general grammar
Dynamic: whole class (in teams)
Procedure:
- Prepare ten to fifteen sentences containing either items of grammar from the unit you are currently working on or areas of grammar which you know students find problematic. Some of them should be correct and some incorrect.
- Write the sentences on the board and explain what an *auction* is (when you sell something to the person who offers the most money).
- Put students into small groups, tell them they have £100 and they need to buy the correct sentences. In their groups, students discuss which sentences they think are correct and decide which to buy and how much they are prepared to pay for each. Don't help or allow students to look at their notes or the Student's Book.
- Take the role of auctioneer and sell each sentence to the group which offers the most money. Keep track of how much each group has spent. Remind students that once they have spent all their money they can't buy any more sentences, so they shouldn't spend too much too soon.
- After all the sentences have been sold, go through them one at a time, revealing which are correct and which are incorrect. Ask students to correct the mistakes.
- The winning group is the one who has bought the most correct sentences. If it's a draw, then the group which has got the most money left wins.

Guess who?

Use: to practise question forms, present simple, present continuous, past simple, etc.
Dynamic: whole class (with optional group/pair extension)
Procedure:
- Tell students that you are thinking of a person and that they have to guess who it is by asking *Yes/No* questions.
- If you wish to practise a specific grammar area, you might tell students that this person is living (for present tenses), dead (for past tenses), etc. Alternatively, you can use this activity to practise question forms in general by not specifying anything about the person.
- Put students into pairs or small groups to brainstorm possible questions. Specify a total number of questions, between five and ten, for the class to try and guess who you're thinking of. Students then take turns to ask you some of the questions they thought of.
- Make sure you reply only with *yes* or *no*, e.g. ~~Yes, he/she is.~~ (correct version = *Yes*) in order not to give away if the person is a man or a woman.
- Students win if they guess the person within the specified number of questions. The teacher wins if students can't guess the person.
- Continue the game either as a class, by asking a student to choose a person and take over from you at the front of the class, or by putting students into pairs or small groups to play.

Classroom whispers

Use: to revise tenses, verb patterns, verb collocations, pronunciation and listening skills
Dynamic: whole class
Procedure:
- You will need a list of short sentences and/or questions which practise the structures you wish to revise. You will need one sheet per three students in the class.
- Divide students into groups of three. All the Student As go to one part of the classroom, all the Student Bs to another, and Student Cs to another.
- Model the activity by standing with the Student As and showing them the first sentence on the sheet. The Student As then walk to the Student Bs and whisper the sentence they have remembered. Make sure the Student Cs can't hear. The Student Bs then go to the Student Cs and repeat the sentence and the Student Cs write down what they heard. Write the correct sentence on the board. Student Cs compare this with what they have written.
- Start the activity by showing the second item on the list to the Student As. The activity then continues as per your model. After the Student As have had two or three turns, they swap roles with the others in their group. The activity continues like this until they reach the end of the list.
- When the students have finished, give each group of three a copy of the sheet and they compare this against what they have written. The group with the least mistakes wins.

Sentence chains

Use: to revise a specific lexical set, e.g. items to take on holiday, etc.
Dynamic: groups/pairs
Procedure:
- Before the class, decide which lexical set you're going to test students on and decide the best sentence to lead in to this. You can use: *Before I went on holiday I packed … (my ticket, a guidebook, my clothes, a map).* However, if you want to revise a different tense as well as the target lexical set, you could amend the sentence as appropriate, e.g. *I came home from holiday and I had spent all my money . I had … (bought a lot of souvenirs, done a lot of sightseeing, stayed in a luxury hotel).*
- Demonstrate the activity with the lead-in sentence and then the first item, e.g. *Before I went on holiday I packed my ticket.* Gesture to a student to repeat your sentence and add a new verb phrase, e.g. *Before I went on holiday I packed my ticket and a guidebook.* Nominate the next student who repeats the sentence and adds another item, and so on until the list is too long to remember.
- Put students into groups of three to five to play together.
- Depending on your students, you may wish to adjust the difficulty of the activity. For example, ask students to include the information about a list of nouns, e.g. *my plane ticket, a heavy guidebook, my beach clothes, a local map.*

Backs to the board

Use: to revise a specific lexical set or general vocabulary
Dynamic: whole class (in teams)
Procedure:

- Put students into small groups of four to five students. If possible, mix stronger students with weaker students so no group is noticeably stronger or weaker than another.
- Tell students in each group to sit close together, leaving space between the groups so they can't easily hear one another. Tell one student in each group to sit with their back to the board and the others to sit so that they can see the board.
- Explain that you're going to write a word or phrase on the board and that the students who can see the board have to communicate the meaning to the student who can't. They can use any method to do this, drawing pictures, mime, synonyms, simple explanations, etc. However, use of their own language will mean they are disqualified.
- When the student(s) with their back to the board think they know the word, they put their hand up. Ask the first student who put their hand up to say the word and, if they are correct, award their group a point. If they aren't, the other teams continue. Any student who shouts out the answer is also disqualified.
- The winning group is the one who has the most points at the end of the game.

Tennis

Use: to revise specific word pairs, e.g. opposite adjectives, past simple / past participle forms, collocations
Dynamic: pairs
Procedure:

- Explain which lexical set you're going to work on, e.g. *travel collocations*. Demonstrate the activity by asking a stronger student to help you. Say the first word of the pair, e.g. *pack* and ask the student to respond with the second, i.e. *a bag*. The student continues with a different first word and you respond with the second. For example **A:** *pack* **B:** *a bag* – *stay at* **A:** *home* – *stay in* **B:** *a hotel* –, etc.
- Tell students that, just like in real game of tennis, it's important not to pause for a long time. If one of the students pauses too long between items, they lose that round, e.g. in **A:** *travel* **B:** *abroad* – *make* **A:** *plans* – *plan* **B:** *ummm ahhh … a holiday,* B would lose.
- Put students into pairs to play together. Tell them they should continue for as long as possible. If one student loses the round, they start again.

Photocopiable activities overview

GRAMMAR

	Target language	Activity type	Dynamic	Teacher's notes
1A	Question forms	Bingo	Pairs	p.179
1B	Present simple and present continuous	*Find someone who*	Whole class	p.179
2A	Past simple	Teacher prompts (Tell me about …)	Pairs	p.179
2B	Past continuous	Story maze	Pairs	p.179
3A	Present perfect or past simple	*Have you ever … ?*	Groups of four	p.180
3B	Present perfect with *just, already* and *yet*	Matching	Groups of three or four	p.180
4A	Present continuous and *going to*	Miming	Groups of four	p.180
4B	*will / won't / shall*	Card game – making offers and suggestions	Groups of four	p.180
5A	*must / have to / can*	Explaining signs	Pairs	p.181
5B	*will* and *might* for predictions	Card game – making predictions	Pairs	p.181
6A	*should / shouldn't*; imperatives	Giving advice from prompts	Pairs	p.181
6B	Uses of *to* + infinitive	Sentence completion / discussing opinions	Pairs	p.181
7A	Comparatives and superlatives	Discussing topics	Pairs	p.182
7B	*used to / didn't use to*	Picture description	Pairs	p.182
8A	The passive: present and past simple	Text completion	Pairs / groups of three or four	p.182
8B	Present perfect with *for* and *since*	True sentences about you	Pairs	p.182
9A	First conditional	Pelmanism	Pairs	p.183
9B	Verb patterns	Class mingle	Whole class	p.183
10A	Second conditional	Class mingle	Whole class	p.183
10B	Quantifiers; *too / not enough*	Completing prompts	Pairs	p.183
11A	Defining relative clauses	Crossword	Pairs	p.184
11B	Articles	Gap fill / sentence jigsaw	Pairs / groups of three or four	p.184
12A	Past perfect	Explaining past events	Pairs	p.184
12B	Reported speech	Passing on messages	Groups of three	p.184

VOCABULARY

	Target language	Activity type	Dynamic	Teacher's notes
1A	Common adjectives	Discussing opinions	Pairs	p.185
1B	Adverbs	Sentence comparison / class mingle	Individually / whole class	p.185
2A	Tourism	Phrase completion / planning	Pairs	p.185
2B	Travel collocations	Collocation matching	Individually / pairs	p.186
3A	*make, do, give* collocations	Using the right collocation	Pairs	p.186
3B	Money	Quiz / sentence completion	Pairs	p.186
4A	Clothes and appearance	Clothes classification / describing people	Individually / groups of three or four	p.186
4B	Adjectives: places	Crossword	Pairs	p.187
5A	Work	Describing jobs	Individually / groups of three or four	p.187
5B	Jobs	Comparing different jobs	Individually / groups of three or four	p.187
6A	Verbs with dependent prepositions	Board game	Individually / pairs	p.187
6B	*-ed* / *-ing* adjectives	Crossword	Individually / pairs	p.188
7A	Life events with *get*	Questionnaire	Individually / groups of three or four	p.188
7B	Health and fitness collocations	Wordsearch / sentence completion / discussion	Individually / pairs / groups of three or four	p.188
8A	Art and music	Crossword	Pairs	p.189
8B	Sports and activities	Table and sentence completion	Individually / pairs	p.189
9A	Education collocations	Wordsnake / *find someone who*	Individually / mingle	p.189
9B	Verbs followed by *to* + infinitive / verb + *-ing*	Matching card game	Pairs / groups of three or four	p.189
10A	Multi-word verbs	Writing answers / matching	Pairs	p.190
10B	Noun formation	Wordsearch / sentence completion	Individually / pairs	p.190
11A	Compound nouns	Dominoes	Groups of three or four	p.190
11B	Adverbials: luck and chance	Sentence completion	Individually / pairs	p.191
12A	Animals	Wordsnake / quiz	Pairs	p.191
12B	Personality adjectives	Sentence completion	Pairs	p.191

WORDPOWER

	Target language	Activity type	Dynamic	Teacher's notes
Unit 1	*like*	Interview	Pairs / groups of three or four	p.191
Unit 2	*off*	Guessing game	Pairs	p.192
Unit 3	*just*	Information gathering / co-teaching	Mingle / groups of three	p.192
Unit 4	*look*	*Find someone who …*	Whole class	p.192
Unit 5	*job* and *work*	Discussion	Pairs / groups of four	p.192
Unit 6	Verb + *to*	Text reconstruction	Pairs	p.192
Unit 7	*change*	Sentence completion	Groups of four or five	p.193
Unit 8	*by*	Guessing game	Whole class	p.193
Unit 9	Multi-word verbs with *put*	Sentence completion	Groups of three or four	p.193
Unit 10	Multi-word verbs with *on*	Guessing game	Pairs	p.194
Unit 11	Preposition + noun	Pelmanism	Groups of two or three	p.194
Unit 12	*age*	Interviews / exchange of opinions	Pairs	p.194

PRONUNCIATION

	Target language	Activity type	Dynamic	Teacher's notes
0	Introduction to phonetic symbols	Matching, wordsearch	Pairs	p.194
1A	Syllables and word stress	Dominoes	Pairs	p.195
1B	Long and short vowel sounds	Sound maze	Individually/pairs	p.195
2A	-ed endings	Peer dictation	Pairs	p.196
2B	was and were	Memory game	Groups of three or four	p.196
3B	Sound and spelling: /dʒ/ and /j/	Shopping game	Groups of four	p.196
3C	Sentence stress	Story telling	Groups of four	p.197
4B	Sound and spelling: /ɒ/ and /əʊ/	Battleships	Pairs	p.197
4C	Sentence stress	Interview	Pairs	p.197
5B	Sound and spelling: /ʃ/	Spot the difference	Pairs	p.197
5C	Sentence stress: vowel sounds	Flow chart	Pairs	p.198
6A	Sound and spelling: /uː/ and /ʊ/	Bingo	Pairs	p.198
6C	Main stress	Matching stress / odd one out	Groups of four	p.198
7B	to + infinitive (weak form)	Logical puzzle	Groups of three or four	p.198
7C	Tones for asking questions	Yes / No game (20 questions)	Whole class / groups of ten	p.199
8B	Word stress	Snap / matching pairs	Pairs / groups of four	p.199
8C	Tones for continuing or finishing	Matching tones	Pairs	p.199
9A	Word groups	Four in a row	Pairs	p.200
9C	Main stress: contrastive	Matching pairs	Pairs	p.200
10A	Sentence stress: vowel sounds	Logical puzzle	Groups of four	p.201
10C	Sentence stress	Personal interviews	Groups of four	p.201
11C1	Checking information	Giving directions	Groups of four	p.201
11C2	Sound and spelling: /ɔː/ and /ɜː/	Sound maze	Pairs	p.201
12B	Sentence stress: that	Role play / Reporting on interviews	Groups of four	p.202
12C	Main stress: contrastive	True / false sentences	Pairs	p.202

Teacher's notes for photocopiable activities

GRAMMAR

1A Question forms

▶ Photocopiable activity on p.204

You will need one bingo sheet for each student and one set of topic cards, cut up, for each pair.

Hand out the bingo sheets and sets of topic cards. Elicit what kinds of words are on the bingo sheet (question words). Demonstrate the activity by taking a card from the set of topic cards and asking the class to think of questions on the topic using the words on their worksheet. Students do not need to use the word on the topic card in the question, e.g.
(languages) *How many languages do you speak?*
(home) *Where do you live?*
(family and friends) *Who is your best friend?*
(music) *Do you like Lady Gaga?*
(films) *How often do you go to the cinema?*

Repeat with a stronger student. This time, answer the student's question, e.g. **Q:** *How many languages do you speak?* **A:** *Four. Russian, French, English and a bit of Spanish.* The student then crosses out the question word on the bingo worksheet and he/she cannot use that question again. The aim is to cross off all the question words on the worksheet.

Students play, taking turns to choose a card and ask a question (which their partner has to answer), until they have crossed off all the question words. Monitor and help as necessary. In feedback with the class, go over good examples of questions and correct any errors.

1B Present simple and present continuous

▶ Photocopiable activity on p.205

You will need one sheet for each student.

Hand out the sheets. Elicit how to form the questions from the prompts using present simple and present continuous, e.g. *Where do you usually live? Where are you living at the moment?* Encourage students to think about the most natural question to ask, e.g. *Do you go to the supermarket more than three times a week?* (Correct version = *How often do you go to the supermarket?*.

Allow students to work in pairs and make notes on the question forms, if necessary. Ask students to mingle with the class and ask each other the questions. They should write students' names and any interesting answers. Ensure students only ask a maximum of two questions per person that they speak to, in order to talk to as many students as they can. Encourage stronger students to ask follow-up questions and make notes on the answers.

Allow enough time for the majority of students to mingle and complete their questions. Monitor and help as necessary. Put students in small groups to compare their findings. Elicit feedback from the class on any interesting answers.

2A Past simple

▶ Photocopiable activity on p.206

You will need one sheet for each student.

Hand out the sheets. Students work individually. Tell students to read the ideas at the top of the sheet and write their response to each one (just one or two words) in one of the shapes on the worksheet. Encourage the students to choose random shapes to write in.

Students work in pairs and show each other their sheets. Students look at the answers/words in the shapes and ask their partner to tell them about five interesting answers e.g. *Tell me about 'France'.* Students explain their answers e.g. *I went on holiday to France last year.* Encourage students to ask as many follow-up questions as possible, e.g. *Did you have fun? What did you do there? Where did you stay?*

Students report back to the class on their partner's most interesting answers.

2B Past continuous

▶ Photocopiable activity on p.207

You will need one sheet for each pair.

Hand out the sheets. Explain to students they are going to use the sentences in the grid to make a story. They should read the sentences in the grid and connect the squares from START to FINISH to create a logical story. (Explain to students that the capital letters at the beginning of the sentences and the full stops at the end have been removed.) Draw an empty grid on the board and show students that they can connect squares up, down, right, left and diagonally (up or down).

Ask students to look at the START square and say which sentence/square should come next. In fact all three squares are possible. Students then work in pairs to make their story in the grid. Monitor and help as necessary.

Then put students into groups of four. Each pair reads the story they created to the other pair. The group decides which story they like best and why.

Students can continue the story in their groups, either with one student writing and the others contributing ideas, or in speech, taking turns to contribute a sentence.

Possible answers

1 I was driving to work when I heard a strange noise. It was coming from the engine of my car. I stopped my car and got out. Smoke was coming out of the back of the car. I didn't know what to do. Then I saw a man walking towards me. He shouted to me, 'Hey! Are you OK?' The man was smiling and holding out his hands. He looked very happy to see me. I was getting back into my car when he suddenly hugged me and said, 'Hello my friend!' I was very surprised and asked 'Who are you?'

2 I was driving to work when I saw a man by the side of the road. He was wearing a bright yellow jumper and he wasn't moving. I stopped my car and got out. A bicycle was lying in the grass. It didn't look broken. I walked toward the man and shouted 'Hey! Are you OK?' Then I noticed he was breathing. I wanted to see if he was hurt, so I was looking into his face when he sat up and said 'Who are you?'
(Other variations are possible)

3A Present perfect or past simple

 Photocopiable activity on p.208

You will need one sheet for each group of four students.

Divide students into groups of four. Hand out the sheets. Students look at the first set of experiences: *Travel*. Check students understand all of the ideas in the first set of experiences. Explain that they are going to find out about the life experiences of the students in their group using *Have you ever ...?* and follow-up questions in the past simple. Demonstrate the activity with your own true answers. Elicit a correct question from the first card: *Have you ever visited New Zealand?* Answer: *Yes, I have,* and tell the group to ask you more questions. Elicit possible follow-up questions and answer them, e.g. *When did you go? What was it like?* Tell students that when they ask the questions in their group, they should write the name of one student who answers *yes* on the line in each square. If more than one student answers *yes,* then the group should decide which was the most interesting or unusual experience.

Students take turns in their group to ask the other students about the travel experiences. Monitor and encourage students to ask follow-up questions. When the groups finish the travel experiences, take feedback as a class. Ask how many squares they filled as a group. The group that has filled the most squares with a name are the most experienced travellers.

Repeat the procedure with each set of experiences on the sheet.

> ### ⚲ VARIATION
> For a shorter activity, cut the sheets into four and give one section to each group. Follow the procedure above. Students report back to the class on their group's experiences and the experiences nobody in their group has had. Discuss these experiences as a class.

3B Present perfect with *just*, *already* and *yet*

 Photocopiable activity on p.209

You will need one sheet for each group of three or four students, cut up to make two sets of cards.

Hand out the two sets of cards to each group. Students put the two sets of cards face down on the desk and spread out the cards into two groups.

Students need to match the sentences in bold (on the smaller cards) with a logical follow-up sentence (from the larger cards). Demonstrate by turning over two cards and reading them out to the class. Ask if the cards match or not. If the sentence on the larger card follows on logically from the sentence on the first card, this means that the cards match and the students can keep them. They can then turn over another small card to try and find another matching pair. If they don't match, the cards are turned over and placed face down again.

The winner is the student who finds the most matching sentences.

> ### ⚲ NO-CUT VARIATION
> Hand out the sheets. Ask students to match the sentences on the left with the correct sentence on the right.

Answers

Can I borrow your car this evening? 4
Shall we make something for dinner? 9
Let's celebrate tonight! 15
Franco and Maria are planning their wedding. 11
I really want a new car. 12
He's very quick. 8
Are we going to eat soon? 6
I can't come out tonight. 5
Did you go to that new café? 10
Let's go for a walk. 13
You're late. 3
He's very sad today. 14
You're early. 7
We haven't got any money. 2
She's waiting for a phone call. 1
You don't need to email the bank. 16

4A Present continuous and *going to*

 Photocopiable activity on p.210

You will need one sheet for each group of four students, cut up.

Explain to students that this is an acting activity: they will need to demonstrate the preparation for a future plan by miming the preparation for the activities written on the cards they will be given. Demonstrate by miming a future plan yourself, e.g. to elicit *I'm going to watch a DVD,* you could mime switching on the TV, looking at some DVD boxes, choosing one, opening the case, putting it in the DVD player/computer, sitting down and getting comfortable.

Put students into groups of four and hand out the sets of sentences A–D, one set to each student. Allow time for students to read the sentences on their card and think about how they will show the preparations. Remind students that the acting should stop before beginning the actual activity – the mimes are about a future plan, not an activity happening in the present.

Student A begins. The group must guess what he or she is going to do. During the guessing process, allow students to use the present continuous to describe what Student A is doing. You may wish to accept answers similar to the given sentence and without the exact future time on the card, e.g. *I'm making a cake tomorrow* for *I'm cooking a special meal tonight.*

> ### ⚲ VARIATION
> Students think of other activities and act out their preparation for their group/class to guess what they are going to do.

4B *will* / *won't* / *shall*

 Photocopiable activity on p.211

You will need one sheet for each group of four students, cut up.

Divide students into groups of four. Hand out the set of sentences and ask students to put them face down on the table. Demonstrate the activity by taking a card and reading it aloud e.g. *I can't find my travel card; I have to leave in five minutes.* Ask students to make you offers and suggestions using *will, won't* or *shall* e.g. *I'll help you find out; Shall I look in the living room?*

Students take it in turns to take a card and to read the sentence to the group. The group must respond orally with an offer, suggestion, promise or decision using *will, won't* or *shall*. Ask students to 'knock' on the table before giving a response. (If students cannot think of any ideas, they can try again with the next sentence.)

The student should choose which response they most like and 'award' the card to that student. The student who has collected the most cards by the end of the activity is the winner. Monitor and help as necessary. In feedback, elicit students' ideas for different offers, suggestions, promises and decisions.

5A *must / have to / can*

 Photocopiable activity on p.212

You will need one worksheet for each student.

Hand out the sheets. Tell students to look at the signs and write down under each one what it means using *have to, don't have to, must, mustn't, can* or *can't*, e.g. *You mustn't run.*

When they have finished, ask the class for suggestions for where they would see each of the three sets of the signs – (set 1 = swimming pool, set 2 = museum, set 3 = railway station). Also elicit some ideas about other possible locations where some of the individual signs could be seen, such as on a coach or train, in a cinema or theatre.

In pairs, students then do a role play for each of the three locations (see below). Encourage them to swap roles so that both Student A and Student B have the opportunity to explain the rules and to listen and ask questions for each situation. The student who is listening should always try to ask at least two questions, e.g. *Can I … ? Do customers/ visitors have to … ?*

1 Student A is the manager of the pool. Explain the rules to a new member of staff (B).
2 Student A is a security guard at the museum. Explain the rules to a visitor (B).
3 Student A is a member of the station staff. Explain the rules to a customer (B).

> **EXTRA ACTIVITY**
>
> Pairs think of a rule and draw a sign for it. They swap with another pair and guess what the sign means.

5B *will* and *might* for predictions

 Photocopiable activity on p.213

You will need one sheet for each student.

Hand out the sheets. Tell students to work in pairs. Explain that the students are going to make predictions about their partner. Ask students to look at the first section: *People* and elicit predictions about you first. Say: *Do you think I'll make some new friends next summer?* Take predictions from the students. Encourage them to use full sentences when they speak and remind them of natural language, e.g. *I think / I'm sure you'll …, I don't think you'll …, I think you might …, You might not …,* etc. Tell students whether you agree with their predictions and why, e.g. *I think I'll make some new friends next summer, because I'm going to …*

Students work in pairs, taking turns to predict their partner's answers and agree or disagree with their partner's predictions, giving reasons. Monitor and help as necessary.

In feedback, ask for any interesting information the students found out about their partner.

> **VARIATION**
>
> Students make predictions about themselves only and explain their answers to their partner. For a shorter activity, cut or fold the sheets so that each pair of students only looks at one section.

> **FAST FINISHERS**
>
> Ask students to write three new predictions about their partner for one topic on the sheet.

6A should / shouldn't; imperatives

 Photocopiable activity on p.214

You will need one sheet for each pair.

Put students in pairs. Hand out the sheets. Explain that they are going to give advice about some problems. Ask students to read problem 1 and elicit advice using *should,* e.g. *You should look for a job; shouldn't,* e.g. *You shouldn't listen to your brother;* and an imperative, e.g. *Tell your parents you are upset.* Ask students to choose which is the most useful piece of advice from the suggestions made and say why.

Ask students to continue to read the other problems and make notes on the advice they would give using *should/ shouldn't* and imperatives. Monitor and help as necessary.

When students have finished, join two pairs of students together to make a group of four. Ask them to talk about the advice they would give. Ask them to decide on the best piece of advice from their suggestions.

In feedback, ask students to share their best piece of advice for each problem. Correct any language errors. Ask the class to vote on which group has the best advice.

> **VARIATION**
>
> Students work in pairs and choose five problems to role play. They make notes on advice they can give using *should/ shouldn't* or an imperative.

6B Uses of *to* + infinitive

 Photocopiable activity on p.215

You will need one sheet for each pair.

Put students in pairs. Hand out the sheets. Ask students to read the sentence beginnings and talk about their ideas on how to complete the sentence. Demonstrate this by reading the first sentence (*At work, it's important to …*) and eliciting some possible ideas for how to complete it, e.g. *not be late, listen to your manager, work hard, be friendly,* etc. Ask the class to choose the best idea from their suggestions and write this on the board in a shape.

Students continue to discuss the sentences in pairs and agree on an ending for each one which they write in one of the shapes at the bottom of the worksheet. Monitor and help as necessary. When students have finished, ask pairs to swap sheets and try to guess which shape/answer goes with which sentence. Pairs then work together to check answers and to confirm their completed sentences.

In feedback, elicit an example ending for each sentence and correct any errors.

7A Comparatives and superlatives

▶ Photocopiable activity on p.216

You will need one sheet for each pair.

Hand out the sheets. Students look at the ten topics and use the words in the boxes to write two opinion sentences on each topic – students must agree on the opinion. One sentence should use a comparative structure and one should use a superlative structure. Demonstrate this by eliciting ideas for the first item (animals), e.g. *Dogs are friendlier than cats; Snakes are the most dangerous animal.* Set a time limit. Monitor and help as necessary. Put two pairs together. The pairs swap sheets and talk about the different opinions. In feedback, elicit students' ideas and opinions about the things in the different categories.

 VARIATIONS

1 Groups write gapped sentences where the comparative or superlative structure is NOT included. Groups then swap gapped sentences and try to complete the other group's sentences with the correct comparative and superlative structures. This alternative could also be done orally.

2 Students work in pairs and complete the sentences. Then they swap worksheets with another pair and explain the reasons for their different opinions.

7B *used to / didn't use to*

▶ Photocopiable activity on p.217

You will need one sheet for each pair.

Put students into two groups: A and B. Hand out picture A to Group A, and picture B to Group B. Explain to students that they have two similar pictures. Picture A shows what a man's life used to be like in the past. Picture B shows the same man today. Elicit a sentence from Group A about the man using *used to* and elicit that he doesn't. e.g. *He used to eat a lot of pizza.* Then ask Group B if the man eats pizza now.

Group A work together to write positive and negative sentences, e.g. *He used to have a pet (bird). He didn't use to read books.* about their picture. Group B students work together to write questions about what the man *used to / didn't use to* do in the past – e.g. *Did he use to drink water? Did he use to listen to music a lot?* – using their picture. Monitor and help as necessary. Encourage students to ask you for vocabulary or use their dictionary.

Put students into pairs: A and B. Students say the sentences/questions from their group and find the differences between the two pictures. Students must not show their pictures to each other. Set a time limit and then allow students to look at each other's pictures.

In feedback, elicit the differences that students found and correct any language errors.

 VARIATION

Put students in pairs: A and B. Give the pair both pictures and ask them to write sentences with *used to* describing the differences between the pictures.

8A The passive: present and past simple

▶ Photocopiable activity on p.218

Put students into pairs. Hand out sheets. Explain that students are going to read some amazing facts. They have to guess what the missing number is in each sentence and complete the gap with the correct passive form of the verb given in brackets. If necessary, read the first sentence with the class and elicit ideas for the number of tigers (5,000) and also elicit the passive form of the verb (are kept). Students work on their own to complete the sheet. Monitor and help as necessary. When they have finished, put students in pairs to compare their ideas and answers.

In feedback, check the passive answers and correct any errors. Then confirm the missing numbers. Award one point to the pair whose numerical answer is closest to the correct answer. The pair with the most points wins.

 VARIATION

Write the missing numbers on the board, so students can choose which numbers are missing from the worksheet.

Answers

1 are kept, 5,000	2 were born, 60	3 was told, 102
4 was saved, 3	5 309, were sold	6 75, are served
7 10, was discovered	8 50, was folded	9 149, were scored

8B Present perfect with *for* and *since*

▶ Photocopiable activity on p.219

You will need one sheet for each pair.

Copy the shapes onto the board. In the shapes, write time references/numbers, e.g. *last summer, ten years, two weeks, December 2012,* etc. Write an example sentence beginning on the board, e.g. *I've lived in my house for …* Explain the sentence is a true statement about your life and ask students to choose an appropriate sentence ending. Elicit whether a time period (e.g. ten years) or a specific time (e.g. last summer) is correct with *for* (time period). Then ask students to guess which is the correct time/ending (I've lived in my house for ten years).

Students work in pairs. Hand out the sheets. Ask students to write eight true sentence beginnings in the present perfect with *for* and *since,* using the ideas in the box at the top of the page to help them. Students should write the sentence endings (i.e. time periods or specific times) in the shapes at the bottom of the worksheet.

Students then show their sentences and times to their partner. The partner should guess which sentence the times go with, e.g. *You've had your mobile since last summer.* Monitor and help as necessary. In feedback, elicit sentences from different pairs/groups.

9A First conditional

 Photocopiable activity on p.220

You will need one worksheet for each pair, cut up to make two sets of cards.

In pairs, students place all the cards face down in front of them and take turns to turn over two cards.

If the two cards make a correct sentence containing an *if*-clause (relating to a possible future situation) and a main clause (relating to result), the student keeps the cards. If not, the student turns them back over.

The winner is the person with the most cards when all the pairs are matched.

> ### ⊘ VARIATION
> Make one copy of the worksheet for each pair of students. Fold the worksheet in half so that only the *if*-clauses are face up. Students work in pairs to complete each sentence with a result clause. When they have finished, they compare their sentences with the ones on the other side of the folded worksheet.

Answers
If I study hard, I'll pass my exams.
If she doesn't get a good mark, she won't be very happy.
If you don't take an umbrella, you might get wet.
If we stay up until the end of the film, you'll be tired at work tomorrow.
If I go to Paris, I might visit the Eiffel Tower.
If my friends go on holiday without me, I'll be lonely.
If the company does well, everyone will get a pay rise.
If the baby is a girl, they're going to call her 'Ruby'.
If he passes his driving test, he's going to buy a car.
If the tickets are still available, I'll get one for you.
If she has enough time, she'll come to visit us.
If I don't get to the concert early, I won't get a seat.

9B Verb patterns

 Photocopiable activity on p.221

You will need enough copies of the worksheet to give at least one question strip to each student. In larger classes, more than one student may have the same question.

Give students one question each and explain that for this activity, they have to move round the class talking to as many other students as possible and asking them the question on their piece of paper. Before you start, you may want to model a question and answer to remind students that some verbs are followed by the *-ing* form and some by the infinitive with *to*, e.g. *What's something you always avoid doing? I always avoid doing the washing up. What's something you often forget to do? I often forget to buy more toothpaste.* Students do the activity, making notes of the responses in their notebooks.

When they have finished, put them into groups and ask them to compare their funniest or most interesting responses.

> ### ⊘ VARIATION
> In larger classes (or where mingling is difficult), students could work in pairs or small groups, taking turns to ask and answer the questions.

10A Second conditional

 Photocopiable activity on p.222

You will need one sheet for each student.

Hand out the sheets. Write the first *if*-clause on the board and complete the sentence with your own idea, e.g. *If I won a holiday for four in the Caribbean, I would take my family with me.* Elicit other alternative possible ways to complete the sentence from the students. Ask students to read the 15 *if*-clauses and deal with any unknown vocabulary. Then, tell them to work alone and complete the sentences with their own ideas.

When students have completed the sheet, tell them they are going to find another student who would do the same thing as them for each item on the sheet. Tell students they cannot read each other's sheets, they must ask questions. Elicit the question for the first item (What would you do if you won a holiday for four in the Caribbean?). Ask students to mingle with the class and ask each other the questions. They should write down the names of other students who have completed each sentence with the same idea. The words do not have to be exactly the same.

Allow enough time for the majority of students to mingle and complete their sheets as far as possible. Monitor and help as necessary.

Take feedback from the class on whose answers were the most similar and anything surprising that they heard.

> ### ⊘ VARIATION
> Students work in pairs. Together they think of three different ways to complete each sentence and write these as options A, B, C. Students work in new pairs and read out their sheet as a quiz for their new partner who has to choose which option he/she would take.

10B Quantifiers; *too / not enough*

▶ Photocopiable activity on p.223

You will need one sheet for each pair.

Explain that students have to think of reasons (excuses) why they *can't, won't* or *couldn't* do the things on the worksheet using *too* and *enough*. They have to think up the best excuses they can for each problem. Provide an example if necessary, or elicit an example from a student, e.g. *I can't go on holiday with my friends because they are too disorganised.* Set a time limit (five to ten minutes) for students to complete the reasons/excuses in pairs.

Ask each pair in turn to read out their reason/excuse for the first thing they can't do and award points. Then go on to the second one, and so on. Award one point for accurate language and two points for the best excuse in each case. This can be the most creative excuse or the funniest excuse. Students must use the words *too* or *enough* somewhere in their excuse.

You could award the points for the best excuse based on a class vote.

11A Defining relative clauses

▶ Photocopiable activity on p.224

You will need one sheet for each pair, cut in half.

Hand out the sheets. Ask students what this game is called in their own language, then ask if they know the English word. If not, introduce *crossword*, and ask the class questions to find out how many students do crosswords in their own language. Explain that students each have half of the same crossword. They must take it in turns to explain the words on their crossword to their partner, and ask their partner to explain words in order to complete the empty rows on their own crossword. Check that students know how to ask which word they want their partner to explain: teach or elicit the questions:
What's one down? What's two across?
Students should describe the words using: *It's a place where …; It's a person who …; It's a thing which/that …*
They can give further help or information if their partner does not understand.

Monitor and help as necessary. When students have completed their crosswords, ask them to compare crosswords to check spelling and any missing words. Go over any errors with the class.

> ### ⚙ VARIATION
> For classes that need more support, put students into pairs and ask them to look at the half-completed crosswords. Students work together to write simple definitions for the answers. The definitions should include relative pronouns.

11B Articles

▶ Photocopiable activity on p.225

You will need one sheet for each pair or group of three or four students, cut up into sentence strips.

Explain to students that they need to work together to put the strips into the correct order to tell the true story of Aron Ralston, whose adventure was made into a film. Monitor and assist with any vocabulary questions.

When they have finished, students take turns to retell the story from memory. Monitor and correct any mistakes with articles.

> ### 📖 VOCABULARY SUPPORT
> *canyon*: a large valley with very steep sides and usually a river flowing along the bottom

12A Past perfect

▶ Photocopiable activity on p.226

You will need one sheet for each pair of students.

Don't hand out the sheets immediately. The aim of the activity is for students to use the past perfect to come up with explanations for the situations described on the sheet. Write the first sentence on the board: *I tried to switch on the lights, but nothing happened.* Ask students: *Why do you think I couldn't switch on the lights?* Elicit possible explanations – e.g. *I hadn't paid the electricity bill* – and write them on the board, paying particular attention to accuracy with past perfect. Say: *What if this were a sentence in a novel or a film?* Encourage more imaginative explanations, e.g. *Somebody had broken all the*

light bulbs. If students need more support, write a few ideas yourself, e.g.
There had been a huge storm. A tree had fallen on the power lines. Aliens had attacked the Earth. They were taking the power into their ship. Ask students to vote for the most realistic explanation and the most imaginative one by raising their hands.

Ask students to work in pairs. Hand out a sheet to each pair. Explain that students should write two explanations for each situation, a realistic explanation under FACT and an imaginative explanation under FICTION. For each situation one pair in the class will get a point for the most realistic explanation in the class, and one for the most imaginative. Monitor the class as they write and help with vocabulary. Encourage fast finishers to add more details to their explanations.

When students have completed the writing, read out the second sentence on the sheet. Each pair of students should tell you their FACT explanation first. If you wish, you can award all grammatically correct explanations a point. Correct any errors with tenses as students read out their explanations. Take a class vote for the most sensible explanation and award the pair a point. Then move on to the FICTION explanations and take a vote for the most imaginative one. The pair with the most points at the end is the winner.

> ### ⚙ VARIATION
> With very large classes divide the students into groups of four or five pairs for the voting stage. Choose one student in each group to read the situations from the sheet and to conduct the vote. Monitor use of tenses closely during this stage.

12B Reported speech

▶ Photocopiable activity on p.227

You will need one sheet for each group.

Put students into groups of three: A, B and C. Hand out the correct part of the worksheet to each student and ask them not to show each other their worksheets. Explain that each group has to deliver a message from Student A to Student B, then from Student B to Student C, and then finally from Student C to Student A. Then ask all the Student As to go to one part of the classroom, Student Bs to another, and Student Cs to another.

Stand with the Student As and demonstrate the activity by going to a Student B and saying a sentence, e.g. *I like chocolate.* Then return to the Student As. Ask Student B to think about the sentence and change it into reported speech, e.g. *He/She said (that) he/she liked chocolate.* Then Student B goes to Student C and says the sentence. Student B returns to his/her group. Student C changes the sentence back into direct speech (I like chocolate) and writes the sentence at the bottom of his/her sheet. Explain that the sentences will be checked at the end of the activity.

Check students understand the procedure and allow students to refer to Grammar Focus on page 165 of the Student's Book, if necessary. Then Student A begins and 'delivers' the four messages. When the four messages have been delivered, it is Student B's turn to deliver the messages to C, then C finally writes the sentence on his/her worksheet. When these four messages have been delivered, it is Student B's turn to deliver the original messages and so on.

Monitor and help as necessary. At the end of the activity, ask students to go back to their original group. They should then check that their sentences match. The group with the most accurate reporting wins. Go over any errors with the class.

EXTRA ACTIVITY

Students write their own statements in direct speech and pass the sentences to another group to report the sentence in reported speech.

VOCABULARY
1A Common adjectives

▶ Photocopiable activity on p.228

You will need one sheet for each student.

For Activity A, give students a time limit, e.g. two minutes, to revise the adjectives in the Vocabulary Focus and then another one minute to write down all they can remember. In feedback, elicit the adjectives and ask students to spell the words or to write them on the board. The student who remembered the most and spelt them correctly is the winner.

For Activity B, divide the class into two groups: A and B. Ask students to work with someone from the same group and explain that they have to imagine that they have visited these places and write their opinion of them. e.g, *The food at Valentino's cafe is delicious*; *The service is awful*. Tell students to include sentences that are positive and negative, and elicit a few examples, e.g. *The rooms at the Carlton hotel are lovely*; *The manager is a bit strange*; *The adventure park is a bit silly, but OK for small children*. Monitor and help as necessary.

For Activity C, divide the class into pairs: Student A and Student B. Tell students they are going to compare their experiences of visiting the two towns Greenwood and Lakeville. Students talk about their towns and decide which one is the best / most interesting place to spend time in.

EXTRA ACTIVITIES

1 Ask students to write a short report about the town using their notes. Encourage them to use headings such as *food, accommodation, shopping, culture* and *entertainment*.

2 Ask students to look up facilities, e.g. hotels or restaurants, in their home town or another, bigger town or city in the area on review-based websites. Encourage students to make notes on what they can understand and to use their dictionaries. Students then write a short report or talk about the facilities in the next lesson.

1B Adverbs

▶ Photocopiable activity on p.229

You will need one sheet for each student.

For Activity A, write a pair of example sentences on the board, e.g.
Tom absolutely loves his job.
Tom is fairly happy with his job.

Ask students to say if the meaning is the same or different. Elicit that the meaning is different and ask students which words in the sentences helped them to work this out. Underline the adverbs *absolutely* and *fairly* on the board.

Students work individually on the eight sentence pairs and compare their answers with a partner at the end. Monitor and help as necessary. Check answers with the class.

Answers
1D 2D 3D 4S 5S 6D 7S 8D

For Activity B, read through the topics and sentence beginnings with students, then tell them how you would complete the first sentence. This activity is fairly open, so encourage students to ask you for any vocabulary they may need or to use a dictionary.

For Activity C, ask students to mingle with the class and compare their answers. Make sure they understand that they should write the names of students who have similar answers to their own in the last column. Have a final feedback where students can tell the class something true about several students, e.g. *Christophe, Marianne and I absolutely love chocolate*.

2A Tourism

▶ Photocopiable activity on p.230

You will need one sheet for each student.

Before students start Activity A, make it clear that the items in the list could belong to them or to other people who live in their home. Then give students a minute or two to go through the list of items, underlining those that they have at home, before comparing their answers in small groups. Get feedback from the class and deal with any pronunciation problems.

For Activity B, tell students to read all the phrases before they choose their answers since there is only one correct answer when all nine verbs are used. Check answers with the class.

Answers
pack your luggage   get a visa   do some sightseeing
decide where you are going to stay   book your accommodation
buy souvenirs   unpack your suitcase when you arrive
check in to your hotel   exchange some money

For Activity C, ask students to work in pairs and agree on the order they would do these things. There is more than one possible order.

Suggested answers
1 decide where you are going to stay   2 get a visa
3 book your accommodation   4 exchange some money
5 pack your luggage   6 check in to your hotel
7 unpack your suitcase when you arrive   8 do some sightseeing
9 buy souvenirs

Finally, for D tell students to compare their answers for C with a different partner. Can they agree on an overall best or most logical order for the activities? If not, which are the items they have different opinions about? Get feedback from the class.

2B Travel collocations

▶ Photocopiable activity on p.231

You will need one sheet for each student.

Begin Activity A by explaining that students should decide whether the words and phrases in the box are mainly connected with cars, planes or both. Some words can go in different columns, so ask students to justify their answers. Monitor and help as necessary. After students have compared in groups, get feedback from the class.

Suggested answers
Cars: hitchhike, give somebody a lift, get lost, traffic jam, set off
Planes: turbulence, land, miss, take off, board, a long queue, a strike
Cars or planes: break down, a long delay, there's something wrong with the engine, crash

For Activity B, use the example to encourage students to use the target vocabulary and include any further information. Monitor the activity to check for accuracy, and then conduct a short feedback on the different reasons.

You can set this up as a competition. Students take it in turns to read their reasons, but they cannot repeat a reason already provided by their partner. The first student to run out of reasons is the loser.

3A *make, do, give* collocations

▶ Photocopiable activity on p.232

You will need one sheet for each student.

Activity A can be done as a race, either in pairs or individually. Draw arrows on the board to help you explain to students that the nine phrases with *make, do* and *give* can run in any direction. The verbs are in bold to make the phrases easier to find. Allow students to call out when they have finished, but encourage the rest of the class to carry on until they have found the phrases. Check answers with the class.

Answers
do well at something, make a joke, make someone smile, give someone a hug, do something nice for someone, give someone a tip, give something away, make a friend, give someone directions, do volunteer work

For Activity B, divide the class into pairs and clarify that in the first six sentences, students should use the phrases in A, but that they can use their own ideas for 7–12. Elicit some ideas for sentence 7, e.g. *I gave the little boy a hug because he looked sad / he had been so good / he was so sweet,* etc. before students begin the activity. Monitor and help as necessary, particularly with 7–12.

Suggested answers
1 made a joke.
2 gave him a (big) tip.
3 gave it away (to a friend).
4 gave her a hug / made a joke / made her smile.
5 didn't do (very) well (at it).
6 gave him directions.
7 fell over / looked unhappy / was crying.
8 I didn't need it / it was old / I don't play tennis any more.
9 lived next door / is good fun.
10 has a lot of free time / hasn't got a job / is very kind.
11 I was happy then / my life is very different now.
12 she's not very well / she's always very kind to us / it's her birthday.

For Activity C, give students a few minutes to compare their answers to B with their partner and then ask for volunteers to read out their most interesting answers. Give feedback on any errors you noted during the monitoring, especially with the forms of the phrases.

3B Money

▶ Photocopiable activity on p.233

You will need one sheet for each student.

You can set Activity A up as a competition by setting a time limit, e.g. five minutes, or by having a race to see which pair can finish the quiz first. Depending on your group, you might want to remind students of how to work out percentages - i.e. divide the number by 100 and then multiply it be the percentage you want to find.

Answers
1 £136
2 £1,800, four and a half months
3 £44 on food, £26 on wine, £70 in total
4 just under nine months
5 £27
6 Not quite. The cost of the car is £1530.

Before you begin Activity B, elicit some examples of words related to money from the class, e.g. *sales, cost, loan,* to make sure they understand what they are looking for. Ask students to underline the word/phrase the first time it appears only. Check answers with the class.

Answers
the sales, cost, (get) a loan, borrow, lend, owe, pay (them) back, bought, euros, special offer, price, spend (on something), save (up), discount, bank account, cash, (can) afford.

Students can complete the adverts in Activity C individually or in pairs. Check answers with the class.

Answers
1 saving 2 offers 3 account 4 lend 5 cash 6 discount
7 afford 8 borrow 9 loan 10 back 11 special 12 save

4A Clothes and appearance

▶ Photocopiable activity on p.234

You will need one worksheet for each student.

For Activity A, students work on their own to complete the table with the clothes words. Give students five minutes for this exercise and monitor the activity. Help with spelling as necessary.

Answers
Feet: boots, high heels, socks, flat shoes, trainers, sandals
Body: shorts, raincoat, jumper, top, tracksuit, sweatshirt
Jewellery: necklace, earrings, bracelet
Accessories: belt, handbag, scarf, gloves, tie

Make sure students read their answers aloud to each other for Activity B in order to check their pronunciation of difficult words, especially *bracelet, necklace, gloves, sweatshirt.* Check answers with the class by drawing the table on the board and asking students to come up and complete it. This will allow you to check spelling and check that students are pronouncing the items correctly at the same time. Drill the words as necessary.

For Activity C, set a time limit of five minutes. Students identify examples of clothing describing their colour /

what they are made of and/or by naming the person who is wearing it/them. Students should only have one example of each item. Monitor and help as necessary.

Begin Activity D by bringing the class together to demonstrate how to play the game. Elicit some examples of descriptions from the whole class before leaving students to continue playing in groups. Monitor and make notes of any mistakes to correct with the class. Check the scores and declare a winner for each group.

4B Adjectives: places

▶ Photocopiable activity on p.235

You will need one sheet for each pair, cut in half.

Ask students what this game is called in their own language, then ask if they know the English word. If not, introduce *crossword*, and see how many students do them in their own language. Explain that students each have half of the same crossword. They must take it in turns to explain the words on their crossword to their partner and to ask their partner to explain words in order to complete the empty rows on their own crossword. Check that students know how to ask which word they want their partner to explain and teach or elicit the questions:
What's one down? What's two across?
Students should describe the words using:
What's the opposite of …?
It's a word that means (the same as) …
Write *crowded* (1 across) and *noisy* (1 down) on the board and elicit possible definitions, (e.g. *It's a word that means there are lots of people; The opposite of quiet*). Monitor and help as necessary. Check answers with the class.

Answers
Across
4 crowded
5 magnificent
9 huge
11 ordinary
12 modern
13 tiny
14 ugly

Down
1 noisy
2 indoor
3 high
6 ancient
7 narrow
8 peaceful
10 pretty

5A Work

▶ Photocopiable activity on p.236

You will need one sheet for each student.

In Activity A, the verbs are in bold to make the phrases easier to find. Students complete the activity individually, then compare with a partner before you check the answers with the class.

Answers
need several years' training, deal with people every day, have a lot of skills, work in a team, deal with serious problems, work long hours, work at weekends, make important decisions, need good qualifications, have a nice working environment, need a university degree, be self-employed

For Activity B, let students choose their jobs or you could assign certain jobs to the class. Give students five minutes to write their sentences; encourage them to include both positive and negative sentences.

Finally, for Activity C, put the students into small groups. They take turns to read their sentences to the group, who tries to guess the job. If the group can't guess the right answer, the student who wrote the sentences must try to give more information.

 VARIATION
Think of another job. Write a short text using phrases in A to describe it, but ask students not to write the name of the job in the text. Students then swap their texts with other students and guess the jobs.

Suggested answers
The people who do this job usually need a university degree and they have a lot of skills. They often work long hours and they deal with people every day. They sometimes have to make important decisions. For example, they decide if students pass or fail a test. *Job*: teacher

5B Jobs

▶ Photocopiable activity on p.237

You will need one sheet for each student.

For Activity A, write the example sentences on the board and tell the class that one job is hidden in each sentence. Underline *driver* in the first sentence, then give students time to find *farmer* in the second. (Note: *driver* and *farmer* are not taught in this unit.) Students can work individually or in pairs to find the remaining eight jobs. Check answers with the class.

Answers
1 actor 2 carer 3 musician 4 IT worker
5 builder 6 vet 7 journalist 8 postman

Students continue to work on their own in Activity B and decide where to put the words in each category. Give students time to write the jobs on the lines. Monitor and help as necessary.

For Activity C, divide the class into small groups to compare their answers. Encourage students to explain and justify their answers. Monitor and make notes on good use of language and any problems.

For the last activity, tell students to add another job to each line, and then compare again in groups. They can select jobs from other categories or any other jobs that they know. Get feedback from the class and point out good uses of language.

6A Verbs with dependent prepositions

▶ Photocopiable activity on p.238

You will need one sheet cut in half, the board game on page 203 and a dice for each pair of students. Divide the class into pairs and give them the cut-up sheet, the board game and the dice. Don't let students look at each other's sheets at this stage. Tell them to look at the first sentence only and think about the verbs and the dependent prepositions for a few seconds. Then, they turn their paper over. Explain to them the rules of the game: during the game, they can't look at all their questions at once. They turn their paper over when it is their turn to play. Students take turns to throw the dice and move to the relevant square. They read out a completed sentence to their partner who checks if it's correct by looking at the answer key on their own sheet. If it's correct, they move forward two squares. If it's wrong, they move back two squares. If they land on 'Go' on four squares or 'Go back' four squares, they obey the instruction. The winner is the person to get to the 'Finish' square first. Monitor and note any mistakes to correct with the class afterwards.

6B -ed / -ing adjectives

▶ Photocopiable activity on p.239

You will need one sheet for each student.

For Activity A, give students a time limit (e.g. five minutes) and ask them to work individually. Remind students that two sentences are correct. Students then compare their answers by spelling the words aloud to each other. Check answers with the class.

Answers
1 surprised
2 disappointed
3 amazed
4 excited
6 shocked
8 embarrassed
9 annoying
10 frightening

The crossword in Activity B is different from standard crosswords in two ways. Firstly, the number of squares at the end of the words is not specified, so students have to decide whether to use an -ed or an -ing ending. Complete clue 1 with the class as an example to demonstrate this. Secondly, on finishing the crossword accurately, students will find another -ed/-ing adjective in the vertical grey squares.

With some classes you may need to point out the difference between *How do you feel?* (e.g. *tired, surprised,* etc.) and *How does it feel?* (e.g. *tiring, surprising,* etc.) in the clues.

Monitor and help as necessary.

Answers

1 tired	2 annoying	3 excited	4 frightened
5 embarrassed	6 relaxed	7 confused	8 disappointing
9 shocked	10 amazed		

word: interested

Demonstrate Activity C by reading a random clue and asking a student to provide the appropriate adjective, ending in -ed or -ing. Monitor and help as necessary.

7A Life events with *get*

▶ Photocopiable activity on p.240

You will need one sheet for each student.

Complete the first sentence in Activity A together by eliciting the correct answer (to get a job) from the group, then give students time to finish completing the statements on their own. Students can compare with a partner before you check answers with the class.

Answers
1 a job   2 paid   3 divorced   4 rich
5 in touch   6 ill   7 a place   8 on well
9 to know   10 better   11 old   12 together

For Activity B, ask students to briefly discuss the first statement in pairs, then ask the class whether they agree or not and why. This exercise is quite open, and students will need time to think about what to say for the rest of the statements. Monitor and make sure that students are not writing too much. Be prepared to help them with any language they require.

Groups will spend different amounts of time on each statement in Activity C, so monitor carefully. If one group finishes quickly, put these students into different groups who are still continuing their discussion. Monitor and make notes of any mistakes to correct with the class.

Get feedback on the topics which students found interesting and correct language use.

7B Health and fitness collocations

▶ Photocopiable activity on p.241

You will need one sheet for each student.

The wordsearch in Activity A can be done individually or in pairs. Explain that there are nine items relating to health and fitness to be found and that the words can run horizontally, vertically or diagonally. When most students have finished, check answers with the class and check pronunciation.

Answers

S	O	H	O	I	S	Y	O	H	J	B	D	N
G	V	A	Y	V	N	M	I	A	R	S	O	P
Y	O	E	R	G	L	S	O	X	S	A	O	R
A	V	B	J	H	O	R	H	K	E	I	P	A
L	E	M	E	E	B	O	W	A	E	S	N	K
L	R	I	N	A	U	B	N	O	P	R	M	E
E	W	E	D	L	X	B	A	A	I	E	R	F
R	E	G	E	T	F	I	T	O	D	G	H	S
G	I	W	A	H	I	S	Y	H	E	I	N	U
Y	G	I	G	Y	S	O	G	V	S	Z	E	G
Z	H	P	U	T	O	N	W	E	I	G	H	T
O	T	L	I	G	I	V	E	U	P	F	O	P
H	L	O	S	E	W	E	I	G	H	T	O	A

For Activity B, start by asking students to quickly read through the articles, so that they understand what kind of text it is (short case studies and advice). Complete the first gap together, then let students work individually on the remaining gaps before they compare in pairs. Check answers with the class.

Answers
1 overweight   2 lose   3 in shape   4 on a diet   5 healthy
6 fit   7 smoker   8 give up   9 allergies   10 put on

Give students a few minutes to read the articles again and decide whether they agree with the advice, or have any other ideas to add. Then divide the class into small groups for the discussion in Activity C. Monitor and make notes of any mistakes to correct with the class. You could open up the discussion to the whole class if students have a lot to say.

8A Art and music

▶ Photocopiable activity on p.242

You will need one sheet for each student.

For Activity A, Students complete the crossword while you monitor and help as necessary. Check answers with the class.

Answers
Across
2 novel   5 written   8 painted   12 classical
13 architecture   14 designed   15 photograph
Down
1 series   3 sculpture   4 directed   6 performed   7 painting
8 play   9 album   10 based   11 poem

In Activity B, students revise the vocabulary from the crossword. Divide the class into new pairs. Students cover the crossword. Then Student A reads out the first clue across for Student B to answer. Student B then reads the first clue down for Student A to answer, and so on.

💡 VARIATION

Write the prompts on the board and ask students to work in pairs and complete the sentences with their own examples.

_____ was painted by _____.

_____ was written by _____.

_____ was directed by _____.

_____ was designed by _____.

_____ is a new album by _____.

_____ is a new TV series.

Students then tell other members of the class what they have written or you could make it into a mini quiz where students leave gaps for the class to complete, e.g. *Sunflowers* was painted by _____.

8B Sports and activities

▶ Photocopiable activity on p.243

You will need one sheet for each student.

For Activity A, move round the class and help students who are having difficulty remembering the words, e.g. you could tell them the first letter of the word. When students have completed the table, they can compare with another pair before you check the answers with the whole class. Check answers and pronunciation with the class.

Answers
in/on the sea: surfing, scuba diving, windsurfing
on land: golf, rock climbing, skateboarding, jogging, athletics, (volleyball)
on snow/ice: snowboarding, ice hockey, ice skating
usually indoors: volleyball, gymnastics, yoga, squash, (athletics)

Activity B can be done individually or in pairs. If students work in pairs, put students in new pairs for C.

Answers
1 jogging (skateboarding)   2 volleyball   3 yoga   4 scuba diving
5 squash   6 rock climbing   7 ice hockey or volleyball (NB: ice hockey has a large number of replacement players, but only six on the ice at any one time.)   8 snowboarding, surfing, skateboarding   9 golf
10 gymnastics, ice skating (windsurfing)

When they do Activity C, make sure students read out their answers rather than just look at each other's worksheets. Elicit answers from the class at the end and discuss any differences.

9A Education collocations

▶ Photocopiable activity on p.244

You will need one sheet for each student.

For Activity A, make sure students understand that there are some words/phrases in the wordsnake which are not related to education (e.g. *healthy*). To make this more challenging, you could make it a race to see who is first to finish. Students work individually and then compare in pairs. Get feedback from the class and check pronunciation.

Answers
engineering, essay, fail, marks, medicine, degree, art, revise, take notes, education, law, psychology

The answers to Activity B are words and phrases students encountered in A, except for *handed (in), get (into)* and *business management*. Monitor and help where necessary, especially with the three phrases not in A. Students can compare in pairs before you check answers with the class.

Answers
failed, essay, revising, marks, notes, handed, get, degree, business management, law, medicine

For Activity C, start with the first sentence and ask students to ask you the question, e.g. *Have you ever failed an exam or a test?* If necessary, elicit one or two more questions until you are confident students know what to do. When students find someone for whom the statement is true, they write the name. Find out who has the most names on their questionnaire, and finish with feedback on the answers and students' language use.

9B Verbs followed by *to* + infinitive / verb + *-ing*

▶ Photocopiable activity on p.245

You will need one sheet for each pair, cut up and the cards kept separate.

Hand out a verb table and a set of cards to each pair of students. For Activity A, ask students to correct the verb table. Check answers with the class. Draw attention to *like* which can be followed by verb + *-ing* and *to* + infinitive.

Answers

Verb + *-ing*	*to* + infinitive
avoid	agree
imagine	arrange
like	like
miss	forget
recommend	manage
regret	promise
	refuse

For Activity B, demonstrate what students have to do with one pair/group. Give each pair/group a set of cards and place them face down on a desk. Explain that the beginnings of the sentences with the verbs are on smaller cards and the endings are on larger cards, and students must find the correct sentence endings for the verb cards – both the meanings and forms must be correct. If they win, they keep the cards. It's important that students put any non-matching cards back in the same position. Monitor and help as necessary.

In feedback, ask students to read out the complete sentences and correct any errors.

This game can also be used as a revision activity later in the course.

 **EXTRA ACTIVITY**

Divide the class into small groups and tell students to put all the verb cards face down in a pile on the table. (They do not need the sentence endings any more.) The first student in each group takes a verb card from the pile and has twenty seconds to complete the sentence in their own words. If the group is not sure whether the sentence is correct or not, they can ask you. Continue until all the cards have been used up.

10A Multi-word verbs

▶ Photocopiable activity on p.246

You will need one sheet for each student.

Demonstrate Activity A by writing the example sentence on the board and eliciting which two of the possible endings are correct. Let students complete the remaining sentences individually, then they can compare in pairs before you check the answers with the class.

Answers

1 the watch   2 my suit   3 the discussion   4 the telephone
5 her hair   6 the marriage   7 at the restaurant   8 ill

For Activity B, you could begin by writing the example question on the board and asking what the situation might be (studying). Then ask students for a possible reply, e.g. *Because I need the qualifications*. Students can then work on their own or in pairs. Monitor and help as necessary. While you monitor, remember that students need to write replies that contextualise the exchanges in C.

Suggested answers

1 (a party) nobody could come on Saturday
2 (the cinema) I had a headache / it was very late
3 (homework) I was very busy yesterday / I forgot about it
4 (a classmate) I want to see her / she's going to help me with my homework
5 (a cat) I'm going on holiday / I don't like cats
6 (a game) it looked fun / I was bored
7 (a couple) they were unhappy / she met someone else
8 (a job/promotion)I wanted more money / I didn't like the new boss

Divide the class into new pairs. For Activity C, start by eliciting some replies at random from different students, and see if the class can pick the question they match with. The students continue in pairs, reading out their answers to Activity B in random order for their partner to match with the correct questions.

Activity D gives students the opportunity to practise the conversations. Monitor and help as necessary.

10B Noun formation

▶ Photocopiable activity on p.247

You will need one sheet for each student.

Students can complete the wordsearch in Activity A individually or in pairs. When most students have finished, check answers with the class and check pronunciation.

Answers

R	E	G	R	E	T	U	N	F
T	Q	F	O	X	C	I	O	D
E	U	E	Y	P	A	T	D	E
N	E	T	K	L	R	A	E	S
J	U	F	P	A	L	E	L	C
O	E	M	L	I	X	S	I	R
Y	O	K	E	N	N	E	V	I
C	E	D	E	C	I	D	E	B
C	H	O	O	S	E	B	R	E

For Activity B, students have to transform the verbs from A into nouns to complete the sentences. Check pronunciation, especially word stress, when you go over the answers with the class.

Answers

1 explanation   2 decision   3 complaint   4 description
5 queue   6 delivery   7 choice   8 enjoyment

Before students work in pairs for Activity C, do some examples with the class using different students. The aim is to practise the verbs and nouns, but also to deliver the questions and answers fluently and naturally. If necessary, ask students to repeat the sentences until they use the correct rhythm. Monitor and help as necessary.

 VARIATION

Ask one student in each pair to read the questions, while the other responds – without looking at the worksheet.

11A Compound nouns

▶ Photocopiable activity on p.248

You will need one sheet for each group of three or four students, cut up.

Demonstrate the activity with one group. Ask students to pick out *OFFICE / SCIENCE* as the first domino and put it on the desk. Then ask students to take four dominoes each and leave the rest face down. The first player must try to complete the compound beginning with *SCIENCE* with one of their own dominoes (the first word of the two on their domino). If they can complete the compound, they place the domino next to the first one and get a point. If they cannot, they miss a turn, but take one of the dominoes from the remaining pack. The next player then tries to complete that compound, and so on.

Monitor to make sure the dominoes are correct. When the groups have finished, ask one group to call out their sequence, so that the class can check their answers.

This game can also be used as a revision activity later in the course.

11B Adverbials: luck and chance

▶ Photocopiable activity on p.249

You will need one sheet for each student.

Demonstrate Activity A by writing example sentences on the board, e.g.
Unfortunately, I didn't see him.
Luckily, I didn't see him.
Ask students to say if the meaning of the two sentences is the same or different. Students work individually and compare their answers with a partner at the end. Monitor and help as necessary. Check answers with the class.

Answers
1S 2S 3D 4S 5D 6D 7S 8D

For Activity B, look at the example with the class and show students that more than one answer is possible. Monitor and help as necessary. Encourage students to ask you for vocabulary if they need it, and also let them use dictionaries. Check answers with the class.

Possible answers
1 it was an accident/mistake
2 it didn't rain
3 I went shopping / to the cinema
4 dropped one/them or broke one/them
5 the shop was closed
6 it didn't break
7 I got it right / I knew it
8 it was still there / someone found it and gave it to me
9 they said no / they didn't
10 he's really horrible / I don't know why he did it

Demonstrate Activity C with a student, then pairs can test each other to see if they can remember their answers to B. Encourage students not to look at their worksheets.

💡 EXTRA ACTIVITY

Ask students to work with a different partner. Student A reads aloud one of their sentence endings, while Student B looks at the sentence beginnings and tries to guess the correct one. For example:

A … it didn't break.

B I dropped my laptop, but luckily …

A Yes, that's right!

Then swap roles.

12A Animals

▶ Photocopiable activity on p.250

You will need one sheet for each student.

For activity A, the students find the animal words in the wordsnake. You could make this more challenging by setting a time limit, e.g. one minute. After that, students could compare with a partner. When you check the answers, elicit the correct spelling, e.g. the singular form of *mosquito* does not have an *e* at the end; and *whale* has an *h*, unlike the country *Wales*. Drill the pronunciation of any items that students are not pronouncing correctly.

Answers
tiger, camel, spider, bee, gorilla, parrot, whale, mosquito

If necessary, pre-teach the verb *bite* for Activity B. The task will be quite challenging if you set a time limit:

tell students they have one minute, but allow it to lapse slightly if nobody finishes in that time. Monitor, but don't make any corrections at this stage.

For Activity C, tell students to read their questions clearly, but quickly. If their partner cannot answer within five seconds, move on to the next question. Check the answers with the class.

Answers
Student A:
1 no 2 yes 3 yes 4 no 5 yes 6 yes 7 no 8 yes
Student B:
1 yes 2 no 3 yes 4 no 5 yes 6 yes 7 no 8 yes

12B Personality adjectives

▶ Photocopiable activity on p.251

You will need one sheet for each student.

Begin Activity A by going through the adjectives in the box with the class, checking meaning. Give students the opportunity to ask you about any words they can't remember. Then ask them to identify and underline words they find difficult to pronounce and drill the pronunciation of these items in particular. With a monolingual group you may know which words are most difficult, but the following are common problems: *reliable, careless, patient, anxious* and *sociable*.

For Activity B, encourage groups not to use any adjective more than twice. This should ensure that all the adjectives have been considered and most will have been used. Monitor and make notes of good language use and any mistakes.

Finally, in Activity C, ask pairs from different groups to compare their answers. Afterwards, you can give language feedback, but also discuss the statements that have produced a range of different adjectives.

WORDPOWER
1 *like*

▶ Photocopiable activity on p.252

You need one sheet for each student in the class.

Tell the students they are going to talk about films. Hand out the sheets to each student. Tell students to look at the film genres (e.g. *horror*) at the top of the sheet. Elicit the names of one or two films for each genre type to check understanding. Model the pronunciation of each genre as you go through them.

Look at question 1 together. Tell students your own favourite genre and some examples, e.g. *I like sci-fi films like Star Wars and Inception.*

In Activity A, students work alone to answer the questions 1–6. Monitor and help with vocabulary as necessary.

In Activity B, divide students into pairs. Tell them they are going to interview each other using the questions. Elicit the necessary change to question 6, e.g. *Do you think I should see it?* Tell students that when they have finished interviewing their partner, they should tell their partner their opinion of the film using *sounds like*. If students need more support, you can drill the phrases with *sounds like* on the sheet.

Monitor and help as necessary.

Students write a film review together. Divide students into pairs or groups according to the genre of film they most enjoy. Each pair/group chooses a film they have both seen and plans a review. To get them started, write on the board:

Title? Genre? Actors? Story?

Students can complete the review for homework.

2 *off*

▶ Photocopiable activity on p.253

You will need one sheet for each pair of students, cut in half.

Hand out the sheets and divide students into pairs. Tell students they are going to make guesses about their partners and fill the gaps in the sentences.

Do the first sentence as an example – ask students *What can you fall off?* to elicit *bicycle, chair, ladder*, etc., and then choose a student and say *I think* (student's name) *has fallen off a bicycle more than once.* Then ask the student: *Am I right?*

Students work alone to complete the sheet about their partner. Give a time limit of five minutes for this. Ask students to talk to their partners to find out how many they got right. Remind students to begin each guess with *I think you …* Tell students to ask *Why?* to get more information from their partners.

In feedback, students can choose the most interesting/surprising facts about their partners and tell the class, e.g. *Maria turns off the TV when a cooking programme is on because she thinks they are really boring.*

3 *just*

▶ Photocopiable activity on p.254

You will need one sheet for each student.

In Activity A, ask students to look at the phrases with *just*. Do number 1 together. Ask students: *What is an expression you've just learned in English?* Encourage individuals to come up with different answers. Students work alone to complete the questionnaire. Monitor and help as necessary.

In Activity B, ask the students to look at number 2. Say to a student *I am just in time for class (about five) times a week. How about you?* Listen to their reply and respond with a follow up question *Why …?* Then ask another student about number 3. *What is an English expression you learned when you were just a child?* Ask students to mingle with the class and discuss their answers. If they hear a new English expression, they should write it down in the space provided and ask their classmate to explain it. Monitor and help students with their explanations.

Divide students into groups of three. Students read out the new English expressions they have found and teach them to the other students in their group.

In their groups, students take it in turns to try to speak for just over a minute on the topic they suggested in question 10. The other students listen and ask questions when the student hesitates or has finished speaking.

4 *look*

▶ Photocopiable activity on p.255

You will need one section of a sheet for each student. Cut enough copies of the sheet into four sections.

Tell students they are going to find a student in the class who does each thing (1–5) on their sheet. Write an example on the board: *Find someone who is from a large family.* Tell students they need to ask questions to find out the information and elicit: *Are you from a large family?* Ask the question to different students until a student gives you a positive answer. Write the student's name on the board and ask a follow-up question *How many brothers and sisters have you got?* Also note the student's answer to this question on the board.

Ask students to mingle with the class and 'find someone who …' by asking questions for each item on their sheet. They should write down students' names and any extra information. Encourage students to ask follow-up questions and make notes on the answers.

Allow enough time for the majority of students to mingle and complete their sheets as far as possible. Monitor and help as necessary.

Put students into groups of A, B, C and D and ask them to report their findings to each other. For example, *Marcel likes looking at old black-and-white photographs. He likes them because they're beautiful.*

5 *job* and *work*

▶ Photocopiable activity on p.256

You will need one sheet for each student.

Tell the group they are going to talk about their preferences for different experiences connected with jobs and work. Tell students to read through all the statements. Ask them to find an experience they like in the list. Take ideas from the class and tell them that there are no right or wrong answers. Tell students to work alone and place the different experiences from best to worst by putting the numbers 1–16 in the 'Me' column.

When students have finished, demonstrate the next stage. Ask a strong student what their number one experience was. Ask why. Tell them your own number one experience and say why. Ask if they agree. Reach an agreement with the student on what your number one as a pair should be. Now divide students into pairs. Tell students to compare their answers and discuss their reasons. Each pair should try to agree on a new order, and write the numbers 1–16 in the 'Pair' column.

Put the pairs into groups of four, and repeat the procedure. This time, students put 1–14 in the 'Group' column.

In feedback, find out what the most popular/unpopular experiences were.

6 Verb + *to*

▶ Photocopiable activity on p.257

You will need one sheet for each pair of students, cut up into strips.

Hand out a set of strips to each pair. Tell students that you have given them a story which they have to put in the correct order. Tell them that the first part of the story has already been identified for them and has been marked *1*. Students work together to reconstruct the rest of the story.

When they have finished, students cover the sheet and retell the story together. Then they look back at the story and find any information they forgot.

Take class feedback on which information each pair remembered and which information they forgot when they retold the story.

 EXTRA ACTIVITY

Read out the questions. Ask students to write answers in full sentences using an appropriate verb + *to*.

1 What did Polly read to Graham?

2 What did Mr Smith refuse to do?

3 What did Graham describe to Polly?

4 What did Polly write to Mr Smith?

5 What did Mrs Smith ask Graham to give to her after the meal?

6 What did Mr Smith know after he ate the meal?

Answers

1 She read the business plan to Graham.
2 Mr Smith refused to lend any money to Polly and Graham.
3 Graham described his favourite fish dish to Polly.
4 Polly wrote an email to Mr Smith.
5 Mrs Smith asked Graham to give the recipe to her.
6 Mr Smith knew that Polly and Graham could sell their food to anybody.

 NO-CUT ALTERNATIVE

You will need one sheet for each pair of students and a few extra sheets.

Put the extra sheets on the walls just outside the classroom. Mark the halfway point in the story on these sheets (after section 6).

Put the class into pairs, A and B. Tell them that A is a reader, and B is a writer. A has to go to the text, read a section, and then come back and tell it accurately to B. B has to write it down. At the halfway point, they swap roles: B reads and A writes.

When each pair finish, hand out the sheets and allow them to check their text against the original. Students should correct their errors. Monitor and help students to decide whether any differences are grammatically correct or not.

7 *change*

▶ Photocopiable activity on p.258

You will need one sheet for each group of four or five students, cut up into cards.

Divide the class into groups of four or five and hand out the cards. Demonstrate the activity by taking the top card from the pile and reading it to the class. *This weekend, I will (BLANK) for a change.* Elicit different ways to complete the statement. Tell students your own answer, e.g. *This weekend, I will go to the cinema for a change.* Encourage the students to ask follow-up questions. *What film will you see? Who will you go with?*

In their groups, students take turns to take the top card and complete the sentences. Monitor, checking understanding of the uses of *change*.

When students have used all the cards, tell them to spread out the cards face down on the table. The first student takes a card at random. They try to remember the information other students told them, e.g. *This weekend, Maria will go to the cinema for a change. She will see a Johnny Depp film. She will go with her sister.* The original student will confirm whether the facts are correct.

If a student picks a card he/she used previously, he/she replaces it and takes another.

 NO-CUT ALTERNATIVE

You will need one sheet for each group of four or five students.

Each group puts the sheet face down on the table. Students take it in turns to turn the sheet over and choose one sentence, following the procedure above. The first student then ticks the square on the sheet and turns it back over. The procedure is repeated until all the squares have been ticked.

When they have finished, ask the students to write down as much as they can remember about the student to their left. Put them in the correct pairs to check one student's answers. Then change the pairs to check the second student's answers.

8 *by*

▶ Photocopiable activity on p.259

You will need one sheet for each student in the class.

If there are more than 15 students in the class, divide them into two groups. Demonstrate the activity using the first sentence. Write on the board. *I think (student's name) likes music by The Black Eyed Peas.* Students work alone to complete the sentences about the other students in the class. Tell students that they must write a sentence about every student in the class/group before they can use a name for the second time. If you wish, tell students they can include your name in their guesses.

Demonstrate the next stage. Ask the student whose name you wrote on the board, *Do you like music by The Black Eyed Peas?* If they answer *yes*, put a tick next to the sentence on the board. If they answer *no*, put a cross. Tell students to mingle with the class and ask each other appropriate questions to find out if their guesses were correct.

 VARIATION

For students who need more support, or a quicker activity, limit the number of sentences they complete to a suitable number.

9 Multi-word verbs with *put*

▶ Photocopiable activity on p.260

You will need one sheet for each student. You will also need two dice for each group (or use a dice app on a phone).

Demonstrate the activity by rolling the dice. Explain that the first die tells them which particle to use with *put* (e.g. *up*, *through*, etc), and the second tells them whether to make a positive, negative, or interrogative sentence. Write a sentence on the board following these rules, e.g. *The school restaurant has put up the price of sandwiches again.* Explain that students should produce detailed sentences. A sentence like *He put his cup down* does not give enough detail; they should include information about who, where, when etc. For example, *Joe put his coffee cup down next to his chair when he came into the classroom.* If the other

193

students don't think a sentence is detailed enough, they should ask questions to get more information.

If a student rolls numbers that have been rolled before, they must make a sentence with a different context. Also, students must not use the same idea twice. For the example above, *Joe didn't put his coffee cup down next to his chair* or *Did Joe put his coffee cup down next to his chair?* are not allowed.

Students take turns to roll the dice and produce sentences. They write their sentences on the sheet. Monitor and correct mistakes related to the meaning or grammatical usage of the multi-word verbs.

End the activity when each student has six sentences. Now students take it in turns to read out their sentences to each other, this time missing out the particle. For example, *The school restaurant has put* (BLANK) *the price of sandwiches again.* The other students have to call out the missing particle.

10 Multi-word verbs with *on*

▶ Photocopiable activity on p.261

You will need one sheet for each student.

Tell the students to work alone for the first part of the activity. Ask students to choose eight of the expressions with *on* to talk about and write one or two key words/ phrases for each answer in a shape on the bottom half of the sheet. Demonstrate if necessary.

When students have finished writing, write your own shape and an idea on the board, e.g. *teaching English*. Ask students: *Why did I write teaching English?* Take guesses by eliciting questions from students, e.g. *Will you carry on teaching English for the next five years / the rest of your life?* etc.

Divide students into pairs and tell them to fold their sheets in half with the shapes on the outside so that their partner can see the ones they have written in. Students take it in turns to ask their partner about the key words in the shapes in order to guess which expression with *on* they relate to. Encourage strong students to ask follow-up questions, e.g. *Why do you want to carry on teaching?*

11 Preposition + noun

▶ Photocopiable activity on p.262

You will need one sheet for every two or three students, cut up into cards.

Divide the class into groups of two or three and give each group a set of cards. Explain the rules of pelmanism. Tell students to place the cards on the table in two piles: one pile for the grey cards and one pile for the white cards. They take turns to pick up cards, one from each pile. If the cards do not make a correct phrase, they are replaced face down. If the cards form a correct phrase, the student uses the noun and preposition in a sentence and then they can keep the cards.

Demonstrate by showing students two cards, e.g. *in* and *love*. Say *My brother is in love with a girl he met last weekend.* Explain that students should produce detailed sentences. A sentence like *He is in love* for example does not give enough information. If the other students don't think a sentence is detailed enough, they should ask questions, e.g. *Who is he in love with?* to get more detail.

The student with the most cards at the end is the winner.

12 *age*

▶ Photocopiable activity on p.263

You will need one copy of the sheet for every two students in the class, cut in half.

Divide students into pairs, A and B. Give half of the sheet to each student.

Tell students that for the first part of the activity they are going to work alone. Students read each statement on their part of the sheet and put a tick or a cross in the 'Me' column according to whether they agree or disagree. Monitor and help students as necessary.

When they have finished, tell students to work with their partner and fill in the 'My partner' column on their sheets. Students take it in turns to read out a sentence and find out if their partner agrees or disagrees. They should ask *Why?* and give their own opinion and reasons. If necessary, encourage pairs who need more support to give reasons and examples by joining in their conversations.

Take feedback by asking if students generally agreed with their partner. Ask if they disagreed strongly about anything and, if you wish, discuss individual statements as a class.

PRONUNCIATION

Introduction Phonetic symbols

▶ Photocopiable activity on p.264

You will need one sheet for each student.

The aim of this sheet is to revise phonetic script. Revise the symbols by writing some simple transcriptions on the board for students to say the word, e.g. /triː/ (*tree*), /maʊs/ (*mouse*), /ˈwɪndəʊ/ (*window*).

For Activity A, ask students to look at the phonetic symbols on page 176 of the Student's Book and find which symbols are the same as alphabet letters (e.g. /w/ and /e/) and which are different (e.g. /θ/ and /æ/).

Students then look at the sounds which are different and underline the part of the word in the table which contains that sound. Drill the target sounds and then drill the words to help students link the sound with the phonetic symbol.

> **Answers**
> /uː/ wh**o**, /ə/ teach**er**, /ɪə/ n**ear**, /eɪ/ l**ate**, /ɜː/ sh**ir**t, /ɔː/ w**al**k, /ʊə/ t**our**, /ɔɪ/ b**oy**, /əʊ/ wind**ow**, /æ/ m**a**n, /ʌ/ b**u**t, /ɑː/ p**ar**t, /ɒ/ g**o**t, /eə/ h**air**, /aɪ/ f**i**ne, /aʊ/ n**ow**, /tʃ/ **ch**air, /dʒ/ **j**ob, /θ/ **th**ink, /ð/ **th**e, /ʃ/ **sh**oe, /ʒ/ televi**s**ion, /j/ **y**es, /ŋ/ si**ng**

For Activity B, demonstrate the activity by eliciting the first sound of an easy word, e.g. *basketball* (= /b/) and a more difficult word, e.g. *themselves* (= /ð/). Ask the students to then find each of these sounds and, once these have been located, to search in the squares around them to find the other sounds that make up the whole words.

Divide students into pairs. They work in pairs to find the transcriptions in the wordsearch. Remind them that words can go across or down. Check answers with the class.

Answers

j	ɪ	s	b	r	ʌ	ð	ə	t	e
uː	θ	ʌ	ɑː	h	t	ʒ	z	v	ɪə
n	p	ɒ	s	ə	b	ə	l	r	e
ɪ	ŋ	æ	k	θ	ɜː	s	t	i	v
v	ɜː	k	ɪ	tʃ	ə	n	ɒ	w	r
ɜː	ɪə	ɒ	t	l	n	r	k	θ	i
s	k	ʌ	b	ə	d	b	t	p	w
ɪ	ʒ	f	ɔː	ɒ	r	ɪ	n	dʒ	eə
t	r	ɔɪ	l	iː	ŋ	tʃ	k	aʊ	h
i	v	ð	ə	m	s	e	l	v	z

💡 **EXTRA ACTIVITY**

Talk about why it is useful to know phonetic script and how the students could use it as a learning tool, for example in being able to read the phonetic script in dictionaries.

1A Syllables and word stress

▶ Photocopiable activity on p.265

You will need one sheet for each student.

Write the words *daughter and learner* on the board and drill them with the class. Explain that both words contain long vowel sounds. Tell students that there are five principal long vowel sounds in English (excluding diphthongs) and that these are:
/iː/ as in tree
/ɔː/ as in horse
/ɜː/ as in bird
/ɑː/ as in car and
/uː/ as in boot.

Give each student a sheet and explain that they need to get from *daughter* to *water* by following those words with the long vowel sound. They can only move one square at a time, horizontally, vertically or diagonally so, each time they land on a square, they should say out loud the words on the squares in all the possible directions around it to determine which has the long vowel sound. Demonstrate with *daughter* in the first square and elicit which of the surrounding words – *love, fish* or *call* – has a long vowel sound (call). Students work in pairs, taking it in turns to choose and pronounce the words. Monitor and help as necessary. Check and drill answers with the class. The maze in Activity B works in a similar way, except here, the students have to follow the words with short vowel sounds. Again, demonstrate the activity by directing students' attention to the first square with word *letter* and eliciting which of the surrounding words – *scarf, leave* or *sun* – has a short vowel sound (sun). Proceed as in the same way for Activity A, monitoring and helping as necessary.

Answers
A daughter, call, heart, laugh, four, teeth, large, horse, aunt, thought, March, bath, door, water
B letter, sun, fish, son, many, spell, clock, cat, egg, kiss, bed, sock, met, wish

💡 **VARIATION**

Put students into pairs. Students take it in turns to identify and say the next word until they reach the end of the maze.

1B Long and short vowel sounds

▶ Photocopiable activity on p.266

You will need one set sheet for each pair of students, cut up into dominoes.

Revise syllables and word stress by writing words on the board and asking students to say how many syllables there are and which one is stressed. For example, *ta-ble* (two syllables), *ho-tel* (two syllables), *dan-ge-rous* (three syllables).

Put students into pairs and hand out the sets of dominoes. Each student takes 15 dominoes. Demonstrate by putting a domino on the desk. Tell students they must find a domino with the same stress pattern as one of the words and place it next to the relevant word. For example:

normally	**engineer**	**magazine**	shampoo

Or:

instructions	**visitor**	**normally**	engineer

Students continue to play the game. If a student can't find a word with the same stress pattern or puts down an incorrect domino, then the other player has another turn. Students take it in turns to play until one of them has used all their dominoes and is the winner. Monitor and help as necessary.

Check answers with the class. Ask students to read out their lines of dominoes.

💡 **VARIATIONS**

1 Hand out the sheet. Students take it in turns to go through the table and read out all the words that have the same stress pattern, e.g. *cupboard, grammar, open, boring, kitchen, football, awful* and *perfect*.

2 Hand out the sheet. Give some or all of the stress patterns below and elicit one word for each pattern. Ask pairs to find the rest of the words with the stress pattern. The pair who finds all the correct words first is the winner.

Answers
Oo: cupboard, grammar, open, boring, kitchen, football, awful, perfect
oO: shampoo, return, asleep, exam, alright, surprise
Ooo: chemistry, excellent, calendar, exercise, customer, normally, visitor, horrible, Saturday, negative, telephone, various, sensible, microwave, document, manager, accident
oOo: delicious, umbrella, directions, excited, instructions, expensive, important, another, potato, remember, tomorrow
ooO: engineer, magazine, afternoon, understand
oOoo: photography, activity, available, American
Oooo: supermarket, centimetre, helicopter
ooOo: information, punctuation, television
oooOo: examination, communication
ooOoo: electricity, international

2A -ed endings

▶ Photocopiable activity on p.267

You will need one sheet for each pair, cut in half.

Put students into pairs: A and B. Give each student their sheet. Tell students to look at the picture. Ask: *Is this a new or an old story? What is the man doing?* and *Which country is he from?* Teach the meaning of *shave* by first pointing to the man's beard in the picture and eliciting the English word for it. Then ask: *How do you say it in English when you remove the hair on your face?* and mime the act of shaving. Tell students to read quickly through the text and underline the past tense verb endings that are pronounced with an extra syllable /ɪd/. The first is done as an example. If necessary, elicit another example – one from a Student A and one from a Student B.

For Activity B, explain that Student A and Student B each have half the story. Students dictate their text to each other until they both have a complete text. Monitor and check they are pronouncing -ed endings correctly. Students then compare texts to check answers.

For C, put students into new pairs to talk about their ideas. Take feedback as a class. **Note:** In ancient Greece, a beard was an important sign that a boy was becoming a man. If a man's beard was shaved off, people would laugh at him and that is why the student didn't want anyone to see him until his beard grew again.

Answer

A long time ago in ancient Greece, a student <u>needed</u> to pass an important test. He <u>hated</u> tests and he was lazy. He <u>visited</u> his friends, <u>chatted</u> with them and <u>invited</u> them to his parties. He went for long walks and <u>painted</u> pictures. He even <u>started</u> to go fishing with sailors. His parents worried about him. They <u>repeated</u> to him again and again that the test was important. His father <u>shouted</u> at him, but it always <u>ended</u> the same way: the student went fishing. Then his mother had an idea. She <u>contacted</u> the sailors and they <u>decided</u> to help the student. When he was asleep on their boat, the sailors shaved off his beard. The student woke up, went home and <u>studied</u> very hard. He didn't leave his house for a month and he passed the test.

2B was and were

▶ Photocopiable activity on p.268

You will need one sheet for each group, cut up into cards.

Put students into groups and give them a set of cards. Elicit some descriptions for each of the cards e.g. *There was some money. There were some dogs.* Drill the sentences and the weak forms of *was/were*. Remind students we usually use the weak forms of *was/were* (with the /ə/ sound) in connected speech.

Give students one minute to memorise the cards, then tell them to place the cards face down on the desk. Ask students to work together and try to remember what was on the cards. Students should write their answers.

Monitor and help as necessary. In feedback, ask each group to read their sentences. Correct any mistakes.

💡 VARIATIONS

1 Hand out the sheets. Give students two minutes to memorise the pictures. They then turn the sheet over and write down all the pictures they can remember using *there was/were*. The winner is the student who can remember the most pictures with the most correct sentences.

2 Hand out the cards. For stronger students, ask them to choose a card at random. Then ask them to describe the picture with a *there was/were* sentence with an adjective, prepositional phrase or an adverb, e.g. *There were some high mountains; There were a lot of people at a party.*

Suggested answers

There was some money.
There was a (round) window (in a wall).
There was a (beautiful) cottage.
There was a plane (flying in the sky).
There was a (birthday) party (with lots of people)./There were lots of people at a (birthday) party.
There was a (pretty/big) hat.
There was a couple./There were two people.
There were some (high) mountains.
There were some mushrooms (in a field).
There were some/different numbers.
There were some cards.
There were some/three (small) dogs.

3B Sound and spelling: /dʒ/ and /j/

▶ Photocopiable activity on p.269

You will need one sheet group of four students, cut up.

Put students into groups of four and hand out the cards. Customer A sits across a desk from Shop Assistant A, and Customer B sits across a desk from Shop Assistant B. Pre-teach any vocabulary items you think students won't know.

Explain that the customers must only buy the things on the shopping list with their sound. Tell As that their sound is /dʒ/ and Bs that their sound is /j/. Ask the customers to underline all the items with these sounds on their shopping lists and the shop assistants to find them on their price lists. Monitor and help as necessary.

Then students go shopping. (If you wish, ask students to look at pages 32 and 33 of the Student's Book and briefly revise useful language for shopping.) Demonstrate by asking one of the shop assistants to buy two kilos of cucumbers and a jumper. Ask him/her what the total price is (£21.20). Monitor and help as necessary whilst the students are shopping. Check they are pronouncing the target sounds correctly. Ask the customer and the shop assistant to check the total price together. Check answers with the class. In feedback, get the students to identify all the words with the /dʒ/ sound (Customer A's shopping list) and the /j/ sound (Customer B's shopping list). Drill all the words.

Answers

Customer A	Customer B
2 cabba**g**es £1.00	½ kilo of c**u**cumbers 30p
apple **j**uice £1.25	3 kilos of n**e**w potatoes £1.20
2 lar**g**e bars of chocolate £2.00	4 **y**ogurts £3.60
1 kilo of oran**g**es 70p	a tin of t**u**na £3.40
sausa**g**es £2.70	a school **u**niform £100
a **j**acket £90	The Times n**e**wspaper £1.50
blue **j**eans £40	a map of **E**urope £3.00
2 **j**umpers £40	a st**u**dent's guide to **u**niversity £9.00
Total = £177.65	a m**u**sic magazine £4.50
	Total = £126.50

3C Sentence stress

▶ Photocopiable activity on p.270

You will need one sheet for each student and one dice for each group of four.

Put students into groups of four and give them a dice and a sheet. Write this story frame on the board:

*It was a **A***

*and I was with my **B** in a **C***

*when a **D E**.*

*I was **F***

*and **G**.*

*It was a **H**.*

Explain that students are going to make a story using the story frame and the phrases on the sheet. Demonstrate with one group. Ask the first student to say the first sentence (*It was a …*) and then roll the dice. The student then completes the first sentence with the corresponding number and phrase in section A. For example, a number three on the dice = 3 *Monday afternoon*, so *It was a Monday afternoon*. The next student continues with *and I was with my …* , and then rolls the dice and completes the sentence with the corresponding number in section B.

Point out that only the words on the sheet are stressed, not the story frame. For example, *It was a **beautiful day** and I was with my **best friend**.* Ask the two students to repeat their sentences using the correct stress.

Groups then complete a story together. Monitor and help as necessary. Make sure they are stressing the correct words (the words on the sheet). In feedback, ask one or two groups to read out their story. Then groups repeat the activity. This can be repeated several times due to the many different options.

> 💡 **VARIATIONS**
>
> 1 Students complete one story together and turn their sheets over. The group work together to retell their story. They can use the story frame on the board, but they need to remember the phrases on the sheet.
>
> 2 Put students into pairs. They make their own story by writing their own phrases to complete the story frame.

4B Sound and spelling: /ɒ/ and /əʊ/

▶ Photocopiable activity on p.271

You will need one sheet for each student.

Pre-teach *cot, rod, soak* and *wok* and drill them. Ask what vowel sound is in each word (/ɒ/ = *cot, rod, wok*; /əʊ/ = *soak*). Tell the students that the words in the list are minimal pairs: they sound the same except for the vowel sound, then give students a few minutes to do Activity A in pairs and decide which word in each pair has the /ɒ/ sound.

Check the answers with the class and then draw students' attention to the grids below and explain you are going to play Battleships. Before they play, ask them to copy the words from the box in the two grids. Explain that they must write the /ɒ/ words in 1–6 and the /əʊ/ words in 7–12. Monitor and make sure they copy the words in alphabetical order. They must have the same order of words in both grids or the Battleships game won't work.

Check this before the next stage and drill the words. Explain how to play. Each student has a number of ships that they should plot on their first chart: one large (six squares), two big (four squares), two medium two squares) and four small (one square). Write this on the board. The students plot their ships on their charts. They mustn't overlap and one ship can't be right next to another one. The aim of the game is to 'hit' and sink all your partner's ships. Students play by taking turns to call out word pairs corresponding to the squares on the grids, e.g. *cot, soak*. If this square corresponds with a square on their partner's grid on which there is a ship or part of a ship, he or she calls out 'hit'. The first student plots this square on the second chart (which is a map of where their partner's ships are) and it is the other student's turn to play. Students continue until one them has successfully plotted/located and therefore 'sunk' all their partner's ships and wins the game.

4C Sentence stress

▶ Photocopiable activity on p.272

You will need one sheet for each student.

Write these sentences on the board and elicit the correct sentence stress (the content word and the negative auxiliary are stressed).

I did the <u>marathon</u>.

I <u>didn't</u> do the <u>marathon</u>.

Drill the two sentences. If necessary, elicit more examples from the quiz and drill the sentence stress.

Put students into pairs to complete the quiz. Student A is the first interviewer. Student A asks the first question and reads the four options to Student B. Student B chooses the best option. Student A should then repeat the option to Student B, and Student B also repeats it. This allows both students to get productive and receptive practice of sentence stress. At the end of the quiz, Student A tells Student B what the answers mean. Then students swap roles and Student B becomes the interviewer.

Monitor and help as necessary. Make sure students are stressing the content words and negative auxiliaries only. Take feedback as a class and drill examples of sentences with positive and negative auxiliaries. Ask students if they agree with what the answers mean.

> 💡 **EXTRA ACTIVITY**
>
> Have a class discussion based on some of the topics. For example, how important is healthy food? (question 2) or how important is sleep? (question 8).

5B Sound and spelling: /ʃ/

▶ Photocopiable activity on p.273

You will need one sheet for each pair, cut in two.

Put students into pairs and give the two different pictures to each pair. Write the words *chef* and *brush* on the board and model the /ʃ/ sound. Elicit the pronunciation of the words in the box, all of which contain the /ʃ/ sound, and drill them. Ask students to label their picture with the words in the box and practise saying the words. They can't look at each other's pictures.

Explain to students that their pictures are similar but there are differences. Explain that they need to talk about their pictures to find the differences. Tell them to use complete sentences. Monitor and help as necessary. Check answers with the class, eliciting complete sentences as above. Drill these sentences, paying attention to the /ʃ/ sound.

Answers
1 The chef is a man/woman.
2 The chef is cutting tomatoes/mushrooms.
3 Someone is washing the floor using a mop/brush.
4 There is fish/meat on the table.
5 There is salt/sugar on the table.
6 The boy is washing dishes/pots and pans.
7 The calendar has a plane in the sky/a ship in the ocean.
8 The customer is wearing shoes/sandals.
9 There is a cushion/no cushion on the chair.
10 The man is reading a book with a white/grey cover.

5C Sentence stress: vowel sounds

▶ Photocopiable activity on p.275

You will need one sheet for each student.

Put students into pairs and hand out the sheets. Tell students they are going to have a phone conversation. Demonstrate the activity with a stronger student. Start with *Hi, is that Lesley?* and let the student follow the arrows and choose an option to respond. Go through a few turns with stronger classes or complete the chart with weaker classes.

Pairs then work through the chart and complete the conversation. Monitor and help as necessary. Monitor how well students use the vowel sounds in *shall, would, could* and *should*. In feedback, drill the sentences with *shall, would, could* and *should*. Then put students into new pairs to complete another conversation. Monitor and correct students as necessary.

 EXTRA ACTIVITY

Students think of different suggestions for the conversation and write their own conversations using *shall, would, could* and *should*. Students read the conversations aloud to the class.

6A Sound and spelling: /uː/ and /ʊ/

▶ Photocopiable activity on p.275

You will need one sheet for each student.

Put students into pairs and hand out the sheets. Read the first exchange to the class and elicit which sounds the underlined words have (/uː/ = *news, you*; /ʊ/ = *good, could*). Drill the exchange. If necessary, read another exchange or ask a stronger student to say it and elicit the sounds. Students then read the exchanges in pairs and decide which sounds the other words in the exchanges have.

Answers

/uː/	/ʊ/
news, music, group, school, cool, do, you, June, soon, soup, spoon, moon, Tuesday, through, rude, move, lose, two	good, could, should, book, would, full, look, stood, foot, pushed, should, sugar

Next, tell the students they're going to play *Bingo*. Each student fills out their two cards with six words of each type, taken from the exchanges in A. Read out words from

the exchanges in A randomly. Students cross out the words on their grid as they hear them. The first student to cross out all the words, shouts *Bingo!* When they do, ask them to say the words and drill the pronunciation with the class.

Students play again in small groups with one student taking your role. Monitor and help as necessary, and note problematic words to drill with the class afterwards.

6C Main stress

▶ Photocopiable activity on p.276

You will need one set of cards for each group. Before the class, cut up the cards.

Put students into groups of four. Revise the concept of main stress by writing the first item on the board with the three different possible stress patterns. Ask students: *How does stressing different words in the sentence change the emphasis?* Ask students to match each variant of the sentence with the appropriate response.

Simon is at university in <u>Manchester</u>. (It's a great town.)

Simon is at <u>university</u> in Manchester. (He's doing economics.)

<u>Simon</u> is at university in Manchester. (That's Sue's brother.)

Divide the class into groups of three and give each student a card. (If there is a group of four, two students could share a card.) Make sure students don't look at each other's cards.

There are twelve rounds. In each round, one student reads the sentence on the Group Card, putting main stress on the underlined word. The student with the appropriate follow up reads their sentence. Demonstrate with the example above. Monitor and help when necessary. As feedback, drill all the sentences on the Group Card. Then get the students to turn over the worksheet, you read out a sentence and see if they can remember the answer or think of another appropriate response to match the sentence stress.

Answers
1C 2C 3A 4B 5A 6B 7C 8A 9B 10A 11C 12C

 VARIATION

You will need one sheet per group. Ask groups to choose the correct option for each number on the Group Card.

 EXTRA ACTIVITY

The students change the main stress in each sentence on the Group Card and write a new response for each.

For example, *The <u>keys</u> were on the table. = The keys for the car./The keys were on the <u>table</u>. = Near the computer.*

7B *to* + infinitive (weak form)

▶ Photocopiable activity on p.277

You will need one sheet for each student.

Tell students that the grid represents a block of flats and that each sentence is a description of a person living in one of the flats. Write the sentence below on the board and ask how *to* is pronounced (the weak form). Drill the sentence. *Tom is in the first flat and he is learning <u>to</u> play the guitar.* Tell students that Tom lives in Flat one and tell them to write *Tom* in the correct square/flat. Put students into groups of three or four. Ask them to take turns reading each sentence aloud to each other and underlining the weak forms of *to*. Monitor and help as necessary. Then ask the groups to read the sentences again and try to work out who lives in which flat. Which group can complete the grid first?

Don't stop the activity when the first group says they have finished (check briefly to see if they have the correct answers and tell them to continue if not) but give the other groups a few minutes more to try and complete their grids. Then check answers as a class.

Answers

21 Phil	22 Jemma	23 Maggie	24 Lara	25 Brian
16 Brenda	17 Mandy	18 Rita	19 Ben	20 David
11 Mike	12 Wayne	13 Emma	14 Jake	15 Sharon
6 Julia	7 Teresa	8 Oscar	9 James	10 Natasha
1 Tom	2 Carla	3 Simon	4 Steven	5 Maria

> **⚦ EXTRA ACTIVITY**
>
> Students work in groups and rearrange the people in the block of flats, so that the people have suitable neighbours. For example, ask students: *Which people have similar interests?* (Steven and Sharon both like watching TV.) Students then compare their ideas.

7C Tones for asking questions

▶ Photocopiable activity on p.278

You will need one set of cards for the class. If there are more than 20 students in the class, put the class into two large groups of ten and give each group a set of cards.

To play the game, each student has to take a card from the set and the rest of the class then asks yes/no questions to find out what the word on the card is. Demonstrate with the 'key' card. Elicit the tone we use when we don't know the answer (*a rising tone*) and the tone we use when we think we know the answer and are checking the answer only (*a falling tone*). Then elicit some yes/no questions for the card. For example,

Is it a person? (rise, we don't know) *No.*

Is it an animal? (rise, we don't know) *No.*

So, is it a thing? (fall, we think we know it's a thing) *Yes.*

Is it big? (rise, we don't know) *No.*

So, is it small? (fall, we know it's not big) *Yes.*

Drill the examples and elicit more examples, if necessary.

Students play the game. Tell students they have a maximum of 20 questions to guess the word. Monitor and help as necessary. Take feedback as a class. Ask some students to model the yes/no questions they asked. Correct and drill as necessary.

> **⚦ EXTRA ACTIVITY**
>
> Students write new words for the rest of the group to ask yes/no questions about. They should choose words from Unit 7.

8B Word stress

▶ Photocopiable activity on p.279

You will need one sheet for each pair or group of four students, cut up.

Write the word *expensive* on the board. Elicit that it has three syllables and that the second one is stressed. Divide the class into pairs or groups of four and give each pair or group a set of cards.

Explain the rules of *Snap*. The aim is to collect all the cards from the other player(s) by finding words with the same stress pattern. The players deal out the cards. They should have the same number. They hold their cards so they can't see the words. One player begins by putting a card on the table. The players then take it in turns to place a card face up, one on top of the other. As they do so, they say the word on the card. If the syllable stress is the same as the previous card, for example *expensive–decided*, the first person to shout *Snap!* takes all the cards on the table. If they are wrong, they miss a turn. The winner is the person who collects all the cards.

Monitor and help as necessary, and note problematic words to drill with the class afterwards.

> **⚦ VARIATIONS**
>
> 1 Hand out the sheet. Ask students to circle and read out the two words in each row which have the same stress pattern.
>
> **Answers**
>
> | seventeen | national | **gymnastics** | doctor | **athletics** |
> |---|---|---|---|---|
> | **weather** | asleep | newspaper | unhappy | **station** |
> | decide | **computer** | magazine | **beginning** | seventy |
> | arrive | **yoga** | beautiful | **surfing** | important |
> | **repeat** | building | elephant | **because** | banana |
> | **hotel** | sofa | **behind** | telephone | amazing |
> | eleven | **windsurfing** | stadium | **usually** | revise |
> | million | between | **Japanese** | remember | **afternoon** |
>
> 2 Put students into pairs. Ask students to take turns to read out all the words which have the same stress pattern. For example, *seventeen*, *magazine*, *Japanese*, *afternoon*. Students could then make a story using those words, *When I was seventeen I used to read a magazine about …*

8C Tones for continuing or finishing

▶ Photocopiable activity on p.280

You will need one sheet for each pair, cut in half. Put students into pairs and hand out the A and B sheets.

Demonstrate the activity by saying these phrases and asking students to complete them if you use a rising tone or say nothing if you use a falling tone.

I want an apple (rise) *and a banana.*
I want an apple. (fall)
I know Jack. (fall)
I know Jack (rise) *so I'm not surprised.*
She came home late (rise) *and her mum was angry.*
She came home late. (fall)

Then drill the phrases with a rise and fall tone.

If necessary, ask one pair to demonstrate using the first phrase on the sheet.

Then Student A starts the activity and Student B chooses the correct response. Monitor and help as necessary. For the second half of the activity, students swap roles.

Check answers with the class and drill the answers using the correct tone.

Answers
1 rise – but it was closed.
2 fall – 0
3 fall – 0
4 rise – but not very often.
5 rise – and cheese and milk.
6 fall – 0
7 rise – but it will be very expensive.
8 fall – 0
9 rise – and I saw a strange light in the sky.
10 rise – so I went to his flat.
11 fall – 0
12 rise – but things got better.
13 rise – so I told him everything.
14 fall – 0

> 💡 **EXTRA ACTIVITY**
>
> Repeat the activity, but ask students to change some of the rise and fall tones. This will test the receptive and productive skills of each student.

9A Word groups

 Photocopiable activity on p.281

You will need one sheet for each pair.

Put students into pairs. Say the first sentence to the class and ask: *What did you notice about the pronunciation?* (a pause between the two clauses, a rise at the end of the first *if* clause, a fall at the end of the second clause). Drill some examples from the sheet. Ask pairs to take turns reading sentences to each other. When the first student reads the sentence, his/her partner should assess if the pronunciation is correct or not. The first student can then correct his/her pronunciation if necessary.

Now play four in a row. Explain the rules. Each student chooses to be an 'X' or an 'O'. The first student chooses one of the sentences from the grid and reads it aloud. If he/she reads it with the correct pronunciation, he/she can mark the square with their symbol ('X' or 'O'). If not, the sentence/square is unmarked and can be used again. The second student then chooses a square and reads the sentence. He/She marks the square if he/she uses the correct pronunciation. The first student with four Xs or Os in a row (horizontally, vertically or diagonally) is the winner.

> 💡 **EXTRA ACTIVITY**
>
> Students repeat the game, but think of their own way of finishing each conditional sentence. For example, *If I become famous, I'll have lots of money.*

9C Main stress: contrastive

▶ Photocopiable activity on p.282

You will need one sheet for each pair, cut up into cards.

Put students into pairs and hand out the sets of cards. Students put the cards face down on the desk in two piles (one with sentences and one with pictures).

Tell students they are going to take turns reading sentences and then correcting the sentences. Demonstrate with a stronger pair. Ask one student to take a sentence card and read the first sentence (e.g. *The film starts at seven o'clock.*). Ask the other student to take a picture card and look at the first picture. The student then corrects the sentence using the information in the picture (*No, it starts at eight o'clock.*). Elicit that we put the main stress on the word that we are correcting, raise the pitch and have a falling tone. Drill the example.

Students then do the activity, and read and correct the sentences on their cards. Note that the cards must stay in the correct order so that the students pick up the correct picture card which goes with the set of sentences they are working on. Students swap roles after each card, so that each student gets practice in using contrastive stress.

Monitor and help as necessary. Make sure students use contrastive stress on the word they are correcting and raise the pitch and have a falling tone. Check answers with the class. Drill all the corrected sentences using contrastive stress.

Answers
1 No, the film starts at <u>eight</u> o'clock.
2 No, it's Gran's birthday on <u>Wednesday</u>.
3 No, the maths homework is on page <u>seventeen</u>.
4 No, they went on holiday to <u>London</u>.
5 No, a ticket costs <u>sixty</u> pounds.
6 No, it's <u>snowing</u> outside.
7 No, you go straight on and turn <u>right</u>.
8 No, Tom loves <u>pizza</u>.
9 No, they've got a <u>cat</u>.
10 No, Susan's got a new <u>motorbike</u>.
11 No, the first letter is <u>B</u>.
12 No, Carl can't find his <u>glasses</u>.
13 No, Kelly wants to buy a new <u>skirt</u>.
14 No, the <u>fridge</u> doesn't work.
15 No, they're travelling by <u>train</u>.
16 No, the pass mark is <u>sixty</u> per cent.
17 No, Alex is having a <u>bath</u>.
18 No, the shop is <u>closed</u>.

> 💡 **VARIATIONS**
>
> 1 Hand out one sheet to each pair. Students take turns to read through the sentences and say the correct response using contrastive stress.
>
> 2 Hand out the cards in the left column only. Students guess where the contrastive stress will be in the response. Check ideas with the class. Award one point for guessing the correct words and one point for using the correct contrastive stress.

10A Sentence stress: vowel sounds

▶ Photocopiable activity on p.283

You will need one sheet for each group.

Put the students into groups of three or four and give each group a sheet. Set the scene by explaining to the students that they are in their local museum near closing time and find an object labelled 'Time Machine' in one of the rooms. Nobody is watching so they decide to see if the 'Time Machine' works. It does! Tell the students to find card number 1 and underline all the examples of *would*.
Where would you like to go?
I would go to the past
I would travel to the future
I wouldn't go anywhere

Elicit the pronunciation of *would* - /ə/ in positives and questions and /ʊ/ in negatives – and drill the examples. To do the activity, the students must go through the cards, discuss the options, make decisions and continue their journey until they find one of the happy endings. Monitor and make sure that they take it in turns to read out the cards and pronounce would correctly. As feedback, get the students to underline all the examples of would on the worksheet and drill them.

 EXTRA ACTIVITY

Put students into new groups to repeat the activity. There are many different options and students will have more practice in using *would*.

10C Sentence stress

▶ Photocopiable activity on p.284

You will need one sheet for each group. You will also need a dice for each group and counters for each student.

Put students into groups of four and hand out the sheets. Ask groups to look at questions 1–4 on the board game. Elicit the sentence stress in these questions (1 *What did you have for breakfast?*, 2 *Can you sing?*, 3 *Do you read a lot?*, 4 *Are you interested in art?*). Remind students that the sentence stress usually goes on *wh-* words, nouns and main verbs. Remind students that functional words, like auxiliaries and pronouns, are usually unstressed. Drill questions 1–4.

Demonstrate the game with one group. Ask a student to roll the dice, move their counter forward to the relevant square and ask the person on their left the question. That person answers the question. Encourage students to give full answers. For example:
What did you have for breakfast?
I don't usually have breakfast, but today I had some coffee and toast.
If that person cannot answer the question, then they lose their turn. Play continues clockwise round the group.

Groups play the game. Monitor and help as necessary. In feedback, correct any mistakes. Ask students what interesting answers others gave.

 VARIATION

Students do not use a dice, but take turns to choose a question on the board that they would like to ask someone in the group.

11C1 Checking information

▶ Photocopiable activity on p.285

You will need one sheet for each group of four, cut up into four.

Put students into groups of four and hand out the maps. Tell students not to show them to each other.

Explain to students they are going to ask each other for directions, so that they can complete the gaps on their maps. Elicit useful language from page 112 of the Student's Book and write some of the phrases on the board. Elicit the sentence stress, e.g.
It's/Go straight ahead.
Go round the corner.
Turn left/right.
Take the first turning on the right.
It's the first on the right.
It's on the corner. Drill the phrases.

Elicit phrases for checking information and write these on the board, e.g.
The second one?
Next to what?
Sorry, can you repeat that? Drill the phrases using a rising tone.

Write all the places on the campus on the board (*art, chemistry, bank, economics, engineering, geography, history, languages, law, physics, sports hall,* and *student services*). Tell students they must give and listen to directions in order to label all the missing places on their own map. Student A starts and asks the group for directions to three places he/she doesn't know. Then Student B asks, and so on. Students give directions from the 'start'.

Monitor and help as necessary. Make sure students are using phrases for checking information with a rising tone. Take feedback as a class. Ask some groups to act out their conversations to the class. Correct any mistakes.

11C2 Sound and spelling: /ɔː/ and /ɜː/

▶ Photocopiable activity on p.286

Write the words *early* and *work* on the board and drill them with the class. Explain that both words contain the target sound /ɜː/. Give each student a sheet and explain that they need to get from *early* to *work* by following those words with the /ɜː/ sound. Demonstrate by saying, *After 'early' would the next word be 'Thursday' or 'East'?* (Thursday). The students can only move across or down. They could do this in pairs, taking it in turns to choose and pronounce the word with /ɜː/. Monitor and help as necessary. Check and drill answers with the class.

Answers

early, Thursday, dirty, were, purse, prefer, worse, hurt, turn, girl, nurse, learn, third, word, shirt, birthday, work

For Activity B, write the words *saw* and *four* on the board and drill them with the class. Explain that both words contain the second target sound /ɔː/. Put students into pairs and ask them to decide which word in each pair has the /ɔː/ sound. They should say the words out loud and make their choice. Ask them to compare answers with another pair before checking as a class.

Answers

four, course, board, wore, poor, more, afford, reward, adore, law, sure

201

In Activity C, the students circle words with the /ɜː/ sound. Check and drill answers with the class.

Answers
journey, church, curtain, first, reserve, third, thirteen, hurt, verb, burn

Finally, for Activity D, the students make their own maze using the /ɜː/ or /ɔː/ words from Activities A, B and C. They then exchange mazes with another student and go through theirs. Monitor and help as necessary.

12B Sentence stress: *that*

 Photocopiable activity on p.287

You will need one sheet for each group of four, cut up into cards.

Ask students: *What do you call a person who looks after animals in a zoo?* When a student says: *zookeeper*, say: *That's right.* Write this sentence on the board and underline *that*. Ask students: *Is this a difficult job?* and *What skills do you need?* When a student gives a good answer (e.g. *you need to like animals, you should know something about biology*), say: *I think that you're right.* Write this sentence on the board and underline *that*. Elicit the two different pronunciations of *that*: the first is a full form, a pronoun; the second is a weak form, after a reporting verb. Drill the sentences.

Put students into groups of four. Set the scene for students. Tell them a zoo needs a trainee zookeeper. There are two candidates, John White and Michelle Peters, and two interviewers. Students quickly decide which role they would prefer or you can assign students to roles. Give students time to read the information on their cards.

Demonstrate the interview by asking one of the interviewer students to ask a question from his/her card to John. The candidate uses the information on his/her card to answer the question whilst the second interviewer makes notes on what the candidate said. Then ask the two interviewers to confirm what the candidate said and write the sentence on the board, e.g. *John said that he works in a pet shop.* Elicit again the unstressed pronunciation of *that* and drill the sentence.

Groups then complete the interviews. The first interviewer asks John questions whilst the second interviewer makes notes on what John said. Then the second interviewer asks Michelle questions whilst the first interviewer makes notes on what Michelle said. Monitor and help as necessary.

Then ask the interviewers to work together and write sentences saying what the candidates said. The candidates listen and correct any mistakes. For example, *I didn't say that. I said that* ... If necessary, again elicit the pronunciation of *that* (first is stressed; second is unstressed).

Then ask the interviewers to choose the better candidate and explain why using reported speech. For example, *John is better because he said that he's sociable and he told us he has some qualifications.*

Take feedback as a class. Ask the class to report what each candidate said. Write the sentences on the board and drill them. Ask why the interviewers choose which candidate.

💡 **EXTRA ACTIVITY**
Students write information for new candidates. Then the interviews are repeated with the two new candidates and the interviewers again choose the better candidate.

12C Main stress: contrastive

 Photocopiable activity on p.288

You will need one sheet for each pair, cut in half.

Put students into pairs and hand out the sheets. Tell students you are going to say some false sentences and ask them to correct you, e.g. *We're having a French lesson. No, we're having an English lesson. It's nine o' clock. No, it's ten o'clock.*

Make sure students use contrastive stress on the word they are correcting and raise the pitch and have a falling tone. Drill the corrected sentences.

Ask students to read the sentences on their sheet to their partner and to correct each other when the information is false. Monitor and help as necessary. Check answers with the class. Drill all the answers using contrastive stress.

💡 **EXTRA ACTIVITY**
Put students into pairs. Students write five more sentences about general knowledge topics with three options (two false and one correct). Pairs then test each other and use contrastive stress when correcting.

Board game

Vocabulary 6A Verbs with dependent prepositions (Teacher's Notes on page 187).

BINGO

How many/much … ?	Did … ?
Where … ?	When … ?
Who … ?	What … ?
Do … ?	What kind of … ?
How often … ?	Which … ?

home	books/ reading	food and drink	sports	family and friends
hobbies	education	music	languages	work/studies
films	the weekend	shopping	relationships	travel

Find someone who ...

Name

1	is living somewhere different from usual at the moment.	_____
2	is spending time with a new person these days.	_____
3	goes to the supermarket more than three times a week.	_____
4	isn't going out much at the moment.	_____
5	never drives to work.	_____
6	generally makes plans by text or instant message.	_____
7	really enjoys talking on the phone.	_____
8	sometimes writes a blog.	_____
9	mainly uses public transport in his/her home town.	_____
10	hardly ever buys clothes online.	_____
11	doesn't send emails very often.	_____
12	is learning something difficult at the moment.	_____
13	rarely looks at news websites.	_____
14	isn't seeing his/her family very often at the moment.	_____
15	likes meeting new people. .	_____

- A person that made you smile yesterday.

- A person you met last month.

- A place you went to in good weather when you were a child.

- A place you went on holiday last year.

- A subject you were good at when you were at school.

- A subject you didn't like at school.

- A book you read and enjoyed in your teens.

- The last song or album you bought.

- Something sad you saw on TV.

- A person in the news yesterday.

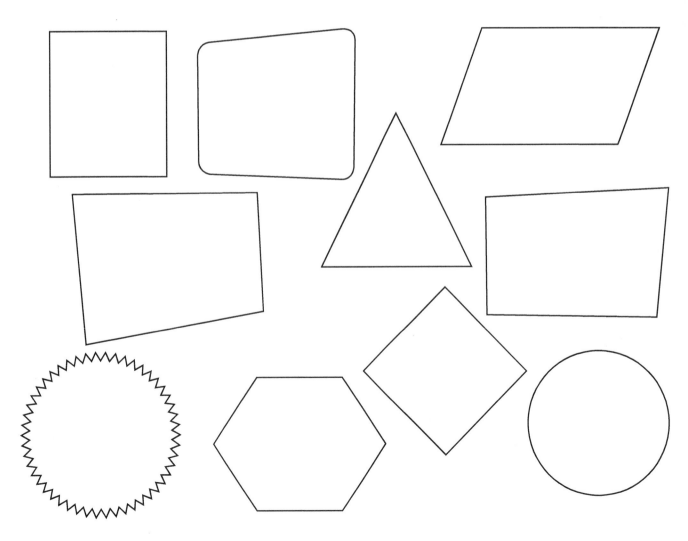

2B Grammar
Past continuous

START

I was driving to work	when I heard a strange noise	it was coming from the engine of my car	my mobile phone was ringing
when I saw a man by the side of the road	when my car broke down	and he wasn't moving	I stopped my car and got out
he was holding a radio and dancing	he was wearing a bright yellow jumper	smoke was coming out of the back of the car	a bicycle was lying in the grass
I was watching him dance when	I didn't know what to do	it didn't look broken	it looked very expensive
he shouted to me	then I saw a man walking towards me	I walked towards the man and shouted	the sun was shining so
What are you looking at?	Hey! Are you OK?	then I noticed he was breathing	I wanted to see if he was hurt, so
the man was smiling and holding out his hands	I didn't know what to say, so I smiled	I was looking into his face	he wasn't wearing any shoes
he looked very happy to see me	I was putting out my hand, to shake his,	and said 'Hello my friend!'	when he sat up and said
I was getting back into my car	when he suddenly hugged me	I was very surprised and asked	Who are you?

FINISH

3A Grammar
Present perfect or past simple

Travel			
visit New Zealand _____	travel abroad for more than three months _____	stay on a river boat _____	sleep overnight on a beach _____
swim to an island _____	spend a night in a jungle _____	walk in the desert _____	drive a car abroad _____

Food and drink			
drink goat's milk _____	eat raw meat _____	cook a meal in a tent _____	taste Marmite or Vegemite _____
catch a fish and eat it _____	make a meal for ten or more people _____	have a meal in a famous restaurant _____	grow fruit or vegetables to eat _____

Sport			
do a watersport _____	ski down a mountain _____	run a marathon _____	play cricket _____
drive a sports car _____	do a bungee jump or sky-dive _____	go mountain biking _____	jump on a trampoline _____

Celebrity and fame			
see yourself on TV _____	read about yourself in a newspaper _____	sing or play music for an audience _____	phone a radio show or write to a newspaper _____
wait somewhere to meet a celebrity _____	take a photo of yourself with a celebrity _____	speak in front of more than 100 people _____	post a blog _____

3B Grammar
Present perfect with *just*, *already* and *yet*

Can I borrow your car this evening?	Did you go to that new café?	**1** He hasn't called her yet. **2** I haven't found a job yet.
Shall we make something for dinner?	Let's go for a walk.	**3** The film's just started. **4** No, I've just taken it to the garage.
Let's celebrate tonight!	You're late.	**5** I haven't finished my homework yet. **6** No, I haven't started cooking yet.
Franco and Maria are planning their wedding.	He's very sad today.	**7** The manager hasn't got here yet. **8** He's already finished writing the report.
I really want a new car.	You're early.	**9** No, I've already cooked it. **10** No, I haven't been there yet.
He's very quick.	We haven't got any money.	**11** She's already bought her dress. **12** All my friends have already got one.
Are we going to eat soon?	She's waiting for a phone call.	**13** It's just stopped raining. **14** His cat has just died.
I can't come out tonight.	You don't need to email the bank.	**15** I've just passed my final exam! **16** I've just done it.

4A Grammar
Present continuous and *going to*

Student A		
I'm going to bed early tonight.	*I'm getting the bus this morning.*	**I'm cooking a special meal tonight.**

Student B		
I'm going to study all day.	I'm going on holiday tomorrow.	*I'm going to see the dentist.*

Student C		
I'm going to go running.	**I'm painting the living room later.**	*I'm having a job interview tomorrow.*

Student D		
I'm visiting someone in hospital this morning.	*I'm starting a new job today.*	I'm taking an exam this afternoon.

1   Oh no! I've missed the bus and it's raining.

2   I can't find my mobile. I know it's here somewhere.

3   I forgot to do my homework. I have to hand it in today.

4   It's Laura and Joe's wedding next week and we haven't bought them anything yet.

5   I passed the end-of-year exam.

6   These suitcases are too heavy. I can't move them.

7   I'm going to move to Australia!

8   I've forgotten my wallet.

9   I'm really frightened of spiders and there's a huge one in the bath!

10 This exercise is really difficult.

11 My babysitter has just cancelled and I need to go out this evening.

12 I've got an awful headache.

13 I'm really bored and there's nothing on TV.

14 It's a lovely day outside.

15 I've got the whole weekend free. What do you want to do?

16 There's no food in the fridge.

17 We have to get there for 8 am tomorrow.

18 It's very cold in this room.

19 There's a horrible smell in the kitchen.

20 We're going on holiday next month. The cats will be alone in the house.

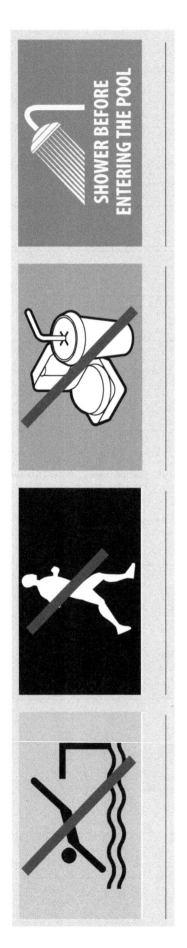

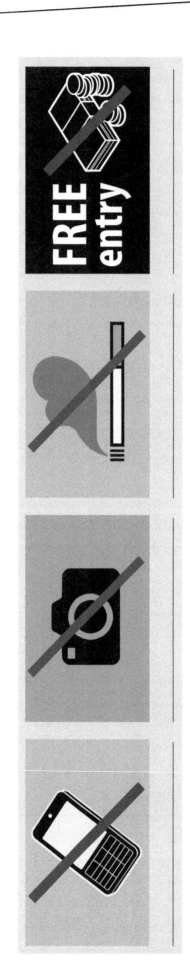

5B Grammar
will and *might* for predictions

People	won't	might not	might	will
make some new friends in the summer				
speak to your mother today				
visit somebody in a foreign country next year				
see a teacher in the street this weekend				
have more than six grandchildren				
say 'I love you' to somebody later today				

Travel	won't	might not	might	will
get a free flight abroad this year				
work abroad in the next five years				
visit every continent of the world in your lifetime				
ever climb mountains in the Himalayas				
go on a two-week holiday next summer				
see a lot of wild animals on your next holiday				

Things	won't	might not	might	will
buy a house in the next five years				
get a new phone this year				
lose something this week				
break something this week				
borrow something from a friend this weekend				
tidy your home tonight				

① My brother has an important job and tells everybody how much money he earns. My parents are very proud of him. I don't have a job and I think they are disappointed in me.

② My parents want me to work in the family business, but I want to go to university.

③ I'd like to have more friends, but I don't know how to meet any new people.

④ I often lend money to my friend and she now owes me over €300. She's got a bank loan and bought a new car. She hasn't paid me back.

⑤ Every time I meet my friend, he/she talks about his/her problems and asks for advice. He/She never asks me about my life.

⑥ My tooth hurts and I can't eat or sleep. I'm afraid of going to the dentist.

⑦ My friend is getting married in another country. I want to go, but the flight and hotel are very expensive.

⑧ My friend and I like the same music. I always download the music and pay for it, then he/she copies it. He/She never buys his/her own music.

⑨ I can't cook very well, but I'd like to learn before I go to university. I've tried learning from cook books, but they're boring.

⑩ I love buying lots of books because I like reading. My apartment is very small and I don't have any more space – and books cost a lot of money.

⑪ I want to celebrate finishing university. I'd like to have a party at my apartment, but I'm worried that my neighbours will complain.

⑫ My friend is visiting from America. He/She has asked to stay with me for three weeks. I would like him/her to stay for one week.

⑬ I'm not very fit and I'd like to get in shape. Exercise classes are too expensive and I'd prefer to be outside.

⑭ My friend is always late. Yesterday, I waited for one hour in a café for him/her. It's very annoying. He/She doesn't think it's a problem.

6B Grammar
Uses of *to* + infinitive

Sentences

1 At work, it's important to …

2 To be good at a sport, you need to …

3 When you move to a new city, you need to …

4 At university, it is easy to …

5 Before you visit a new country, you should try to …

6 When you are learning a new skill, you shouldn't expect to …

7 If you are looking for a new job, it is a good idea to …

8 When you go on holiday, don't forget to …

9 People in my town are usually happy to …

10 When starting a new course/job, most people want to …

Your sentence endings

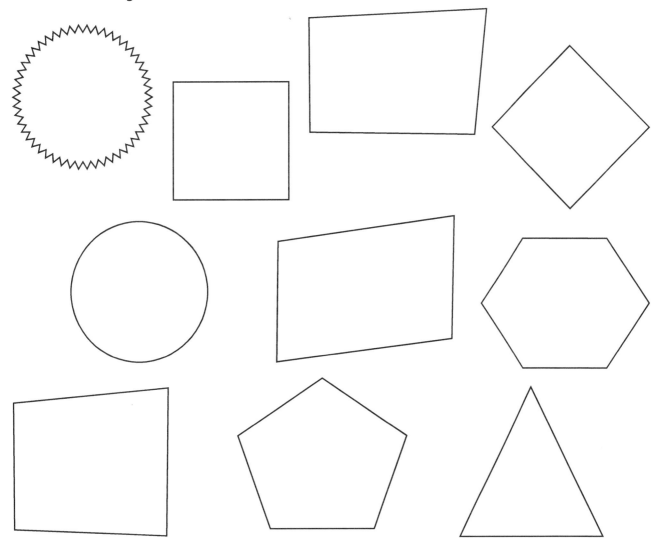

7A Grammar
Comparatives and superlatives

1 ANIMALS

friendly good pet dangerous cute beautiful interesting

Comparative / (not) as … as:

_____

Superlative:

_____

2 FAMOUS PEOPLE

interesting funny attractive clever annoying

Comparative / (not) as … as:

_____

Superlative:

_____

3 FOOD AND DRINK

delicious (un)healthy rich expensive boring

Comparative / (not) as … as:

_____

Superlative:

_____

4 HISTORY / ART

important exciting embarrassing successful

Comparative / (not) as … as:

_____

Superlative:

_____

5 SCIENCE AND TECHNOLOGY

useful frightening unhealthy fast expensive

Comparative / (not) as … as:

_____

Superlative:

_____

6 SPORT

relaxing fun exciting easy tiring

Comparative / (not) as … as:

_____

Superlative:

_____

7 ENTERTAINMENT (FILMS / TV / MUSIC)

funny interesting boring exciting sad

Comparative / (not) as … as:

_____

Superlative:

_____

8 BOOKS AND READING

funny interesting boring exciting sad

Comparative / (not) as … as:

_____

Superlative:

_____

9 EDUCATION

useful boring interesting difficult easy

Comparative / (not) as … as:

_____

Superlative:

_____

10 COUNTRIES AND TRAVEL

beautiful friendly good food expensive

Comparative / (not) as … as:

_____

Superlative:

_____

7B Grammar
used to / didn't used to

Student A: Luke – Ten years ago

Student B: Luke – Today

Grammar
The passive: present and past simple

① More wild animals _____ (*keep*) in American homes than in American zoos. It's estimated that there are at least ▮▮▮▮▮ tigers in private homes.

② **A man's son, granddaughter and great-grandson _____ (*be born*) on the same day when he was aged ▮▮▮▮▮. His wife, daughter and granddaughter gave birth at the same time.**

③ A man who was ill with cancer _____ (*tell*) he had six months to live. Ten years later, he went back to his doctors to say he was still alive – but all the doctors were dead. He died aged ▮▮▮▮▮.

④ The life of a woman who ordered pizza every day _____ (*save*) by a delivery man. The delivery man noticed that the woman hadn't placed an order for ▮▮▮▮▮ days.

⑤ **Only $ ▮▮▮▮▮ worth of tickets _____ (*sell*) in 1997 for a film called *Trojan War*. The film cost $15 million to make.**

⑥ ▮▮▮▮▮ burgers _____ (*serve*) in a famous international fast food restaurant every second.

⑦ An old box that contained $ ▮▮▮▮▮ million in gold coins _____ (*discover*) by a couple walking near their home in Sierra Nevada.

⑧ **If a piece of paper _____ (*fold*) in half ▮▮▮▮▮ times, its thickness would be three-quarters the distance from the Earth to the Sun (*71 million miles*).**

⑨ A record number of ▮▮▮▮▮ goals _____ (*score*) in one football match in 2002 in Madagascar, when the team AS Adema beat their rivals Stade Olympique de L'Emyrne.

8B Grammar
Present perfect with *for* and *since*

be married   cook for yourself   do regular exercise   drink coffee   drive to work/college

have your driving licence   have your mobile phone   live in your house   not go on holiday

not buy/eat a particular type of food   not see my brother/sister   not take the bus or train

own a cat   study at this language school   study a language (not English)   work in your current job

1 _____

2 _____

3 _____

4 _____

5 _____

6 _____

7 _____

8 _____

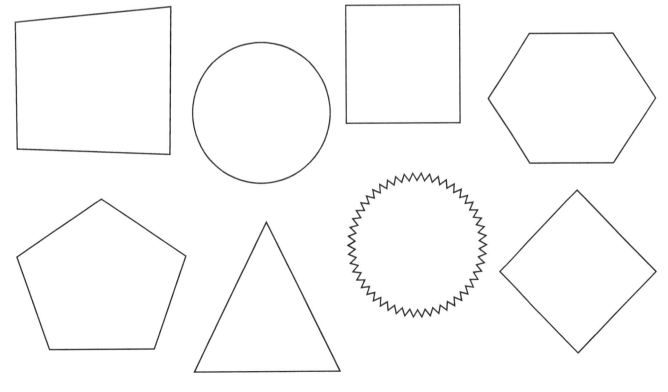

9A Grammar
First conditional

If I study hard,	I'll pass my exams.
If she doesn't get a good mark,	I'll be lonely.
If you don't take an umbrella,	he's going to buy a car.
If we stay up until the end of the film,	you'll be tired at work tomorrow.
If I go to Paris,	she won't be very happy.
If my friends go on holiday without me,	I might visit the Eiffel Tower.
If the company does well,	everyone will get a pay rise.
If the baby is a girl,	I won't get a seat.
If he passes his driving test,	you might get wet.
If the tickets are still available,	she'll come to visit us.
If she has enough time,	I'll get one for you.
If I don't get to the concert early,	they're going to call her 'Ruby'.

9B Grammar
Verb patterns

1. What's something you always avoid doing?

2. What's something you often forget to do?

3. What's something important you decided to do last year?

4. What's something you stopped doing when you left junior school?

5. What's something you hope to do in the future?

6. What's something you're expecting to do next year?

7. What's something you would like to do at the weekend?

8. What's something you don't mind doing, but would prefer not to do?

9. What's something you hate doing?

10. What's something you finished doing recently?

11. What's something you promised to do but didn't do?

12. What's something you need to do today?

13. What's something you worry about doing?

14. What's something you enjoy doing in the evenings?

15. What's something you're learning to do?

10A Grammar
Second conditional

	What would you do?	Name
If I won a holiday for four in the Caribbean,		
If I saw my favourite celebrity in the supermarket,		
If I saw somebody stealing my bicycle,		
If I broke a window with a football,		
If I found a large spider in the bathroom,		
If I missed the last train home,		
If I failed an important exam,		
If I didn't have enough money to get home,		
If I needed a lot of money to start a business,		
If I wanted to give my best friend a nice surprise,		
If I saw somebody cheating during an exam,		
If I thought a friend was lying to me,		
If I found out somebody was organising a surprise party for me,		
If I arrived late for a job interview,		
If I spilt a cup of coffee on my work computer,		

① I can't meet my friends later …

② *I didn't do my English homework …*

③ I haven't cooked dinner this evening …

④ **I'm not going to clean the house this weekend …**

⑤ *I don't go to the gym …*

⑥ I can't talk to you now …

⑦ **I haven't learnt to drive …**

⑧ **I don't cycle to work …**

⑨ *I didn't get good results at school …*

⑩ **I don't like going to the city centre …**

⑪ I didn't buy a new Smartphone …

⑫ *I was late for work …*

⑬ **I'm not good at sport …**

⑭ I couldn't phone you last night …

⑮ *I can't come to your party …*

11A Grammar
Defining relative clauses

Student A

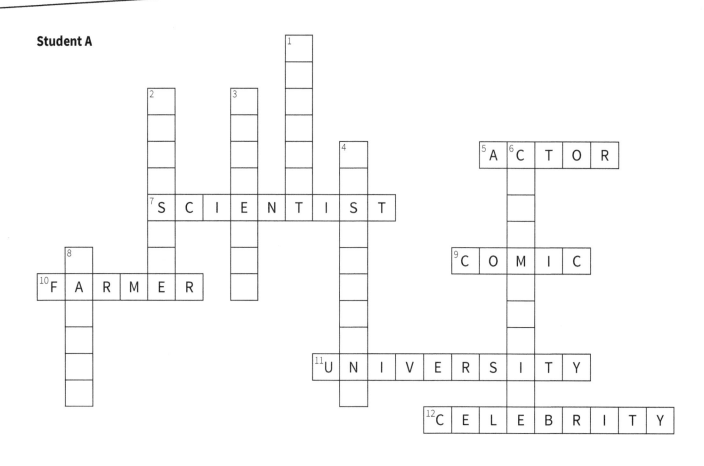

Student B

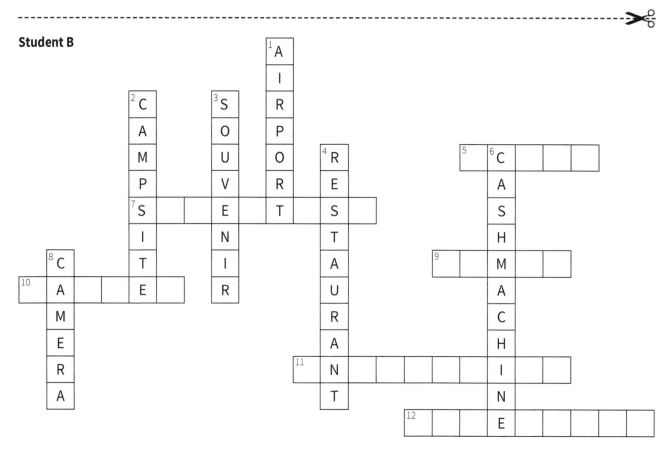

The film *127 hours* is based on a true story.

He hopes that the girls he met while he was travelling to the park will hear him if he shouts, but he soon realises that nobody can hear him.

Today Aron still goes climbing, but he always tells someone where he is going.

He knows the water won't last a long time. He will die if he can't escape from the canyon.

It's the story of a young man who loves adventure, danger and excitement.

The young man, whose name is Aron Ralston, decides to go climbing by himself in Canyonlands National Park in the USA.

He uses the knife to cut his arm free and climbs out of the canyon.

The rock lands on Aron's arm. His arm is stuck. He can't move.

He tries to push the rock away, but it's too heavy.

Aron has a small bottle of water, no food and a small knife.

By chance a pair of walkers is passing close by and they help him reach a hospital.

He has to make a very difficult decision, his arm or his life.

Aron has spent 127 hours stuck in the canyon. He is weak. His arm is bleeding.

He doesn't tell anyone where he is going. While he is climbing in a canyon, a large rock falls down.

12A Grammar
Past perfect

1 I tried to switch on the lights, but nothing happened.

FACT: _____

FICTION: _____

2 I walked into the office and saw that a stranger was sitting at my desk.

FACT: _____

FICTION: _____

3 Her hands and face were covered in dirt, but she was smiling.

FACT: _____

FICTION: _____

4 I waited for my friends to arrive for the party, but nobody came.

FACT: _____

FICTION: _____

5 I looked up at the sky and saw my name written in the clouds.

FACT: _____

FICTION: _____

6 I opened the envelope and inside there was a cheque for £10,000.

FACT: _____

FICTION: _____

7 It was 5 pm on Saturday, but the streets were completely empty.

FACT: _____

FICTION: _____

8 The waiter smiled and told me that there was nothing to pay.

FACT: _____

FICTION: _____

9 The crowd were all shouting my name.

FACT: _____

FICTION: _____

10 I arrived home and tried to unlock the door, but my key didn't seem to fit the lock.

FACT: _____

FICTION: _____

12B Grammar
Reported speech

Student A

1 I like watching TV online.
2 I don't want to go to the park on Saturday.
3 I can speak three languages.
4 I saw your brother yesterday.

Sentences from Student C

1 _____
2 _____
3 _____
4 _____

Student B

1 I'll see you later.
2 I have been to Mexico three times.
3 I'm trying to learn a new language.
4 I can't swim very well.

Sentences from Student A

1 _____
2 _____
3 _____
4 _____

Student C

1 I talked to my manager last week.
2 I'm sure you'll pass your exams.
3 I can play the piano very well.
4 I haven't finished washing up.

Sentences from Student B

1 _____
2 _____
3 _____
4 _____

1A Vocabulary
Common adjectives

A Look at the adjectives in the Vocabulary Focus on page 133. Close your book and quickly make a list of the adjectives. Compare your lists with a partner. Who can remember the most adjectives?

B Work in two groups: A and B. You are going to write a report for tourists about a town you visited. Group A: You visited Lakeville. Group B: You visited Greenwood. Complete the table with sentences about the places in the town you visited, using the adjectives in the box.

e.g. *The food at Bicco's restaurant / Valentino's café is delicious / awful / alright.*

horrible	rude	gorgeous	ugly	perfect	awful	boring
alright	strange	amazing	silly	serious	delicious	lovely

LAKEVILLE	GREENWOOD
BICCO'S RESTAURANT food service	**VALENTINO'S CAFÉ** food service
PANORAMA HOTEL the hotel the manager	**CARLTON HOTEL** the rooms the receptionists
LAKESIDE SHOPPING MALL the prices things to buy	**GREENWOOD INDOOR MARKET** the prices things to buy
HISTORY MUSEUM the building things to see	**ART GALLERY** the building things to see
WATER PARK the prices things to do	**ADVENTURE PARK** the prices things to do

C Work in pairs: Student A and Student B. Talk about the towns you visited. Which place do you prefer? Why?

1B Vocabulary
Adverbs

A Is the meaning in a and b the same or different? Write S (same) or D (different).

1. a We **hardly** ever go out on Sundays.　　b We **never** go out on Sundays.
2. a I'm **really** into classical music.　　b I don't like classical music **very much**.
3. a Dad **rarely** comes to see us.　　b Dad **often** comes to see us.
4. a I **don't usually** wear jeans to work.　　b I **don't normally** wear jeans to work.
5. a The visitors are **mainly** tourists.　　b **Most of** the visitors are tourists.
6. a The town is **fairly** busy today.　　b The town is **particularly** busy today.
7. a It's **pretty easy** to understand.　　b It's **not difficult** to understand.
8. a It's **generally** cold at the moment.　　b It's **especially** cold at the moment.

B Complete the questionnaire for you.

Topic	You	People who like or do the same things as you
Sport	I particularly like _____	
Music	I'm really into _____	
Food	I absolutely love _____	
Free time	In the evenings or at weekends, I normally _____	
Holidays	I hardly ever _____	
Friends	We generally _____ We don't generally _____	
Studying	I think studying English is pretty _____	
Home	I invite people to my home, especially _____	

C Compare your answers with other students. Write the names of the students who like or who do the same things as you. How many students are similar to you?

2A Vocabulary
Tourism

A <u>Underline</u> the items in the box that you or your family have at your home. Which items are yours? Which items belong to someone else? Compare your answers in groups.

e.g. We've got two backpacks. My father's got a large backpack and I've got a smaller one.

backpack	sunglasses	map of your country	suitcase	passport
guidebook for your town		suntan lotion	foreign currency	souvenirs from another country

B Complete the phrases below with the words in the box. Use each verb once.

decide	check in	pack	exchange	get	buy	book	unpack	do

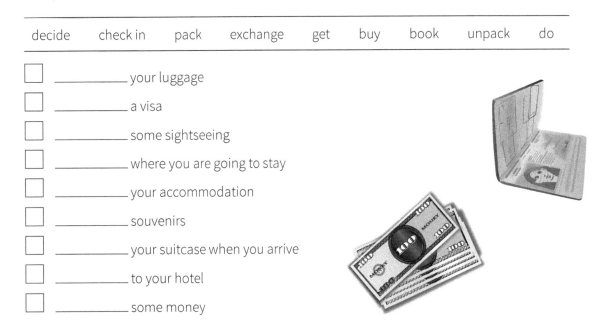

- ☐ _____ your luggage
- ☐ _____ a visa
- ☐ _____ some sightseeing
- ☐ _____ where you are going to stay
- ☐ _____ your accommodation
- ☐ _____ souvenirs
- ☐ _____ your suitcase when you arrive
- ☐ _____ to your hotel
- ☐ _____ some money

C Work in pairs. You are planning a holiday. Put the activities in B in the order that you do them.

D Find a new partner. Compare your answers in C. Are they the same?

2B Vocabulary
Travel collocations

A Complete the table with the words and phrases in the box. Then compare in groups.

break down	land	crash	set off	hitchhike	get lost	take off

break down   land   crash   set off   hitchhike   get lost   take off
long delay   a strike   turbulence   a traffic jam   a long queue   board
give somebody a lift   miss   something wrong with the engine

Cars	Planes

B Work in pairs. Complete the sentence with eight reasons for being late. Use the words and phrases from A.

e.g. *I'm sorry I'm late, but the plane took off an hour late.*

1 _____

2 _____

3 _____

4 _____

5 _____

6 _____

7 _____

8 _____

C Find a new partner. Take it in turns to read your reasons for being late. You cannot repeat the same reason.

3A Vocabulary
make, do, give collocations

A Find nine phrases with *make, do* and *give* in the wordsquare, e.g. *do well at something*. The phrases can run in any direction.

do	someone	smile	give	someone	a	friend
well	make	hug	someone	a	make	give
at	something	a	for	tip	away	someone
make	give	someone	nice	give	something	directions
a	joke	do	something	work	volunteer	do

B Work in pairs. Complete 1–6 with phrases in the table in A in the correct forms. Then complete 7–12 with your own ideas.

1 Everyone was very serious, so I _____ .

2 The waiter was excellent, so I _____ .

3 I had $200 but I didn't need it, so I _____ .

4 She was looking sad, so I _____ .

5 I didn't study for the maths test, so I _____ .

6 He asked me where the post office was, so I _____ .

7 I gave the little boy a hug because he _____ .

8 I gave my tennis racket away because _____ .

9 I made friends with Jack because he _____ .

10 Stephan does volunteer work because he _____ .

11 We talked about the past and it made me smile because _____ .

12 Let's do something nice for Monica because _____ .

C Work with a different partner. Talk about your sentences in B. Are they the same?

3B Vocabulary
Money

A Work in pairs. Complete the maths quiz.

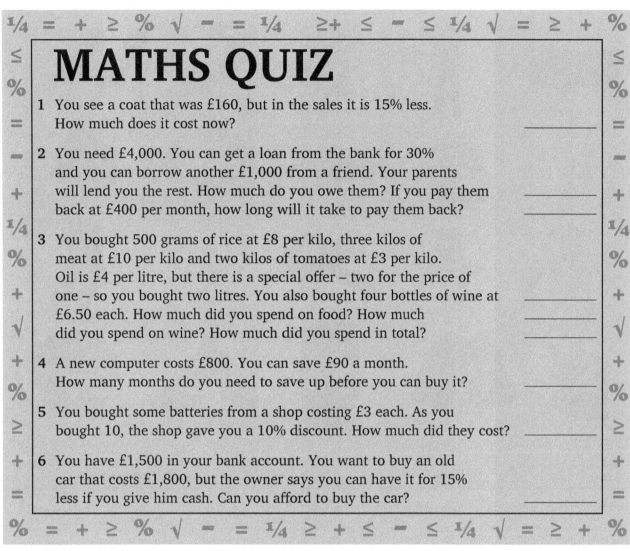

MATHS QUIZ

1 You see a coat that was £160, but in the sales it is 15% less. How much does it cost now? _____

2 You need £4,000. You can get a loan from the bank for 30% and you can borrow another £1,000 from a friend. Your parents will lend you the rest. How much do you owe them? If you pay them _____ back at £400 per month, how long will it take to pay them back? _____

3 You bought 500 grams of rice at £8 per kilo, three kilos of meat at £10 per kilo and two kilos of tomatoes at £3 per kilo. Oil is £4 per litre, but there is a special offer – two for the price of one – so you bought two litres. You also bought four bottles of wine at _____ £6.50 each. How much did you spend on food? How much _____ did you spend on wine? How much did you spend in total? _____

4 A new computer costs £800. You can save £90 a month. How many months do you need to save up before you can buy it? _____

5 You bought some batteries from a shop costing £3 each. As you bought 10, the shop gave you a 10% discount. How much did they cost? _____

6 You have £1,500 in your bank account. You want to buy an old car that costs £1,800, but the owner says you can have it for 15% less if you give him cash. Can you afford to buy the car? _____

B Work with a different partner. Underline all the words related to money in the text in A.

C Complete the adverts with words from the text in A.

Are you (1) _____ up for a holiday? Come to SunTours and see our special (2) _____ .

Open a bank (3) _____ today and we will (4) _____ you money today!

SHEILA'S SHOES

Pay by card or with (5) _____ . Our prices are already low, so please do not ask for a (6) _____ .

Need a bigger flat, but can't (7) _____ it? Come and visit us today – don't delay!

RDS BANK Need to (8) _____ some money? Get a (9) _____ from us. Pay it (10) _____ over ten years.

Come to **Scala Superstore** today and see our (11) _____ offers! You can (12) _____ £££££ on meat and fish this Christmas!

4A Vocabulary
Clothes and appearance

A Look at the pictures of different types of clothes and complete the table with the clothes words.

Feet	Body	Jewellery	Accessories
		bracelet	

B Work in pairs. Take turns to read your answers.

C Look at your class and make a list of all the items in A that you can see. Do not include more than one example of each item.

e.g. *Carla's silver bracelet, Pavel's blue and white scarf*

D Work in small groups. Take turns to describe items of clothing that people in your class are wearing. You can't say the name of the item. Other students have to say what it is. The first person to give the correct answer wins a point and it's their turn to describe something.

They are beautiful and made of gold. Ana's wearing them.

Ana's earrings?

Yes! Your turn

They're red and white and Marco is wearing them on his feet.

4B Vocabulary
Adjectives: places

Student A

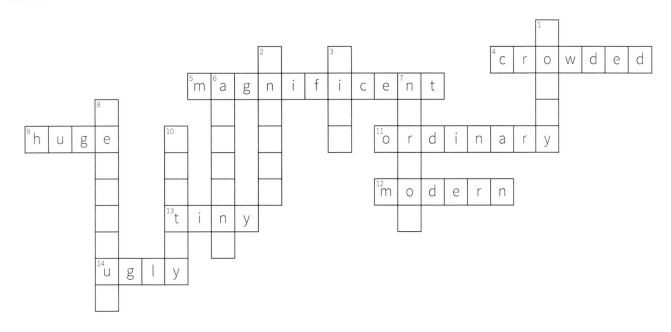

✂

Student B

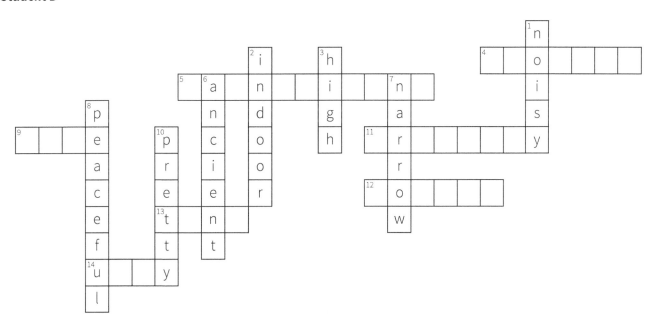

5A Vocabulary
Work

A Find twelve phrases related to jobs and work in the wordsquare, e.g. *earn a good salary*. The phrases are vertical ↓, horizontal →, or horizontal and vertical →↓.

earn	a good	long	hours	be
need	salary	**work**	**work**	self-
several	**work**	in	at	employed
years'	training	a team	weekends	**need**
deal	**deal**	with	serious	a university
with	day	**make**	problems	degree
people	every	important	**have**	environment
have	skills	decisions	a nice	working
a lot	of	**need**	good	qualifications

B Choose one of the jobs in the box below. Write four sentences to describe the job.

gardener   hairdresser   plumber   scientist   lawyer   accountant   electrician   banker

e.g. 1 *You need good qualifications.*
     2 *You earn a good salary.*
     3 *You work long hours.*
     4 *You make important decisions about people's health.*

1 _____

2 _____

3 _____

4 _____

C Read your sentences in small groups. Can the other students guess your job?

5B Vocabulary
Jobs

A Find and <u>underline</u> the names of eight jobs hidden in sentences 1–8.

e.g. Is *this a goo<u>d river</u> to catch fish in?*
Can you tell me how <u>far Merc</u>edes walked today?

1 Does Martina act or sing in the musical?

2 Is that the car Erica and Johan bought?

3 Is that the kind of music Ian plays?

4 This machine: how does it work, Eric?

5 They're going to build Erin a new house.

6 I've taken Andrew's watch back to the shop.

7 The best journal is the one you've got: 'Zoo Biology'.

8 Can you post Mandy's birthday card, please?

B Put the jobs in order from *very* to *not very*.

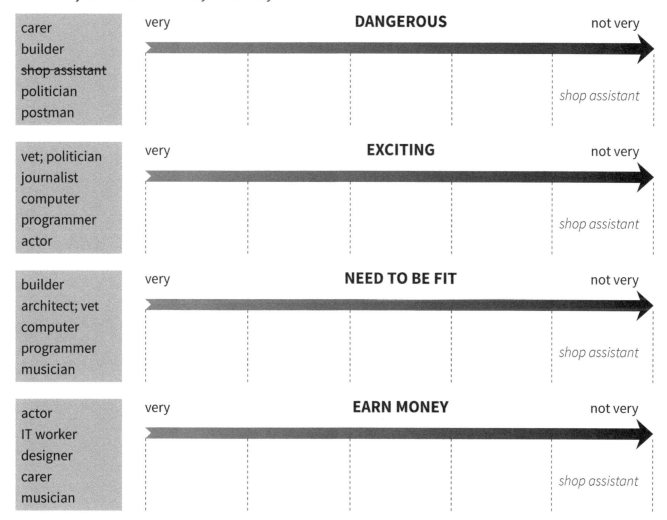

carer builder ~~shop assistant~~ politician postman	very **DANGEROUS** not very *shop assistant*
vet; politician journalist computer programmer actor	very **EXCITING** not very *shop assistant*
builder architect; vet computer programmer musician	very **NEED TO BE FIT** not very *shop assistant*
actor IT worker designer carer musician	very **EARN MONEY** not very *shop assistant*

C Work in groups and compare your answers.

A postman's work is quite dangerous – dogs sometimes attack and bite them.

Yes, but I think a builder's job is more dangerous.

D Add one more job to the lines in B. Ask your group if they agree with you.

6A Vocabulary
Verbs with dependent prepositions

STUDENT A: Complete these sentences with the correct dependent preposition or the missing verb. Then play the boardgame on page 203.

1 You have to deal _____ the problem quickly.

2 Don't look out of the window! _____ on your work, please.

3 I _____ some money from my father to buy a car.

4 Can you ask your teacher _____ the answers to the exercise?

5 Julia paid _____ the theatre tickets and I bought the meal afterwards.

6 I often think _____ my family when I'm not at home.

7 Do you ever _____ to music when you're studying?

8 I had to _____ for Jim outside the office. It was very cold.

9 They _____ at the party about two hours late.

10 Don't look _____ your watch every five minutes!

11 I like talking _____ Tino. He's very funny.

12 Can you _____ of three ways to stop smoking?

Student B's answers
1 to   2 pay   3 for   4 of   5 ask   6 looked   7 deal   8 talk   9 on   10 think   11 from   12 at

-- ✂

STUDENT B: Complete these sentences with the correct dependent preposition or the missing verb. Then play the boardgame on page 203.

1 Did you listen _____ that radio programme about dogs yesterday?

2 Did you _____ for the meal in cash or by debit card?

3 We waited _____ the bus for over two hours.

4 I must think _____ a way to earn more money.

5 I'm going to _____ my brother for a lift to the station.

6 Everybody _____ at me when I fell over in the street.

7 How do you _____ with difficult people in your job?

8 I want to _____ to my teacher about my progress.

9 It's difficult to concentrate _____ studying at the moment.

10 Do you _____ about your girlfriend when she isn't there?

11 We had to borrow $400 _____ my sister to buy the tickets.

12 What time did you arrive _____ the office this morning?

Student A's answers
1 with   2 Concentrate   3 borrowed   4 for   5 for   6 about   7 listen   8 wait   9 arrived   10 at   11 to   12 think

6B Vocabulary
-ed / -ing adjectives

A Find and correct eight spelling mistakes in the sentences. Two of the sentences have no mistakes in them .

1 *... and we were very sorprised because ...*

2 ... so they were disapointed when they...

3 **I was really amased and I ...**

4 *... the children were very exited and started ...*

5 ...it was confusing; I didn't understand ...

6 ***She was so chocked when she saw the bill ...***

7 If you are tired, go and ...

8 He told me he was very embarased and wanted ...

9 *... the man on the bus was very anoying ...*

10 *... was a frightning experience.*

B Complete the crossword using -ed and -ing adjectives in A.

Clues

1 This is how you feel if you work for 12 hours without stopping.

2 Some children keep ringing your doorbell and then running away. How does that feel?

3 This is how you feel when something really good is going to happen.

4 You are walking in the country and suddenly a snake falls out of a tree in front of you. You are _____ .

5 You meet a neighbour in the street and say, Hello, Joaquin! Later you remember his name is Jaime. You feel _____ .

6 This is how you feel after you spend a week on holiday, sitting in the sun.

7 This is how you feel in a city you don't know when all the roads look exactly the same and you can't understand any signs.

8 Three different people tell you about a new restaurant where the food is fantastic. You go for a meal and it's not very good. It's very _____ .

9 You hear that your favourite actor/actress has died suddenly. How do you feel?

10 You find out that you've won a new laptop. How do you feel?

C Work in pairs. Student A: Read five different clues (not in order) to your partner.
Student B: Don't look at your worksheet. Can you remember the adjectives? Then swap roles.

7A Vocabulary
Life events with *get*

A Complete the opinions using a word or phrase in the box. Use each word or phrase once.

on well	a job	to know	divorced	old	rich
in touch	together	ill	better	a place	paid

1 It's easy for young people to get _____ when they finish school.

2 Nurses get _____ well in my country.

3 50% of married couples get _____ .

4 It's easy to get _____ – you just have to work hard.

5 People often get _____ with you when they need your help.

6 People sometimes get _____ because they're stressed.

7 Anyone can get _____ at university if they work hard at school.

8 Most children get _____ with their parents.

9 Facebook is fun, but it's difficult to really get _____ people online.

10 My English is getting _____ every year.

11 When people get _____ , they forget things all the time.

12 When two people first get _____ , they think everything is perfect.

B Do you agree with these opinions? Why / Why not? Make notes for the questions.

C Work in small groups. Talk about your ideas.

A Find nine more words or phrases related to health and fitness in the wordsearch. The words are horizontal →, vertical ↓ or diagonal ↗.

S	O	H	O	I	S	Y	O	H	J	B	D	N
G	V	A	Y	V	N	M	I	A	R	S	O	P
Y	O	E	R	G	L	S	O	X	S	A	O	R
A	V	B	J	H	O	R	H	K	E	I	P	A
L	E	M	E	E	B	O	W	A	E	S	N	K
L	R	I	N	A	U	B	N	O	P	R	M	E
E	W	E	D	L	X	B	A	A	I	E	R	F
R	E	G	E	T	F	I	T	O	D	G	H	S
G	I	W	A	H	I	S	Y	H	E	I	N	U
Y	G	I	G	Y	S	O	G	V	S	Z	E	G
Z	H	P	U	T	O	N	W	E	I	G	H	T
O	T	L	I	G	I	V	E	U	P	F	O	P
H	L	O	S	E	W	E	I	G	H	T	O	A

B Complete the articles using words and phrases in A. Compare in pairs.

Lucy Atherton wrote to ask us for help. She tells us that she is very (1) _____ and she needs to (2) _____ about 20 kilos. 'I do try to keep (3) _____,' she says, 'but I am a busy, working mother with five children, so I don't have much time. I need to go (4) _____, but there are so many different ones. What's best for me?'

We say: Lucy, you need to start eating a (5) _____ diet: fresh fruit and vegetables, fish and absolutely no sugar. You could take your children to the park and play games with them every day. That will help you to get (6) _____. Good luck!

Q **Marius Tomasz** is a bus driver who is a regular (7) _____ – up to 40 cigarettes a day. He wrote to us after his doctor told him he had to (8) _____ smoking completely, but didn't give him any help. Marius also has (9) _____ to different kinds of food and drink, especially milk and eggs, which make him quite ill. 'I know I need to stop smoking,' says Marius, 'but it's really difficult!'

A **We say:** Marius, smoking is a big health problem – good for you for wanting to stop. Try to smoke one cigarette less every day for forty days. And be careful that you don't eat too much. When people stop smoking, they often (10) _____ weight. Good luck!

C Do you agree with the advice in B? Can you think of any other ideas? Talk about your ideas in groups.

8A Vocabulary
Art and music

A Work in pairs. Complete the crossword.

Across

2 A long written story, using characters who are not real.

5 *A Tale of Two Cities* was _____ by Charles Dickens.

8 The *Mona Lisa* was _____ by Leonardo da Vinci.

12 I love _____ music especially Mozart and Bach.

13 The study of designing buildings.

14 The building was _____ by Gaudi.

15 You take one of these with a camera.

Down

1 *CSI Miami* and *The Wire* are famous TV _____ .

3 This is an example.

4 The film *The Godfather* was _____ by Francis Ford Coppola.

6 The symphony was first _____ in Vienna in front of 2,000 people.

7 *Sunflowers* by Van Gogh is a famous _____ .

8 You see this at the theatre.

9 *Thriller* is a best-selling _____ by Michael Jackson.

10 The film is _____ on a true story.

11 A piece of writing in beautiful language, often with short lines.

B Find a new partner. Student A: read the Across clues for Student B to answer. Student B: read the Down clues for Student A to answer.

8B Vocabulary
Sports and activities

A Work in pairs. Look at the pictures. Complete the table with the sports and activities.

In/On the sea	On land	On snow/ice	Usually indoors

B Complete the sentences with words in A.

1 I often go _____ in the streets near my house.

2 We play _____ indoors in the winter, but sometimes on the beach in summer.

3 _____ helps me to stay calm.

4 I tried _____ , but I didn't like having my head under water.

5 _____ is a fast game and the friend I play with is very fit, so I usually lose.

6 The instructor told me not to look down when I was _____ .

7 You start with a team of six for _____ .

8 _____ first became a sport in the Winter Olympics in 1998. It was developed from _____ on the sea and _____ on land.

9 _____ is such a slow game: it can take about four hours to complete 18 holes.

10 I love watching _____ . You need to be very strong, but it looks so beautiful.

C Work in pairs. Take turns to read your sentences in B. Are they the same?

A Find and circle the words and phrases related to education in the wordsnake.

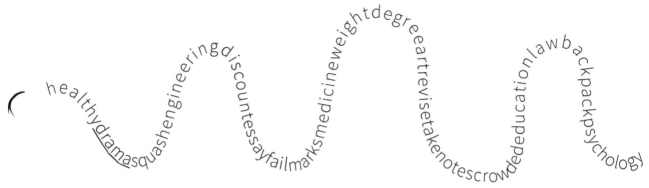

healthydramasquashengineeringdiscountessayfailmarksmedicineweightdegreeartrevisetakenotescrowdededucationlawbackpackpsychology

B Complete the sentences in the questionnaire with the correct words. Most of the answers (but not all) are in the wordsnake in A.

Find someone who ...   Name

1 has never **f**_____ an exam or a test.   _____

2 has written an **e**_____ this month.   _____

3 is **r**_____ for an exam at the moment.   _____

4 has got good **m**_____ in a test recently.   _____

5 takes **n**_____ in every English class.   _____

6 has **h**_____ in some work late to their teacher.   _____

7 would like to **g**_____ into university.   _____

8 has done a university **d**_____ .   _____

9 would like to study **b**_____ **m**anagement.   _____

10 has studied **L**_____ .   _____

11 knows someone who has studied **m**_____ .   _____

C Work in groups. Ask each other questions to complete the questionnaire in B.

> Kim, have you ever failed an exam or a test?

> Yes! I failed my driving test the first time, but I passed the second time.

> Roman, have you written ...

9B Vocabulary
Verbs followed by *to* + infinitive / verb + *-ing*

A Work in pairs. Correct the verbs that are in the wrong column in the table.

verb + *-ing*	*to* + infinitive
avoid	agree
forget	arrange
imagine	manage
like	miss
recommend	promise
refuse	regret

I ALWAYS AVOID	speaking to Tim. He's very boring.	**I ALWAYS FORGET**	to bring my dictionary to class.
I MANAGED	to carry my suitcase, but it was very heavy.	**I CAN'T IMAGINE**	living without a car. I use mine all the time.
I DON'T RECOMMEND	staying at that hotel. It's not very clean.	**I REALLY REGRET**	moving to London. I was so happy in Paris.
SHE AGREED	to lend me her car for the day.	**SHE DISLIKES**	being so far from her family.
WE ARRANGED	to meet at six o'clock, but they didn't come until seven.	**I MISS**	working with Mr Elliott. He was very funny.
HE REFUSED	to give me any money.	**SHE SEEMS**	to be very busy. I'll speak to her later.

10A Vocabulary
Multi-word verbs

A <u>Underline</u> the two possible ways to end each sentence. Which ending is NOT possible?

e.g. He plans to carry on <u>*working*</u> / *leaving* / <u>*studying*</u>.

1 *The marriage / The watch / The relationship* broke up last year.

2 I wanted to put off *my suit / the meeting / the party*.

3 Tom handed in *the bag / the discussion / his homework* yesterday.

4 I told him to pass on *the message / the information / the telephone*.

5 She asked me to look after *her hair / her cat / her handbag*.

6 I don't know why he turned down *the invitation / the job / the marriage*.

7 They want me to come round *tomorrow / when I'm free / at the restaurant*.

8 I feel like *something to eat / ill / an ice cream*.

B Read the questions and decide what the situation is. Then write a reply.

e.g. **A** (Why do you want to carry on?)   **B** (Because I need the qualifications.)

1 **A** (Why did you put it off?)   **B** (Because _____ .)

2 **A** (Why didn't you feel like going?)   **B** (Because _____ .)

3 **A** (Why did you hand it in late?)   **B** (Because _____ .)

4 **A** (Why do you want her to come round?)   **B** (Because _____ .)

5 **A** (Why can't you look after it?)   **B** (Because _____ .)

6 **A** (Why did you want to join in?)   **B** (Because _____ .)

7 **A** (Why did they break up?)   **B** (Because _____ .)

8 **A** (Why did you turn it down?)   **B** (Because _____ .)

C Work in pairs. Read your B replies in a different order. Can your partner guess the correct questions?

D Work in pairs. Practise the exchanges. Student A: ask the questions. Student B: give your replies. Then swap roles.

10B Vocabulary
Noun formation

A Find eight more verbs in the wordsearch. The verbs are horizontal →, vertical ↓ or diagonal ↗.

R	E	G	R	E	T	U	N	F
T	Q	F	O	X	C	I	O	D
E	U	E	Y	P	A	T	D	E
N	E	T	K	L	R	A	E	S
J	U	F	P	A	L	E	L	C
O	E	M	L	I	X	S	I	R
Y	O	K	E	N	N	E	V	I
C	E	D	E	C	I	D	E	B
C	H	O	O	S	E	B	R	E

B Complete the exchanges with nouns formed from the verbs in A.

1 **A** Did someone tell you how the system works?

   B Yes, one of the IT staff gave us an _____ .

2 **A** Do you know what you want to do next year?

   B Yes, I've made my _____ . I'm going to Rome.

3 **A** Did you tell them you were unhappy with the food?

   B I didn't, but Gaby made a _____ .

4 **A** Did you tell him what the suitcase looked like?

   B Yes, I gave him a _____ .

5 **A** Did you have to wait long?

   B Yes, we were in the _____ for ages.

6 **A** Will they deliver the fridge?

   B Yes, the _____ is next Friday.

7 **A** Can you decide the colour you want for your tablet?

   B Yes, they give you a wide _____ of colours.

8 **A** Do you like computer games?

   B No, I don't, but they give some people a lot of _____ .

C Work in pairs. Practise the exchanges in 2. Then swap roles.

11A Vocabulary
Compound nouns

OFFICE	SCIENCE	FICTION	CASH	MACHINE	STREET
LIGHTS	TELEVISION	PROGRAMME	ROAD	SIGN	SHOE
SHOP	ADDRESS	BOOK	BOOK	SHELF	KEY
RING	MOUNTAIN	TOP	ROCK	STAR	COMPUTER
SCREEN	COFFEE	CUP	TEA	BAG	SHOPPING
CENTRE	CAR	PARK	KITCHEN	DOOR	BREAD
KNIFE	BOTTLE	TOP	TICKET		

11B Vocabulary
Adverbials: luck and chance

A Is the meaning in a and b the same or different? Write *S* (same) or *D* (different).

☐ 1 a It was cold. **Fortunately**, I had a coat.   b It was cold. **Luckily**, I had a coat.

☐ 2 a I was very **surprised** that he passed the test.   b **Amazingly**, he passed the test.

☐ 3 a I told him her name **on purpose**.   b I told him her name **accidentally**.

☐ 4 a It was a **mistake**.   b I didn't do it on **purpose**.

☐ 5 a I met him at the hotel **as expected**.   b I met him at the hotel **by chance**.

☐ 6 a **Surprisingly**, the hotel was next to a bar.   b **Unfortunately**, the hotel was next to a bar.

☐ 7 a I saw Miki yesterday **by chance**.   b I **didn't plan** to meet Miki, but I saw him yesterday.

☐ 8 a **Luckily**, he had the money with him.   b **As expected**, he had the money with him.

B Work in pairs. Complete the sentences.

e.g. They gave me a big box of chocolates, but unfortunately …
     I'm on a diet / I dropped the box / my sister ate them.

1 He didn't send the text on purpose – _____ .

2 I forgot to take my umbrella, but fortunately _____ .

3 I met John and Lucy by chance when _____ .

4 I was carrying the glasses carefully, but I accidentally _____ .

5 We went into town, but unfortunately _____ .

6 I dropped my laptop, but luckily _____ .

7 The teacher asked me for the answer and surprisingly _____ .

8 I left my bag in the park, but amazingly _____ .

9 I asked the children to help me, but as expected _____ .

10 He took my mobile phone on purpose – _____ .

C Work in pairs and test your partner. Student A: read the sentence beginnings.
Student B: say your sentence endings – do not look at your worksheet! Then swap roles.

12A Vocabulary
Animals

A Find and circle the names of eight animals in the wordsnake.

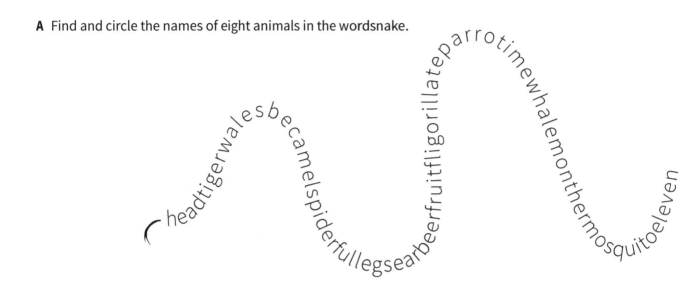

B Work in pairs: A and B. Quickly answer your questions. Do not look at your partner's questions.

Student A

1 Can tigers talk?	yes / no
2 Do spiders have eight legs?	yes / no
3 Do whales live in the sea?	yes / no
4 Are camels green?	yes / no
5 Do bees make honey?	yes / no
6 Can mosquitoes fly?	yes / no
7 Do parrots have four legs?	yes / no
8 Do gorillas eat leaves?	yes / no

Student B

1 Can parrots talk?	yes / no
2 Do bees live in the sea?	yes / no
3 Do whales live a long time?	yes / no
4 Can camels swim?	yes / no
5 Can tigers climb trees?	yes / no
6 Are gorillas intelligent?	yes / no
7 Do spiders have six legs?	yes / no
8 Do mosquitoes bite?	yes / no

C Work in pairs. Student A: read your questions for Student B to answer quickly. Then swap roles.

12B Vocabulary
Personality adjectives

A Look at the adjectives in the box. <u>Underline</u> the words that you find difficult to pronounce.

sensible	confident	reliable	strict	careless	patient
generous	fair	creative	honest	serious	funny
fun	selfish	anxious	easy going	shy	sociable

B Work in groups. Complete the sentence beginnings with adjectives in A. Do not use the adjectives more than twice.

A good parent should be _____ and _____ .

A good parent shouldn't be _____ or _____ .

A top sportsman/sportswoman should be _____ .

A top sportsman/sportswoman shouldn't be _____ .

A good driver should be _____ .

A good driver shouldn't be _____ .

A teacher should be _____ and _____ .

A teacher shouldn't be _____ .

A politician should be _____ .

A good friend should be _____ and _____ .

An artist should be _____ .

A tour guide should be _____ .

C Find a partner from a different group. Compare your answers.

Unit 1 Wordpower
like

A Answer the questions.

1 What kind of films do you **like**? Can you give examples?

horror   action   comedy   sci-fi

crime   drama   musical

'I like action films like James Bond.'

2 What was the last film you saw?

_____

3 **Was** it **like** another film you've seen? (Which one?)

_____

4 **What was** the story **like**? (exciting? funny? boring? difficult to understand?)

_____

5 What did the actors in this film **look like**?

_____

_____

6 Do you think your partner should see it? Why / why not?

*I think you'd **like** / **wouldn't like** this film because …*

_____

_____

B 💬 Use the questions 1–6 in A to interview your partner. Then tell your partner your opinion of the film they described. Use the phrases below to help you.

It **sounds like** you really enjoyed it / didn't enjoy it.

I**'d like** / I **wouldn't like** to see it myself.

It **sounds like** a (really) good/bad/interesting/exciting film.

Unit 2 Wordpower
off

I think my partner ...	Right or wrong?	Why?
1 has **fallen off** a/an _____ more than once.	☐	_____
2 **set off** for work/school at _____ today.	☐	_____
3 only buys _____ when there is **money off**.	☐	_____
4 never **switches off** his/her phone in the _____ .	☐	_____
5 **runs off** when he/she sees a/an _____ .	☐	_____
6 **turns off** the TV when _____ is on.	☐	_____
7 will **be off** today at _____ .	☐	_____
8 feels _____ when a plane **takes off**.	☐	_____

--✂

I think my partner ...	Right or wrong?	Why?
1 has **fallen off** a/an _____ more than once.	☐	_____
2 **set off** for work/school at _____ today.	☐	_____
3 only buys _____ when there is **money off**.	☐	_____
4 never **switches off** his/her phone in the _____ .	☐	_____
5 **runs off** when he/she sees a/an _____ .	☐	_____
6 **turns off** the TV when _____ is on.	☐	_____
7 will **be off** today at _____ .	☐	_____
8 feels _____ when a plane **takes off**.	☐	_____

Unit 3 Wordpower
just

A Write down …

1 an English expression you have **just** learned

_____

2 how many times a week you are **just in time** for class

_____

3 an English expression you learned when you were **just a child**

_____

4 a time you **just** passed a test and how you felt

_____

5 an English expression which is **just like** a phrase in your language

_____

6 how you feel when you are **just about** to have a test

_____

7 an English expression you might say when you have **just** finished your homework

_____

8 a piece of English grammar you **just about** understand

_____

9 an area of English you are **just about to** study

_____

10 something you can talk about in English for **just over** a minute

_____

B Talk to other students in the class and find out their answers to A. Write down
any new expressions the other students tell you and ask them to explain the meaning.

_____   _____   _____

_____   _____   _____

_____   _____   _____

Unit 4 Wordpower
look

A Find someone who ...   **Name**   **Extra information**

1 is **looking forward** to the weekend   _____   _____

2 never **looks up** English words on a phone   _____   _____

3 doesn't like **looking after** animals   _____   _____

4 always tries to **look** interested in class   _____   _____

5 likes **looking at** black and white photographs   _____   _____

B Find someone who ...   **Name**   **Extra information**

1 never **looks up** English words on a phone   _____   _____

2 isn't **looking forward** to tomorrow   _____   _____

3 likes **looking around** old buildings   _____   _____

4 **looks up** restaurants online before going to them   _____   _____

5 sometimes **looks after** older relatives   _____   _____

C Find someone who ...   **Name**   **Extra information**

1 sometimes **looks after** a younger brother or sister   _____   _____

2 enjoys **looking around** other people's houses   _____   _____

3 thinks you **look** happy   _____   _____

4 never **looks at** social media websites   _____   _____

5 **looks up** English words in a paper dictionary   _____   _____

D Find someone who ...   **Name**   **Extra information**

1 **looks for** funny videos to watch online   _____   _____

2 thinks you **look** clever   _____   _____

3 is **looking forward** to a holiday   _____   _____

4 doesn't like **looking around** shops   _____   _____

5 likes **looking at** graffiti   _____   _____

Unit 5 Wordpower
job and *work*

Order from best (1) to worst (16)	Me	Pair	Group
Having a job in a fast-food restaurant			
Finishing work for the week			
Starting your first job			
Looking for work			
Having a job in an office			
Being the last person at work in the evening			
Doing jobs around the house all weekend			
Your phone stopping working			
Your computer stopping working			
Having a job outside in summer			
Arriving at work and finding your workplace is closed for the day			
Having a job outside in winter			
Doing a lot of hard work in the garden			
Working out how to get a pay rise			
Working in politics			
Working out how to do something new			

Unit 6 Wordpower
Verb + *to*

The Restaurant

1 Two years ago, Graham was working as a cook in a small café. But he dreamed of opening his own restaurant with his friend Polly. The only problem was, they didn't have enough money.

- ✂ - - -

☐ Polly studied business, so she worked out how much money they needed to borrow and wrote a business plan. She read the plan …

- ✂ - - -

☐ … to Graham. He didn't know very much about business, but he thought it sounded good. The next day he went with Polly to the bank. They explained their idea …

- ✂ - - -

☐ … to Mr Smith, the manager, and showed him their plan. They thought the interview was going well; however, Mr Smith refused to lend the money …

- ✂ - - -

☐ … to them. He said that there were already a lot of places to eat in the town. He was worried that they wouldn't be able to pay the money back …

- ✂ - - -

☐ … to the bank. But Polly and Graham didn't give up. Polly said to Graham, 'If Mr Smith tries your food, he might let us borrow the money. We'll ask him to bring his wife …

- ✂ - - -

☐ … to dinner with us on Saturday evening. What is the most amazing meal you can cook?' Graham thought carefully and described his favourite fish dish …

- ✂ - - -

☐ … to Polly. She knew that he was a great cook, and that this was their last chance to get the money, so she wrote an email …

- ✂ - - -

☐ … to Mr Smith, and invited him and his wife to dinner that Saturday evening. Graham cooked the meal perfectly. Mr and Mrs Smith loved it. Mrs Smith even asked Graham to give the recipe …

- ✂ - - -

☐ … to her. But Graham said it was a secret. He might tell her the ingredients if Mr Smith agreed to the loan. Everybody laughed. Mr Smith knew that Graham and Polly could sell this food …

- ✂ - - -

☐ … to anybody. He believed their restaurant would be a success. The next week Mr Smith's bank lent enough money …

- ✂ - - -

☐ … to Polly and Graham for them to open their first restaurant. Mr Smith and his wife became regular customers.

Two years later, Polly and Graham are just about to open their second restaurant. It's hard work, but they are very happy.

Unit 7 Wordpower
change

I usually have some change with me because …	The last time I changed trains was …	I often change my mind about …
I usually change into different clothes when …	Next year, I will _____ for a change.	The best place to change money near here is …
When I change something in a shop, I feel …	When a shop assistant gives me my change, I …	The last time I changed my mind in a restaurant was …
The first time I changed planes was …	Tonight, I would like to go to _____ for a change.	The last time I changed money was …
The worst station to change trains is …	One day, I would like to live in _____ for a change.	I sometimes give some change to …
Next week, I would like to eat _____ for a change.	I often keep my change in a …	I never change my mind about …

Unit 8 Wordpower
by

Correct or incorrect

1 I think _____ likes music **by** _____. ☐

2 I think _____ can learn things **by heart**. ☐

3 I think _____ can make _____ **by hand**. ☐

4 I think _____ never does anything **by mistake**. ☐

5 I think _____ thinks that _____ is **by far the tastiest** food in the world. ☐

6 I think _____ doesn't like paying for things **by credit card**. ☐

7 I think _____ always **gets home by** _____. ☐

8 I think _____ would like to **live by** _____. ☐

9 I think _____ likes books **by** _____. ☐

10 I think _____ thinks that _____ is **by far the best** singer in the world. ☐

11 I think _____ never washes clothes **by hand**. ☐

12 I think _____ sometimes breaks things **by mistake**. ☐

13 I think _____ doesn't like learning irregular English verbs **by heart**. ☐

14 I think _____ likes to **sit by** _____ in class. ☐

Wordpower
Multi-word verbs with *put*

⚀	on	⚁	up	⚀ or ⚁	+
⚂	down	⚃	back	⚂ or ⚃	−
⚄	through	⚅	off	⚄ or ⚅	?

Write your sentences here.

1 _____

2 _____

3 _____

4 _____

5 _____

6 _____

Unit 10 Wordpower
Multi-word verbs with *on*

- Something you have to get **on** with this weekend
- Something annoying that a friend **keeps on** doing
- Something you bought from a shop but didn't **try on** first
- Something you will **carry on** doing for the rest of your life
- Something special you would **put on** for a party
- Something naughty you **went on** doing when you were a child
- Something you **tried on** in a shop but didn't buy
- A mistake you **go on** making in English lessons
- Something you have to **get on with** this evening
- Something annoying that a relative **keeps on** doing
- Something you would **put on** for the first day at a new job
- Something you will **carry on** doing for the next five years

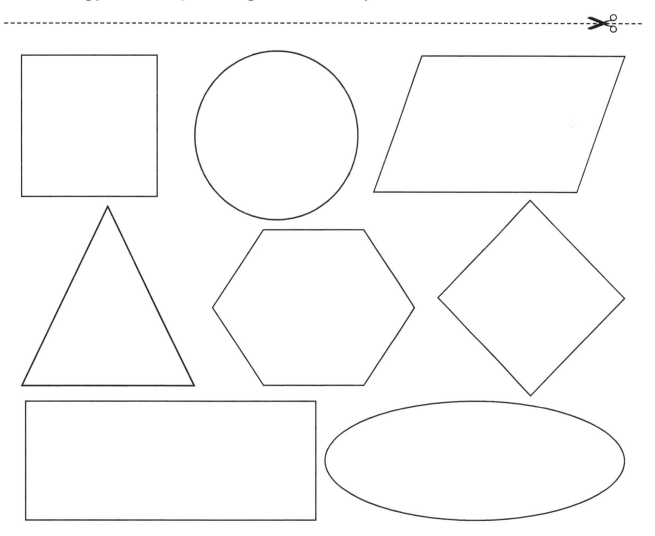

Unit 11 Wordpower

Preposition + noun

on	business	in	bed
on	purpose	by	car
on	time	by	plane
on	holiday	by	mistake
on	foot	by	credit card
in	advance	by	chance
in	love	for	sale
in	hospital	at	university
in	school	at	home
in	prison	at	work

Unit 12 Wordpower
age

Student A

Agree or disagree?	Me	My partner
Couples who are **far apart in age** shouldn't marry.		
People should start working **at an early age**.		
I get on best with people **about my age**.		
People who are **middle-aged** rarely have exciting lives.		
It is easier to study with people who are **of a similar age**.		
I don't want to be like my parents are **at their age**.		
People should stop working **in their early sixties**.		
I want to live alone **in my old age**.		

Student B

Agree or disagree?	Me	My partner
People shouldn't get married until **their late twenties**.		
When they were **my age**, my grandparents had more problems than I do.		
People **of a similar age** usually worry about the same things.		
In old age, it is best to live in a care home with other old people.		
It is difficult for parents when their children are **far apart in age**.		
I started learning English **at an early age**.		
Middle-aged people don't understand **teenagers**.		
Children need friends who are **about their age**.		

Introduction
Pronunciation
Phonetic symbols

A Work in pairs. Look at the phonetic symbols. Some of the symbols are the same as alphabet letters and some are different. In the 'different' row, underline the parts of the words that have the sound of the phonetic symbols.

Same	i e p b t d k g f v s z m n h l r w
Different	iː cheap uː who ə teacher ɪə near eɪ late ɜː shirt ɔː walk ʊə tour ɔɪ boy əʊ coat ɪ chip æ man ʌ but ʊ put ɑː part ɒ got eə hair aɪ fine aʊ now tʃ chair dʒ job θ think ð the ʃ shoe ʒ television j yes ŋ sing

B Find the phonetic script for the words in the wordsearch. The words can be horizontal or vertical.

basketball   brother   cupboard   everywhere   kitchen
orange   possible   themselves   thirsty   university

j	ɪ	s	b	r	ʌ	ð	ə	t	e
uː	θ	ʌ	ɑː	h	t	ʒ	z	v	ɪə
n	p	ɒ	s	ə	b	ə	l	r	e
ɪ	ŋ	æ	k	θ	ɜː	s	t	i	v
v	ɜː	k	ɪ	tʃ	ə	n	ɒ	w	r
ɜː	ɪə	ɒ	t	l	n	r	k	θ	i
s	k	ʌ	b	ə	d	b	t	p	w
ɪ	ʒ	f	ɔː	ɒ	r	ɪ	n	dʒ	eə
t	r	ɔɪ	l	iː	ŋ	tʃ	k	aʊ	h
i	v	ð	ə	m	s	e	l	v	z

Pronunciation
Syllables and word stress

delicious	chemistry

excellent	cupboard

directions	customer

normally	engineer

exam	centimetre

manager	alright

television	asleep

understand	document

microwave	supermarket

helicopter	afternoon

grammar	calendar

international	open

horrible	expensive

magazine	shampoo

exercise	photography

return	electricity

instructions	visitor

perfect	telephone

American	sensible

communication	available

activity	umbrella

boring	excited

football	another

punctuation	remember

important	kitchen

negative	information

potato	Saturday

tomorrow	awful

various	examination

surprise	accident

1B Pronunciation
Long and short vowel sounds

A Move through the maze from *daughter* to *water* using words with a long vowel sound on the stressed syllable. You can move horizontally, vertically or diagonally.

daughter	love	kiss	fun	hot	fit	box
fish	call	very	carry	book	food	wet
leg	heart	luck	clock	sit	sub	fact
bad	six	laugh	bit	cook	hot	carry
nice	mum	four	lips	egg	March	spell
love	red	teeth	head	thought	spell	bath
sit	pull	large	much	aunt	cut	door
dead	good	sock	horse	since	desk	**water**

B Move through the maze from *letter* to *wish* using words with short vowel sounds on the stressed syllable. You can move horizontally, vertically or diagonally.

letter	scarf	bad	one	lose	seat	sit
sun	leave	turn	heart	hat	green	feel
horse	fish	taught	grass	girl	boot	soon
bird	sharp	son	warm	laugh	kiss	fast
teach	rude	many	class	egg	choose	bed
ship	horse	spell	spoon	cat	sleep	sock
mean	shirt	teeth	clock	talk	word	met
ugly	aunt	boot	tree	choose	week	**wish**

2A Pronunciation
-ed endings

Student A

A Work on your own. Read the phrases from a story and <u>underline</u> the past tense endings which are pronounced with an extra syllable /ɪd/.

B Work in pairs. Student A: read your first phrase. Student B: listen and write the phrase in the first gap in your story. Then Student B reads the first phrase in his/her story and Student A writes, and so on.

A long time ago in ancient Greece, _____
_____ . He <u>hated</u> tests
and he was lazy. _____
_____ and invited them to his parties.
_____ .
He even started to go fishing with sailors. _____
_____ . They repeated to
him again and again that the test was important. _____
_____ . but it always ended the same way: _____
_____ . Then his mother had an idea. _____
_____ and they decided to help the student. _____
_____ , the sailors shaved off his beard. _____
_____ . He didn't leave his house for a month and he passed the test.

C Work with another pair. What do you think happened to change the student's attitude?

Student B

A Work on your own. Read the phrases from a story and <u>underline</u> the past tense endings which are pronounced with an extra syllable /ɪd/.

B Work in pairs. Student A: read your first phrase. Student B: listen and write the phrase in the first gap in your story. Then Student B reads the first phrase in his/her story and Student A writes, and so on.

_____ ,
a student <u>needed</u> to pass an important test.
_____ .
He visited his friends, chatted with them _____
_____ . He went for long
walks and painted pictures. _____
_____ . His
parents worried about him. _____
_____ . His father shouted at him, _____
_____ : the student went fishing.
_____ _____ . She contacted the sailors
_____ . When he was
asleep on their boat, _____ .
The student woke up, went home and studied very hard. _____
_____ .

C Work with another pair. Talk about what happened to change the student's attitude.

3B Pronunciation
Sound and spelling: /dʒ/ and /j/

CUSTOMER A

Food	Clothes
2 cabbages	a jacket
1 kilo of oranges	blue jeans
½ kilo of cucumbers	2 jumpers
a cheese sandwich	a school uniform
a jar of strawberry jam	a yellow scarf
sausages	
apple juice	Other
4 yogurts	The Times newspaper
2 large bars of chocolate	a French language course
a tin of tuna	a map of Europe
3 kilos of new potatoes	a student's guide to university
	a music magazine

CUSTOMER B

Food	Clothes
2 cabbages	a jacket
1 kilo of oranges	blue jeans
½ kilo of cucumbers	2 jumpers
a cheese sandwich	a school uniform
a jar of strawberry jam	a yellow scarf
sausages	
apple juice	Other
4 yogurts	The Times newspaper
2 large bars of chocolate	a French language course
a tin of tuna	a map of Europe
3 kilos of new potatoes	a student's guide to university
	a music magazine

SHOP ASSISTANT A

Food	Clothes
1 cabbage (50p)	a jacket (£90)
cucumbers (60p/kg)	blue jeans (£40)
a jar of raspberry jam (£1.50)	a jumper (£20)
apple juice (£1.25)	a school uniform (£100)
a large bar of chocolate (£1.00)	a purple scarf (£10)
new potatoes (40p/kg)	
oranges (70p/kg)	
a chicken sandwich (£2.50)	
sausages (£2.70)	
yogurts (90p each)	
a tin of tuna (£3.40)	

Other

The Times newspaper (£1.50)

a Spanish language course (£8.00)

a map of Europe (£3.00)

a student's guide to university (£9.00)

a music magazine (£4.50)

SHOP ASSISTANT B

Food	Clothes
1 cabbage (50p)	a jacket (£90)
cucumbers (60p/kg)	blue jeans (£40)
a jar of raspberry jam (£1.50)	a jumper (£20)
apple juice (£1.25)	a school uniform (£100)
a large bar of chocolate (£1.00)	a purple scarf (£10)
new potatoes (40p/kg)	
oranges (70p/kg)	
a chicken sandwich (£2.50)	
sausages (£2.70)	
yogurts (90p each)	
a tin of tuna (£3.40)	

Other

The Times newspaper (£1.50)

a Spanish language course (£8.00)

a map of Europe (£3.00)

a student's guide to university (£9.00)

a music magazine (£4.50)

3C Pronunciation
Sentence stress

A
1 beautiful day
2 cold morning
3 Monday afternoon
4 boring day
5 crazy week
6 hot summer

B
1 best friend
2 great-grandmother
3 ten children
4 pet lion
5 tennis coach
6 boss

C
1 small restaurant
2 cheap hotel
3 shopping centre
4 dark forest
5 museum
6 railway station

D
1 young woman
2 famous film star
3 good friend
4 police woman
5 horrible man
6 dangerous man

E
1 said 'Hello'
2 phoned me
3 texted me
4 screamed
5 shouted, 'Hey!'
6 arrived

F
1 very surprised
2 really excited
3 angry
4 bored
5 feeling bad
6 busy

G
1 said, 'Oh no!'
2 ran away
3 fell asleep
4 didn't understand
5 did nothing
6 smiled

H
1 dream
2 strange day
3 bad decision
4 nice idea
5 funny situation
6 good experience

4B Pronunciation
Sound and spelling: /ɒ/ and /əʊ/

A Look at the minimal pairs below. Each pair of words has an /ɒ/ sound (e.g. *hot*) and an /əʊ/ sound (e.g. *so*). Underline the words with an /ɒ/ sound.

coat – cot	goat – got	road – rod	want – won't
cost – coast	not – note	sock – soak	wok – woke

B Work with a partner. Write all the words with /ɒ/ sounds in the left column of each grid. Write all the words with /əʊ/ sounds in the bottom row. The words must be in the same order (alphabetical order) in both grids.

C Play Battleships. Your teacher will explain the rules.

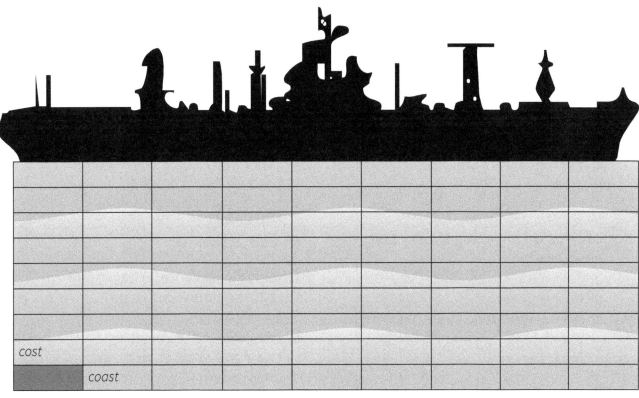

You

Your partner

Work in pairs. Read the questions and each of the four options to your partner.
Underline his/her answers. Then tell your partner what the answers mean.

Are you in good shape?

1 How far can you swim?
a) I can swim more than a kilometre.
b) I can swim a bit.
c) I can't swim.
d) other answer

2 What do you have for breakfast?
a) I have fresh fruit.
b) I don't have breakfast.
c) Four eggs, three sausages and fried bread.
d) other answer

3 Did you do anything sporty last weekend?
a) Yes, I did a lot.
b) No, I didn't do much.
c) Yes, I played World Cup 2018 on my phone.
d) other answer

4 Do your friends think you are a healthy person?
a) Yes and we often do sport together.
b) Go and ask them.
c) I haven't got any friends.
d) other answer

5 How do you relax after work/ studying?
a) I do some exercise.
b) Relax? What do you mean?
c) I fall asleep at my desk.
d) other answer

6 How much water do you drink every day?
a) I drink two litres of mineral water.
b) I don't know.
c) I can't stand water, but I love milkshakes.
d) other answer

7 When you wake up, what is the first thing you want to do?
a) I want to go running.
b) I don't want to do anything.
c) I want to go back to sleep.
d) other answer

8 Do you sleep well?
a) Yes, I can sleep anywhere and any time.
b) No, I can't fall asleep for ages.
c) I sleep during lessons.
d) other answer

Answers

Mostly a): You are in great shape! Well done!
Mostly b): Well, no one is perfect. You definitely aren't.
Mostly c): Join the gym today. Walk there, don't take a taxi.
Mostly d): You seem very confused! What's the matter?

5B Pronunciation
Sound and spelling: /ʃ/

Student A

Label the picture using the words in the box.

chef	cushion	dishes	fish	shoes	wash

Now compare your picture with your partner's picture and find the ten differences.

In my picture, there's a chef and …

✂

Student B

Label the picture using the words in the box.

brush	chef	mushrooms	ocean	ship	sugar

Now compare your picture with your partner's picture and find the ten differences.

In my picture, there's a chef and …

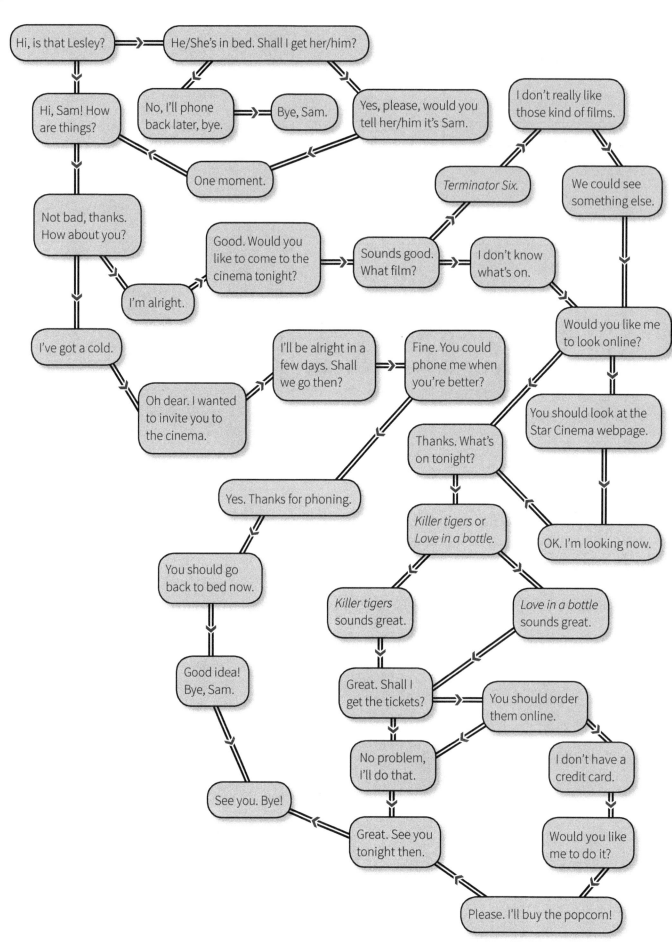

6A Pronunciation
Sound and spelling: /uː/ and /ʊ/

A Work in pairs. Look at the underlined words in the exchanges below. Which sounds do the words have, /uː/ or /ʊ/?

a) Have you heard the <u>good</u> <u>news</u>?

b) No, <u>could</u> you tell me what happened?

a) I'm in a <u>music</u> <u>group</u> at <u>school</u>.

b) <u>Cool</u>! What <u>do</u> <u>you</u> play?

a) Let's go in <u>June</u>.

b) Fine, but we <u>should</u> <u>book</u> <u>soon</u>.

a) Do you want anything with your <u>soup</u>?

b) A <u>spoon</u> <u>would</u> be nice.

a) There's a <u>full</u> <u>moon</u> this <u>Tuesday</u>.

b) I'll <u>look</u> at it <u>through</u> the window.

a) Oh! Who <u>stood</u> on my <u>foot</u>?

b) I'm sorry. Someone <u>pushed</u> me.

a) My neighbour is very <u>rude</u>.

b) You <u>should</u> <u>move</u> house.

a) Do you want any <u>sugar</u>?

b) No, I'm trying to <u>lose</u> <u>two</u> kilograms.

B Play *Bingo*.

Bingo card for /uː/

Bingo card for /ʊ/

6C Pronunciation
Main stress

Group Card

1 Simon is at university in <u>Manchester</u>.
2 The keys <u>were</u> on the table.
3 I can <u>read</u> French.
4 I gave the <u>jumper</u> to Sarah.
5 Is skiing <u>popular</u> in Pakistan?
6 <u>Jane</u> goes running every morning.
7 She <u>wrote</u> a big book about cooking.
8 Can <u>I</u> ask you a question?
9 Maria is flying to <u>Rome</u> tomorrow.
10 Can you <u>lend</u> me fifty euros tomorrow?
11 Does <u>anyone</u> have an answer to number five?
12 There were <u>some</u> mistakes at the beginning.

Student Card A

1 That's Sue's brother.
2 The keys for the car.
3 But my speaking is not very good.
4 It was a nice, warm one.
5 Not really.
6 It's a great way to keep fit.
7 Not my favourite topic.
8 It's my turn now.
9 I mean Thursday.
10 I'll give it back to you.
11 There may be different answers.
12 They did a lot of things wrong.

Student Card B

1 He's doing economics.
2 Near the computer.
3 I'm quite good at it.
4 Not the skirt.
5 I know they like cricket.
6 Have you met her?
7 There were 800 pages.
8 Just one question.
9 She lives there.
10 That's a lot of money.
11 It's on the next page.
12 It was a bad start.

Student Card C

1 It's a great town.
2 They aren't there now.
3 It's a beautiful language.
4 It was a present.
5 There isn't much snow there.
6 She likes running.
7 She is a well-known author.
8 You know the answer.
9 She's our manager.
10 I need it then.
11 It's a difficult question.
12 But not very many.

- Lara doesn't want to live next to a flat that has dogs.
- Mike wants to know why the woman below him wakes up very early.
- Oscar lives next to James and he really needs to see the dentist.
- Wayne lives between Mike and Emma, but he refuses to speak to them.
- Steven lives next to a marathon runner, but he prefers to watch sport on TV.
- Maria lives in the bottom-right flat and she loves to cook.
- James lives in flat nine, but he used to live in a big house.
- Carla tries not to listen to her neighbour's terrible guitar-playing.
- Natasha likes to visit the flat below her and have some great food.
- Brian is where Rita used to live.
- Teresa can't get to sleep, because the man next door is crying in pain.
- Emma would like to have a friendlier neighbour.
- Julia lives in flat six and has to get up very early every day.
- Brenda is in number 16 and she is getting ready to go out.
- Maggie in number 23 has six dogs and she would like to have more.
- Jake is in number 14 and he is going to be a famous actor, so he reads scripts aloud.
- David wonders why the woman downstairs needs to have her TV on all the time.
- Phil is in 21 and he is going to have a barbecue on the balcony.
- Sharon is in the middle row, on the right, and she loves to watch TV.
- Ben is glad he doesn't have to share with the man downstairs who talks to himself.
- Rita is in flat 18, but she used to live in number 25.
- Mandy likes to go out with Brenda next door.
- Jemma should phone the fire service, because there is smoke or a fire next door.
- Simon is in flat three and he is going to run the London marathon.

21	22	23	24	25
16	17	18	19	20
11	12	13	14	15
6	7	8	9	10
1	2	3	4	5

key	shoe	uncle	boat
breakfast	snow	leg	ice-cream
money	bike	chess	holiday
cat	picture	shower	film
doctor	night	ball	tea

8B Pronunciation
Word stress

seventeen	national	gymnastics	doctor	athletics
weather	asleep	newspaper	unhappy	station
decide	computer	magazine	beginning	seventy
arrive	yoga	beautiful	surfing	important
repeat	building	elephant	because	banana
hotel	sofa	behind	telephone	amazing
eleven	windsurfing	stadium	usually	revise
million	between	Japanese	remember	afternoon

8C Pronunciation
Tones for continuing or finishing

Student A

A Work in pairs. Read your statements with a rise or fall tone. You get a point if your partner gives the correct response – i.e. nothing (after a fall) or finishing the sentence (after a rise).

1 I went to the shop … (rise)
2 It was a beautiful day. (fall)
3 Then she ran to the station. (fall)
4 Sometimes we go to the café … (rise)

5 She needs some eggs … (rise)
6 The stranger took off his coat. (fall)
7 It's a lovely idea … (rise)

B Now your partner will read some statements to you. Listen for the rise tone or fall tone and choose the correct way to respond: 0 = nothing (after a fall) or finish the sentence (after a rise).

8 … but I haven't got time to read it.
9 … and I saw a strange light in the sky.
10 … so I went to his flat.
11 … and go to sleep.

12 … but things got better.
13 … so I told him everything.
14 … but I didn't answer it.

Student B

A Work in pairs. Your partner will read some statements to you. Listen for the rise tone or fall tone and choose the correct way to respond – i.e. nothing (after a fall)
or finish the sentence (after a rise).

1 … but it was closed.
2 … and I was very happy.
3 … because she was very late.
4 … but not very often.

5 … and cheese and milk.
6 … and sat down.
7 … but it will be very expensive.

B Now it is your turn to read these statements to your partner. You get a point if your partner gives the correct response: nothing (after a fall) or finishing the sentence (after a rise).

8 It's an interesting book. (fall)
9 I was driving home … (rise)
10 Sam wanted to meet me … (rise)
11 Go to bed. (fall)

12 It was a terrible start … (rise)
13 My dad wanted to know … (rise)
14 Then the phone rang. (fall)

If I have ten children, I'll need a big house.	If I get the chance, I'll study in America.	If there is a good film on TV, I'll watch it.	If it rains, I'll take an umbrella.	If I have a sports car, I'll drive very fast.	If it tastes strange, I'll throw it away.
If we have any questions, our teacher will answer them.	If she works hard, she'll pass the training.	If I get a bad headache, I'll lie down.	If I forget my dad's birthday, he won't like it.	If I find a good business partner, I'll start a business.	If I feel sick, I'll stay at home.
If it snows tomorrow, I won't be able to go to work.	If I'm wrong, I'll say sorry to you.	If I go to the city centre, I'll buy you a present.	If there isn't any milk, I'll get some.	If my friend invites me to a party tonight, I'll go.	If I need a holiday, I'll go to Spain.
If you're not there by 6 pm, we'll go without you.	If I wake up at 10 am tomorrow, I'll be late for work.	If I can speak English well, I'll get a good job.	If it's hot this weekend, I'll go swimming.	If I'm not sure, I won't do it.	If I move house, I'll get a cat.
If I win this game, I'll buy you all a coffee.	If I'm lucky, I'll finish work early.	If everyone is ready, we'll begin.	If I want to look completely different, I'll grow a beard.	If there is a test next week, I'll revise tonight.	If it's cheap, I'll buy it.
If there is a choice, I'll take the red one.	If there is a problem, I'll text you.	If the baby is asleep, I won't wake her up.	If you don't want to cook, I'll order a pizza.	If I don't know a word, I'll use a dictionary.	If it's true, I'll be very surprised.
If I become famous, I'll be on TV.	If I move to a different country, my parents will be sad.	If my boss is angry with me, I won't get a promotion.	If I need some money, I'll ask you.	If no one enjoys the programme, we'll stop watching it.	If I don't like my new job, I'll find another one.

A

1 The film starts at seven o'clock.

2 It's Gran's birthday on Friday.

3 The maths homework is on page sixteen.

B

4 They went on holiday to Barcelona.

5 A ticket costs sixteen pounds.

6 It's raining outside.

C

7 You go straight on and turn left.

8 Tom loves pasta.

9 They've got a dog.

D

10 Susan's got a new mountain bike.

11 The first letter is P.

12 Carl can't find his keys.

E

13 Kelly wants to buy a new jumper.

14 The microwave doesn't work.

15 They're travelling by car.

F

16 The pass mark is fifty per cent.

17 Alex is having a shower.

18 The shop is open.

A

B

C

D

E

F

7 You walk down the street. An old man stops you and asks you for 2000 zlogs. What would you say?

I would give him some dollars. (20)

I would run away. (15)

9 The farmer does not understand you. He is afraid of you and your ideas.
It would be better if you started this game again.

14 You walk away, but the robot that owns the car sees you. You tell it your story. The robot would love you to take the car to the present and show people.
If I were you, I'd do this. Happy travelling!

20 The old man is very surprised. He remembers his great-grandfather had some dollars. You tell him your story. He would like to go back in time with you.

Would you take him (16) or wouldn't you (8)?

18 There are traffic police in the future! They stop you.

I would tell them I am from the past. (4)

I would apologise and park the car. (13)

19 The woman gets better quickly and everyone is very pleased.
If I were you, I would go back to the present while everyone is happy! Your time travelling ends here.

1 The time machine works! Where would you like to go?

I would go to the past. (17)

I would travel to the future. (6)

I wouldn't go anywhere. (2)

8 The old man is disappointed, but he understands that it would be difficult. You would like to see that flying car again.

Go to (13).

2 Boring! Choose again.

Would you like to go to the future (6) or would you prefer the past (17)?

17 You are in a village.

Would you go inside one of the houses (3) or do you think this would be dangerous (21)?

3 A woman inside is very ill with a temperature. You have some aspirin in your bag.

Would you give the aspirin to her (19) or wouldn't you (11)?

21 You go past the houses and into some fields. Suddenly a big farmer's dog is running across the field.

Would you run to one of the houses (3) or would you give the dog a chocolate biscuit (5)?

13 You are in front of the flying car. Hmm… It would be nice to 'borrow' the car and take it back with you.

Would you leave a note for the owner and take the car (15) or would you walk on (14)?

10 Good idea – the farmer wouldn't understand you.
Wait! The time machine is moving again and you are going forward in time.

Go to 6.

15 That wasn't very nice! Your journey in time was not very successful. Think about what you would do differently next time.

6 You are in a street with lots of strange cars flying around. One lands near you. You could get in the flying car.

Would you (12) or wouldn't you (7)?

11 The woman gets worse.

I would give her the aspirin. (19)

I would leave the house quietly while no one is looking. (15)

5 The dog eats the biscuit and a friendly farmer comes out. You have an idea – talk to him about technology, so he will be a famous scientist in the future!

I would tell him. (9)

I wouldn't tell him. (10)

16 You travel back to the present with the old man. He loves the present and becomes very famous. He wouldn't like to return to the future, so he stays here with you. A happy ending!

4 The police think you are very strange and take you to a hospital for tests. It would be better if you started this game again.

12 You are flying! What would you do next?

I would fly as fast as I could. (18)

I would stop and park the car. (13)

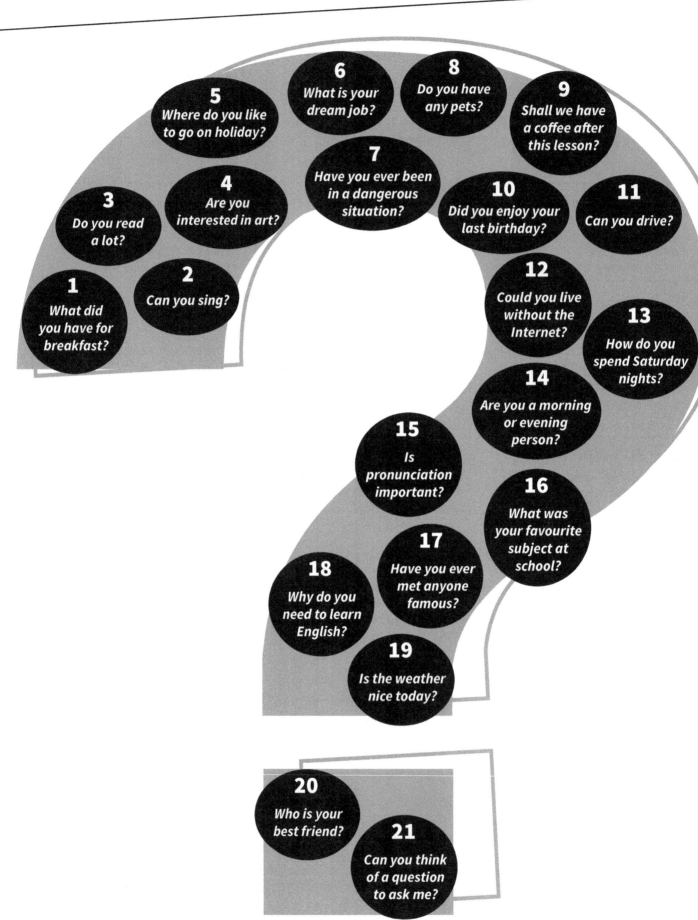

5 Where do you like to go on holiday?

6 What is your dream job?

8 Do you have any pets?

9 Shall we have a coffee after this lesson?

7 Have you ever been in a dangerous situation?

3 Do you read a lot?

4 Are you interested in art?

10 Did you enjoy your last birthday?

11 Can you drive?

1 What did you have for breakfast?

2 Can you sing?

12 Could you live without the Internet?

13 How do you spend Saturday nights?

14 Are you a morning or evening person?

15 Is pronunciation important?

16 What was your favourite subject at school?

17 Have you ever met anyone famous?

18 Why do you need to learn English?

19 Is the weather nice today?

20 Who is your best friend?

21 Can you think of a question to ask me?

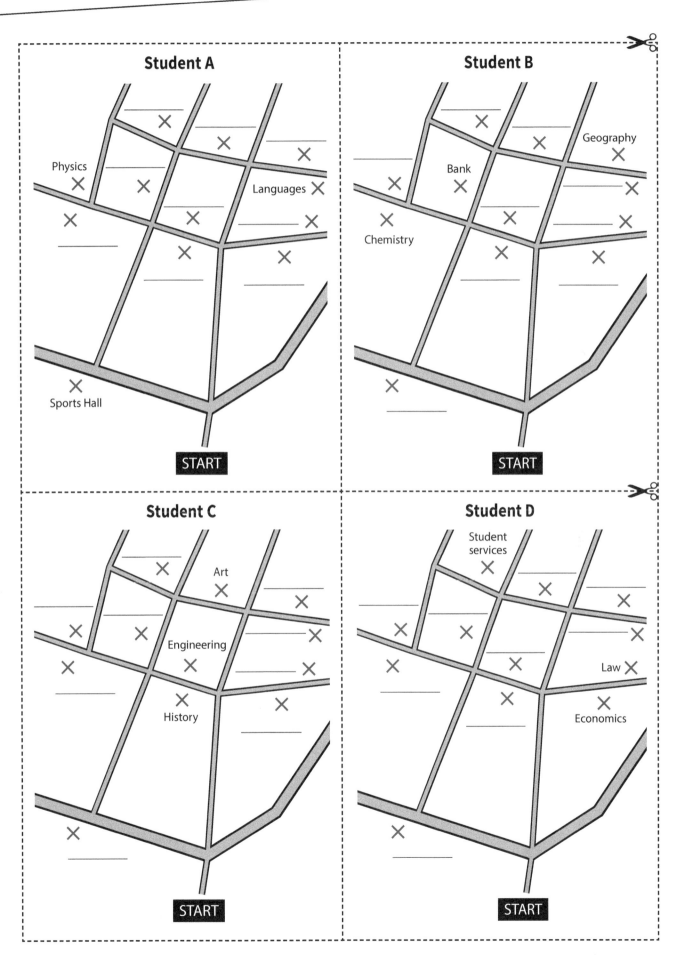

11C2 Pronunciation
Sound and spelling: /ɔː/ and /ɜː/

A Find your way from *early* to *work*. You can move across or down through squares where there is an /ɜː/ sound. Say the words.

early	Thursday	mean	hurt	turn	girl
east	dirty	pear	worse	tune	nurse
where	were	purse	prefer	heart	learn
dream	bread	there	read	word	third
leave	sharp	car	art	shirt	present
best	short	ear	part	birthday	work

B <u>Underline</u> the word in each pair that contains an /ɔː/ sound.

four / fear   course / nurse   board / bird   wore / were   pair / poor   more / among
afraid / afford   journey / reward   allow / adore   laugh / law   sure / sew

C Circle the words in the box with the /ɜː/ sound and practise saying them.

money   journey   bear   cheese   church   curtain   kitten   first   more   reserve   there
think   third   thirteen   verb   won't   warm   burn   born   really

D Make your own maze with words from A, B and C. You can choose if you want to focus on the /ɜː/ sound or the /ɔː/ sound. Exchange it with another student's maze and find your way through theirs.

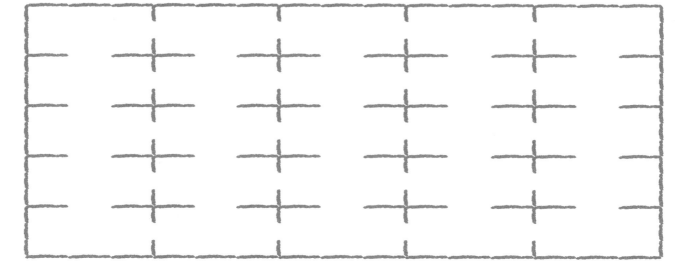

John White

I work in a pet shop.
I like to talk about animals with customers.
I think it's sad when customers buy the animals and the animals leave the shop.
I want to be a zookeeper because I love animals and have qualifications in animal care.
I love birds, especially parrots.
I don't like mice and rats.
I've got three dogs.
I watch nature programmes on TV in my free time.
I'm friendly and sociable.

Michelle Peters

I am a science teacher.
I like to watch videos about animals with the students.
I don't like the long hours I have to work.
I want to be a zookeeper because I live near the zoo and like gorillas.
I love all animals.
I don't like dangerous animals.
I don't have any pets.
I like reading and visiting zoos in my free time.
I'm clever and caring.

Interviewer 1

1 What do you do?
_____

2 What do you like about your job?
_____

3 What don't you like about your job?
_____

4 Why do you want to be a zookeeper?
_____

5 What is your favourite animal?
_____

6 Are there any animals you don't like?
_____

7 Have you got any pets?
_____

8 Do you have any hobbies?
_____

9 How would you describe yourself?
_____

Interviewer 2

1 What do you do?
_____

2 What do you like about your job?
_____

3 What don't you like about your job?
_____

4 Why do you want to be a zookeeper?
_____

5 What is your favourite animal?
_____

6 Are there any animals you don't like?
_____

7 Have you got any pets?
_____

8 Do you have any hobbies?
_____

9 How would you describe yourself?
_____

12C Pronunciation
Main stress: contrastive

Student A

A Work in pairs. Read the sentences to your partner. Your partner will guess if the sentences are correct or not. (The correct answer is in brackets.)

1 The shortest month is April. (No, February)

2 King Henry VIII of England had eight wives. (No, six)

3 The most common letter of the alphabet is *A*. (No, *E*)

4 The 2012 Olympics were in London. (Yes)

5 Swimming is the last event in a triathlon. (No, first)

6 Bill Gates invented the Internet. (No, Microsoft)

7 A 'dozen' eggs is ten eggs. (No, twelve)

8 Hamburgers were first made in Germany. (No, the U.S.A.)

B Now it is your turn to answer. Choose the correct answers from the options. Use contrastive stress when your partner's sentences are false.

9 a Yes, that's correct.	b No, it's Ottawa.	c No, it's Vancouver.
10 a Yes, that's correct.	b No, he writes songs.	c No, he writes novels.
11 a Yes, that's correct.	b No, we have 30.	c No, we have 36.
12 a Yes, that's correct.	b No, they're red.	c No, they're green.
13 a Yes, that's correct.	b No, it's Chinese.	c No, it's Spanish.
14 a Yes, that's correct.	b No, it's Neptune.	c No, it's Venus.
15 a Yes, that's correct.	b No, it's 13 February.	c No, it's 8 March.
16 a Yes, that's correct.	b No, he's a runner.	c No, he's a basketball player.

Student B

A Work in pairs. Your partner will read some sentences. Choose the correct answers from the options. Use contrastive stress when your partner's sentences are false.

1 a Yes, that's correct.	b No, it's February.	c No, it's October.
2 a Yes, that's correct.	b No, he had four.	c No, he had six.
3 a Yes, that's correct.	b No, it's *E*.	c No, it's *O*.
4 a Yes, that's correct.	b No, they were in Beijing.	c No, they were in Sydney.
5 a Yes, that's correct.	b No, it's the first.	c No, it's the second.
6 a Yes, that's correct.	b No, he invented Microsoft.	c No, he invented the iPhone.
7 a Yes, that's correct.	b No, it's twelve.	c No, it's fourteen.
8 a Yes, that's correct.	b No, they come from Britain.	c No, they come from the USA

B Now it is your turn to read the sentences to your partner. Your partner will guess if the sentences are correct or not. (The correct answer is in brackets.)

9 The capital of Canada is Montreal. (No, Ottawa)

10 Stephen King writes poems. (No, novels)

11 We have thirty-two teeth. (Yes)

12 Buses in London are yellow. (No, red)

13 The most spoken language in the world is English. (No, Chinese)

14 The nearest planet to Earth is Pluto. (No, Venus)

15 Valentine's Day is on 14 February. (Yes)

16 Usain Bolt is a famous footballer. (No, runner)